From Fargo to the World of Brands

Also by David Aaker

- *Brand Relevance: Making Competitors Irrelevant*
- *Spanning Silos: The New CMO Imperative*
- *Brand Portfolio Strategy*
- *Brand Leadership* (with Erich Joachimsthaler)
- *Building Strong Brands*
- *Managing Brand Equity*
- *Strategic Market Management* 9th ed. (also published in hard-cover as *Developing Business Strategy*)
- *Marketing Research* 10th ed. (with George S. Day and V. Kumar, and Robert Leone; a modified version also published as *Essentials of Marketing Research*, 2nd edition)
- *Advertising Management* 5th ed. (with John G. Myers and Rajeev Batra)
- *Brand Equity and Advertising* (Edited with Alex Biel)
- *Multivariate Analysis in Marketing: Theory and Applications* 2nd ed. (editor)
- *Consumerism: Search for the Consumer Interest* 4th ed. (edited with George S. Day)

From Fargo to the World of Brands

My Story So Far

David Aaker

From Fargo to the World of Brands: My Story So Far

First edition, revised.
Published by Iceni Books®
1760 East River Road, Suite 145
Tucson, Arizona 85718 U.S.A.
www.icenibooks.com

Publisher's Cataloging-in-Publication
(Provided by Quality Books, Inc.)

Aaker, David A.
    From Fargo to the world of brands : my story so far /
by David Aaker.
    p. cm.
    Includes index.
    LCCN 2005925704
    ISBN 1-58736-494-8 (hardcover)
    ISBN 1-58736-495-6 (pbk.)

    1. Aaker, David A. 2. Marketing—United States.
3. Businessmen—United States—Biography. 4. College
teachers—United States—Biography. I. Title.

HF5415.1.A25 2005   658.8'0092
            QBI05-200110

Contents

Preface

I wrote this book for two reasons. First, the exercise was a good chance to relive some good times and some difficult times, an excuse to talk to people that have been important to me at one time or another, and a reason to review the many picture albums and files that have been gathering dust. The journey has been awesome. I recommend it to anyone.

Second, I wanted my children and their children and perhaps others that have crossed my path from Fargo to the "World of Brands" to have a record of what happened to me and why. What was it like to develop a career, to experience events, to see a family grow, and to enjoy friendships in the times and places in which I lived? What people crossed my path? I know that I would have appreciated such documentation from those that came before me. It is a bit sad to think that all those events, emotions, opinions, and relationships will so soon be lost to posterity.

I have four concerns. One is that others will feel that I am presumptuous to think that my life story is of interest and worth writing, and that reflecting on the good things that have come my way will appear as bragging rather than telling a balanced story. A second relates to the discomfort in sharing my life in such detail, sanitized though the story may be. A third is that there are a host of people important in my life whose photos and even names do not appear because I forgot some details or was missing some information or a photo. I'm afraid they will make the wrong attribution to this omission. A final concern is that that no one will read the book because they do not know it exists or, worse, they have no interest. At the end of the day, the book went forward despite these concerns.

The book covers everything. It is not limited to a period or a particular part of my life such as my professional background or my family life. It addresses questions like:

- What was it like growing up in the Midwest in the 40s and 50s?
- Who were the Aakers going back two generations? What did they do and value? How did they influence me?
- How did a Fargo boy in over his head survive at MIT and Stanford?
- How did three highly qualified entrepreneurs fail? Why was failure a good thing?
- What is an academic life like? What processes and people populate it?
- How did my academic research stream evolve toward the study of brands? Why did portions of my research lack impact?
- What were the drivers that led to new research directions or to impactful work?
- Who were the five key Aaker coauthors and what were their roles?
- Why is academic research interesting, even fascinating?
- What is life as a public speaker and author like? What are my eight speaker rules?
- What is it like to have a second professional home in Japan?
- What is Prophet, and what role do I play in growing this small consulting company?
- How did the Aaker family with three daughters evolve over forty years?
- What were the activities, the lifestyles, and the relationships that represented those forty years?

- What makes a good friend, and what are the characteristics of a successful marriage partner (according to Dave Aaker)?

I have tried wherever possible to provide not only detailed descriptions of activities, events, and people with anecdotes to illustrate and inform, but also the associated feelings. I wanted, where possible, to get beneath description and offer insight into who I am, why I did what I did, the passions that motivated me, and the nature of the relationships that I developed.

The book is structured in topic sections so that it would be easy for the reader to skip or skim parts that are less relevant to them, although many of the insights into my personality are sprinkled here and there. Many of the sections will span wide time periods because spreading them out over multiple chapters would make the narrative more difficult to read.

I have had books that have sold in the tens—even hundreds— of thousands. I am not sure if this book will have an audience beyond my friends, relatives, and family. The sales may be measured in the dozens. In the unlikely event that there are any net royalties, they will be donated to charity.

My thanks to the pros at Iceni Books. Nathaniel Birdsall, a fellow Fargoan, did a nice job copyediting. Atilla Vekony helped me understand photo scanning and encouraged me through the final stages of writing. Finally, Susan Wenger, a patient, friendly, and talented production editor, made the book become a reality.

My thanks to all those who have helped me grow, live, and achieve. There are a host of people to acknowledge, starting with my parents, my wife Kay, my three kids, our friends (especially the DeJonghe family), and my professional colleagues that have been especially meaningful and supportive. Thanks to those that helped me with the creation of the book. My daughter Jennifer, in particular, read the manuscript in detail and pushed me to improve it. However, despite that help, the book is what it is.

Credits

The cover picture was taken by Mr. Takayuki Watanabe, Manager, Creative Management Division, Dentsu Inc.

The image of the cover of *Strategic Market Management* (first edition by David Aaker, copyright 1984 by John Wiley), and *Marketing Research* (second edition by David Aaker and George Day, copyright 1983 John Wiley) are both reprinted with permission of John Wiley & Sons, Inc.

The image of the cover of *Absatzwirtschaft* is used by permission of the publisher and the artist, Christian Eckert.

The images of the covers of *Consumerism* by David A. Aaker and George Day; *Managing Brand Equity* by David A. Aaker; *Building Strong Brands* by David A. Aaker; *Brand Leadership* by David A. Aaker and Erich Joachimsthaler; and *Brand Portfolio Strategy* are all reproduced by permission of The Free Press, a Division of Simon & Schuster Adult Publishing Group. All rights reserved.

The image of *Three Men in a Boat* by Jerome K. Jerome copyright 1957 by Penguin Books is reproduced by permission of Penguin Books and the illustrator, Ken Cox.

The image of *The World's Religions* by Huston Smith copyright 1991 by Huston Smith reprinted by permission by Harper/Collins.

The first stanza of the poem "Seaside Golf" by John Betjeman from *Collected Poems* is reproduced by permission of John Murray Publishers.

1 Growing Up in Fargo

My adventure in Fargo, North Dakota, started February 11, 1938. In 1938, the nation, under the leadership of Franklin D. Roosevelt, was still trying to find an exit to a depression nearly a decade old. North Dakota, a farm state that had suffered through the mid-1930s from droughts and dust storms (black blizzards), was no exception. North Dakotans were frugal by necessity and inclination. Many were Scandinavian immigrants or their descendents who had left tough economic times in their homeland. Stable jobs, such as being a postal worker, were prized. Yet people in Fargo, at least in my parent's circle of friends, seemed to be active, happy, and good at enjoying simple pleasures.

Fargo

Fargo, with some 33,000 people, was on the eastern edge of North Dakota, separated from the Minnesota town of Moorhead, with its 8,000 or so people, by the Red River of the North (which actually flows north). It was the largest city in North Dakota and the largest city between Montana and Minneapolis. Its regional prominence was reflected by the presence of two major railroads, the Northern Pacific and the Great Northern. The primary industry was farming, with the rich Red River Valley generating grains such as wheat, oats, and barley (with global warming the crops have lately shifted to corn, sugar beets, and soybeans). The terrain was flat, and there was no semblance of a hill for miles—the only trees to be seen were by a river or those planted by the government during the Depression to provide windbreaks. The

1

whole state was like a tabletop. The Red River was a quiet, dirty stream that erupted into a serious flood every four years or so.

Fargo was the regional metropolis but modest in shopping and available activities. The downtown was about ten blocks long and ended at a large park inexplicably called Island Park despite the fact that there was no island. It featured three department stores, Hearst (where my brother Paul once got lost at age two and was found at the police department), Moody's, and DeLendrecies, six menswear stores (such as The Fargo Toggery), eleven women's clothing stores (The Store Without a Name being one), and numerous mom and pop grocery stores, three of which were near my home and within a few blocks of each other. There were three colleges, North Dakota Ag College (now renamed North Dakota State University), Concordia (supported by a branch of the Lutheran Church and founded in 1890), and the Moorhead State Teacher's College (now Moorhead State).

For adult activities there were six or seven movie theaters, an outdoor drive-in theater (where a speaker was attached to your car), a few bowling alleys, the library, the Elks club, assorted churches, two golf courses, and a fairgrounds that held a county fair each year that had animal awards, rodeos, and rides. The municipal golf course, Edgewood, was on the north side of town, while a country club was on the other side. Our family was an Edgewood, northside-type for sure. The Aakers knew their place economically and socially; it was not at the country club.

The top cuisine was found in a few hotel restaurants: the Powers, the Graver, the Gardner, the F-M Hotel, and a few steak-houses in Moorhead. The F-M had a "view" restaurant on the top floor of what I believe was an eight-floor building. Moorhead had a big edge over Fargo because in North Dakota you could not serve drinks in restaurants (except at private clubs like the Elks). The Moorhead steakhouses thus enjoyed a price premium, although the décor was more plastic then upscale. Fargo did have some ethnic fare. Maybe six times a year, we patronized a Chinese restaurant, ironically called the "Fargo Café," that specialized in chicken chow mein. A Norwegian smorgasbord offered Norwegian dishes such as meatballs, herring, and cheese. Remarkably, given today's scene, there was not one pizza restaurant. This was definitely not an Italian area, and the pizza chains had not gotten traction. Round Table and Pizza Hut were not even around in the forties and fifties. The absence of more good restaurants did not bother my parents because they did not eat out often.

Fargo is very different today. It is over four times as large, with some 175,000 people in the area. There is a million-square-foot mall, indoor tennis, an indoor driving range, a dome that houses events of all sorts, and a host of museums. The revived downtown includes renovated hotels, boutique hotels, and a variety of trendy restaurants. The nicest theater of my day, the Fargo Theater, has become a historic art deco theater with a live organ and classic movies.

Fargo has always made the lists of the best cities to live or do business in, mainly because of its people, the safe neighborhoods, the Midwestern values, the cost of living, and the work ethic. Fargoans are proud of where they live, even if they do occasionally complain about the weather. The area was especially inhospitable in the winter for adults in my era who, unlike their kids, did not tend to play in the snow and go skating. The winters were long—very long—and punctuated with storms that brought heavy snow, high winds, and bitter cold. Shoveling the walks and driveways was a challenge. Actually shoveling snow was not only difficult but dangerous. Our class golfer, Norm Vennerstrom, was one of many who had a heart attack while shoveling snow. People stranded on highways by a storm could and did freeze to death. A family friend recalls the deadly storm of March 14, 1941, with its dirt, winds, extreme cold, and several deaths that hit while my parents were at her house playing bridge. I (then three years old) was home with a baby-sitter. Despite advice to the contrary, my father covered his face and walked five blocks to relieve my baby-sitter, a risky undertaking.

The summers with welcome warm weather were wonderful except for the humidity, the mosquitoes, and the thunderstorms. Late in the day, the mosquitoes would "eat you alive" unless there was a rare breeze to keep them down or you escaped into a screened porch. Thus, it was usually hard to enjoy the warm evenings. There were frequent, sometimes unpredictable, thunderstorms that could affect picnic plans. And there was the rare tornado. In 1957, one hit Fargo and tore the roof off the Andrist house (Mabel Andrist was a golfing friend of my mother, and her daughter Kay would become my wife—more on that later). We survived, and we found a phonograph record in our tree the next day. Summers were also a time when there was ongoing concern whether the farmers had too much or not enough rain.

Fall and spring would come in fits and starts. April, May, October, and November could see wide day-to-day variations in weather. The weather report was always news in Fargo, unlike San Francisco, where the weather forecast is nearly always the same.

The Early Days

In 1942, my parents bought their first house, 1045 Second Street North, a corner house fifteen blocks from "downtown." It was my home during my Fargo days. The house always seemed secure and comfortable. The entryway faced a staircase that led to two bedrooms of modest size (but which seemed roomy to me at the time) separated by a bath. A cozy den off the living room held a piano and desk. A dining room looked out onto Horace Mann, the school I attended from the first through the seventh grade, and the school where (future wife) Kay Andrist's father taught. The roomy basement contained a ping-pong table, a pinball machine, and, later, a knotty pine bedroom. The single-stall garage was separated from the house, and the walk from one to the other in the winter could be uncomfortable. I can't imagine carrying groceries on a windy day with below zero temperature. A corner house meant that the sidewalk involved three times as much snow shoveling in the winter. My bedroom window was only a few feet from a bedroom of the house next door. When I was about seven or so I had some romantic conversations with Jo Lobb, a girl one or two years my senior, protected by the space between us.

When I was in college, at my mother's insistence, we moved about two blocks into a more "modern" house on 1213 First Street. A single-story, rambling home in a newer (but not new) neighborhood, it was a step up for sure. The most notable amenities were a fireplace in the living room, a connected dining/living room,

1045 Second St. North

a third bedroom, a "modern" kitchen, an attached garage, and hallways. For some reason Ida craved hallways, which Oscar felt was simply wasted space. (Like Oscar, I get inordinate pleasure out of using space efficiently.) I felt that part of my childhood with its memories, experiences, and heritage had been take away. And I was in no way consulted about the decision. In retrospect, I should have been happy for my mother, but I was not blessed as a young man with such sensitivities (which, of course, I now have in excess).

The first record of my impact on the community was on May 5, 1942, when a picture of the Aaker family examining the first sugar ration books issued in Fargo during World War II appeared on the first page of the *Fargo Forum*. The start of rationing was big news, but not the only news that day. Japan attacked Chungking using the Burma Road; fighting was fierce in Corregidor and Madagascar; the Nazi forces executed 127 people in France and Holland; and some 400 products were deprived of iron and steel needed by the war effort. Closer to home, a

The first sugar ration book in Fargo—1941

prize was available for the jitterbug contest at Eddie's Nightclub, dresses were being sold for under two dollars at Penney's, and a two-quart container of milk sold for nineteen cents at Vic's Supermarket.

There were plenty of neighborhood children to play with. I did well with women early on. The picture of myself in a parade at age four playing a drum between two cute girls shows I was no male chauvinist. Another picture taken a year later shows me at a party, the only boy with five girls, wearing a rather debonair sweater and jacket. Another of my outfits that same year, 1943, was a military uniform complete with hat. I may have sensed that women of the day were attracted to uniforms.

There was a limit to my patience as a boy. My mother always liked to go out after Sunday church at First Lutheran for a Sunday dinner (as opposed to the light evening supper). One of her favorite places for this outing was the Powers Hotel. Although their free "popovers" were delicious, I always lobbied hard against

At age 3—not
a chauvinist

Age 4—ready
for World War II

this monumental waste of time. I much preferred to get home and into some comfortable clothes and start some serious playing.

My mother tells a story about an incident when I was six or seven. We were waiting for the bus to take us home from church. Gasoline was rationed during the war, so the bus was a very reasonable alternative for the fifteen-block ride. But I did not like to wait very long, and one day—and in the midst of a large group of churchgoers—I bolted out to the street, peered down the block, and asked angrily, "Where is that damned bus?" My mother has no idea where I could have learned such a word. Another story of the same vintage had me observing during a dinner at our neighbors', "I don't eat this kind of soup at home."

I had my first girlfriend in the second grade, but she moved away and our love did not survive. My romantic interests then receded until the fifth grade, when my friends and I again discovered girls. We then had wheels—bicycles—that allowed us to escort the girls home. One time after school we were a bit too forward—I guess we buzzed them on our bikes—and we were called before the principal. It was an uncomfortable time. In the sixth grade we wrote lists of the girls that we liked. These lists were entrusted to unreliable people, so leaks were inevitable. It was most embarrassing when these very private lists became public information, and very sad when one of the less popular people would have an unattainable list exposed, thereby becoming a subject of derision.

My folks did not travel much, undoubtedly the preference of my father. But on one occasion they did try a major trip without me. They went to California, where the high-lights were a stay on the Queen Mary, berthed near San Diego, and a trip to Coronado Island. I stayed with an older couple that had a musty house and a tightly organized schedule that included listening each night to H. V. Kaltenborn, the evening anchorman

Brother Paul

of the day, pontificate on political issues with a very distinctive speaking style.

Paul, my cute redheaded brother, born in 1946, was eight years my junior. Where the red hair came from was a mystery until my father grew a red beard during the Fargo centennial when most Fargo men grew beards in order to relate to the early pioneers. Paul shared my room until high school, when our dad built a room for me in the basement. I don't recall any major sharing problems—that was simply the way it was. We had a small library in the room and both liked to read. However, I do recall being glad to get my own room in the basement somewhere in my teens, even if it was a bit dank.

When I got old enough to baby-sit, I became the first option. One Christmas my folks had a social event every night for two weeks, and on each of those nights I was called on to watch Paul. I didn't mind baby-sitting or the low pay, but I did mind being tied down every night. I had a social life as well. I got frustrated, and one night when Paul was asleep I snuck out to play hockey. As luck would have it, that was the night I was tripped and cut my chin. I went to our neighbor, Don Warren, to see if I should go to the doctor. He advised against it. Big mistake—I still have the scar. When my folks returned, I emphasized my injury to divert attention from shirking my duty. My folks were perturbed that I'd left Paul, but they also felt guilty for imposing on me, and they did not have, as usual, the disposition to engage in any meaningful discipline.

In the summer most people had a garden in which they raised fresh vegetables, always including iceberg lettuce (which was served in wedges with thick French dressing over it) and tomatoes that were incredibly flavorful. I recall the victory gardens of World War II that appeared when I was six or seven. They were more significant undertakings on a major plot of land several blocks from my house. The idea was to raise food so that more resources could be diverted to the war effort. My father tried his hand but lacked a green thumb. A "friend" put up crosses to commemorate Dad's dead tomato plants. I once tried tomatoes with the same result—green thumbs are apparently genetic.

A staple of every backyard was rhubarb. It was a fast-growing reddish stalk with a wide leaf. The taste of the stalk when eaten raw was sharp and sour, but flavorful. However, it was usually served as a dessert, either in rhubarb sauce or rhubarb pie. In either case the product was heavily laced with sugar. There was a time when rhubarb was my favorite pie, although it later lost out to banana cream (with piles of real meringue—no cream tops for me).

Meals at my house tended to feature hearty meat and potatoes. Meatloaf and pot roast were frequent main courses. I suspect I was served potatoes nearly every day in Fargo. Liver and onions with bacon made its appearance about once a week because of its health value. Steak was regarded as something of a luxury. When steak was served, my mother bought cheap cuts and made sure it was well done. As a result, it was neither tender nor tasty. To this day I have never liked steak, so it has not been a hardship to avoid red meat. When freezers were introduced, deciding whether to buy one was a huge topic of conversation. The killer app (application) of the day was to buy a side of beef—either a quarter, half, or whole steer. The freezer and meat purchase represented a big investment, but the payoff seemed worth it. My folks finally bought a freezer and settled for a quarter side of beef. The quality

Dave at Horace Mann ...

It got cold in Fargo!

of the meat probably improved, but, unfortunately, the preparation did not.

Horace Mann School

Kids and parents were serious about school in our part of town. Although kids will be kids, most teachers had a relatively easy time with discipline. The parents were under control as well (unlike some Orinda parents)—there was not a lot of pressure for first-graders to start establishing a record that would lead to Stanford. The school simply reflected the Midwestern school work ethic.

Music at Horace Mann was not one of my things. The music teacher, Miss Ellifson, had a system. She put the best singers in the rear, the second best in the second to the rear, and so on. The logic made sense. People would have an incentive to achieve the recognition of moving toward the rear. Further, the poorer singers could be "helped" by listening to those behind them. However, being branded as the worst did not make the class a barrel of laughs. Further, the music teacher made a big deal of the Christmas show. She spent months priming students for "that night." I was one of three or so to whom she gently but directly suggested that it might be better if we moved our lips but didn't actually sing. From the first through the third grade, I got A's and B's in ten subjects, but C's and D's in music. How harsh is that? Giving a first-grader a D in music is not a confidence builder.

We did not progress as fast at reading as students do now. I recall that in the second grade I could not read a lick. However, I once offered to pick out the next book that the teacher would read aloud to the class. I went up to the bookshelf and with great concentration pretended to mull over the selection, when, in fact, I could not read the titles. In the third grade, small circles of students would read aloud out of material that was not very demanding. I don't believe that I could read with any real fluency until the fourth grade.

I did better in "auditorium" (a combination of literature and dramatics) under the guidance of a no-nonsense teacher, Mabel Garman. My biggest achievement was memorizing and performing "Casey at the Bat," a very emotional story of a local baseball hero that struck out. I recall the teacher insisting that two stanzas would be enough, but I found other audiences that would listen to the whole thing. I still get called on to recite it. I found the poem in our twenty-volume *Book of Knowledge*. Every family that wanted their kids to be successful had to have an encyclopedia. I actually spent hours reading its wide selection of poetry. I especially liked poems with a beat, such as those of Robert Service.

Horace Mann was the site of marble competitions before and after school. You would put a desirable mooney (clear marble) down, and others would try to capture it by hitting it from a distance that would be fixed depending on the desirability of the mooney (usually based on its size). You would collect the misses and could accumulate a lot of marbles that often tended to fall out of very full pockets in school. As there was no referee, arguments would ensue. In contrast, my father had a different take on marbles. His schoolboy group would put marbles in a circle. The goal would then be to knock them out of the circle by flipping a "shooter" marble with a thumb. I could never master the flip.

Living across the street from the school had several implications. I could leave for school later and thus sleep in more than others. The upshot was that I was frequently late for school. I could always go home at lunch for a hot meal. Campbell's soup and toasted cheese sandwiches were frequently on the menu. Horace Mann was also a convenient recreation facility. I practiced basketball on the outdoor courts. My father got out on rare occasions to demonstrate the underhanded technique of the 20s, but I was usually by myself when I practiced my shots. Later, when I took up tennis, I spent hours using the side of the brick building to refine my tennis strokes. It was hard because the ball would come off at angles.

My best friend, Roy Smillie, lived a block away. When I was nine, in 1947, he and I celebrated New Year's by playing Monopoly until midnight under my grandmother's watchful eye—a very adult evening. For several years we would say "good luck" when parting, but, finally, that seemed too childish.

Sports

Even in elementary school, sports were an important part of my life. The major winter activities were skating and hockey. We tried skiing, but we were short on equipment and hills. When we got older we skied behind cars in the country, a dangerous activity because the sides of the road were not designed with skiers in mind—you could hit a culvert. So skating it was. I'm sure that I skated virtually every day all winter (around five months per year) from the second to the sixth grade. The rink was an easy three blocks away. I would swing my skates over my hockey stick and trudge down the streets crusted with snow. The exceptions were those days when the rink closed because it was colder than fifteen below or storming hard. I recall the exhilaration of hitting the ice for the first time each day. There was such a feeling of speed, control, and accomplishment. And the warming hut, where snacks and hot chocolate were available, was small but warm and filled with friends.

I was good at the coordination aspects of hockey but short on aggressiveness and personal courage. Depending upon your viewpoint, I relied upon skill and finesse rather than brute force, or I was a coward fearing for physical safety. In fact, I played center and was one of the best skaters and stick handlers in my grade at our rink, where I played with Bruce Larson, Tom Wright, and others who also were into skill rather than intimidation. However, in the sixth grade we advanced to the point of playing boys from a rougher part of the northside who were aggressive and did not abide by our gentlemanly rules of no checking or lifting the puck into opponents. We were totally intimidated. A player from this group caused the scar on my chin the night I was supposed to be baby-sitting by tripping me from behind after I had embarrassed him with a particularly good play.

The prime activity in the summer was baseball. I was usually the captain because I was a great talker and organizer—not because of my ability. Although I had good footwork as a catcher or first baseman (not important skills), I could not throw, field grounders, or hit (skills that were important). Because of my weak arm, I was limited to playing first or second base. As a catcher my throws to second base involved a bounce, as an infielder I always

With Mike McLain,
set to battle the
elements

thought that grounders would bounce up and hit me in the face, and as a batter I feared getting hit by a pitch. Despite my lack of potential, the games were important to me. I once imposed on my father to interrupt our lake vacation to drive sixty miles to one of my Little League games.

Swimming was another summer activity. But it was strictly recreational—there were no swim teams in Fargo. The main swimming outlet was a large municipal pool at Island Park, in the middle of town. I would ride my bike the two miles or so to get there. We would pay our fifteen cents and receive a metal wire container in which we would place our clothes. The number of the container would be attached to an elastic band that we placed around our ankles. It was rather like going to prison. The pool itself seemed enormous but on a hot day was completely full of people—there was no way you could swim two strokes without bumping into someone. I didn't enjoy swimming that much.

At the behest of my parents, I also tried scouting. The meetings were OK because we played ping-pong. And the Boy Scout camp I attended over two summers was fun with a lot of water sports. There I learned the backstroke, breaststroke (or frog), crawl, and sidestroke. While the sidestroke never became an Olympic event, it can be very helpful when swimming a long way. However, the merit badge route required real time and effort. It was basically a lot of crafts and camping, and I never liked either activity. So after maybe three years I was still a tenderfoot.

An important part of our house was its basement with its pinball machine and ping-pong table. I played countless games with my parents and with several friends such as Tom Wright and

John Altenburg. We kept track of scores, and I did well against both Tom and John. Once, when I got some boxing gloves, the basement became the site of a boxing match with Tom. Boxing, which requires a modicum of personal courage and reckless physical abandon, was definitely not my sport—I lost quickly and retired from the sport. Our basement was also where I learned to pass a basketball behind my back with either hand by using the concrete wall as a backboard. That skill was satisfying to develop but virtually useless except in the hands of a player like Bob Cousy, Pete Maravich, or Jason Kidd.

During the winter months we found things to do inside. One of our friends, David Scott, had a large house that included a billiard table and assorted other games. We spent hours there mostly learning billiards. I felt rather worldly playing such a grown-up game.

There were no African Americans in Fargo, so my parents had no firsthand knowledge of them. I recall my father using the phrase "darkies" when, even then, that was not politically correct. My mother once suggested that I not play so much with Bruce Larson because he had kinky black hair and might therefore be part "Negro." I went apoplectic, making sure that my mother realized how prejudiced I thought she was, and I deliberately made my association with Bruce more frequent and visible than ever.

Entertainment and Activities

There was no television during the 40s, but there were a host of radio shows that commanded a loyal following. *The Buster Brown Show* with Buster Brown and his dog Tye was an early favorite. We then graduated to mysteries like *The Lone Ranger* ("It's the masked man with his big horse Silver"), *Superman* ("It's a bird, it's a plane, no, it's Superman!"), *The Shadow* ("The Shadow knows"), and comedy shows like *Jack Benny*, *The Great Gildersleeve*, *Fred Allen*, and *Can You Top This*, a joke show. *The Hit Parade* had a countdown for the top seven songs of the day. I remember throwing a tantrum once when I was not permitted to listen to one of my favorite shows. I think my folks learned from that incident not to fool with me—I usually got my way after that. The theme song of *The Lone Ranger*, the *William Tell Overture*, was my only exposure to classical music.

Saturday morning movies were a great attraction. We would walk, bus, or bike to a theater to see a movie for all of twelve cents; often it would be a Roy Rogers or Gene Autry western. In addition, there was an extra show, a serial that would be spread over about eight weeks. It would always stop at a crucial time with the hero in an impossible situation. You simply had to return the following week to see what happened. These serials provided the inspiration for *Raiders of the Lost Ark* and its sequels.

Our first TV set came sometime around 1950. Much of the day you just got a test panel, a geometric design that allowed you to tell if the picture was centered and clear. When there was programming, you could access three or four channels, many of which would be snowy. There was some art to adjusting the rabbit-ear antennas to improve reception. Some of the early shows were transferred from radio. Some radio personalities like *Jack Benny* and the *Lone Ranger* made the transition to TV well, but others, like Fred Allen (who was an authentic wit and a

The skis were
different then

The swing has not
improved

friend of the father of my son-in-law, Andy), struggled in the new medium. *The Hit Parade* worked on TV but could get repetitive when a song like "How Much Is That Doggie in the Window?" was number one for the fourteenth straight week. There were also new faces such as Lawrence Welk (who was a North Dakota boy and mother's favorite), Milton Berle (whose slapstick comedy really worked on TV), and Ed Sullivan, a newspaper columnist who became MC of a variety show that introduced both Elvis Presley and the Beatles to American television. In 1956, Elvis sang "Hound Dog" and "Love Me Tender" on an *Ed Sullivan* show that 82.7% of the U.S. television audience watched. The cameras did not show his hip movements, as they were considered by some to be too suggestive. Times have changed.

North Dakotans appreciate summer—whatever there might be of it. It was a time for picnics in the park. And golfing. Golfing was an activity in which I was included at an early age. I would get to follow the group and hit balls. Eventually, I would play Edgewood with my folks. I enjoyed then and today the challenge of hitting that stationary ball and the feeling that comes with connecting.

Another Saturday activity was to go to the library. I always checked out the maximum: four books. I remember the smell of dusty shelves and old books—somehow it was comfortable and pleasant. I recall my joy when I learned that there were books of fiction about sports. The Clair Bee series of books featuring Chip Hilton with titles like *Touchdown Twins* and *No-Hitter* were terrific—I read some many times. *The Hardy Boys* by Franklin Dixon, a series of some eighty-five books written between 1904 and 1985 about two brothers who experienced incredible adventures, was another staple. *Nancy Drew* was also a big seller for girls, but the appeal was definitely gender specific. I would not read a Nancy Drew book.

Very few "new" kids arrived in Fargo when I was growing up. Larry Swenson was one of the few. He moved in and tried immediately to get "in" with our group, the prestige group, consisting I suppose of Tom, John Altenburg, Mike McLain, and Roy Smillie. Larry tried everything. I recall him on a black bicycle racing past the girls and us. He had the best bike and was probably the best cyclist, but we were not impressed. Over time, Larry finally was accepted, but it was a bit of a battle, perhaps partly because he was not the sort that just blended into a crowd unobtrusively, and in part because, like most schoolkids, we were not secure enough to welcome others into our midst.

During high school and college, Larry was a clothes salesman and dealt in used cars. A natural politician, he was a fixture on the student council during high school. After graduation, he worked for several years for General Motors as a district manager (the youngest appointed to that post in the history of GM) before beginning a career as a car dealer. He owned a series of automobile dealerships—Ford in Huron, South Dakota, and Willmar, Minnesota, Chevrolet in Fargo, and Cadillac/Oldsmobile also in Fargo. He and his lovely wife now live on a lake at Park Rapids, a Minnesota town not far from Fargo. He organized a golf outing there a few years ago for Tom Wright, our Ben Franklin basketball coach, Donovan Nelson (who incidentally married one of our classmates and is still remarkably fit), and myself.

Larry has always been fun to be with. He has opinions, is never boring, and is always good for an adventure. However, he often speaks with a serious, sincere voice that some (not me of course) occasionally label in a good-natured way as pompous. Larry is the very definition of a good friend. When Roy Smillie got melanoma in the mid-1980s, Larry was there for him during the last year or so getting him involved in a business venture and finally helping to care for him. Friendship does not get better than that.

Vacations

Our vacations most years were local and modest, reflecting the frugality of my parents and my father's reluctance to take long trips. We never, for example, escaped the long winter by going to Arizona or Florida. Flying would have been way too extravagant, and driving would take too long given my father's limited vacation time. So we mainly stayed around home exploiting the Minnesota lake country.

Many families had a cottage on one of the numerous lakes around fifty miles away, such as Pelican, Melissa, Cotton, or Detroit—but not the Aakers. My parents regarded a lake cottage (like the country club membership and even dining out) as an unnecessary extravagance. But even without owning a cottage, the lakes still played a role in our summer life.

Our vacation always included one or two weeks at a rental cottage on Broadwater Beach on Lake Pelican, about sixty miles east of Fargo. A two-bedroom cottage, it was primitive in the early years with an outhouse with the worst odor imaginable and an icebox. Every other day or so my father took a wheelbarrow to the local icehouse

Where is the game?
The Pelican cabin

about a block away, picked up a block of ice, and hauled it to the kitchen. However, the cottage did finally get indoor facilities, an extra bedroom, and a refrigerator—luxuries that were not taken for granted.

The prime activities were swimming, boating, fishing, and playing with neighbors. There was a floating platform about thirty yards from shore to which we often attached an inflatable boat that was tipped over. It could be used as the basis for tag and hide and seek as well as diving and sunning. My greatest thrill, however, was getting to run our boat with its 3.3 hp Evenrude outboard motor by myself. What a feeling of independence that was! It was superior to my first bike or first car. You could start and stop it at will, go anywhere, turn sharply—it was great. I would take it on long fishing trips to Fish Lake, perhaps two miles away, nestled around a point. However, the trip was more important than the fishing, which was just OK unless the sunfish (which would put up a vigorous fight) were biting. Being accepted by the neighbors was also important. It helped that I was good at the ball games that they tended to play. I remember one year that we had rain every day of our vacation. I just played outside with the neighbors, but my folks must have really suffered.

My friend Roy Smillie had a cottage across the lake and I would motor across—a forty-minute trip. What an adventure! And there were no life vests in those days. When I got to the other side, the first task was to travel along the shore looking for his cottage. I could never hit shore very close to it. At the Smillie cottage, we would play badminton, ski, or surf behind his big ten-horse, and be spoiled by his mother. Now, of course, kids use nothing smaller than seventy-five hp outboard engines. On one occasion, an electrical storm came up as I was returning. The waves and whitecaps were a worry, but the possibility of being hit by lighting, a very real likelihood in an aluminum boat, was really frightening. I made it, but the last twenty minutes were among the longest in my life. My mother was very glad to see me.

There were other vacations oriented around the Minnesota lakes. Each summer we also had a gathering of the Aaker family at Lake Bertha, a subject for the next chapter. In 1952, we had a vacation from hell when, with three other families, we took over a house on an island on Lake Lizzie, accessed by a rickety barge. First, the power went out, so we had no lights, refrigerator, or water pressure. Then there was an explosion in the gas stove just before the gas ran out. We stored the food in the well until we realized rats were eating it. A storm prevented us from leaving. However, it was hard to complain about the nightmare experience because the owner of the island, a local church, had offered it to us "free." "Free" was a big upside for my family and friends.

With two exceptions, our travels never extended beyond the Black Hills in South Dakota or Duluth, Minnesota. The first exception was a trip to the West Coast to visit my mother's cousin, Gaylan Larson (who was then studying to be an optometrist), in Eugene, Oregon, and her aunt (Ann Larson) in Tacoma. I recall packing the '38 Chevrolet for the trip. There was barely enough room on one side of the backseat for a small boy. There was no air conditioning, and the trip was hot and long. We would pass the time by attempting to spot state license plates from as many states as possible. We saw Yellowstone, Glacier National Park, and the Pacific Ocean, all breathtaking after a life on the Dakota prairie.

The other exception was in 1952 when, at age fourteen, I joined my parents on a trip to Detroit, where my father was attending a meeting connected to his work at the telephone company. One of the biggest thrills of my life was seeing my first major league baseball game. The Yankees played the Tigers, and Yogi Berra hit two home runs. It was awe-inspiring. In addition to the game, I recall my mother being nervous about driving on Detroit's bewildering freeway system filled with huge trucks. I wrote a letter to my grandparents detailing our visit to the Ford Museum, a showplace for the heritage of the Ford Motor Company and the marvels of the production line pioneered by Henry Ford.

Junior High Years

My junior high years were good for me both athletically and socially. I spent seventh grade at Horace Mann, which was then a school that spanned first through eighth grades. The eighth and ninth grade were spent at the newly constructed Ben Franklin Junior High, about a mile from my house. The new school was spiffy and up-to-date. It felt good walking in those doors.

My big achievement in the seventh grade was making the basketball team. In fact, I was perhaps the best seventh-grader in basketball. Although I didn't realize it then, it was to be the pinnacle of my basketball career. I also made the team in the eighth and ninth grades, but the talents of my contemporaries continued to improve, whereas mine seemed to have plateaued. I was strong at the fundamentals of passing and shooting but never got comfortable with team play. Still, I was on the team and got to go to practice. By high school, I dropped basketball (or more accurately, basketball dropped me) as an active participant. But in junior high I was one of the athletes.

I also played football and ran track in junior high at the insistence of our basketball coach, who felt that the experience would sharpen our talents. I had no talent for either sport. In football I was too nearsighted and weak-armed to play quarterback and too slow for much of anything else. So I played guard, but my small size and fear of getting hurt were handicaps. In track I developed great high jump and shot-put form but had zero talent. My performance was a joke. In my view, the reason people don't excel is often mistakenly attributed to a lack of practice or coaching when it is really a simple lack of talent. My track efforts (and piano playing for that matter) are a case in point. The basketball coach made me give up hockey as well (because we might get hurt—as if the team would notice). In retrospect, I had far more potential in hockey than basketball had I gone that route.

Eighth grade at Ben Franklin

Manager—Sam Norris
Coach—Don Nelson
Tom (32), Dave (29), Roy (28)

"Hooking" cars or buses, which consisted of hanging on to the rear bumper and sliding along the snowy street, provided both transportation and recreation. Every morning John Altenburg (who lived on First Street in the house that my folks ultimately bought) and I would attempt to hook a bus from Second Street up to Seventh Street, where Ben Franklin was located. We never considered riding the bus for such a short trip. Sometimes the drivers would smear grease inside the bumper to discourage us. Tom and I would often skip our Saturday morning confirmation class to hook cars as well. I'm sure that hooking cars is no longer an option in Fargo. In those times, the streets were continuously covered with a coat of packed snow. Now, there is much less snow, and the use of salt reduces the number of days that the roads are covered even when the snow is heavy.

I was fairly successful socially in junior high, even dating a cheerleader. A group of popular girls had arrived at Ben Franklin eager to meet the fabulous Horace Mann boys who impressed with suave personalities, cool wardrobes, and dazzling self-confidence. A lot of the social whirl revolved around the skating rink. We would ask girls to skate and would circle the rink holding the girl around the waist. It was terrific fun! A ploy that Tom Wright and I employed was to meet our dates in the balcony of the theater. That meant, of course, that we didn't have to pay for their ticket. It also meant that we could arrive whenever we felt like it. I still recall our girls sitting with Swenson and others and leaving them to come to us when we arrived. My romance did not survive high school, where she had better pickings.

In our class there was a boy named Fred that was different. We were amazed to learn that he had memorized the telephone directory, and he could demonstrate his knowledge by giving us our number knowing only our name or address. Shy with a gangly body that was not always coordinated, Fred did not fit in, and some teased him, causing him considerable discomfort. We now know that he was autistic, a person who finds social interaction confusing and scary, and who had special skills, in this case an ability to memorize numbers. Such a person, termed an autistic savant, was the subject of the movie *Rain Man* with Dustin Hoffman and Tom Cruise. I like to think that schoolchildren today would handle such a classmate in a more understanding manner than we did then.

A big project during the summer prior to entering high school was to begin the insect collection that was to be assigned for high school biology, which would be taught by Art Dronen in the following fall. John Altenburg was determined to get an A and collected hundreds of specimens. Working with John was a mixed blessing. On one hand, I got a lot of insects just by using his duplicates. On the other, I got into the project far more than I wanted. It was this project and the subsequent course that convinced me that I was not destined for medicine. The grade was based upon the number of insects collected. Ladybugs were the best. They came with different numbers of spots on them, and I figured that the number of spots was the way that one species was distinguished from another. It turned out that the teacher disagreed.

John followed his science interest by becoming an ophthalmologist after marrying an attractive Fargo girl. He retired after practicing in the Air Force, and he and his wife Sue moved to Florida, where he developed a successful private practice doing operations on eyes. We see them periodically and hear about their travels. He and his wife take off three or four times a year, going to exotic places to view and take pictures of animals. Africa and Asia are common destinations, but one trip took them to Antarctica.

I was not that well informed about current events as a junior high student. Harry Truman sacked General Douglas MacArthur in June of 1951 for speaking in public about using nationalist Chinese troops in Korea. I recall being puzzled at the time and uncertain who was the hero of that decision. I was not alone, of course, as MacArthur got a ticker-tape parade in New York. When Senator Joseph McCarthy of Wisconsin claimed in 1950 to have a list of 205 communist spies in the State Department, I wondered, like many others, why the government allowed spies to hold jobs in the government. Of course, thanks to television, McCarthy's excesses finally become public in 1954, and he was brought down. However, for a time, few stood up to him. I was nervous about the nuclear threat and recall wondering, like many of those in Fargo, whether a bomb shelter would be worthwhile. Given that Fargo would never be a target and that any shelter would be next to useless, there was not much logic in those thoughts. But, as a young boy with superficial knowledge at best, the fear was real.

Confirmation class, a two-year Saturday morning commitment preparing young people for full church membership, was something most Lutheran children went through. My class was under the supervision of Revered Berge, a stern Lutheran minister that set the standard for boring. He did not have a knack for making the scriptures and Lutheran dogma interesting and persuasive. The goal of the two-year course was to memorize large chunks of material, much of which was passed off as "truth" by Reverend Berge. The climax was a test in which the students would stand up in the aisle of the sanctuary in front of an audience of apprehensive parents. The minister asked questions to the "candidates," and a memorized response was expected. I had bluffed my way to the point that he thought I actually knew the stuff. So I got the hard questions, and my memory was not up to the task. It was a disaster. The whole experience, I suspect, was intended to make us better and more committed Lutherans. It did the reverse. Memorizing answers to questions that seem irrelevant just created doubts and skepticism.

Since that time my religious feelings have evolved. I consider myself a believer in God and a Christian. I find a relationship with a higher being comforting, uplifting, and helpful in creating life priorities. Further, parts of the Bible—such as the twenty-third psalm—can be a friend in difficult times. Christianity, to me, means that a concern for others in thought and deed— whether it be family, friends, or disadvantaged people at home or abroad— is an obligation, an opportunity to enrich lives, and a source of rewards and warm feelings. It provides an inspiration to do the right thing when others are involved. Easter and Christmas, whether based on reality or myth, help put life's daily happenings into perspective. I have been a fairly regular churchgoer for much of my life and usually find the sermons to be stimulating and the music inspiring. Christianity is like a kind, empathetic, principled friend, and role model.

Having said all that, I do have reservations about the dogma and intolerance sometimes associated with organized religion. Reverend Berge insisted that any who were not Christian would not get to heaven, and he implied you had a much better chance if you were a Lutheran or at least a Protestant. That made no sense to me then or now. I have no issue with those Christians (or Muslims or those of the Jewish faith) that have beliefs that differ from mine on interpretations of the Bible, on social issues, or on how people should behave or dress. However, I get annoyed when they signal that their way is the only right way and attempt to impose it on others. Of course Christians, at least in this country, no longer have the Inquisition, the Salem witch trials, or similar mechanisms to enforce adherence to the dogma of the day and place, but I too often observe an intolerance about the beliefs and actions of others that makes me uncomfortable.

High School Years

In retrospect, my high school experience was a good one. There were no protests or drugs in the 50s, so the school and associated activities were relatively placid and goal directed. Although, like many, I struggled socially on occasion, there were plenty of fun times. It was also productive with solid academics, opportunities with class politics, and the debate team experience.

My high school was the venerable Fargo Central, an older school that housed some 950 students in a solid, imposing structure, with three large staircases in front, about three miles from my home. Our nickname, the Midgets, was coined in 1911 when the championship football team averaged 138 pounds. During my sophomore year, I mostly walked the three miles home—even in blizzards—although there was a bus option. As a junior and senior, however, I drove my car. Fargo Central burned down in 1966 (ten years after I graduated) and was replaced by two modern schools, one on each side of town.

I was on the debate team all three high school years and have long felt that this activity provided the single most important learning experience of my life. Each year there would be a new topic, and we would research one side with great diligence. In my senior year the topic was federal aid to education. Except for the first speaker, every participant had to be able to adapt remarks or rebuttals to what the opponent had said. Thus, there was a great premium on organizing thoughts under pressure, as well as on exposition.

Howard Erickson

Larry Swenson

Jack Bergene

John Altenburg

Dave Aaker

Tom Wright

Larry Dodge

Lyle Baker

Roy Smillie

In my junior year I had Howard Erickson as a partner. The team, which included David Papermaster and Lois Ivers (both of whom went to Harvard), did exceptionally well that year. For example, we got second in a regional tournament with some forty-five teams held at Concordia College. And we won the prestigious state tournament. In my senior year great things were expected from Lyle Baker, my new partner, and myself. To the great delight of my "friends," we barely won at all—in fact we accumulated an amazing string of losses culminating with a solid 0-5 record in the state meet. Sandra Daley, a witty, bright junior on the team, made the losing trips more bearable.

A highlight of high school was my first and last foray into the theater. I played Laurie in *Little Women*. I recall my entrance line: "What ho! Within there, what ho!" I really got into it. During the big scene I cried actual tears on cue. In contrast, the girl playing Amy opposite me, Faith Smith, a veteran of many plays, would always break up and laugh. Musicals were a big deal at Fargo High but were, of course, out of my competence arena. The school put on *Desert Song* and *Naughty Marietta* during my last two years with casts that included Roy and Larry, but not me.

I enjoyed academics and usually got the three A's needed to be on the second rung of the honor roll. My high-water mark was in the spring of my junior year, when I finally got up the courage to take a fifth solid and got all A's. My best subjects were probably math and history, and my worst were the sciences. I remember a very colorful French teacher, Theodore Vavrina, who had a strong French accent. I did learn to read and write French but was hopeless at speaking or understanding other speakers.

In high school I discovered minor sports, namely golf and tennis, that seemed to place a premium on raw coordination, did not require speed or physical strength, and involved little competition. It was clear that the sports were not only labeled as minor, but were second-class on all dimensions. The letters awarded were half the size of those of the "major" sports, and letter winners were not eligible to join the National Athletic Scholarship Society unless you won multiple letters.

In my sophomore year I played on the golf team with about a fourteen handicap. There were two or three golfers who had real talent, but then it dropped off fast. My parents taught me golf when I was around seven. Their advice was to keep the left arm straight, right elbow in the side, and swing slow. That was it. No lessons from pros. With that as background, I learned by reading books and playing. I enjoyed golfing with my folks because it seemed to be the only adult activity besides card games in which I was included. It was also a good outlet when I got stale playing tennis, always my priority sport. I recall once playing in a local golf tournament at the Fargo Country Club where I was paired with Bill Weaver, the local TV sports announcer for WDAY, who always signed off by winking and saying, "Win or lose, be a good sport." I got my first taste of hypocrisy in the media when I saw him curse, be rude, and even throw clubs. Welcome to the real world.

In my junior year I was on the tennis team; in fact, Tom Wright and I won the state doubles title. I suspect anyone on the current Miramonte girls junior varsity would have beat us. A picture of us in the *Fargo Forum* showed us topless—we were not into style. In our senior year we interrupted our graduation weekend to drive to Jamestown to lose our title (despite the fact that we represented ourselves as serious players by carrying two rackets onto the courts), again to the delight of our "friends." Larry Dodge, who beat me in the finals of the intramural tourney in both my junior and senior year held the singles spot. Through high school and college summers I must have lost thousands of sets to Larry without winning any. More on this remarkable streak in chapter three.

Tennis in Fargo was a three-month activity at Island Park's five-court complex. The hard-core players and others would hang around all summer. The social center was a shack manned by a court coordinator who sold soda. The courts were concrete and featured gaps that followed the lines. As a result, there would be frequent weird bounces, especially on the serves. There were also unforgiving metal nets, which did serve the function of surviving the severe spring weather.

I started to play tennis regularly when I was a sophomore in high school. I still recall the thrill when I realized I could rally with one of the better players. We were all self-taught; there were no pros or lessons. An active summer tennis league had four-person teams populated mostly by a cadre of older gentlemen. One,

Warner McNair, who owned an ice cream store, had a big spin serve. The challenge was to pass this group and become number two or number one on the team so you could play better players. There were three big tourneys each summer: the all-city, the state championship, and the Red River, which would attract players from South Dakota and Minneapolis. It was not until after high school, when I got some coaching in college, that I became competitive in these settings.

In my junior year, I ran for class president and lost to my friend John Altenburg, but I was elected vice-president as a consolation prize. We were both considered noncontroversial choices. All the boys voted for John and all the girls for me—there were more boys voting. I remember John was concerned that the remaining officers, Jan Burdick (the daughter of Senator Quentin Burdick and future Homecoming Queen) and Sharon Williams, might have felt funny because they voted for me instead of him—I never did understand that. Being an officer was really a boost to my ego. The job entailed a lot of activity, much of it associated with raising money for the prom that was the responsibility of the junior class. The mainstay was frequent dances. The surefire formula was a school auditorium and a cheap band. The big winners were dances around basketball tournaments. For one tournament we sold some 900 tickets for our program of dances. I really enjoyed playing the role of politician, executive, and organizer. Associating with two of the school beauties, even if they were beyond my reach, was a pleasant extra benefit.

I was very involved in creating skits for the rallies held before big football or basketball games. We would always push the boundaries of good taste if there was a good chance for a laugh. Making fun of a campus personality usually worked well. Larry Swenson, the football team's punt returner, once let the football go between his legs and roll far down the field. A skit was devoted to remembering the incident. A laugh was a laugh. Of course, I would have loved to have had the talent to be on the football team like Larry.

In June of 1955, after my junior year, I attended North Dakota Boy's State with some 525 other high school students, and I was an active politician. When it appeared that I could not get my party's nomination for governor, I started to create deals. I got my friends in our party to agree to support a rival for governor in exchange for controlling most of the other nominations. In the process I made sure that one statewide slot, the attorney general office, was reserved for me. Ironically, the "deal" tainted our party's gubernatorial candidate, and he lost. The taint did not extend to me, so with some active campaigning I won. This political microcosm was not unlike the real world. The democratic system may be better than alternatives (as Churchill noted), but it is not perfect. You get to vote, but only for the names that make the ballot, and often the process that generated those names can be shady and lack visibility. In this case, the details did not make the Boy's State newspaper.

As the attorney general candidate, I got to give a campaign speech and to be a pretend lawyer prosecuting a court case in which the defendant in a speeding car killed a person on a bicycle. To discredit the defendant's auto expert, I went to a gas station and asked a mechanic to give me two facts about a car that most would not know. The next day I got the defense expert to build himself up and then sprang the questions and made him look ridiculous. It was a Perry Mason moment. But it was only a partial victory because the defendant was only found guilty in the second degree. I had aspirations of being a lawyer and a politician, but this was my high point in the legal arena. My legal aspirations went downhill from there.

I ran for president of the senior class with little expectation of winning. My opponent (and good friend), Jack Bergene, was not only a star on the basketball team—he was taller, wittier, and more popular than me. To top it off, he was even brighter, with better grades. He proposed that we limit campaigning to three signs to save effort. Since I lacked not only energy but also supporters and resources, I immediately took him up on the offer.

I did become one of the speakers at graduation. Jack was the MC, and we used that event to exchange witticisms that I'm sure others thought were inappropriate at best. In my talk, I encouraged us to dream, to set high goals, and then to achieve those goals with hard work and persistence. I quoted Henry David Thoreau, who suggested that after building castles in the air, you need to put foundations under them. It was the only speech I have ever given that was memorized. Thank goodness it was short, because it must have sounded both presumptuous and boring. It was a conventional talk for a conventional time.

Social Life

Social life revolved around dances during high school. On Friday nights, the teen canteen was the place to be. The canteen was held at the Crystal Ballroom, a large dark hall at the foot of Broadway. On special occasions, it would draw as many as 700 students from local high schools. There was often a dance on Saturday night as well, sponsored by the junior class. The dancing was mostly the fox trot until the jitterbug arrived. The twist was not far behind. There were several formals during the year, including the prom.

I was not very successful with women in high school, in part because I was on the fringe of the in-student group and was not sufficiently appealing to the most popular girls. I recall that my junior prom date needed to get in early so (I found out later) she could go on a late date with another student, Don Enabnit, who was really cool but a bit of a party animal. To impress guys he would pass gas and set it on fire. He used other techniques to keep girls entertained. He ultimately fulfilled his ambition to own a Fargo bar, where he practiced his hanging-out skills. My prom date wrote in my yearbook, "Sorry about you know what." It was definitely a low point. For the senior prom I was the odd man out and ended up going with a girl from Moorhead. She did not have a late date, so it was a big step up over the junior prom. High school can certainly be a tough time socially—and not just at prom time.

In the summer, the dances and all social life moved fifty miles east to Detroit Lakes, where there were several beer halls and a large dance pavilion. In addition, most families had a lake cottage. Jack Bergene and I were among those without a cottage, but that didn't bother us much. We would spend a good deal of time driving from friend to friend and picking up a lot of meals and places to stay. Generally, the girls—like Joyce Ivers, whose family owned a point on Pelican—were by far the most hospitable. We could always impose on people like Roy and Tom (who had a cottage on Cotton Lake), but the flak we took was sometimes intense. As we drove up we were always greeted with terms like "lunch is over" and "we are busy today." But we were persistent. One of our best days

was when we both successfully skied together behind an underpow-
ered boat and Roy and Tom, the experienced skiers, could not.

It's really a wonder that we survived that time considering the
wild driving that went on over dark and hilly roads, often in less
than a perfectly sober condition. More on Jack and lake escapades
in chapter three.

The 50s had distinct music that people recognize even today.
Like most people who have a special attachment to the music from
their high school and college years, I still love the music of the
50s. The best was Bill Haley's "Rock Around the Clock" (from the
movie *Blackboard Jungle*, starring Glenn Ford and Sidney Poitier, a
disturbing story about a gang disrupting a high school) that stimulated the jitterbug craze. I was into the jitterbug and have since
impressed my girls by teaching it to them. We danced to that one a
lot. Charlotte Tomlinson was one dance partner that made me look
good. But there were other favorites such as "Memories Are Made
of This" (Dean Martin), "The Wayward Wind" (Gogi Grant),
"Sixteen Tons" (Ernie Ford), "Seventeen" (Fontaine Sisters), "Catch
a Falling Star" (Perry Como), "Everybody Loves a Lover" (Doris
Day), "Love Me Tender" (Elvis Presley), "The Rock and Roll
Waltz" (Kay Star), "Chantilly Lace" (The Big Bopper), "Love and
Marriage" (Dinah Shore), "The Great Pretender" (The Platters),
"Day-O" (Harry Belafonte), and "Love Letters in the Sand" (Pat
Boone). Other favorites were folk singers such as The Brothers
Four ("Greenfields"), Glenn Yarbough ("If I Had a Hammer"), The
Kingston Trio ("Tom Dooley"), and The New Christy Minstrels
("Green, Green").

Our graduation celebration consisted of a weekend at the lakes.
Our group spent it at Roy Smillie's cottage on Pelican. We stored
the beer in the large minnow storage area at the end of the dock.
I'll never forget Jack Bergene breaking everyone up at four in the
morning by barking the order, "You with the army boots, out of
the pool." The Smillie player piano played "Red Sails in the Sunset"
and "Dardenella" (songs of yesteryear) again and again and again.

Winter in North Dakota depicted in the movie *Fargo* was
severe, but it didn't seem to bother us. I remember that once
when school was closed because of the worst snowstorm in years,
some friends and I drove out to the Kilfoyl farm to tell them that

the storm was bad. We barreled through drifts in the road that must have been higher than the hood of the car. It was probably Swenson's idea. He was crazy about cars. Yet I remember once he looked me in the eye and said with all seriousness, "You need to keep two hands on the wheel at all times."

Tom, Dick Johnson (the star fullback on the football team), and I would go to Holloway Hill to ski. When approaching the hill, we would open the windows to get used to the cold. Go figure. On days when it was very cold, under twenty below, you could only stay out for twenty minutes or so before you had to get warm. Holloway Hill had a pathetically short run that ended at a lake. Nevertheless, we charged down the hill looking for any bump that would get us some air. The rope tow was difficult to use. I recall getting so tired at the end of the day I could no longer hold on to the rope. I would go through a pair of mittens each day I skied. After that experience I really appreciated chair lifts—which my kids of course take for granted. During one trip, Dick strained to remove the cap from a container. After Dick failed, Tom removed it effortlessly after an appropriate buildup. Dick was crushed. Tom never tired of reminding Dick about the incident. We all used long skis—the longer the ski, the better the skier. The better skis had metal edges and bottoms that did not stick, but cost more. We also used "long-thong" bindings, which was the only way to get good control with the old leather boots. The only problem was that any fall held a great risk of an ankle injury. There were no release bindings that worked.

Among our circle of high school friends, I was probably closest to Tom Wright, although I would say that among high school boys (as opposed to girls) there is more of a hanging-out relationship than a best-friend relationship. Nevertheless, Tom and I have always enjoyed the same sense of humor and had a lot in common. He was the best man at our wedding and I am the godfather of Dianne, his second girl. We had Dianne visit us in California. She now, coincidentally, lives in Fargo, where her husband manages a major Home Depot store.

Tom married Sharon Elliott, a wonderful girl and friend. She was one of the school's elite; she was named the most representa- tive girl (the school's highest honor), a homecoming attendant,

Tom, Dave, Sharon, and Kay

Girl's State rep, and was just a sweetheart of a person. (I complimented Tom for marrying over his head.) After spending two
years in the army (where he was basically a tennis pro based, I'm
sure, on his personality rather than his tennis talent), he attended
North Dakota State—quite an accomplishment, considering that
he had two kids by then. He then began a very successful career
at New York Life, interrupted by a tour as an executive for a St.
Paul insurance company. He lived in an idyllic setting on Lake
Minnewashta in Minneapolis. My kids loved to visit Tom and
Sharon because it was a rare chance for them to water-ski, and
because they enjoyed the Wright family, especially the two boys,
Tom and Jason. Remarkably, his oldest son, Tom, now lives in a
house on Minnewashta next to the house in which he grew up.

Tom and Sharon retired early and spent months each year in
a home they built in the middle of Baja. I once visited them there
when on a Prophet company outing to the tip of Baja. It was a
wonderful Spanish home designed and furnished by Sharon right
on the Sea of Cortez with great diving (one of their favorite activities) out their front door. A highlight of my visit was an adventure
on their four-wheeled cycles that allowed us to go to some rugged
backcountry. But to get to their place you have to drive on rutted,
unpaved, two-lane roads through small remote villages. They
have since traded that home for one in San Diego plus a condo in
Minneapolis where their kids and old friends reside. We play golf,

and it is especially painful when I lose to Tom, because we both know I am the better golfer.

The Working Man

Thanks to Tom Wright's father, Clarence, who was superintendent of buildings and grounds for the school board, I was hired to wash school windows after my sophomore year. I started at seventy-five cents per hour and received a nickel an hour increase each month. It was nice to make all that money and to get to know the teachers, who were fellow workers, but it was not exactly stimulating. I got into trouble the following fall by calling my typing teacher and fellow summer worker by his first name in class. The next summer I was moved indoors to a wood shop where I sanded for three months. That was a total disaster. It was depressing to be inside, and I was never (to this day) interested in working with my hands. I was so bad that the boss, a crusty carpenter, recommended that I not be rehired the next year. I'm sure that Clarence breathed a huge sigh of relief when I told him that the next summer I would work at Culligan Soft Water—more on that experience in chapter three.

On to College

My overall impression of my first eighteen years is very positive. I had a solid Midwestern upbringing. My home was loving, stable, and secure. Links to the Aaker clan that will be outlined in the next chapter, and to my family's friends, added warm, fun relationships. Outdoor activities for a growing boy were plentiful, and a love of books provided recreation and learning. The Fargo schools were not academically strong by some standards, but it was good enough to get me through the freshman year at MIT. The debate and public speaking activities provided me with a considerable edge. I was a very lucky guy.

2 Roots

Roots are important, especially growing up. And I had roots—Midwestern and Norwegian roots.

Halsten and Josie Olsberg, the parents of my mother Ida, were an ongoing part of my early life. They lived in Valley City, North Dakota, less than sixty miles away from Fargo. Ole and Marie Aaker in Minnewaukan, a tiny town in North Dakota that was too far to easily visit, raised my father, Oscar. While Ida was an only child, Oscar had two sisters and four brothers, and they and their families were also big parts of my early years. In many ways my grandfathers, Ole and Halsten, are the center of the roots story. Both left their home and family in Norway attracted to the promise of a new country and open lands. They both settled in North Dakota at the turn of the century where the farming was difficult and the winters harsh. The story of these two and their families are the stuff of legend. They definitely shaped the lives and values of Oscar and Ida. The Ida and Oscar story will be told because it represents roots, and because my parents define and explain many of my characteristics—a fact that I never fully realized until this book came along. But first we need to describe the Olsbergs and the extended Aaker family.

Valley City—The Olsbergs

I was blessed by being able to grow up being close to Halsten and Josie, who lived in a super house in Valley City. Grandparents, at least these grandparents, provided a sense of security and a link to my roots. If anything happened, I could always go to Valley

Josie with Ida

Halsten as a young lawyer.

Halsten and Josie

Valley City home

City. The house, the surrounding land, and the people felt warm and secure. I was very lucky.

The trip to Valley City in the black 1938 Chevrolet, which occurred maybe six times a year, would take about one and a half hours if Dad drove, as he thought fifty mph was the right speed. Mother, who sped along at fifty-five mph, would get us there faster. The trip seemed interminable as we had to pass through West Fargo, Casselton, Buffalo, Tower City, and Wheatland to reach Valley City, a major town of about 5,000 people (it is now around 7,000 with homes well under $100,000).

One of the best things about Valley City was their house, the next thing to paradise for a young boy. It had two stories with an attic and a porch with pillars. The attic contained a wonderful collection of old trunks filled with clothes and assorted prized antiques. I would easily spend four or five hours there by myself making discovery after discovery. The porch was just about as good. It had Grandpa's library, with hundreds of old books. I was an avid book lover and would again and again browse the collection. He had history books—especially of the prairie—and a rather complete selection of Arthur Conan Doyle's Sherlock Holmes stories. In the winter my stay could only be minutes, since the porch was unheated and it could easily be below zero.

The three upstairs bedrooms had armoires instead of closets.

The outside of the house, involving well over an acre of land, was even better for a young boy. It was set on a rise just above a river inlet. The water and the acreage gave the house a sense of being in the country. The river was the source of considerable entertainment. In the winter, snow would be cleared off for ice-skating. In the summer, Grandpa would fashion a wicker/wood love seat in some bushes on the water in which I could sit and read and

Halsten's swing

be close to the water. Grandpa would also build a crude swing in one of the tall trees. The house was beside a road that led up to the hills surrounding Valley City. The road was terrific for sledding during the winter, as it demanded great skill to maneuver around the sweeping curve. In the summer I would hike up the road to the open hills above. I felt adventurous and independent, I suppose much like children venturing in the hills of Norway centuries ago.

The main business section involved two streets, each about three blocks long, about one and a half miles from the Olsbergs'. I would enjoy going downtown on my own and shopping at the five and dime and the ice cream store.

Valley City was usually where we gathered for Christmas. The holidays involved a lot of whist, an excellent training ground for bridge. It was my first serious effort to be an adult card player. We would open the presents after a dinner and cleanup that would always take forever. One Christmas was particularly memorable as I asked for four "big" presents—expecting to get one—and actually got them all. I was stunned. One was a flat board with netting at the corners, allowing a sort of pool game.

As I got older and moved into high school, I played golf with my parents on the local course. It was just below a high railroad bridge linking two hills. I also then got to know some Valley City high schoolers and even served as MC at one of their variety shows. I loved being MC, as you could be the center of attention without doing anything requiring talent—of which I had little.

It is interesting and somewhat humbling to realize the life that my grandparents led. It is very different than ours for sure.

Josie

Josie was born in 1881 at Newburg, Minnesota and died eighty-one years later. Her parents, the O. A. Johnsons, soon moved to Fort Ransom, North Dakota, a small town not far from Valley City, where they operated a farm. Josie's mother was attractive as a young woman (as was Josie). Josie's father looked stern in photos, but everyone seemed to take serious pictures in those days. The farmhouse was a sturdy though small two-story house in the middle of the prairie. Her grandmother, Anna Thompson, who became a centurion in 1916 and died two years later, was born in Telemarken, Norway, and emigrated to Rushford, Minnesota, in 1867. In 1881, Anna moved to Kathryn, North Dakota, close to Fort Ransom. Despite raising eleven children and having thirty-two grandchildren, she was reported to be a great reader.

Josie married Halsten on May 30, 1908, when she was twenty-seven and he thirty-nine. Judging from the letters written by Halsten prior to their marriage, they had a deep expressive love affair going on for several years. On March 25, 1904, Halsten writes: "My beloved Josie ... I do wish that you would either work in Kathryn or come to Valley City this summer and not work on a farm; as that will cause so much inconvenience to see you ... my beloved, good bye. I am as ever yours." Later, in August of 1904, a hint of jealousy creeps into the correspondence as Halsten writes, " ... wish I could have reached you every Sunday and stayed with you. Yes, it is pleasure to be with you, for you know I love you, which I have told you so many times. Did you ever for a moment think that I mistrusted you? No, that idea could never enter my head. If you had a hundred boys around there trying to take you out driving and if you rode with them every Sunday, I couldn't make myself believe that you were capable of dividing your love. I have an implicit trust in you, and even if time should disappoint me in this confidence, I would love you still."

Ida was an only child; Josie had a sister Ann, who married Ben Larson and had three boys, so Ida did have cousins. Ann and Ben lived in the Seattle area, as did two of their boys, Cliffton and Duane, and they had little contact with us. But the other, Gaylan Larson, became a Moorhead optometrist. He and his wife Joyce, a vivacious mother of five kids (the youngest, Ann, a gifted and creative person, was killed in an automobile accident when still a teen) and an avid bridge player, became close friends. I remember telling Gaylan that he should not give us discounts on glasses because we were captive customers. Even then I did not have the frugality of my parents.

Josie was a great cook—plenty of meat and potatoes and cookies. Her specialty was orange drop cookies with lemon frosting. There was nothing better, especially if you could help by putting extra frosting on. Her daughter, Ida, had a chocolate version. In addition, pickled pig's feet, herring, goat cheese (a sweet brown cheese), and flatbread gave us a taste of Norway. Josie would always have some soda for a snack—I usually selected orange crush. She struck me as a gentle, kind person who was a good homemaker. Unlike Grandpa, who barely tolerated church, Josie enjoyed the local Lutheran church and its circle activities.

Halsten

Halsten was born in Rendal, Norway, on September 12, 1869, and passed away eighty-seven years later in 1956. He had five siblings—Ragnild (b. 1968), Ole (b. 1872), Anna (b. 1874), Carl (b. 1878), and Johanna (b. 1880). These five produced eleven children, Ida's cousins, all of whom lived in Norway. His father, Andress, passed away in 1921 at the age of eighty-six, and his mother, Ingeborg, died three years later at ninety. As was the custom in Norway, the Olsberg name came from a farm on which the family lived. The father's name had been Gjelten.

Halsten came to the United States in 1891 at the age of twenty-two. He graduated from Valley City State Teachers College in 1899 and from the University of North Dakota Law School in 1902 when he was thirty-three. For the next twenty-nine years, after a brief stint as a teacher in rural schools, he practiced law in Valley City and for most of that time was a city alderman. In 1931, at the age of sixty-two, when most people would retire, he began a twenty-six-year career as Barnes County judge that was undoubtedly important financially. In 1931 the Depression, which was to last until 1940, was in full swing. Further, the judge probably did not save a great deal during his days in private practice. Early in his practice, a partner absconded with a substantial amount of his assets. Further, there is evidence that he was not very firm about collecting debts from clients.

Some insights into Halsten's personality and writing style come from his description of his trip back to Norway in the summer of 1935 at the age of sixty-six. He writes of his stopover in New York, "I never had any hankering for the sight of large cities ... I feel lost in that maelstrom of humanity and as a certain man said, in the city you feel like an atom in a congregation while in the country you feel like a congregation of atoms ... after dark, when all the city lights were on, it was a magnificent sight, but as I looked up into the star-studded heavens, I thought, how small, after all, is the handiwork of man."

And in Norway, "I had the time of my life roaming around over the valleys and hills, over the uplands and the mountains, the scenery continually changing. No need of going thirsty on any of these jaunts. Everywhere the finest and purest. And the rivers, running swift and deep with waters crystal clear. When I thought of the scarcity of the water here [1935 was a time of drought] I could but regret that nature had been so discriminating in the distribution of this life-giving and life-sustaining element." A relative in Rendal, Norway, reported that Halsten retained fluency in Norwegian despite being away from it for forty years.

Perhaps Halsten's most fascinating possession was a Model A Ford of around 1929 vintage (they were made from 1928 to 1931 and many are still running). It had the most charming mellow sound as it chugged along. Starting it required the ability to handle two manual adjustment devices by the steering wheel that regulated the choke and gas. As backup there was a crank that you inserted into the engine and manually turned it over—a very dangerous device, as the engine could send the crank flying backwards. The garage was below the house and part of the fun was to careen down the hill at relatively high speed—at least my mother and grandmother claimed that it was at high speed. The best was when we would get into the car to ride across town to visit a park and an ice cream cone establishment.

Halsten was always making things out of wood by "whittling." His specialty was canes. He would find and uproot small trees and fashion functional and sometimes ornate handles out of the root structure. The canes were invaluable as we went for walks. He also made flutes out of wood. His knives were kept sharp by a huge grinding wheel about thirty inches in diameter that was operated by a foot mechanism. A key element to this machine was a leaky can positioned so oil would drip upon the wheel as it turned. He also built a very rustic log cabin way out in the woods near Kathryn. It was primitive with a dirt floor but was still used by Ida and her friends as well as Halston both in the winter and summer (although Ida's group would spend the nights at relatives in Kathryn as it was too rustic for them). A picture of a winter outing shows them with what looks to be eight-foot skis. Skis in those days were very different.

Halsten and I were prime examples of the remarkable association that can be created between a very young boy and a very seasoned man. When I was eight he was seventy-six years of age. We got on exceptionally well, sharing a host of interests and activities. He had a collection of old coins that he kept at his courthouse office that I never tired of examining. Among his other antiques was an old ornate clock that, after considerable research, was determined to be of modest value.

Halsten had a gruff manner with most, including his wife and daughter. I think he found it convenient to create an image of not being excessively social. I recall Halsten once leaving church after the offering, muttering that the service after the offering was not very important. However, with me he was quick to laugh and always ready to create swings, slides, or whatever it took to

Halsten's cabin—Those were skis!

entertain a small boy. He also took me to the "Elks" where he
clearly enjoyed companionship. When I was six or so, I broke
everyone at the Elks up by insisting upon bourbon and Seven-Up.
They provided the seven-up.

It was fun to visit the courthouse. I would often go with
Grandpa after his daily post-lunch nap and stay for the afternoon.
I would always have a Coke and a bag of peanuts for a snack. It
was the only time I can recall enjoying Coke. When I was in
junior high school, he hired me for forty dollars or so to replace
his secretary for a week. So I was typing formal legal documents.
Needless to say, there was not a lot of pressure upon me. I think
that he did want to expose me to the law, and in fact, as noted in
chapter one, there was a time in high school when I aspired to be
a lawyer. In 1945, at age seven, I signed a legal financial agreement
that read: "For value received, I promise to pay you $1.00 when I
get ready with interest at the rate of 25% per week." The debt is
still unpaid and is probably now worth billions.

A friend made the following observation about Halsten in
February of 1946: "He's nice people. I like Judge H. A. Olsberg. It

took us a long time to get acquainted, and I don't see him often, but he impresses me as a quality person. I first thought he was a sourpuss; but actually, he isn't at all. He has a sense of humor all his own, and when you get past that mask there is really a solid personality underneath. He's so quiet, has so little to say, that at first meeting you think he is crabby. No again. And I get a continuing kick out of him and his Model A coach. Rain or shine, in snowy times or horrid weather, he gets around in his sturdy Ford. Like the old judge, who is always in his office, his Ford always seems to run. They make quite a pair."

The Extended Aaker Family

My father, as noted, grew up in Minnewaukan, North Dakota, as part of a family with five brothers and two sisters plus two nieces from Norway who arrived at age twelve and fourteen when their mother died and their father (Syver the younger) was too occupied with his farm to raise them. These brothers and sisters were really a remarkable group in many respects. And their children, my seventeen cousins, were an important part of growing up.

My dad's oldest (and also the tallest by several inches) brother, Sig, born in 1901, lived in Sauk Centre, where he was superintendent of schools. He passed away in 1995. Sauk Centre, the home of Sinclair Lewis and the setting for his famous novel *Main Street*, was (and is) between Fargo and Minneapolis, and was a convenient place to stop to break up a trip to the Minneapolis area. Like many Minnesota towns, it contained a lake, where Sig would enjoy fishing. It also contained two completely different cousins. John, two years my senior, shared my interest in books and in intellectual discussion. Bud, two years my junior, shared my interest in sports and physical activity. I had a great time with both. Their mother Blanche, warm and loving, always seemed glad to have me around and was always good for cookies. She never forgot my birthday; there was always a card from Blanche.

Among the cousins, John has had by far the most interesting career. He has been a drum major for Concordia College (where he would strut at football games), was involved in the theater designing costumes, started and operated a private school in a

The seven Aaker kids—mid 1950s
Al, Mabel, Ted. George, Oscar, Stella, Sig

The cousins at a 1993 reunion
Bud, Steve, Dave, Joan, Doug, Bob, Karen, Paul, Janet,
Bill Neilsen, Linda, Margaret, Ed, Bill, Cameron, Carol
(not shown: John, Ellen, Dick)

low-income minority section of New York City, and ran seminars for people who deal with "people problems" in society. In essence, he has always been on the firing line as far as the needy in spirit are concerned. John was gay but really never came out until the end of his fight against AIDS—he was one of the early victims. Bud turned out to be a salesman (of class rings, real estate, and water well-drilling operations) and entrepreneur (including a go-cart track). He settled in Spokane and became a successful real estate broker and developer. One of his kids, Tom, became a high-powered investment banker in Hong Kong and, later, in London and Africa, and a very active marathoner participating in events all over the world.

The next child was Stella, born in 1902, who died in 1959 after a long illness caused by her childhood bout with rheumatic fever. Visiting her home in Sauk Rapids, just outside Minneapolis, was a great adventure because it had a fabulous garden. The fun part was crossing the streams by jumping from rock to rock. Her husband, Clarence, was a local banker. They had two kids, both older than I. Cameron was the oldest cousin, eight years my senior and really too old for me to know well—he worked as an accountant for General Mills. Joan was a bundle of energy with an excellent sense of humor. I always enjoyed talking with her and getting some hints at wild times to come at college. She married a local car dealer and pursued her considerable talents in piano and bridge.

The next Aaker brother was my father, Oscar, born in 1904. Then came George, born in 1905, an accountant who worked in Washington DC until 1951 when he moved to San Rafael, just north of San Francisco where he became the regional auditor for the U.S. agency HEW (Health, Education & Welfare). George joined the Navy during World War II and served in the Pacific theater as a paymaster aboard the carrier *Saratoga* in the Pacific. At Iwo Jima his boat was attacked by five kamikaze pilots and he was lucky to be one of the survivors. All the Aaker boys married late, but George, who was around his mid-forties, was the latest of all. He married Alice—a girl who always had a smile—in 1950. George had three boys whom we saw only rarely since they lived so far away. Ed, the oldest, became an aeronautical engineer, Bill was in sales, and Dick in construction. George died prematurely in the spring of 1966 of a heart attack at the age of sixty-one.

The fourth brother and fifth child was Ted, born in 1907, who became a dentist in Gaylord, Minnesota, just sixty miles or so south of Minneapolis and died some ninety-five years later. An accomplished musician, he played the clarinet in a Gaylord band. Ted was the dentist of choice for our family whenever we could get near enough to visit. I think he was a good dentist (I've since had other dentists attest to his craftsmanship), but I suspect he also undercharged his brother—an attractive attribute to our family. Ted explored hypnotism. My mother was one of his best subjects, and I was not that far behind. I still recall the story he used. I was coming down a long staircase out of the clouds into a huge field of flowers that I could actually smell. It really took the mind off the considerable discomfort. I can still put myself in that field but prefer to rely upon Novocain to make sure that the pain is under control. My brother, Paul, figured out the dentist thing and would run away when the time came. The whole family had to scour the town to find him. Ted closed his dentistry practice in 1982 after forty-nine years. Ted and George both looked enough like Oscar that as a young boy I more than once ran to the wrong father.

In 1937, Ted married Arleen, a warm, sweet woman. The oldest of their four children was Janet, perhaps one year my junior. She was relatively quiet and has turned into a very successful English teacher in Brooklyn Park, a suburb of Minneapolis. She cared for Ted during his last days and told me what a joy that was, a sentiment I came to understand when I did something similar for my mother. Janet's younger sister, Karen, was attractive, outgoing, and about three years my junior. She married David Minge, who had a career in Congress that involved me—more on that later. The two younger boys, Doug (now an orthodontist in St. Cloud, Minnesota, and an avid outdoorsman) and Steve (who teaches and practices dentistry in Minneapolis and is a committed golfer) were around nine years younger than I.

The second daughter, Mabel, was born in 1914. The baby girl got a lot of attention. She tells of how, at age fifteen, her brother Ted took her to Minot for a Minnesota Symphony Orchestra concert. The 150-mile trip in Ted's 1931 Chevrolet was an adventure at that time. The trip was in part the inspiration to get serious about her piano playing. She subsequently did well in some local contests and became the family's piano player.

Mabel moved to Washington DC in 1935 to take a typist job in the government when the family decided that she would have to drop out of the University of Minnesota for a time because of lack of funds. Two years later she met Bjarne Nielsen, who was a butler at the Norwegian embassy. Her Norwegian came in handy as he knew no English. They married in 1940. Bjarne may be my all-time favorite person. Everyone had fun when Bjarne was around—there was no way to avoid it. He had (and has) boundless enthusiasm, curiosity, and humor. It was just a treat to be with him. And he was impressive. Arriving from Norway, he learned the language and won Mabel's heart. Later, he became a successful operator of a Culligan Soft Water dealership in Gaylord, demonstrating hands-on product knowledge, exceptional people skills, and a commitment to customer service. Mabel and he were incredible parents of five cousins and contributors to the cohesiveness of the extended Aaker family.

Ted deserves much of the credit for getting Bjarne into business in Gaylord. Ted discovered the opportunity, sold Bjarne on it, and arranged the financing from a wealthily retired farmer. I can still recall one evening—it must have been around 1947—when I was visiting at Ted's and listening to Oscar, Ted, Sig, and Grandpa Aaker discuss Bjarne's new business venture. Clearly, Bjarne had a support team. Bjarne started with two accounts (one of them being Ted) that he serviced from Minneapolis, where he was then living. Bjarne was just special. When a competitor opened a business, Bjarne welcomed him to town and introduced him to the local service clubs. Amazing.

The oldest of the Nielsen's five children was Margaret, who was just three years younger than me and a favorite companion. She had her father's cheerful disposition even though she suffered from polio and the numerous operations and crippled limbs that went with it. Now a professor of social work at Michigan State, she has my admiration. Bob (a school teacher in Minneapolis) was a bit younger and Bill (now an American Airlines pilot) was of the same vintage as Doug and Steve. I enjoyed playing with all of them during my trips to Gaylord. The next two kids, Linda and Carol, were younger. All five, remarkably, went to St. Olaf College in Northfield, Minnesota.

The baby and daredevil was Alvin, born in 1916 when his parents were forty-six. As a boy he constructed a ski jump off the barn roof. At age twelve he biked four miles to work on a farm for $.50 per week. He married a Norwegian girl, Halene, and had a daughter named Ellen, now a nurse. Not much of a student, Al moved to Washington in the mid-1930s and for a time lived with George and Mabel. He drove a cab and worked with Bjarne as a waiter at the Norwegian embassy. He later became a pilot in the World War II flying thirty-five B-24 missions over Germany. Later, he became a flying photographer in Washington. A dashing figure, he fit the image of a World War II pilot. He subsequently also went into the Culligan Soft Water Business in Fairfax, a town near Gaylord. Al appeared somewhat flamboyant to me when I was young. One summer he turned up at a family get-together in a yellow Ford convertible.

Family Reunions

The family, including the nineteen (counting Paul and myself) cousins, got together frequently. There were always events such as weddings and funerals that prompted trips that would cause the clan to gather. The most regular event was an annual summer week at the Sunset Knoll resort. The resort was in Northern Minnesota on Lake Bertha, off Whitefish Lake and near Pequot Lakes, a small town just north of Brainerd, the home of Paul Bunyan. Started around 1949 by Sig and Bjarne, it expanded the next year to include everyone and lasted for eighteen years. Probably the best part of the experience was the feeling of family togetherness, the sense of collective roots.

The Bertha weeks represent many memories. Ted would fry fish on Friday, when we were lucky enough to have caught enough fish to fry. The key ingredient in his recipe was beer—which contributed to tasty meals. Blanche started making oatmeal that became a big hit among the kids, who would never touch the stuff at home. My father was the supplier of popcorn. There was always a shuffleboard tourney, and several years I did well even though it was an aiming sport in which I lacked talent (my lack of putting skill holds back my golf game). I was definitely competitive.

The lake, however, was the center of activities. The mail was delivered in a large, bulky, "speedboat" which circled the lake. One day each summer we would ride the mail boat on its rounds. My mother especially liked to be in the boat and see the lake. As we got older we graduated from swimming in the shallow shoreline to fishing to water skiing and ultimately to driving into a nearby town to attend a play in the summer theater.

I've often felt that these seven brothers and sisters and their spouses were a remarkable group. All professionals or married to professionals, they came from modest circumstances from a very small North Dakota town which featured harsh winters, short summers, and an uncertain economy. To understand how this set of families emerged it is useful to discuss my father's parents.

Marie Olsdatter Jeglum Aaker— My Grandmother

Marie was born on the Jeglum farm on February 24, 1870, in a "township" called Hol in a larger area termed Hallingdal that represents a valley high in the mountains between Oslo and Bergen in Norway. Somehow over the years the name Jeglum morphed into the name Geilo, and the farm became the city of Geilo. In fact, the room in which she was born with its fireplace is now a part of a hotel in the middle of Geilo—it is called the fireplace room. There is now a town called Hol about fifteen miles away.

Marie reported that she had a happy childhood living on the farm with her parents and four brothers and sisters. However, her childhood was cut short when her mother, Gro Losdatter Tufto Kvisla (1828–1880), died when she was ten, and, perhaps more tragically for the little girl, her father, Ols Asleson Nygaard (1822–1885), died when she was only fifteen. On her own, she became a house helper on the nearby Eker farm to "earn her bread." In 1891, at the age of twenty-one, she moved to Chicago just in time to see the World's Fair. In an 1897 diary she describes her life in Chicago where she worked at a laundry ironing clothes: "I had both sorrows and gladness, set-backs and sicknesses. I earned good money and spent good money." In the diary, she describes getting homesick and making a six-month visit to Norway in 1897 where she clearly enjoyed seeing her siblings (one brother she had not seen for twelve years), relatives, and friends. She recounts coming up to the farm of a sister she had not seen for nine years and having her niece guess who she was—an emotional moment. Both she and her sister had changed so much that neither recognized the other. Marie observed that life in Norway, especially for the women, was very hard, and that her life in America was much more comfortable and rewarding. In 1900, Ole—passing through Chicago when returning from a trip to Norway—proposed (for at least the second time—she had doubts about prairie living) to Marie, and they were married in December of that year. He was thirty-one and she thirty.

Ole's Homestead Farm—1893–97

From pictures I can say that Marie had great beauty as a young lady, although she clearly had a substantial frame—she looked like she hold her own with physical work. As a mature woman she became heavyset. She certainly must have had a demanding life raising a large family in primitive conditions by our standards. Mabel writes about what a great mom Marie was—always a friend, always there for an afternoon snack or to act as audience for piano practice. Never out of sorts or cross. She and Ole raised seven children plus two girls from Norway. Wow!

I did not really know her, as one of my earliest memories is of a family gathering in Minnewaukan for her funeral in June of 1946. Her daughter, Mabel, helped Ole care for her during her last year when she was incapacitated by several strokes. All of eight, I recall that Sig drove up in a new car on the day of the funeral.

Marie
and
Ole
Aaker

Ole Syverson Aaker—My Grandfather

Ole the Elder, my grandfather (one of his brothers was also named Ole), was born in 1869 on the Aaker farm that is a few miles out of what is now Geilo. It was then also described as being in Hol, Hallingdal. A farm boy, from age eleven Ole spent many of his summers herding cows and goats in their grazing areas high in the mountains called the Aaker saetre—about two days journey from home.

When he was a boy, his father taught him a lesson about tobacco. When Ole pleaded for chewing tobacco, his father finally gave him some but only on the condition that he bite off as much as he could get into his mouth and chew and swallow it. He got so sick that he never touched tobacco again.

After two winters without work, Ole decided to move to America at the age of twenty. He was joined by three friends, one of which, Ole Rodning, also ended up with Ole in Minnewaukan, a small town near Devil's Lake, northwest of Fargo. In his first summer in St. Peter, Minnesota, in debt from his ticket to the U.S. and desperate for work, he hired himself out to a demanding farmer. It was tough, arduous work involving workdays from twelve to twenty hours a day for five months—all for $85. Ole honored this commitment even though he received a much better employment offer only days later.

Four years later, after some schooling at Luther Academy at Albert Lea, Minnesota, he homesteaded in Wells County, North Dakota. He describes breaking the land with a plow pulled by four oxen and the overpowering thirst caused by the plowing and the shortage of water. Years later, he recalled the joy and relief of a cold quart of fresh milk. In 1897, in his fifth year on the farm, a July 9 hailstorm wiped out his crop and he moved to Minnewaukan. There he bought a mercantile store by signing a note for $400. The Aaker children all worked in the store unpacking, serving customers, and delivering (sometimes one or two items). Farmers obtained goods in part on credit and in part in exchange for their cream and butter. Their bills would be settled after the harvest (when the harvest was adequate). Ole was too softhearted to be good at collecting.

Ole and Marie owned a single-seated buggy that was their transportation and weekend recreation during this time. In 1919 Ole bought a new Oakland Touring Car with removable side-curtains that could be used only in the summer when it was not too wet. Before an outing (and often during as well) the spark plugs needed cleaning and the tires needed pumping.

After running this store for twenty years, at the age of fifty-two in 1921 he sold out (receiving a small farm as partial payment) and became the postmaster of the town. The postal clerk position provided a job for the kids thereafter.

He was so conscientious that he missed the marriage of Sig and Blanche because of his obligations. Ole was elected to the North Dakota legislature in 1906, but one term was more than enough for him. Ole lacked the time and resources to return to Norway. However, in May of 1937 the kids, with George as organizer, sent Ole and Marie to Norway on the *S.S. Bergensfjord* for a return to their roots, a generous gesture in the midst of the Depression. A picture of them on the boat shows them beaming.

I didn't know Grandpa Aaker well. Although he lived with Bjarne and Mabel during his last thirteen years, he was quiet and always wore dark glasses to protect his eyes. However, his children, who are all winners, and his grandchildren, many of whom were my childhood friends, enriched my life. There follows a description of his family that provides insights into his and my roots. He passed away in 1959 at the age of ninety.

The Aaker Roots—Geilo

The Aaker and Jeglum families had a lot to do with the development and growth of Geilo, now a prosperous resort town attracting downhill and cross-country skiers in the winter and hikers and horseback riders in the summer. Not too many decades ago, half the people or more were related to me.

We trace the beginning to Ole Aaker's father, who was named Sjugurd Sjugurdson (son of Sjugurd) Reinton (1830–1912), but who was called Syver Aaker because he moved onto the Aaker farm (records of which go back to 1588) and adapted the Aaker name. He took over the farm from his uncle, who had no children. He and his wife, Gro Mikkelsdtr (daughter of Mikkel)

The Aaker farm in Hallingdal

Syver (Elder), Syver (Younger), Mikkel,
Grandfather Ole, Embrikk

sore Slettemoen, (1832–1919) had seven children, Syver the Elder, Mikkel, Embrikk, Ole the Elder (my grandfather), Syver the Younger, Ole the Younger, and Guri. A picture of five of the boys in vests in 1937 shows that three of them sported neatly trimmed grey beards.

The farm was by custom passed on to the oldest son, Syver the Elder (1856–1944). He in turn was followed (by the oldest son rule) first by Sigurd (1882–1972) and then Sverre (1913–). Sverre Aaker, who had no children, had a serious bike accident in 1984, and his nephew, Harold Hagen (1952–), was on the farm in 1985 when I visited. Harold spoke excellent English and took me all around the farm. His great grandfather and my grandfather were brothers.

When I first visited Geilo in 1985, the sight of the farm really hit me. The farm basically consists of three buildings and two barns on about forty acres of sloped land. No one knows how old the original building is. There is a horse ring attached to one of the two wood pillars that has the inscription ("SOS 1847") and a carving ("OLA 1900") made by Ole the Younger. The house contains several paintings by Syver the Elder, including one of the Aaker saetre. The doors were short, around four and a half feet, suggesting that people of the mid-1880s were of smaller stature. In the "living/dining room" there was a loft in which all the kids slept. I frequently bore my three daughters, who assume all kids need their own room plus a playroom, by reminding them of their great-grandfather's lot.

There are actually two farms associated with this first generation of Aakers. Mikkel (1865–?) bought the Haugen farm in 1892 and thus became Mikkel Haugen (he was taller than his brothers for what that is worth). Mikkel, in addition to farming, was a blacksmith who repaired and built farm tools. The Haugen farm was passed on again by the oldest son rule to Olav (who suddenly passed away in April of 1984) and to Olav's son, Bjorn Haugen. I met two of Mikkel's seven children in 1985. Sverre Haugen, a former ski jump champion, had a career as a truck driver. Hendrik Haugen, a delightful gentleman who wore a white beard (to protect his face, which is sensitive to the cold), worked in a general store before opening a shoe/clothing store in 1936 that he operated until the early 80s. He was reportedly a conscientious and frugal businessman who never married. He always tried to schedule dental appointments, for example, after store hours.

Embrikk (1873–1958) was the merchant. He operated a general store for over forty years. The store was a co-operative; the customers basically owned it and shared in the profits according to their purchases. Syver the Younger (1859–1955) bought and sold cattle. Ole the younger (1871–1950) lived in Geilo but made several visits to the U.S. and was tempted to move there. Guri (1863–1920) was a schoolteacher.

The picture of the Ole Aaker family mirrors that of Geilo. They were people who worked with their hands—farmers, carpenters, craftsmen, or shopkeepers. Their life revolved around the rural farm life of the times, a very different lifestyle than ours. It was much less comfortable with more physical, repetitive work. But it also included simple pleasures such as local social events and hiking with vistas that were both peaceful and dramatic. Ole's life in Minnewaukan followed the pattern—but without the vistas.

Oscar and Ida—the Early Days

Ida, born on July 18, 1909, grew up in Valley City as a cute, petite young girl with long dark curls. She and her friends did a lot of hiking, boating, and camping. The river was important for both boating in the summer and skating in the winter. One hike to Tower City, ten miles away, made the local paper. There was little dating then (go figure) but a lot of slumber parties (what did they talk about?) and attending basketball and football games. A train trip to Fargo was an adventure. She, like many of her era, took piano, an activity she enjoyed her whole life.

During the summer, a big event would be the Chautauqua held over several days in a big tent. In the early 1900s through the 20s (before radio and movies), it provided to small towns a dose of entertainment and culture with singers, magicians, variety acts (such as educated dogs), and lecturers. William Jennings Bryan, a two-time presidential candidate and the attorney for the state in the famous monkey trial (famous also for his "cross of gold" speech), was one of the stars, but I suspect that he never hit Valley City. The event, which would be announced by streamers and publicity, drew people from a wide area.

In 1930, her high school classmates voted Ida the most beautiful girl. She attended the practical Valley City Teacher's College for two years (which was above the norm for women's education at that time and place), and took a job as a secretary at the school. I suspect her father was not a big women's rights fan and did not push her college ambitions.

The advent of driving was liberating. Her friend Margaret Halvorson, with Ida and their mothers, drove Margaret's new 1933 Pontiac to Yellowstone Park. The trip with muddy roads and inadequate maps was a cut above Lewis and Clark's trip but nothing like today's travel. She took up golf in earnest, playing on the sporty Valley City course. Pictures of her golf attire show dresses that extended to the ankles.

Oscar, born December 5, 1904, was raised in Minnewaukan. The town now has around 150 homes and just over 320 people, but back then it was a town of note with 500 people, a railroad station, four general stores, two photo studios, and several hotels. The Aaker house, the school, and the church were all surrounded

Minnewaukan Basketball Team—1921
Oscar with ball; George second from right

Four boys Sig, Oscar, George, Ted

by a lot of land. It was farm country. Work on the farms in the summer, especially during harvest, was a part of life. A wonderful picture of the road out of town shows a single-lane dirt road through a field of grain with no sign of trees or hills.

Three of his brothers, Sig, George, and Ted, were roughly his age. Once, when Oscar was nine, he and Sig tied a rope to the tail of one horse and linked it through a window to another horse and almost caused the barn to be torn down. Its hard to visualize the Aaker boys as rough, but there is a story that Sig and Oscar got into a fight while doing janitor duty at church, which resulted in Oscar getting poked with a broomstick and losing two front teeth. He wore a "flipper" until Ted made him a bridge.

In my 1985 trip to Geilo, Ole's niece, Ester, who lived with the Aakers in Minnewaukan, told me that Sig, Oscar, and Ted were mischievous, that Oscar was nice, and that George was handsome and had to fight off the girls. She also told of how Ted and Sig would sit out back of the store when they were supposed to be working. Ole caught one of them and put the book he was reading in the oven—the culprit later recovered it and went on reading. Grandpa didn't sound so tough.

Oscar, who was unaccountably called Heinie in high school, was a good basketball player. He was captain of the team in his senior year. A picture of his eight-man team shows them wearing caps and long socks. Their team won the district small-school tournament and went to the state tourney only to lose to Hillsboro (a small town near Fargo) in the first round. One player during the district tournament was in jail for bootlegging and had to be bailed out for the game. Prohibition, which ran from 1920 to 1933, has been judged a failure on all counts, but it did provide work for enforcers. A colorful time.

Oscar attended the University of North Dakota at Grand Forks, where he received a degree in electrical engineering in 1929. College for the kids was a cooperative affair. Most of the siblings dropped out of school for a year or even more to earn money for themselves and for the others. Oscar was no exception. He dropped out of college for a year to help support two of his brothers. The most common job was working for their Dad as a postal clerk for $85 a month. Mabel, Oscar's younger sister, recalls

Ida

The courting days

Oscar

that in 1934, when she was attending Jamestown College, she would receive $25 a month from Oscar to help supplement her baby-sitting and provide a livable income. The thought of sacrificing a year to help a brother or sister tells a lot about the family.

A member of the Tau Sigma Rho fraternity house at the university, Oscar had a social bent. He organized the engineering moonlight dance at the local armory and apparently made sure that the lights failed during the event so couples could enjoy darkness. Engineers are nerdier now. During the summer, he would use the family Oakland Touring Car to take out his girl friends (to where, I wonder). He was an ROTC member in college but going into the army was a non-issue because it was the time of downsizing—the Great War was long over.

Radio was just coming to rural North Dakota. A friend, Selmer Rodning, tells of being at the Aakers' one evening in 1927 trying to pick up the world heavyweight rematch when Jack Dempsey was trying to regain his title from Gene Tunny. They took turns listening to the crystal radio set through earphones trying to catch a word or two about the "fight of the century." Tunny won that fight because Dempsey failed to retreat to a corner after knocking his opponent down, thereby generating the famous "long count."

Oscar took a position with Northwestern Bell (NW Bell) in 1929 that turned out to be the beginning of a lifetime career. He began by climbing poles in Valley City. In those days the college grads were not pampered, but were expected to learn the business from the ground up.

Oscar and Ida connected in Valley City and had an active courtship. They played a lot of golf, winning some local tournaments. Oscar had a car so there was no reason that they could not visit Fargo, the big city. Oscar tells of how on a tennis outing he hit a spin serve to Ida that discouraged her from playing him. Ida has never denied the story.

They married December 22, 1935, in the midst of the Great Depression when Ida was twenty-six and Oscar thirty-one. Ida reportedly wore a wine-colored velvet gown with a Queen Anne collar (whatever that is) and a short veil. All of Oscar's brothers and sisters were there and added some spice to the wedding by kidnapping Ida and bringing her to Fargo, then a considerable journey. It sounds frightening, but to them it was the best joke. Practical jokes on newlyweds were part of the culture. When Sig and Blanche were married there was also a kidnapping, plus sewed-up pajama bottoms and nightgowns. I think people had more time in those days.

The couple moved to Fargo, where they lived for over thirty years until they retired in December of 1968 when Oscar had served for thirty-nine and a half years at NW Bell. The warmth of Sun City, a retirement community just outside of Phoenix, Arizona, attracted them, and they moved to 10502 Roundalay Circle. During their married life, they shared common interests in bridge, dancing, golf, cribbage, family traditions and events, the challenge of raising two children, and special relationships with relatives and friends.

Dancing was a source of fun and exercise. In Fargo, they had a regular dance outing called the Y-dance, held at the YMCA. And in Sun City, they had plenty of chances to do ballroom and square dancing. Golf too was a favorite outing during the short summers in Fargo and the long winters in Sun City.

But the centerpiece of their activities together and their social life was bridge. Both had good card sense and were reasonably good players. Ida was steady and predictable while Oscar had a touch of flair and unorthodoxy that sometimes backfired. He was known as an aggressive bidder and at least one person called him "the Shark." But the real fun was in the socializing that went along with it.

While in Fargo, there were three couples—the Petersons (Maynard Peterson was from the engineering department at NW Bell), the Paulsens, and the Knutsons (Bud Knutson owned the pinball machines in town, which explains in part why we had one in our basement)—that regularly got together with Oscar and Ida for potluck meals and bridge over the years. This same group celebrated Thanksgiving together. But there were dozens of other couples that were part of the Aaker bridge network. And the list expanded when they got to Sun City.

Oscar and Ida did not have a "drop in" culture. I used to admire Joyce Larson, Ida's cousin-in-law, who would spontaneously and effortlessly entertain a dozen people. People did not

25th Anniversary—1961

tend to come over to our house without advance planning. And Oscar and Ida did not pop in on others, even on relatives. They avoided ever being unwelcome in any way. I was expected to share this reticence and avoid having friends hang out at home or stay over. As a result, I resolved that my home would be different, that my kids would always feel completely open to having their friends over and that, further, their friends would regard our house as a second home. I think that goal was achieved and, as a result, I got to know some great kids growing up and had a better relationship with my own three daughters.

I think they had a solid marriage. I never heard either of them express anything resembling regrets. They appreciated the couple activities that involved church, meals, and vacations as well as bridge. Ida expressed many times how much she missed Oscar after he passed on in 1982.

On February 29, 1980, my wife Kay and I organized a surprise celebration for Oscar and Ida on the occasion of their forty-four and one-sixth anniversary (we did not want to wait for the fifitieth). It was held in Sun City at the Lakes Club, a dining club to which my folks belonged. We asked all invitees to contribute a memory of Oscar and Ida.

Oscar and Ida enter their fourty-four and one-sixth
anniversary party

I prepared a three-volume memory book filled with pictures and stories from 120 contributors, supplemented with a host of pictures from the family archives. The book covered their early days, their kids and grandkids, their parents and relatives, Oscar's career, and life in Fargo and Sun City. Preparing the book was truly one of the most rewarding and enjoyable creative projects I have ever had. It was particularly fun to add captions to some of the pictures—a friend, Keith Turner, was the best at this.

The party itself was a total surprise to Oscar and Ida. I was having dinner with them at the Lakes Club when Kay and our three girls appeared. What a shock! Shortly thereafter Paul made his appearance, followed by Kay's mother, Mabel. And finally we went into another room where around one hundred people had gathered, including our best friends, Tom and Marty DeJonghe (who surprised Kay and I), Ida's cousin Gaylan Larson, and two of Oscar's brothers—Sig and Ted. The delight in the faces of Oscar and Ida as they came into that room, captured on film by Marty, is priceless. It was an incredible moment for me.

Oscar, the Father

Oscar, upon his move to Fargo, worked in the plant department of NW Bell, which was called on to create and service the infrastructure of the telephone system. Each winter, his cohorts and he would handle crises precipitated by the North Dakota sleet storms, working through the night to restore telephone service caused by fallen wires, sometimes climbing poles in extreme cold.

For much of his career, he had the important job of supervising the engineers in the plant department. I believe that he was a good, empathetic manager. One engineer recalled that Oscar provided support in a difficult time by saying "Don't worry, you can always work for me." He played a part in some truly impressive accomplishments of the 1930 to 1960 period. During this time operators were replaced by dial telephones (1937–1944 period), "party lines" shared by several homes disappeared, and telephone lines were replaced by microwave and underground cables. The business was guided by a set of objective measures or indices. Each month they would be examined and unsatisfactory numbers would be discussed, stimulating action plans. I often wonder if we are better off with so many firms and technologies competing for phone service. NW Bell got the job done.

An incident in the 30s gives a glimpse of working life. Oscar and a colleague were attempting to improve service around Devil's Lake. They shared a room at the Northern Hotel and were disturbed by Oscar's $1.00 pocket watch—it was too loud. After Oscar was assured that no one would steal such a cheap watch, they put it outside the room. They clearly did not travel first class.

Safety was important to NW Bell and to Oscar. Their motto (that is on my wall in memory of Oscar) asserted, "No job is so important, and no service is so urgent that we cannot take time to perform our work safely." An AT&T movie on defensive driving helped my driving—although as many will attest, it is still very bad. Oscar always avoided ever backing up because he had learned that most accidents happen when a car is in reverse.

Oscar contracted crippling arthritis when a young man of thirty-seven. For several years at a key point in his career, the arthritis was severe, affecting his ability to work and his career path. He visited the Hot Springs in Arkansas for relief, if not a cure. His arthritis later receded enough so he could walk with a limp and even dance and play golf. It must have been very frustrating and painful, yet I never once heard him complain about it. His usual response to my frequent queries was "Its' fine," or "It's a little stiff today." At times, he would have to take Prednisone, which was a miracle drug in terms of removing the stiffness and pain, but which also had unpleasant side effects. He pushed himself to regularly exercise, from walking several miles to work in Fargo to bicycling in Sun City. Surely his long struggle with this disease was nothing short of courageous.

He enjoyed a golf game that would occasionally venture into the eighties. Even with arthritis, he still played regularly in Sun City with a swing that was adapted to his stiff wrists. But it was a challenge for him. I vividly recall one summer day when I was in high school; my father and I were on the elevated tenth tee at Edgewood and were assigned to play with another father/son pair. My dad asked me to hit his drive, saying that he would then get a better start on the hole. The other father said that his son would love to hit his ball, implying that they were in a competition. I thought that the other father should in fact be thankful that he did not have arthritis rather than bragging about how well he was competing. I also thought that such a remark must have hurt Oscar's feelings, but he never let on if it did.

Oscar enjoyed fixing and building. He built a bedroom for me in our Second Street Fargo home and a knotty pine recreation room when we moved to First Street. One of those electrical engineers who could actually do electrical work, he was the electrician on several major family building efforts, including the summer cabins of Ted and Bjarne. In retirement, he worked with rocks, creating bolo ties and other jewelry in one of Sun City's fine craft centers. A wall clock with embedded rocks he made still adorns our home in Orinda. He never involved me in his projects so I never developed the motivation or skill to be a fixer or builder. The feeling of satisfaction that others get from working with their hands has not been a part of my life. I don't know if he was protecting me or if he lacked the patience to deal with me.

Oscar loved to fish, and there were plenty of opportunities. The challenge was always to find the right spot. And if there were four in the boat, as happened on "Sig's" lake once when Sig, Ted, and Clarence (Stella's husband) were fishing together, there could be four opinions as to where the magic spot was. Oscar was also a pheasant hunter in the fall. I can recall tromping in the cornfields in late fall with him, but I could never understand the appeal. Duck hunting, which Oscar rarely participated in, was really even more of a puzzle to me—you got up in the middle of the night to sit in the wet and cold hidden in an extremely uncomfortable setting (called a blind) waiting for ducks to fly over. Why?

He followed the Fargo-Moorhead Twins Class C baseball team. I can still hear him tell my mother, who would as usual be hoping for a sparkling conversation, "I'll turn on the radio just to get the score." The announcer, Manny Margett, would simulate an away game based on continuous Teletype feed from the game site, often making up facts to provide color. One year the Twins had a home-run hitter named Frank Gravino who hit sixty or so home runs. He probably was buried in Class C because he had trouble with good curve balls. Later, the Minnesota Vikings earned Oscar's loyalty, especially when they played a North Dakota boy in the backfield. The Vikings in the playoffs was an exciting time.

Oscar vocalized strong views on few subjects. With Paul and me, he would vigorously defend Republican Party polices and principles. We had some tense times, as did many families during the Vietnam War, when Oscar believed that we needed to support our president. He also never tired of discouraging us from drinking carbonated beverages or getting too much sun (he was ahead of his times). When he wanted to disparage a weak argument, a foolish policy or action of government, or a son, he would say something that sounded like "Puff" and push his hand forward.

He was honest and fair. At age twenty-one he embarked with a memorized pitch to sell reference libraries in a rural community (using Sig's car). After his initial easy sale he realized that the product was not really needed by his potential customers, and he abruptly decided he was not comfortable selling it. I never saw him try to shortchange anyone. I'm sure he was influenced by his father, who once fulfilled a large debt to a contractor despite the fact that the contractor had died and there were no local relatives.

Oscar had a happy childhood, but resources were very limited, involved hard work and good fortune, and needed to be carefully allocated. His early career years were in the Depression when many were out of a job and nearly all were short of money. Because of this experience, and because of his simple wants, he avoided needless or extravagant expenditures. It was always difficult to get him to buy clothes—in fact, to buy much of anything—shopping and buying were not his thing. There was no thought of having a second car. If Ida needed a car, she would take Oscar to work if he did not walk. At Christmas, his reply to desperate queries as to suggestions for a present was, "I'd like a tie."

Oscar's frugality was coupled with a disciplined savings program influenced by his college roommate, an accounting major. He invested in stocks and bonds and held them for the long pull. In a note to me written in 1966 or so, he observed in his understated manner that his savings were more than they would be had he been a spendthrift, and that stock investments had done all right over the long run. His careful records and graphs of his expenses and income over time were evidence of his attention and discipline in managing his saving and investment program. He did not encourage extravagance in others either. Although AT&T (where he bought stock at a employee discount) was the major part of his portfolio, he owned a dozen other stocks—his records indicate that a $745 investment in IBM in 1958 was worth nearly $6,000 less than ten years later. Oscar was able to provide a comfortable life for his family and still feel secure in retirement. During his twelve-year retirement, he was able to more than double his annual income—a remarkable achievement.

Oscar loved home wherever home happened to be. You couldn't find a more loyal Fargoan. He was found of saying that North Dakota featured ten days of cold, ten days of hot, and that the rest were delightfully in-between. After retiring, he was proud to display Sun City activities and landmarks to all who came through. For many years, when Phoenix got too hot, his summer home became the college campus in Logan, Utah, where he picked berries, made jam, visited the nearby lakes, and, of course, played bridge. He loved to be with us at Christmastime in Orinda where harvesting and cracking nuts was one of his things. But he was always ready to return home. Because home was so enjoyable, he was a most reluctant traveler. If he did drive somewhere, he liked to keep going. It was difficult for Ida to get him to stop, although the prospect of a pancake breakfast or pie and ice cream, preferably at Sambo's, was enticing.

In retirement he returned to his Norway roots, where he got ample opportunity to practice his rustic Norwegian. Among the few Norwegian phrases he passed on to Paul and me were "tak for maten," "mange tak," and "pas die gut."

I have endured a reputation for being absent-minded that is, in my view, greatly exaggerated, despite incidents like driving off with a billfold or other items on top of a car, leaving a locked car running for hours in a parking facility, failing to pick up my friend Tom DeJonghe in another parking facility after a vacation (an honest miscommunication), bringing an expired passport to the airport, and regularly forgetting to deliver messages or packages from one family member to another. People never forget incidents that happen decades ago. My claim is that my forgetfulness is only a bit above average and that it is completely unfair for my kids every time they screw up to bring up my name and imply that any errors are caused by the Dave Aaker part of their personality. Oscar had a similar problem. He once wore with pride new shoes—but had brown and black socks on. Another time he forgot to take off his overshoes when going on a dance floor. Still another time, he went to rescue two colleagues stranded during a huge blizzard, only to realize that he was wearing slippers. And his shoes (perhaps because of his arthritic ankles) were never tied. His stories, like mine, seem to have an extraordinarily long life.

Another characteristic that I share with Oscar is a reluctance to "chat-up" strangers. He and I both instinctively feel that those we do not know may not have an interest in talking to us or simply may have other things to do. As a result, we feel that starting conversations may be seen as an imposition. There is also the risk that a stranger may be very boring and any exchange may be awkward to terminate. Thus, we are not chatters when strangers are involved. My two grandfathers also shared this quality; Ole was quiet and Halsten gruff, but neither would seek out strangers for conversations. In contrast, many of my friends, such as biking companions (to be introduced later) like Bob Blain, Mike Kelly, and Tom DeJonghe, never seem to pass up a "chat-up" opportunity. When I am with them, I am usually either impatiently waiting for them to get chatted out or trying to help them terminate a discussion that is delaying the event of the day. On balance, they have the right idea, and I wish I had the patience and social aggressiveness to be more of a "chat-up" person—especially when I was younger and interested in meeting women. But I, like my father, lack that proclivity.

Oscar was comfortable to be around, met people easily, and was a good conversationalist, but he was always much more of a listener than a talker. He tended to find ways to remove tensions from the air when they surfaced. My strongest overall impression of my dad was that everyone liked him, from new acquaintances to fast friends. I once asked him what was his most lasting achievement and was surprised to hear him answer that it was being successful at raising two children.

Oscar started to have health problems not too long after the 1980 anniversary event and died less than two and a half years later, in June of 1982 at the age of seventy-eight. His last months were very difficult because his short-term memory began to go. I once traveled to Sun City to make sure that the doctors were doing all they could and that Oscar's arthritis was under control. In one fateful meeting with a doctor everything changed. I realized at that moment that improvement was not going to happen and that final decisions were instead upon us. It was such a shock and source of sadness.

I learned of Dad's passing while on a Caribbean sailing trip with Marty and Tom DeJonghe and Marty's parents. It was nice to be among friends at a time in which I felt particularly sad, reflective, and mortal. Writing down my thoughts was, for me, a good way to get closure. So on the boat I wrote a letter to my three kids describing Oscar and my relationship to him. Our oldest daughter, Jennifer, then age thirteen, contributed a written tribute to Oscar in the form of a poem that read in part:

Memories to rejoice that's what there for.
To bring life and sunshine, forever more.
Memories of love filled with need and care.
Of good times and hard times each moment's rare.
Moments to remember, however long one lives
Of the times shared together, oh, how much joy that gives.

Ida, the Mother

Ida was a stay-at-home mom, the norm in those days. As far as I know, there was never a thought that she should work. So she had a lot of time to fill with activities with other housewives, often involving bridge, sports, and church.

Bowling in the winter and golf in the summer were a big part of Ida's life in Fargo. She had excellent coordination (but limited strength—no one worked out in those days). She did well as a bowler in two leagues (one being a telephone ladies league), once posting a 538. She was always one of the best golfers in her peer group, occasionally venturing in the forties. She would contend for the ladies club tournaments. Edgewood, Fargo's excellent municipal course, was the course of choice. As already noted, the Aakers were never country club material. One attraction of Sun City was the longer golf season, and Ida and Oscar regularly tootled out to the course in their golf cart. Ida's game was consistently down the middle but never long enough for her. Even five months before she passed away, during her last golf outing, she forcefully lamented that her eighty-yard drives were too short.

Church was also important in Ida's life. The First Lutheran Church on Broadway in Fargo was a regular fixture on the Aaker weekly household calendar during the Fargo years. Church also meant a variety of activities such as circles—women's groups that involved worship, gossip, bake sales, and cookbooks, not necessarily in that order. Oscar and she made a smooth transition to the American Lutheran Church in Sun City, where everyone arrived thirty minutes before the service started to get a seat. Go figure. They usually organized a group for lunch afterward.

Ida had a few expressions that often surfaced: "my stars" when she was surprised, "forevermore" when she was pleased, "that's the berries" when something went wrong, and "uff da" when she was disgusted.

Ida, like Oscar, had some trouble understanding what an academic did. Ida, in particular, was always unclear. She would always ask about teaching, even in the summer, as if that was all I did. And when I got a paper accepted she seemed let down when there was no money attached to it. She could never figure out what we did when not teaching.

Ida loved to travel but did not do much because of Oscar's reluctance. Oscar and Ida did make it to Norway to check out their roots, but a major trip was the exception. From 1982, after Oscar passed away, Ida took off!! She had trips that ranged from Russia, Helsinki, the Holy Land, and England to New Zealand, Japan, Tahiti, and places in-between. She would find a companion and a tour and go. All the pictures and brochures would be preserved—and Ida did take pictures. The family joked about how long she would take to actually snap the photo—she would join in the laughter. Less than a year before she passed away, she enjoyed an Aaker family reunion in Minneapolis and visited her high school friend in Valley City.

Ida, like Oscar and probably others who experienced the Great Depression and were not blessed with riches, was frugal or cheap, depending on the circumstance. Coupled with a price perspective apparently locked in the 50s, shopping for clothes, cars, furniture, and even food with her was a challenge. She would vigorously disparage anything she felt was over-priced, no matter how useful it might be or how much it would improve her life-style. She would donate small amounts to charity appeals and give to her church regularly, but she avoided large gifts even when it became feasible to do so. She was afraid of running out and told Paul and me to donate when she was gone (which we did). I did not share this frugality, but her need for activity and her indecision did spill over to me.

Ida needed social stimulation and activity. She was most happy in the midst of a game, a trip, a family party—events involving others. And she always had several more planned for the future. Some are sitters and watchers, and some are goers and doers. Ida was a goer and doer. She wore us all out. For better or worse, I have inherited this quality. A quiet time sitting on the beach that others seem to long for is not for me. I do not crave alone time and try to fill each day with physical activity, nearly always involving a companion.

One of Ida's most endearing (or frustrating, depending on your perspective) characteristics was her indecision. A firm pronouncement that she was going on a trip or even going on an errand was not a good predictor of what she would actually do. She would go back and forth over what to us seemed like easy decisions. Changing her mind was a fundamental personality trait. We all got skilled in forcefully encouraging her to pursue a planned outing in the face of hesitation. I have also inherited this trait, which means that, on reflection, I am more like my mother than I would ever have predicted when growing up. I am always looking to refine a decision, whether it is to accept a speaking engagement, the length of a vacation, the exact return flight of a business trip, or the route to a restaurant. I drive my wife Kay, who is extremely decisive, to distraction.

Ida had a wonderful relationship with the three granddaughters. They would visit Sun City and play miniature golf, drive the golf cart, and feed the birds. She and Oscar would join us at holidays. She also came to love the grandsons-in-law, Andy, Rich, and Brian. She explicitly said multiple times that they had a lot more patience than David (an attempt to teach her to use an Internet access program tested my patience—and my patience failed). During her last years, everyone would agree that her favorite was her great-granddaughter, Samantha (Sami), and she always wanted to know when Samantha would come over.

Ida spent her last three years at Waterford, a nice living facility in Walnut Creek (about ten miles from our home in Orinda) that included a dining room with very good food, all the bridge that you could play, sponsored outings and events, and several close friends. As frosting on the cake, the fathers of the DeJonghes, Everett and Harry, were at Waterford, so we gathered for meals there many times. It was in the middle of Rossmoor, a retirement community with a golf course and other amenities. Ida had the support and companionship of Kay and me, along with the three girls and their husbands, plus Sami. She was vigorous and active until her last six months, playing golf, taking a train to Reno, and joining our vacations. A lifelong Lutheran, she was adjusting to the convenient Rossmoor Methodist Church that was a great source of support during her last months.

My mother and I had a difficult relationship from my earliest time. The basic problem was that her advice always seemed directed at me and, to my eyes, was excessively frequent and relentlessly repetitive. I could have been more graceful. In 1957, when I felt that her backseat driving and other pieces of wisdom deserved a label, I coined the term "tips from the top." It was not meant to be complimentary.

When Ida moved to Walnut Creek, I was apprehensive about our relationship because we were going to be in relatively close quarters for the first time since I'd left college. It turned out to be one of the best things that could have happened to me. I was amazed and delighted that I loved having my mom close and enjoyed spending time with her. Her repeated comments and suggestions became charming and cute rather than annoying. Spending quality time, getting her on the golf course, taking her to dinners outside Rossmoor, playing cards, meals at the Waterford, and planning with her—the next trip, the next week, the medications, the appointments—were fun, rewarding, and precious. It was all about having a mom. I was blessed.

Everyone liked Ida. Most people who knew Ida, even those with limited exposure, would spontaneously tell me how much they liked her. I think it was due to her ready smile and twinkling eyes, her interest in people, her ability to engage in conversation (even with people she was meeting for the first time), her exuberance when it came to activities, and her incredible energy. Whatever the reason, being liked is not a bad legacy.

At Ida's 2002 funeral, Jennifer penned a poem entitled "Ida, Dancing" that captured her spirit. It was stimulated by a picture of Ida laughing while dancing at an event at her Rossmoor facility:

Live, live, live—those were the words she lived by
Every time I saw her—a twinkle in her eye
People—they would say that Ida made their day.
And she was always interested—"You don't say?"

She had that hop in her step—and a smile on her face
She was engaged and so lively—and never ever out of place
And boy was she quick—sharp as a tack
She moved here, she moved there—and she never looked back
Always intent—Ida never missed a beat.
She searched out fun—and she always kept us on our feet.
With Oscar she found love—and created a family
Life was full—and they lived happily
Playing, singing, loving—and romancing
That was her in life—Ida, dancing

My Midwestern/Norwegian roots certainly helped define my character and propel me on my way. My home was loving, stable, and secure. Links to the Aaker clan and to friends of my family added warm, fun relationships. I was a very lucky guy.

The next phase was to be an adventure at MIT; the North Dakota boy ventured east with a sense of excitement and trepidation.

3   The MIT Years

I was wide-eyed as I arrived in Boston in the fall of 1956—like a character in a Dickens novel. Just off the train, I was face-to-face with the Boston Garden, the home of the Bruins and the fabled Celtics, where Bob Cousy and Bill Russell dazzled the basketball world. The hustle and bustle of Boston was all around. A taxi took me across the majestic, boat-filled Charles River, a far cry from Fargo's muddy Red River of the North. My first glimpse of the signature MIT domes made me realize that I had arrived—I was a MIT student.

In the shadow of the MIT dome

As I walked onto the campus for the first time, I felt pride and awe, but also apprehension. The challenge ahead was intimidating. The students all seemed like geniuses to my eyes. I felt that I was out of my league for sure. Although it seemed unlikely that I would survive the grade standards of a scholarship student, I was determined to give it my best shot and be an "overachiever." I knew it would be a great educational and cultural experience, even if for only a year, and North Dakota State was a fallback.

The Decision

As a high school senior, I applied to Harvard and MIT. Harvard sounded prestigious, was far from home, and had a freshman, Lois Ivers, who was a high school debate colleague and surrogate big sister. (Lois ultimately introduced me to pastrami sandwiches in Harvard Square—a heady experience.) MIT, in addition to being prestigious, was an engineering school, and I wanted to follow in my father's footsteps and be in engineering management—this in spite of a prophetic vocational preference profile in 1955 that indicated extremely high orientation toward "persuasive" and "literary" and low interest in "scientific" and "mechanical."

My parents, particularly my mother, thought it nonsense to go so far when perfectly good colleges existed in Fargo. And if I really needed an adventure, I could go to the University of North Dakota at Grand Forks (Oscar's alma mater) or even to a school in Minnesota (my mother suggested Concordia in Moorhead, which would not exactly represent an out-of-town experience). Further, MIT and Harvard were both prohibitively expensive. My father was less opinionated but, as usual, did not really take issue with my mother or her ideas.

Today, high school students routinely apply to a large set of schools screened by making campus visits throughout the country with the aid of councelors and fellow students. Incorporated in the list are aspirational schools that are long shots, schools that are acceptable, and fallback "sure thing" schools. My experience had no resemblance to this pattern. I had been east of Minneapolis only once when, as a grade-school student, Ida and I accompanied my father on a business trip to Detroit. There was no thought of visiting campuses, no consideration of sure things or even reasonable choice schools, and no help except for a few older students.

I got into both schools. The Harvard acceptance was "diploma" ornate and impressive, while the MIT notice came in a simple, to-the-point postcard. My acceptance to Harvard became my most impressive achievement in the eyes of Jennifer, my oldest daughter, when she started applying to colleges. She did not realize that my acceptance was mostly due to the fact that Harvard and MIT did not get many applicants from the Dakotas and that they aspire to have a diverse student population. It was a thrill to get into Harvard, and I fantasized about going there, but MIT offered a full tuition scholarship of $1,300 ($200 of which was to be applied to dorm fees). The scholarship meant that MIT, while still a stretch financially, was no longer completely infeasible.

My folks were unconvinced, but after considerable discussion and a few emotional outbursts, they finally signed off on MIT. The deal was that my father would give me $1,000 per year (which was close to 10% of his pre-tax salary), and I would pay $1,000 per year from my savings and summer jobs. I was firm on avoiding working during school, arguing that it would be really dumb to spend so much for education (which could be reduced to an hourly cost) and for the cultural experience and then waste precious hours working at low wages on a nothing job. I wanted the full experience, every hour. I further argued that I needed the time to achieve the B average that I had heard was required of scholarship students. I stuck to my guns and did not work during the school year while at MIT.

Going to the East for school was rare in Fargo. The only person in my class that ventured east was my good friend Mike McLain, the only child of a Congregational minister (who was a Catholic priest before he got married). I would describe his father as both cool (he never talked down to us) and warm. Mike, after graduating from Yale and entering the Navy, died in a summer rock-climbing accident in Yosemite. I recall him telling me how safe the sport was. His parents never got over it. He was their life.

I never regretted the MIT decision. The place was truly inspirational. Norbert Weiner could be seen walking around campus.

Niels Bohr was once ahead of me in a cafeteria line. Some of the professors were celebrities in their field. The electricity and the standards of the place permeated everything. And the MIT degree opened doors, most importantly into the PhD program at Stanford. Further, my four years were an incredible cultural experience for a boy who knew only the plains of North Dakota. Exposure to Boston, the Pops, the debutante balls, the Bruins, the Red Sox, Harvard, and, most of all, students from all over the States and the world qualitatively broadened my perspective—as I had known it would.

Few described MIT as having a "pretty campus." It had a concrete motif with limited grass. But to me the signature domes were symbols of something special, and the Charles River provided charming views of sailboats and rowers in addition to the dramatic Boston skyline.

The Fraternity Scene

Part of the MIT experience would be getting to know fellow students from around the world. I reasoned that this was more likely to happen in a fraternity (I learned to never call it a frat) where you have dozens of built-in close relationships. I therefore decided to attend the fraternity rush held during the week prior to fall classes, even though I suspected that my budget would not tolerate such a luxury.

I decided, for several reasons, to pledge the Phi Beta Epsilon fraternity, despite the financial stretch. Most importantly, it was one of two fraternities that housed prep school graduates used to Boston society circles. I had no interest in living in a clone of a Midwest fraternity. Second, it was one of four (of twenty-eight) on-campus fraternities, which meant that I would not have to walk across the Mass Avenue Bridge in the winter when the wind chill was comparable to North Dakota winds. As important, it was next to a dorm, and I made arrangements to sleep in the dorm and live in the fraternity, thereby accessing the $200 dorm scholarship that I could ill afford to pass up. It would have been easy to occasionally sleep in the house because I had a bed there, but every night I returned to the dorm, not wanting to even be accused by the "authorities" or by Phi Beta Epsilon members of

Phi Beta Epsilon 1956

cheating on the receipt of the $200. It was a blessing in disguise because I got to meet some of the dorm students and see their lifestyle.

Phi Beta Epsilon was perfect for me. I wanted a cultural experience as different from my Midwestern background as possible. And I got it. The prototypal Phi Bete member was extremely wealthy, had a sports car, had attended a New England prep school, and was from South America, Europe, or some prominent U.S. family. A host of DuPonts, for example, were prominent MIT benefactors and Phi Betes all. Phi Bete pledges got invited to the Boston society cotillion dances when they were short of men. The dance I attended was another world—it was Gatsby reinvented. From the outset it was clear that I was an outlier, the marginal recruit. But I thrived.

The norms in our house were compatible with the background of our members. Phi Betes were (with one other prep school fraternity) the only MIT students to wear coats and ties to class and to dinner. I wore the same olive sports coat for two years to every class and dinner—very efficient, if a bit gross. Further, our sit-down meals were pictures of decorum. Everyone waited for the table head (the president) to sit before sitting themselves. Candles made a regular appearance. I was especially struck by the fact that if something was being passed, you never took any as it went by you but, rather, said, "After you, please" and waited for it to go to the recipient and come back to you. Very inefficient with thirty-five people at one table but also very genteel—I tried to transfer this bit of upscale manners to my family with little success. And the demi cup of coffee after dinner was a touch of old-money class.

The fraternity was a warm, friendly place. The living room had large comfortable leather furniture, a huge fireplace, and an audio system (which played *My Fair Lady* or the Kingston Trio over and over at one point). There was a game room with a pool table that doubled as an extra high ping-pong table. There was a cozy TV room in the back that got a lot of attention. It is now a small theater with Dolby surround sound. On floors three and four, where women were excluded (except one weekend each year), we had three-person suites and a few singles. Each suite had a study room with three desks (In 1986, my daughter Jennifer's sorority at Berkeley had no desks in their rooms—go figure) and an adjacent room with two bunk beds—so studying was separated from sleeping. The house now has a fifth floor with a large balcony that has a spectacular view of the Charles, the Boston skyline, and the MIT campus. A great setting for parties, it is a draw for new pledges that undoubtedly visualize impressing women.

The house did have some people from the Midwest, such as Jon Bulkley from Kansas City, Ron Koetters from Cincinnati, and Alan Pike from Bismark, North Dakota, but that was the exception. Most had a prep school background and were memorable for one reason or another. Al Hobart, an unassuming, short, slight person with a flashy sports car, was the grandson of a U.S. vice-president, and he ultimately opened a ski area to train racers in Vermont. Les Hopton was the grandson of the founder of the house. Another brother opened a factory in South America and gave his wife a course on the classics so she could make up for educational deficiencies.

Tom Stockman was a stocky EE major who never studied before any test he ever took—he would go to a movie, or so the legend goes. He was one of the developers of the technologies behind digitized music and voice, and he became such a preeminent researcher that he was on the cover of *Time* as one of the scientist trying to recover the famous erased part of Nixon's tape during the Watergate scandal. He and his group found that there were six separate incidences of erasures that meant the theory that a secretary accidentally pushed the wrong button was faulty. Tragically, he was diagnosed with Alzheimer's in 1994 and passed away a decade later.

The star of our pledge class was Jon Shirley, an extremely bright student with a prestige prep school background, who partied from the moment he arrived. He did well that first semester and flunked out the second when he started getting material he had not had in prep school—while he partied even harder. The legend at MIT was that the most successful students got straight *A*s effortlessly or flunked out because they were creative and bored with engineering thinking. Jon transferred schools and contributed to the legend by surfacing later as president of Radio Shack and still later as the COO of Microsoft.

About a quarter to a third of the house was from outside the states. Rudy Segovia, a charismatic and confident chemical engineer, was the heart of a nightly bridge game (I would have liked to have joined but could not spare the time), an All-American goalie on the MIT soccer team, and, later, the head of the oil ministry in Columbia and, still later, an influential board member of Occidental Petroleum. Knut Hauge, a terrific skier, was a large, jovial Norwegian that was a bit older because of military service. Per Bugge-Asperheim, also from Norway, was a serious EE student. Alberto Solis from Cuba and Roberto Peccei from Italy both added personality and color. Andres Bardoes, who escaped from Hungary during the revolution that was crushed by the USSR, was very bright but struggled with the enticement of TV and the memories of the harrowing Soviet occupation. He ultimately worked in optics (lasers, holography, and fiber optics). Colin Clive, an older student from England who had some military experience, had a quiet sense of humor and started a successful private equity firm before that was common. Alan Weiss, another Brit, ultimately became a forest manager out of London. Still another Brit in my suite one year played opera arias that I grew to like—but it did not stick. Another was Raul Karman.

Raul Karman

Raul, my best friend at MIT, was a terrific companion and someone that would do anything for you. One year my junior, Raul was tall, lanky, and a gifted athlete. A member of the Cuban Davis Cup team, he was a welcome addition to the MIT tennis team, of which I was a part. I vividly recall his freshman year when he was paired in a freshman team match with a Bob Bowditch of Harvard, a top-ranked junior from New England. The audience, larger than any seen at a MIT varsity match, included Jack Kramer, a tennis legend (90% of all players including me played with Jack Kramer-endorsed rackets). For some reason, Bowditch played to Raul's backhand, which was a graceful, flowing, powerful, and reliable stroke. Raul killed him to the surprise and chagrin of the Harvard folks, who never expected such quality out of an MIT freshman match. Watching was so fun.

Raul went on to play number one as a sophomore and compiled a remarkable record against the best number one players in the East. In addition to an exceptional backhand, he had a huge serve. He also could serve underhand by looping his racket in a big arch and hitting the ball as the racket was going up. The resulting serve would hit and immediately skid to the left, staying only a few inches from the ground. It was both unnerving and unhittable to anyone unfamiliar with it. However, our coach, Ed Crocker, would not let Raul use it in a match because he felt it would be disrespectful to the opponent. Raul got burned out on tennis and the coach, and as a junior he switched to golf, which he had grown to love.

Raul Karman

Raul was very laid back and very Caribbean when he arrived at MIT. We shared a Phi Beta Epsilon suite one spring during the tennis season of my junior year. Tennis practices were held late afternoon and the weather was typically humid, which meant that practice uniforms were soaking. Dinner at Phi Beta Epsilon was always "on-time," and most drifted down from a relaxing pre-dinner gathering in the living room. However, Raul and I would race over from practice (which was across the street from our house) toss our wet clothes on the extra bed, quickly change, and get to dinner in a matter of minutes. The next day we would sort through the wet clothes to find something to wear to practice. It was truly disgusting. But to wash clothes was very time consuming and would only provide a solution for a few days because we only had two or three sets of uniforms (consisting of MIT t-shirts and shorts).

Raul was relaxed about everything. If you loaned money to him or borrowed from him, he would promptly forget about it. If he owed you money, you simply borrowed that amount from him later. In my senior year, Raul and I (with Andres) got a flat on Beacon Hill's Myrtle Street, number thirty-six, fifth floor. Three others (Colin Clive, Alan Pike, and Alan Weiss) were in the same building but in a decidedly more organized and neater apartment on the third floor. A couple on the fourth floor would sometimes engage in violent arguments in the middle of the night, allowing us to share in some of the intimate details of their relationship. A small schoolyard was next door, and a convenience store and laundry were across the street. Myrtle Street at that time was in-between—within two blocks of Boston slums and two blocks in the other direction from Kennedy-level Boston opulence.

Our meals were informal to say the least when Raul and I were involved—and Andres was worse. At one point Andres ate only potatoes (probably to save money but also because he had eccentric ideas about diets). We each did have our specialty; mine was "French" hamburger featuring a consommé and sour cream sauce. Raul did Cuban dishes that reduced his homesickness for Cuba. Our friends in the other apartment had much more gourmet fare. Once they invited the local wine merchant who supplied Phi Beta Epsilon with its considerable booze needs. He brought three bottles of wine, and I got my first taste of really good wine—the difference was discernable, but that also did not stick, as I could not leverage that experience into the life of a wine connoisseur.

Raul did not take to cold. One winter day, I took him to Mad River Glen, a Vermont ski area catering to advanced skiers. We immediately went to the top where the only way down was a black diamond run. That was where I taught or tried to teach Raul to ski. It was a nightmare. All Raul could say over and over was "I am sooooo cold." He did get down without injury, but I never forgot my lack of judgment and teaching skill. Ironically, much later, Raul came to enjoy skiing and organized family outings to ski areas from his home in Puerto Rico, where he built an air conditioning business. But this had to be in spite of a rocky start.

In my junior year, Raul invited me to spend Christmas in Havana to play golf and see Cuba. My parents acquiesced, even though it meant having the traditional Christmas without me for the first time. It was an incredible experience for someone who knew nothing outside of Boston and North Dakota. We stayed at the Miramar home of Maria, who was Raul's sister. The home with its marble floors was to me palatial—I told my folks it was the most impressive home I had ever been in. On Christmas Eve there was a huge party featuring a pig roasted over a spit for a whole day. I especially enjoyed fried bananas, a terrific dessert made with "Cuban" bananas. Christmas was somewhat subdued because Fidel Castro, who was in the hills, had issued an edict against cinemas, nightclubs, and shopping. The only places that you saw Christmas trees and festive decorations were in police stations—everyone else was so low key it was eerie.

The featured activity was golf, where I learned to keep score and say nice shot in Spanish—bueno balle. We played every day at a terrific private club, which seemed to operate normally, although you had to wonder about the sentiments of the help who could see the excesses of the rich up close. One day we were playing in the usual hot and humid weather with two of Raul's friends, one of whom was extremely fastidious and hyper-conscious about germs. At the turn we were all hot and looked forward as usual to a wonderful, refreshing pineapple slush to get us through another nine holes. Raul got four of these incredible drinks, passed out two, took a sip of the third, and visibly stirred the fourth drink earmarked for his germ-conscious friend with his unwashed finger. Raul had a second drink for himself; his friend collapsed in a fit of frustration, and the rest of us were convulsed with laughter.

Just before I was to leave Havana, on New Year's Day, 1959, the revolution erupted. Fidel Castro's guerrilla army entered Havana to replace the corrupt government of Fulgencio Batista. Maria and her husband had left for Miami several days earlier in anticipation of this event. I suspect they had moved money long before then, but their plantations were lost to the new government. My trip back, like that of many others (there were some 12,000 Americans on Cuba), was delayed a few days until I got the jump seat in a flight. It was a hectic time with no government in place.

My letter to my folks described my observations of New Year's Day, 1960, when Raul and I took an ill-advised drive around a quiet city:

> Everyone is happy, celebrating, yelling greetings, and wearing the red and black of the revolution. The cars have the Cuban flag, the flag of the revolution, and heavily armed passengers. The bearded ones from the hills, some in their early teens, arrived. They are clean, polite, earnest, well armed, and look like effective fighters. They stay at the best hotels, are constantly on TV, and are regarded as the heroes that they are. They direct traffic, often with a sub-machine gun resting on their shoulder. When they turn their back to you, the barrel of a gun is staring at you.

I suspected that the country club life and the lifestyles of the very rich would change markedly.

The revolution was popular, as corruption was rampant. It was common knowledge, for example, that most of the money earmarked for roads went into the pockets of corrupt officials. However, I felt at the time that the current hero might eventually disappoint the Cuban people. Batista, in fact, was the big hero of a 1933 revolution. You never know. Some forty-five years later the verdict is cloudy. Cuba is certainly not the social and economic paradise envisioned by Castro. But the bulk of the people do have schools and healthcare that are exceptional in comparison to other developing countries and pre-Castro days.

The Cuba revolution—January 1959

The experience was one of the most illuminating of my life. The contrasts were so vivid. The lifestyle of the Cuban wealthy was so sharply different from anything I had known in the States—and from the poverty evident in Havana. The stories of corruption as an accepted part of society were eye opening. The way that the rebels won and then took over was so different than our system. But it was not clear that our system would work in Cuba. Would there be the culture and systems in place to allow it to work? Even if a fair election were held, might the end result be another corrupt dictator? Hitler once won a fair and free election. It was not clear to me. More questions than answers were raised.

Tennis and Other Sports

I graduated from Fargo High School with a tennis game that was only a few years old. I was without coaching and could be described as being anywhere from weak to pathetic. Despite this background, I decided to try out for the freshman team and became an inspiration for other "walk-ons" that would follow. I barely made the freshman team as the ninth player out of a nine-man team. In addition to lacking skill, I lacked commitment because grades were a priority and because my prospects did not look so good. But I got coaching for the first time. The coach, Ed Crocker, encouraged me to get my racket back even before the ball crossed the net, and to swing from low to high. As a result, I developed "Crocker" ground stokes that eventually led to a tendency to make very few errors.

At the end of the season, I was invited to a freshman tourney

The 1959 MIT tennis team
Bottom—Dave, Bob Hodges, Tom Cover,
Raul, Jack Klapper

by the coach, who observed that since I had little chance of playing on the varsity, I should take the trip. I declined. I could not take a weekend away from studying.

During the summer I played at Fargo with Larry Dodge, one year my junior and a talented player, and improved enough to make the varsity as a sophomore. When the spring season of my sophomore year started, I was playing number six, ahead of all but one of the freshman that I had played behind the prior year. I was a backboard, always getting the ball back in singles, and I had a reasonably good net game in doubles. So I played in all the matches, had more coaching, and improved considerably.

In my junior year, again benefiting from a summer playing the Fargo-Minneapolis tennis circuit with Larry Dodge, I played number five behind two seniors plus Raul at one and Jack Klapper (who was once a national-ranked junior from Colorado) at two. Thus, I had passed all eight people ahead of me on the freshman team, including Bob Hodges, my doubles partner, who played at number six, and Tom Cover, who got more interested in physics than tennis. It was by far the best MIT team during my tenure at MIT, and we had to be among the best MIT teams of that era. We did well in our spring trip and finished the regular season ten and four with wins over Williams and Army. Two of our losses were to Harvard and Dartmouth, both with strong teams. In the New England championships we were tied with Yale for second behind Harvard. Karman finished in the top four in the individual competition.

In my senior year, Raul escaped to the golf team and the two seniors were gone, so I played number two behind Jack Klapper. I was just ahead of two other seniors, Bob Hodges (again my doubles partner) and Fred Kayne, who had a great (my style) sense of humor and became a close friend. Incidentally, all three became presidents of their fraternity, thus proving that I did not hang out with the nerds (although, to some, all MIT students are by definition nerds). We still had a great time, but we were decidedly weaker. The main schedule was short but intense for an academic place. I recall that in my senior year I played fifteen matches in thirty days, and half were away. All matches were on clay, so you would learn to slide as you played.

Tennis was a blast. During the winter we would play indoors on hardwood, very different from the clay that was the dominant surface during our season. Hardwood was terrific for me because on that surface my pathetic service was a boomer—it would hit the wood and skid. I felt like Pancho Gonzales (the big server of this era). In the spring when the snow was still on the ground, we would head south for a week and play schools like North Carolina, Davidson, Georgetown, and North Carolina State. We would drive down in a van, eat wonderful food, and play tennis at great venues. It was a bonding time and a wonderful tennis experience. When the season started there would be road trips

Fred Kayne

to some great campuses like Wesleyan, Dartmouth, and Army. The camaraderie was wonderful. What could be better—hanging out with friends, traveling with all details organized, seeing attractive campuses, and playing two matches a day (one singles and one doubles).

Tennis was not my only athletic endeavor. During my freshmen year, in an effort to try anything to extend my cultural experience, I joined the freshman fencing team and learned lunging and countering. Fencing, a world onto itself, was cool—like being in the old fencing movies. But it took a lot of time, and tennis seemed more promising, so I turned my back on a career as a struggling apprentice fencer. Also as a freshman I pursued debating, one of my most successful high school activities. In one event, my partner and I beat teams from intimidating Harvard (the home of JFK and God knows how many famous jurists) and Wesleyan. However, debating also was a casualty of time constraints.

Intramural sports were a good release from academics (which were locally described as getting a drink from a fire hose). I played football, basketball, hockey, ping-pong, volleyball, and softball for the fraternity team. By far the most successful team sport for the Phi Bete house was hockey. We had three Norwegians and several others with some skating experience, and many of our opponents fielded a lot of people that could barely skate. My youth, where I played hockey nearly every winter day from the second through the sixth grade, came back. When playing one team that really could not skate, I scored twelve goals. One year we won the championship, and we were always contenders. The varsity coach asked me to join the varsity, an exceptional request—I'm sure that would not happen at Michigan.

Ping-pong had to be my best individual sport. It requires quick reflexes, good eye/hand coordination, and places no premium on foot speed (of which I am not blessed to say the least) or a throwing motion (as a fraternity quarterback, all routes had to be within fifteen yards). We had several good players, and, as a result, I played a lot of ping-pong. Because of our unorthodox table (higher than regulation and with a constrained area), we had a significant advantage in the intramural leagues and did very well. I once played one hundred games in three weeks. At one point I was ahead of Raul and his heavy topspin forehand forty-five games to thirty-nine despite the fact that he had gone on a big winning streak.

Skiing was a prominent part of every winter. I would manage to get up several times and always during winter break. It is a bit ironic that someone who was scraping by on a scholarship and a small parent stipend not only turned his back on getting a job but found the resources to ship skis to Boston and engage in such an expensive hobby. But it was great to get away into the country, and there were plenty of skiers in my house. The snow, however, was generally terrible—you always seemed to be skiing on ice. One year we reached Stowe one evening only to learn that it was exceptionally icy on the slopes. We just kept going until we hit some areas outside Montréal. In one, at Mount St. Sauveur, the lift fee was two dollars at what was then a local hill in the shadow of larger areas.

Classes, Learning, Grades

Academics were important to me. I fundamentally liked classes and school, especially when a course took me into new areas. It was a kick to learn something that was new and challenging. Further, all the bright, motivated people around me were intimidating. One of them, Sam Norris, had preceded me from Fargo High by one year (in chapter one, Sam appears as manager of our junior high basketball team). But Sam's presence was hardly reassuring because he had done much better academically than I in high school. I realized that to excel, even to survive, I would have to give it my best effort. In addition, I felt that good grades would increase my options later on with respect to jobs and graduate school. I knew I was not the brightest student and thus had to be the hardest working and the most organized. I was right up there in disciplined study habits, often involving the hours from eleven to three in the morning—I was a night person.

My letters home, which were extensive (and saved by my mother), always talked about my latest test results and the class average. Tests were frequent and important in my life. And class average was huge. I clearly wanted some distance between the class and me. Grades arrived in the mail after the semester, and although I always had a fair idea of what I would get from test results, there was some uncertainty, and the letter was a big deal. While I was looking for B's and some A's, I recall a fraternity brother saying that he could do badly or could get C's—a different frame of reference.

In my first semester, I was very proud to have gotten all B's (in calculus, physics, chemistry, foundations of Western civilization, and creative thinking) plus a C in ROTC (which was like getting a C in gym in the sixth grade). A 3.94 average (where 5.0 is an A) put me roughly in the top third of my class—this before grade inflation. During the first two years I found calculus (where I relied on an excellent book and rarely went to class) and physics (basically applied algebra) very easy, humanities hard, and chemistry (mostly memorization from my vantage point) very hard. After some ups and downs and a relaxed senior spring semester, I finished with something close to a B average that was just good enough to qualify me for Tau Beta Pi (national engineering honor society).

Each term I took one humanities course, which was hard for someone who did not write well. I always put extra time into humanities because I believed that I was missing something by not being at a liberal arts school, and I wanted to compensate as much as possible. During the first two years we had a foundations course that started with Plato and systematically marched through the centuries. In the fall of my senior year, my humanities elective was "Religions of Man" taught by Huston Smith, who wrote the clearest book on religions ever (I recommend it to anyone wanting an understanding of the world's major religions—it is now titled *The World's Religions*). The first of two six-page book reviews written for Smith's course covered *Gandhi* by Fischer and was labeled a good piece of work (and given an A-), but the

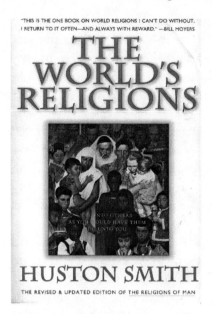

"THIS IS THE ONE BOOK ON WORLD RELIGIONS I CAN'T DO WITHOUT.
I RETURN TO IT OFTEN—AND ALWAYS WITH REWARD." —BILL MOYERS

THE
WORLD'S
RELIGIONS

HUSTON SMITH

THE REVISED & UPDATED EDITION OF THE RELIGIONS OF MAN

My top undergrad text

second was judged too descriptive (and received a B). I recall both required an enormous amount of effort. I was not the only student impressed with Professor Smith, as he was asked to be our commencement speaker.

In the last semester I took a philosophy course on symbolic logic taught by the famous Noam Chomsky, later an internationally known activist critical of the actions of the U.S. government. I loved the course and did not find it hard, but it was there that I received my only D at MIT. Go figure!

I really liked electrical engineering—or course six, as it was called. At MIT all majors, courses, buildings, and classrooms were given a number using decimals. The first EE course is called 6.01, for example. A course by a Professor Guillemen on circuit theory (the design of logic circuits for computers) was so simulating and fascinating that for a month during my sophomore year I decided to switch to EE, my father's major. I wrote about having so much fun finding the resistance between two nodes in a system of meshes that have connections extending to infinity. Sounds nerdy in retrospect. After a month in EE, I went back to Course fifteen (the Sloan School of Management) because I really loved marketing and advertising. Further, I observed that EE students had no social life, were incredibly smart, and, worst of all, had spent their childhood building radios (when I was playing baseball or hockey). I figured that I would not excel there.

Course fifteen was full of interesting professors and great content. For the first time, I was with students outside my house that wore ties—it felt professional, like real business people. I was impressed with my advertising professor, Gerald Tallman, who did consulting and told about how his clients, to his surprise, expected him to travel first class. I especially enjoyed advertising and marketing and the case assignments. I also enjoyed organizational behavior, an interest that reflects my ongoing curiosity on the impact of organizational structure, culture, people, and processes on business effectiveness.

Several professors clearly were impacting management thought and practice. Professor Douglas McGreger had pioneered some organzational behavior ideas. He developed the concept of Theory Y (a supportive management style) in contrast to the prevalent Theory X (authoritative style). However, much of the MIT path-breaking work of the time involved quantitative modeling using the emerging power of the computer. For example, Professor Jay Forester was doing visible work applying EE systems ideas to business. In marketing, Professor Arnold Amstutz had created an elaborate computer simulation of market response modeling consumers, retailers, and manufactures with hundreds of variables and relationships—a simulation that was the forerunner of many others.

I have a compulsive drive for efficiency—an annoying or colorful trait, depending on your perspective—that in part can be traced to a course on work simplification (a remnant of Frederick Taylor's scientific management using time and motion studies) that I took. I recall an assignment in which I attempted to make the task of brushing my teeth more efficient. The idea is to remove all wasted time from the effort by combining and reordering the subtasks involved.

This efficiency compulsion takes many forms. When traveling, I am always looking to change flights to get home faster. I try not to be too early to any engagement so that time is not wasted. When watching TV (always using the picture within picture) or listening to the radio, I am always changing channels in order to make sure I don't miss a better selection. I dual-process (eating while reading, etc.). If a service provider is being inefficient, I usually make helpful suggestions for improvement (even when my kids strongly encourage me to use some will power and let it go). I even suggest to my regular golf companions to go to the next tee stand before entering the score. I often think that I need to learn to value "slow" and consider efficiency in a broader context, but that doesn't seem to be easy for me.

David Butterfield

My course fifteen thesis was done jointly with Dave Butterfield. We failed to find an interesting topic like exploring some substantive issue in information systems or marketing. So when a professor of business statistics had a topic for us, we jumped on it. The task was to write a computer program to explore the use of the Type B Gram-Charlier series, a variant of the well-known (in some circles) Poisson distribution, as an approximation of the binomial distribution. It was as bad and useless as it sounds. We found by brute force (trying the approximation under many varies of "p," the key parameter of the binomial) that indeed it was better. The thesis was in retrospect a complete waste in that we learned little (beyond some programming) and the results were of no interest to anyone. When I told my Stanford advisor, a real statistician, the title, he was kind to avoid indicating that it was a joke. But we didn't know it at the time and it got us through with a satisfying pile of printout. Dave is now the vice chairman of LPL, an investment advisory service with nearly 5,000 representatives, where he has developed the systems that are the backbone of the firm. I suspect that thesis did him more good that it did me, but not much.

ROTC was compulsory and a graduation requirement. Midway in my sophomore year, I convinced the ROTC program to stop wasting time and money (to say nothing of morale) on a person that would be prevented because of eyesight from ever serving. So I got a waiver of this requirement for graduation. ROTC was horrible. You dressed up in a neat little uniform and marched around the field. And the "successful" students got to shout orders. You had to feel sorry for them. Actually, my high school friend, Roy Smillie, was a naval officer out of ROTC. After five years he got a Northwestern MBA and went to work for a manufacturer that sent him at a young age to turn around a plant in the South. I always felt that his military ROTC management style was one reason that he never had a chance—the union people simply ate him up (not too long after that he contracted melanoma—from which he never recovered—a legacy of his Minnesota summers, his love of sailing, and his light skin).

Politics and Politicians

I was interested in campus politics as I had been in high school. In the fraternity, I was treasurer, rush chairman, and, ultimately, president in the fall of my senior year. I took the job seriously—running a thirty-five-person house with a staff and regularly scheduled events was not trivial. I got a gavel that remains a nice memento. I recall urging my friends Dave Butterfield and Fred Kayne to start such a tradition in their fraternity the year before they would become presidents—so they would also get a gavel. But both were too principled to take my suggestion.

With respect to the campus, my political vehicle was the IFC (Inter-Fraternity Conference) that represented the fraternities to the campus and also dealt with issues spanning the twenty-eight individual houses. I was the IFC representative as a junior and an IFC vice-president and member of the executive committee as a senior. The IFC during that year expanded a cooperative buying program, helped organize some IFC-wide charity events, supported rush week, and lobbied the campus on issues relevant to fraternities. However, the most visible task was to organize the IFC weekend, especially the Friday-night dance. On the executive committee with me was John Sununu, who went on to become a prominent national politician—three-term governor of New Hampshire, chief of staff of George Bush the first, host of CNN's *Crossfire* program, and faculty member of Harvard's Kennedy School. Who would have guessed?

Among the movers and shakers were Linda Griener and Chris Sprague. Linda was the first female editor of the *Tech*, a newspaper that came out twice a week. She was scary bright, funny, energetic, a wonderful hostess, and a fun person to hang out with. She lived in an apartment because the first women's housing unit was not built until 1960. After hearing complaints about her drinking from her neighbors, she arranged with friends to leave an empty bottle in the waste every morning for months just to let "them" talk.

Chris Sprague, who later married Linda, was one of the brightest people I have ever known. He was editor of *Voo Doo*, the monthly humor magazine, and later became president of the student body. *Voo Doo* at the time seemed racy, irreverent, and fall-down funny. Now with *MAD* and *Saturday Night Live* in the culture, *Voo Doo* seems a rather banal part of the placid 50s. But it was one of the "you-had-to-be-there" things. It was a pleasure to spend time with both Chris and Linda. Chris, after starting a family with Linda, tragically had a stroke and could only move his eyes. I think of him often, especially when I am tempted to complain about my lot. Linda became a dynamic professor of organizational behavior at Vermont.

Social Life

My social life was restricted by my study habits. During my first year I would only allow myself one night off. I was so disciplined that I did not participate as a freshman in the annual spring fraternity weekend. The dates I did have tended to be study dates. However, I did attend some mixers at Radcliffe and Wellesley. I recall entering a stuffy room with coffee being served and attempting to screen women and then getting up the nerve to approach them. There was the real risk of either being rejected or getting involved with a loser. And it took a lot of time away from studying. It was a lose-lose-lose situation. A better option was to be fixed up, but that too had substantial risks. It did not help that the women at Radcliffe and Wellesley tended to look down on MIT men. Of course, there were a million lesser schools around Boston with students that were only too willing to deal with the MIT image. Significant trade-offs needed to be addressed on a weekly basis.

As a sophomore and junior I relaxed a bit. I dated a MIT coed, Sheila Evans (now Sheila Widnall) who was one of the few MIT women undergraduates (they represented something under 4% of the student population). Later, she was the first woman appointed to the MIT engineering faculty, the first to be chair of the MIT Faculty, and the first female Secretary of the Air Force serving from 1993 to 1997. A gifted researcher in aeronautics, she made significant advances in understanding aircraft turbulence and spiraling air flows. I had lunch with her at Berkeley in the early 1990s and she was definitely a confident, forceful, bright, and still attractive lady.

As the years went by, I got more socially active. By my senior year, I was a full participant in the social life—which means that I often took two weekend nights off. (I recall being shocked at learning from Jennifer that at Berkeley Thursday night was added as an extra party night). But study dates were always OK and had the advantage of neutralizing the "have to study" excuse for not dating me.

During my senior year I really enjoyed the fraternity weekend. I was dating a Chicago native from Wellesley—a great girl named Alice Kanlian whom I left behind because I was not ready for a commitment (she was also dating a Harvard PhD student, so it is not clear that I had a choice anyway). On the Friday night of the party weekend, in particular, I stayed up most of the night and consumed a lot of alcohol-based drinks. The next day I had a tennis match against Army. During warm-ups I had such a headache that I sat behind a far windscreen instead of hitting. However, at number two singles, I played one of the best matches of my college career, wining easily while the number one and three players struggled. I was so focused on the ball and so trying to avoid running that I simply made no unforced errors the whole match. My take is that training is overrated—the ability of Babe Ruth, Mickey Mantle, and Joe Namath to excel after wild nights is confirmation.

Frequently, we would take off during the evening and go to Elsie's, a sandwich shop in Harvard Square about four miles away. It provided terrific sandwiches (the roast beef was always featured), the Harvard Square ambiance, and a chance to procrastinate. We would sometimes stop at a drive-in along the way and get coffee frapes—Eastern for milk shakes. So a car was needed, but there were plenty at the house—many of which were expensive sports cars. This was not Dorothy's Kansas.

There was no shortage of events to attend in Boston. The Tech night at the pops was a really cool date event. I would always go to a few Bruins and Celtics games. Sitting in the cheap seats at a Bruins hockey game really got you close to the "real" Boston. The Bruins fans made the Oakland Raiders fans seem serene, even monk-like. They were involved, loud, and had violent tendencies. The Celtics with Russell, Cousy, Sharman, and Don Nelson (who is now better known as a successful coach) were more of a ballet in action. Then there were the Red Sox with Ted Williams in an intimate, now demolished, Fenway Park.

Assorted friends from the house invited me to their homes during vacations. Bill Butcher's family in Staten Island opened their doors to me during my first Thanksgiving away from home. Also during my first year, I visited Washington DC where Uncle Al and his wife, Helena, entertained me. We flew over the city (Al was a professional pilot/photographer), hit the museums, and had clams-on-the-half-shell, a first for me. I saw the anti-trust subcommittee headed by Estes Kefauver, famous for his coonskin hat and his run for the presidency. North Dakota Senator Usher Burdick chatted with me about Jan, my schoolmate in Fargo, who was his daughter. Senators, at least North Dakota senators, were more accessible in those days.

When school ended, many would head off to the Cape for a celebration. We would find a house to crash and just party. One year I was less than stable and walked into a ditch and bruised my leg. I recall that I had trouble finding a female that would give me the sympathy I needed. On the weekend there would be the Phi Beta Epsilon reunion where well over one hundred alumni of the Phi Bete house would gather. Everyone believed that our house was tighter because it was the only chapter—there were no competing "national" events. It was a bonding time, especially for the older alumni.

A popular activity was to park along the Charles at night to watch the submarine races. More than a little naive, I recall the first time I heard the line I had to think it through—how can you watch a submarine race if the boats are under the water and at night when you could not even see a regular boat? But I finally got it.

The Fargo Connection

Christmas vacation was a special time because I got to come home. Although I fantasized about taking a plane for all or part of the journey, the train always was the practical choice. Practical but not easy—switching trains in Chicago in the middle of a thirty-six-hour trip spanning a night and two full days. But it was so cool getting close to Fargo with visions of home, family, and friends. The anticipation during the last few hours of the trip was palpable.

Getting to school in the fall and returning in the spring was also by train when I was a freshman. A friend's car became an option when I was a sophomore, and a car that I inherited from Oscar became the transportation of choice during my junior year and the fall of my senior year. I prided myself on driving without the use of maps—just bearing east (or west) and using the signs. During one trip, I was crossing Ohio in the middle of the night and tried to drink coffee, but it just didn't work—even at that hour the taste was terrible. It was not Starbuck's quality, of course.

During one trip a series of loud noises signaled that the car had a serious problem. It happened within miles of Gaylord, the home of two of my uncles, Bjarne and Ted. What are the chances? So we had a day layover in Gaylord while friends of Bjarne fixed the car, and we were treated like royalty by Mabel and Arleen, my aunts. The timing of the car breakdown was truly a miracle.

I needed to earn money to pay my one-third of the school expenses. During the summer, I worked for Culligan Soft Water, owned by a family friend, Don Warren, a crusty manager who did not believe in overpaying, in admitting mistakes, or in employing a motivational, supportive managerial style. Those with whom I worked were not summer college interns. One sometimes failed to turn up because he had been on a bender the night before, and another, on his best day, never bathed. We carried heavy tanks into homes and removed those in place so they could be recharged by running salt water through them. It was an unpleasant job and hard on your back. I once fell asleep driving the big "double-clutch" truck back from a nearby town in the late afternoon but woke before the accident happened. And I still have a broken toe caused by a falling tank. But it was money.

After my junior year at MIT, I got to be an engineer at the Northwest Bell Telephone Company where my dad worked in the plant department. The conditions were much better, no heavy lifting except for the "manual." The engineering involved looking up things in huge books of tables—for example, how far microwave towers should be apart under various conditions. The people were kind to me in part because they liked my dad. It was an indoor coat-and-tie job, although I did take one field trip to survey for microwave towers. Occasionally I would have lunch in my suit and tie with Larry Swenson, who was selling clothes at Straus Clothiers. Exhibiting big-time executive behavior, we fought over the bill. Once Larry grandly tore my five dollars in half, saying my money is no good here, and paid the bill with a flourish.

After work and on the weekends I would play tennis or golf or go to the lakes. I enjoyed golf, but tennis was my first priority. Tennis was at Island Park where Larry Dodge, the "manager," would monitor the five cement courts, sell soda and snacks, hang with his friends, and play tennis. I always felt that his job was a lot better than hassling with Culligan tanks. I must have played thousands of sets with Larry (as he did not have a lot of competition), always getting from two to four games but never winning any. None! When I would get close he would elevate his game a notch—he was competitive and never choked. We played doubles in the local tournaments in Fargo and Minneapolis and were ranked three or so in the Northwest one year, in part because we got to the finals of a big Minneapolis tournament. I would lose to Larry in the finals of most Fargo tournaments. The *Fargo Forum* reported in July of 1960 that Larry captured his fourth successive men's singles championship in the state tennis tourney beating the bespectacled (what has wearing glasses got to do with it?) Dave Aaker 6-4, 6-2 with a strong net game and a potent serve. Larry ultimately became a California developer and architect and a nationally ranked senior player winning some national tournaments. For a time, his doubles partner was Whitney Reed, once ranked as the top U.S. player but equally well known for avoiding all semblance of healthy living.

My parents were not into tennis and rarely came to watch, even when I was in a tournament. And of course, there was never a thought given to see me play on the MIT tennis team. Their disinterest in my tennis always puzzled me, although it did not anger or upset me. It was in part due to the norms of a time in which there was relatively little involvement in the sports activities of the kids, and most fathers had no compulsion to relive their youth through their kids as we do now. Most families' social schedule now works around the practices and games of their kids, starting in the first grade. The lack of parental interest in my tennis was in sharp contract to my own involvement, as detailed in chapter seven, in my daughter Jolyn's athletic career.

The lakes, including Pelican, Detroit, Melissa, and Cotton, were less than one hour away, and I would go down sometimes for an evening. Summer nights in Minnesota by a lake are incredible, especially when there is a breeze to repel the mosquitoes. One night after my freshman year in college I needed to escape from Fargo but my only option was to use a clunky old Chevrolet that my father had bought just so I would have transportation around town. He explicitly said not to take it to the lakes because it might break down. I decided to risk it. On the way home, I blew something and a tiny noise became a bang as I finally got home. My father reminded me of the deal, and I had to get along without a car for the rest of the summer.

My usual companion on lake trips, as in high school, was Jack Bergene, introduced in chapter one as bright, witty, and a prodigious beer consumer. I recall us taking dates to the dance held each weekend in Detroit. We used to carry four spares because the tires were so threadbare that we would have several flats each night.

We also consumed a lot of beer. Jack, in particular, liked beer in quantity, starting with breakfast. This practice probably anticipated an alcohol problem that I understand he has battled. In any case, our driving and drinking habits were scary. And the two-lane gravel roads in the lake country were dangerous, full of blind hills and curves. I recall driving a Casselton girl I was dating home so smashed I had to close one eye to avoid seeing a double road. This was way before seat belts or designated drivers. Remembering those times made me want to make sure my kids never had similar experiences.

Jack was a successful engineering student at UND despite, according to his accounts, spending close to zero time studying and much time partying. We had (what we assessed to be) an incredibly funny correspondence during our college years—so funny that we always talked about using the letters as the basis for a book. I now realize in reviewing his letters that we over-estimated their quality (although mine are lost to posterity— probably a good thing) and that the subject matter (some of our best friends could easily take them the wrong way) and tone (a bit crude) would make it hard for the humor to come through, especially forty years later.

Jack on my writing quality and quantity: "Your handwriting and spelling has been condemned ... try to improve this sad state of primigenial (look it up in Uncle Billy's Whiz Bang iggermance) as well as your tennis game which I trust is in its usual sad state of affairs ... I must again remind you that there is such a thing as the alphabet. In your next epistle I would appreciate its use in communicating your nonsensical remarks. The days of Sanskrit are over, my boy ... realizing your inability to scrawl readably (and intellectually and humorously) I hereby send you an informative paper on the subject of better scribbling ... notice how I thought-fully corrected parts of this epistle for benefit of easy reading. Please do similarly in your forthcoming letter, which I shall expect shortly. The last one was sent to Fort Yates (an Indian reservation) for translation where it was misinterpreted as a letter from Boston proclaiming war."

In the letters he kept me up to date on those entering the armed forces (at least a dozen, led by Tom Wright), those getting married (led by Larry Swenson, whose marriage in Perley was attended by Jack, who expressed the hope that we would attract one-eighth the people, one-half as rich when we got married), those looking for jobs (1958 was a recession year for summer jobs), and those finding jobs (Larry going into the used car business). A constant theme was his lack of studying, parties (he signed the letters as horizontally yours), our friends, the limitations of the Ivy League, and my writing deficiencies. He once described himself as being from Lower Fargovia.

My folks came to Boston twice, the first time to pick me up after my freshman year. Oscar, Ida, and Paul got to see MIT, Boston, and, most importantly, Phi Beta Epsilon and the fraternity brothers with whom I had gotten close. We then went to New York to see the sights, a first for everyone in the family. The second time was for my graduation. At that time my Chevrolet, the Oscar hand-me-down, was not in good shape. One side was bashed in and only two of the four doors worked. I recall a lady once wrote a note saying she bumped my car not realizing that the other side was a wreck. The most serious issue was the brake pedal. It pushed in OK but to get it out you had to pull on an attached rope. Over time the rope had to be pulled harder and harder until it required two hands and considerable effort. Driving it was an adventure. When my folks called from the suburbs of Boston, I went down to the car and drove it to the car pound and calmly walked home. They never saw it.

The Job

Senior year was a time to find a job. I thought about going to Harvard for an MBA and even talked to a counselor there. However, my family, particularly my mother, thought that four years at an expensive school was quite enough and that I needed to get serious and get a job.

Interviewing was fun and challenging. I received offers from NW Bell Engineering Department in Minneapolis thanks to my father's influence and despite the fact that I was perceived as a bit arrogant. I also had offers from AT&T Long Lines in Kansas City and manufacturing positions at both GE and Johns Manville. For one interview I went by sleeper train to New York. I felt important, verging on being a celebrity. However, my trip to Texas Instruments in Houston sold me. First, it was in a warm climate, and at that point anything without a winter seemed south enough for me—I did not distinguish between Houston and Los Angeles. Second, it was in the electronics sector, although the Houston Instruments part of TI was not exactly cutting edge. Third, the

The first trip to New York for the Aaker family—1957

other options were not that exciting—so TI it was. The pay was around $550 a month, a very attractive sum in those days.

I took a few weeks off, but the need to get on a payroll and start a career was on my mind. So I was off to Houston to begin a new era in the life and times of yours truly.

4   The Houston Years

I arrived in Houston for my first job at Texas Instruments (TI) in early July 1960, a real eager beaver. Most rational people would have taken a few months off to enjoy the Minnesota summer, visit friends and relatives, and spend time with the family. Most rational Europeans would take a year off even in those days. It was clear that soon I would be in a very time-constrained schedule with only two weeks vacation each year. Why would you rush off to start the job only two weeks after getting home from college?

Two motivations stand out. First, I wanted to get started on my career. I was going to learn, work hard, be creative, impress, and advance up the corporate ladder (hopefully to CEO). There was not a moment to lose. Second, I was interested in getting on a payroll. Every week on my own meant money being spent, and, having scraped through college, money was valued. I needed to replace the old family Chevrolet that my father had given me and to begin an investment program. These goals reflected the values of my Norwegian immigrant heritage, my family that never had a lot of extras and exhibited frugality at every turn, and perhaps the materialistic 50s as well.

The Job

TI was a major semiconductor company located in Dallas. TI Houston, an extremely minor part of TI, designed and manufactured test equipment. It liked to exaggerate its importance by noting it was the "instruments" in Texas

Instruments. The TI Houston legacy was oil well instrumentation, and one business group still marketed to the oil fields. Another group, eventually to be my TI home, made analog strip-chart recorders, devices that would record anything that could be transformed into electrical signals.

My first assignment, which lasted around three or four months, was designed to provide an overview of the manufacturing operation. The job title, "dispatcher," meant that I physically moved parts from one manufacturing area to another, expedited rush jobs, and located missing parts and equipment. It was really a bottom-of-the-barrel job, but I liked it because I learned a lot about tools and equipment and met some nice people with very different backgrounds than I. But manufacturing? In retrospect, I cannot think of any job less appropriate for a person that opted out of electrical engineering because I wasn't practical enough to do simple lab work.

My next assignment was in accounting, in retrospect another "off-brand" job. It involved a lot of manual posting and even helping to conduct a physical inventory—activities I then believed were wasting my prodigious potential. I recall making myself learn how to use an adding machine by touch just so my time would not be a complete waste. But I liked to learn new areas and I realized then— and still believe—that accounting and related planning activities represent one of the most practical business skills. Anyone in business will benefit from knowing cost accounting.

I was a rather pathetic go-getter. In order to make a mark, I got involved in the self-appointed project of evaluating whole dollar accounting. I estimated how much we would save by forgetting the pennies in any transaction and analyzed the resulting complications and potential problems. My memo, recommending that we adopt whole dollar accounting, was probably greeted with a "who is this guy?" reaction. In any case, it was not adopted. One time I even came in on Sunday, and the suspicious manufacturing manager stopped by and asked what I was doing here (probably thinking that I was embezzling or something equally nefarious). I showed him my wit by promptly asking him what he was doing here. My wit and diligence were unappreciated. Of course, manufacturing managers, in fact all TI managers, were not hired for their sense of humor or people skills.

My third and final assignment was as a requirements engineer (retitled "product sales manager" in 1963), a slot I was destined to be buried in for the rest of my five-year tenure at TI. The job was to support the field sales force and customers. We processed orders, corresponded with customers, handled delivery and service issues, and acted as the interface between the engineering staff and the field. In theory, we had more product knowledge than the salesmen who were covering other product groups and could go into the field and answer customer questions. What it really meant was that we could call on engineers with whom we had a personal relationship to get questions answered.

We were also expected to communicate to the engineering group what new products or product modifications would appeal to customers. In that respect, we contributed to the long-range strategic thinking. What really happened was that we tended to divert the attention of the engineering group to modifying products to help get a large order rather than doing long-range product development—not a good thing in the long run.

By far the most positive aspect of five years at TI was that I learned to write. I wrote some five to fifteen letters a day to customers, plus numerous memos. All this writing had inconsequential content, but it was writing. I got good at putting sentences and paragraphs together simply by doing so much of it. I think my writing skill ultimately helped me get through graduate school, write articles, and eventually write books.

I worked next to Herb Roehrig, a career product marketing salesperson. He was just a terrific colleague. Herb and I had a similar sense of humor, and it was great fun to exchange thoughts on customers and organizational gossip involving salespeople and other employees. More than a bit cynical, we joked that we sure did not want to be in a hospital where doctors were relying on our equipment. When confronted with an irate customer, I would turn him or her over to our "boss." Herb would pick up the phone and authoritatively promise to solve the problem and imply that the incompetent would be harshly dealt with. I would do the same for Herb.

Two of the salespeople were particularly good with women, and we would live vicariously through them. One was open and detailed about his escapades while the other was more secretive, only hinting at his adventures. Both made our relatively boring lives more interesting. During a business trip to Houston in the early 90s I learned that Herb had died of a heart attack not too long after he retired. A shame.

For over a year we had a likable boss, an excellent field sales representative named Charles who was promoted to be the product-marketing manager. Whether running meetings, handling simple customer tasks, knowing relevant product or process content, or exercising people skills, he was way over his head. He just had no feel for management. He didn't even seem to detect disparaging remarks or actions in his direction. The division manager, who brought him in with all the transfer costs, could not very well fire him immediately, so we lived with him for over a year.

He was not the first bad manager I'd ever had (I recall the shop foreman on my school board job and the Culligan owner, both of whom lacked people skills), but he was the first in my post-college world. The experience might have stimulated me toward a lifelong interest in what makes a good manager different from a bad one.

Just over two years after I arrived, Ed Hill, the manager of the recorder business, and the marketing manager, Orm Henning, concluded that I was due for a change, a conclusion that I, of course, had also arrived at. But what change was available within the confines of the recorder group? The answer was field sales. Accordingly I was offered a field sales position in either St. Louis or Orlando. But selling just wasn't my thing. Calling on leads and living in hotels did not seem stimulating, broadening, interesting, or fun. So I said no. The only other job opening in Houston was as an industrial engineer. However, the manufacturing manger desired someone that not only knew something about the job (which disqualified me already) but someone with experience. There was no access to jobs in Dallas so my TI career stayed stagnant.

In an effort to advance myself in the face of a job that did not exactly challenge, I turned to education. I enrolled in the University of Houston graduate EE program. I took two courses toward a master's before realizing that a master's in EE would not really advance any reasonable career trajectory. I also enrolled in a Dale Carnegie (win friends and influence people) course. I learned how to remember people's names and how important that is. Unfortunately, its impact seemed to be short term because my inability with names has remained a problem despite the course.

The "glamour" part of my job was to travel to the field to support the sales offices. I could fly to new places (all places would be new to me) and stay in fancy hotels (all hotels were fancy to me). However, because Ed Hill thought that meeting customers was important, he tended to take the trips. I did make one West Coast trip and fell in love with Northern California. My Uncle George, my father's younger brother, who lived in San Rafael, just north of San Francisco, took me on a tour. He was extremely proud of the San Francisco area and showed me the bridge, Chinatown, Alcatraz, Fisherman's Wharf, and the rest of the sights. It reminded me of my introduction to Washington DC by Uncle Al while I was at MIT

In spring of 1963 we lost two salesmen in LA, and I was selected to fill the breach. I found an apartment near Hollywood (not so seamy in those days but still very LA) and was on my own. My crowning achievement, which I suspect they are still talking about, was my trip to a desert government research facility to demonstrate our cryogenic (ultra-low) temperature measurement device. I had to drive to the Ontario airport where a private plane (functional, not plush) took me to the client location. I set up the demo, turned it on ... and nothing. I tried to make it work, called the engineers in Houston, and tried again. Finally I got it to go for a few seconds, after which it exploded in a puff of smoke. The customer group was sympathetic but did not give me the order. It might have been the all-time worst demo in the history of technical sales.

Back in Houston, in late 1963, the manager of the recorder group made me an unofficial strategic planner in part to compensate for the limitations of my boss, but also to allow me to be more than a product sales manger. The recorder group was going nowhere—TI had many better places to put money. Nevertheless, I charged ahead in the assignment I had dreamed of since college—to chart the strategic course of a business. Of course, I knew little about strategic planning and was definitely feeling my way (I did write a book on the subject, but that was nearly two decades later). I would develop projections of the various subcomponents of the market, do competitor analysis, discuss new product options, and suggest R&D priorities. I would even suggest acquisition candidates that in the larger picture must have made little sense. This "staff" job made the time seem less wasteful—but wasteful nevertheless.

In my strategic planning role, as usual, I expanded the job description by developing an (unasked for and unwanted) external "Strategic Information Planning System" in which information that flowed into the firm from trade shows, trade magazines, customers, etc. would be systematically collected, organized, and disseminated. During my strategy period of the 1980s, I wrote an article around the system that was published in the *California Management Review*. I still think it was a good concept, but the system (like my whole dollar accounting plan) was never used at TI.

A related aspect of the job was to be involved in applications engineering. In early 1963, I wrote a three-page memo detailing the potential of providing marketing guidance to engineering for planned and in-progress projects, and of having marketing input to product planning efforts. I wrote a lot of memos giving unsolicited and ignored advice.

I was rather desperately looking for ways to stand out, and for opportunities to learn within the context of my job. (There is a theme here—I was not inspired by my job and my lack of growth and advancement.) As a result, I became motivated to write technical articles, the ostensible purpose of which was to provide PR support for our products. I liked the idea of being a published author (a motivation that eventually influenced my choice of an academic career). Although I received little encouragement, I plunged ahead and ultimately published four articles. They probably had little impact with respect to sales leads or to adding to the stature of our products, but I enjoyed seeing my name in print, and it also gave me something to mention at the end of the year during the time for performance review.

The articles largely described the characteristics and applications of our strip-chart recorder line. They were published in the trade magazines *Electromechanical Design*, *Electrical Design News*, *Quality Assurance*, and *Analytical Chemistry*. These were not pieces that pushed the frontiers of knowledge but, rather, discussed some basic descriptions of the product or an application. The *Analytical Chemistry* paper (which was also presented in May of 1965 at a Pittsburgh conference) was the longest and explained the sources of error in a strip-chart recorder. Others described a Litton Systems application for a four-channel recorder (a high margin item), provided a tutorial on how to select the optimal recorder, and discussed how a recorder should be connected.

Part of my motivation to come to TI in the first place was to avoid the draft, since my educational deferment would lapse and I would become 1-A (it happened in July, 1960). Avoiding the draft sounds unpatriotic, but the fact was that the nation was at peace, there was no compelling enemy to fight, and only a small percentage of unlucky people got called. Still, there was a draft and working as an engineer for a defense-related company provided the possibility of getting an occupational deferment. My aborted experience with ROTC made me realize that the armed forces were not compatible with my temperament. And I did not want a two-year diversion from my career. I figured that even two years in a nothing job was better than two years in the army.

Each year that I was at TI, I therefore wrote to the Selective Service Board in Fargo, supported by a letter from a TI representative, requesting an occupational deferment. My first letter, July 26, 1960, described what TI was doing for the military and how indispensable a "manufacturing engineer" was to their efforts. Every summer the same set of letters were sent, except that my job description changed from a manufacturing engineer to a "requirements engineer." It was always granted, but each year I had some apprehension that the Fargo board, perhaps resenting another local boy that had fled the harsh winters, would see through my thin reasoning and say that I should join the army. I suspect that their quota was low and that thus they had little incentive to challenge requests, weak though they may be.

The Entrepreneurial Dream

It was clear early on that TI was not going to be the optimal long-term career. Even had the job been challenging and appealing, and had I been moving up the ladder, I would still be working for a large company. As a result, there would be inherently little chance to exert real entrepreneurial initiatives, almost no chance to accumulate capital, and no control over my time. My dream was thus to create my own firm and use it as a base to build an empire and a lifestyle that would allow as much vacationing as desired. Think Virgin's Richard Branson or Dell's Michael Dell. With no money, limited skills and knowledge, and a full-time job, I needed help and companionship in this venture. They came in the form of two colleagues of like mind at TI, Steve Shaper and Charles Gillespie.

A TI recruit out of Rice and the Harvard Business School who arrived about the same time that I did, Steve Shaper became one of my best friends. Steve's family had developed a business called Metal Window Products that involved manufacturing and installing metal windows and associated products. The business was significant and profitable, but also tough because contractors would squeeze margins with open bidding. Steve had considerable exposure to all aspects of the business and thus had some real background in fabrication, selling, and running a small business.

Steve also had an entrepreneurial mindset. TI was just a way station on his way to creating interesting business ideas. He was, much later, extremely successful at building businesses, including a major truss (the structure of a building roof) firm. His big winner, however, was TeleCheck Services, a firm that approved checks for retailers. He became involved in the mid 1980s when it was small and helped grow it to a very profitable firm doing over $400 million dollars. But, unfortunately, his successes came after his association with me. I like to think that the Aaker experience and association were helpful to him (by helping him learn what not

Steve Shaper

to do), but that is a stretch. Steve and his wife, Sue (who became a PhD in philosophy and then a patent lawyer), raised four kids with impressive careers and credentials.

Charles Gillespie was a young manufacturing engineer at TI with considerable talent in all aspects of manufacturing. He had a delightful dry sense of humor and was a pleasure to hang with. He also believed that the corporate world was not an attractive life and wanted to strike out on his own. He thus joined Steve and me, and we all began to explore options to get the first business base. We all thought that if we could get one off the ground the rest would soon follow. The first was the key.

The effort to find the big idea absorbed 1961 and much of

Sue Shaper

1962. Steve spent about six months in Europe in 1961. Rather than putting our efforts on hold, we formed the firm Importing Associates and charged Steve and Sue with finding hot products in Germany to import and identifying needs that could be filled by exporting products to Germany. In August of 1961, Steve became excited by a light that was selling like hot cakes for $.50 each at fairs, carnivals, and wherever a large crowd gathered at night. With a hidden battery, the light would appear like a little electric lantern hanging in mid air. Another import prospect uncovered by our intrepid colleagues was "Krusta" baking pans, a hot-selling item in Germany. An export possibility was Frisbees, a concept that had not hit Germany. These ideas were among a large set that were not seriously pursued.

We also considered a host of "domestic" products and ideas. One of the more promising, a tennis wrist band made out of sponge so you could periodically wring it out, was a terrific product in Houston where it was so humid that a conventional wrist band would only last a few minutes. We conducted research on customer and trade reaction but ultimately decided not to pursue it. Another idea was getting a Lawn Boy franchise and selling lawn care equipment. Still another option was selling metal greenhouses.

One idea, to design and manufacture redwood plant containers, became our first venture. They were simple, elegant wood-slated cylinders designed to be used to house large plants in office buildings and the like. They came in three sizes and four finishes and sold for prices ranging from $40 to $60. There was a nice brochure from our company called UAS Design. ("U" stood for a designer named Uffer that was part of this team, and Aaker and Shaper represented the rest of the catchy brand name.) We sold some, but as I recall they had quality issues as the slates would fall off. It was not our springboard company.

We had explored buying a small company throughout this period. This direction bore fruit. We settled on a small metal fabricating company called Precision Fabricating and Engineering, a modest firm run out of a run-down plant (by some people that could be also described as run-down). It had sales of around $60,000, equipment equity of around $15,000, a crusty, ancient owner, and an experienced foreman.

Our logic was as follows: the NASA effort in Houston was associated with a host of high tech firms, all of which needed precision sheet metal work—basically metal stuff made to high tolerances as opposed to the sheet metal used in buildings for heating and air conditioning. Thus, there should be a growing demand with few firms with the capability of responding. Second, if we provided an active salesperson we should be able to increase sales sharply in a company that had relied on existing customer contacts. Third, with our expertise and professionalism, we could surely improve operations and thus margins. So we made the plunge.

Rather than buy the firm, which would have required more money than we wanted to risk, we proposed to join the firm, adding our expertise and effort. We would pay $5,000 for a one-third interest initially. If our sales goals were met, we would be able to exercise options such that our one-third interest would be converted to a two-thirds interest. The target was sales of $10,000 for each of three consecutive months with a 16% profit level. The agreement stated that Charles would become the full-time president and Dave and Steve would work without compensation. The prior owner was to continue working at an agreed salary. In addition, the foreman was given an equity interest in the firm. The deal was finalized in August of 1962.

There were a host of plans for the firm. The sales role of Charles was a cornerstone of the future, but there was much more. We expected to improve the layout and production methods, add a quality program, improve the turnaround, and develop a cost control system. The latter task was one of my assignments, given my cost accounting background at TI.

We spent a lot of time on the business. Steve and I must have averaged nearly twenty hours per week working nights and Saturdays (that effort may have contributed to my lack of success at TI). We had great camaraderie and an enviable working relationship between the three of us. Although wearing and often discouraging, it was also fun and educational. I learned what all the machines did and could even estimate fabrication jobs and deal with issues involving the manufacturing staff. Of course, it turned out that this "education" was not useful given my eventual career path, but I did not know that at the time.

Steve believed in having and living a cost-conscious culture. My sharpest memory is of Steve using the back of adding machine tape and conserving paper clips. Charles and I considered these efforts a bit bizarre, and Steve got a lot of flack over providing leadership on the cost front.

After about one and a half years, we gave up. We had significantly advanced sales to $100,000 or so, but the additional margins did not result in that much more profit given the salary of Charles and other expenses. On February 1964 we offered to sell our interest in the business for $3,000 plus a note for $4,500 paid at $75 per month. We subsequently settled for the note plus $1,000. We were out of the business, and it was a relief.

Why? How did such talent and effort fail? One reason was that the product was basically a commodity that could be and was delivered by small firms with crude operating methods, unprofessional managers, and low costs. The jobs went to the lowest bidder and we had competitors that did not live high on the hog. There was really nothing that we contributed that added customer value to justify higher prices or that reduced costs. And there was no compelling quality or reliability story that would prevent the lowest price from prevailing. A related reason was that the firm was so small and it turned out to be difficult to grow this business from such a small base. If the challenge instead had been to turn around a large operation, we would have had more leverage for our efforts—but that was not the task. Another related reason was that the big spurt of NASA-stimulated sales simply did not happen. We had made an assumption that as NASA grew, so would the demand for high-tolerance fabrication. Wrong.

Potential learnings. Make sure that your value-add really matters given the context. Be realistic about the nature of the business and the competitors, especially if you cannot introduce a new way of doing business. Make sure the growth potential is real.

I do not regret the effort because I can say that I gave the dream of building my own major firm a shot. It was not a token effort, as it involved over three years a broad exploration phase and enormous sweat equity. In retrospect, it is a good thing that I failed in this endeavor (just as it was lucky I was unsuccessful at TI) because I ended up in an incredible career and lifestyle. Things have a way of turning out for the best. Someone may have been looking out for me.

Social life in Houston

Social life in Houston for my first three years (before Kay) was somewhat mediocre. I was a nerdy engineer coming into a foreign land with no friends and contacts. So I had to build from my colleagues at work, my neighbors, and my tennis contacts. The social life revolved around tennis, golf, sailing, bridge competition, neighborhood parties, and society parties.

Tennis was a big part of my life and an excellent way to meet people. I started playing immediately after arriving in July by promptly signing up for a tennis tournament. I was fresh from a full tennis season at MIT and was on the top of my game, such as it was. I played the number-one seed in the local park tournament. He won, but it was not the easy first-round match he was expecting. A three-set match, it must have lasted two and a half

hours in heat well over one hundred degrees on the clay courts—
along with the normal Houston 100% humidity. I now wondered
what I was thinking by playing. But I left the tournament with
the names of several people with whom
I could play tennis.

I developed a set of tennis partners
that became a core set of friends. One
was Ron Latta, a stockbroker who was
also a weekend DJ for a jazz program.
Another player, Art Foust, decided
that I would make a good doubles
player because of my reflexes at the
net (not because of my service, which
remained pathetic), and we entered
a bunch of tournaments. It was nice
to have friends, even though they
probably enjoyed my company because
of my tennis and not my personality.

The MIT tennis
player arrives

The highlight of my tennis adventures in Houston—indeed,
of my entire tennis career—was my entry into the River Oaks
Tennis Tournament. River Oaks was a real old-money country
club with beautiful cypress trees and a great golf course that I
never did play. Their clay court tennis courts were impeccable.
Each year the River Oaks tourney was one of the major tournaments in a time in which each week there were no competing
events. The draw for the 1961 tournament was as strong as the
U.S. Open. Sixteen touring players got automatic byes into the
tournament, including Rod Laver (then the number-one player
in the world and in some people's eyes one of the all-time great
players—also the ultimate tournament winner) and Roy Emerson
(another top player and the finalist). There was a qualifying tournament with sixty-four players vying for the other sixteen spots.

Most of the sixty-four qualifying players were from the world
tour. However, there were a few slots for local players, and Ron
Latta and I made that group. The River Oaks pro was the tournament manager and saw a way to get his son into the thirty-two
draw. He paired him with a fictitious name in the first qualifying

round, and with the winner of a match between me (a complete unknown) and a very weak player in the second round. I beat his son 4 and 4, to his deep disappointment.

I was therefore in the tournament and appeared in the program—in fact my name was next to Rod Laver. In the first round of the tournament proper, I played Bill Talbert, once a top-ranked player but way past his prime. I was so nervous that I did not play well and lost 6-1,6-1. Talbert, a class guy, reported the score as 6-3, 6-3. In the next round, he managed to get five games off of Laver, so he still had some talent. It was a real high to walk around the ground in a tennis

Laver wins River Oaks—   Bill Talbert upsets Aaker
1961

outfit during the tournament and have kids ask for my autograph.

Although tennis was my primary social and exercise outlet, I did have other activities as well. I played golf occasionally, usually with people from TI. Although I did have an eighty-six that got me top marks at a TI company tournament, my game was more often higher. In the summer the heat and humidity was a challenge, even when teeing off early in the morning.

A colleague at TI had a twenty-five-foot sailboat that he raced in Galveston Bay, and I joined him for a series of races. The racing was definitely absorbing, and the competitors really got into race tactics and the skill of changing sails during a race. The lack of exercise on the boat and, again, the hot weather, was inhibiting for me, but I did enjoy a new experience. Some of the races involved a whole day in rather high winds.

Bridge was a major activity during my first year in Houston. I lived with two TI engineers, Johnnie Smith and B. J. Long. B. J. was older and a bridge fanatic. So we teamed up and entered the active duplicate scene in Houston that featured some of the best players in the world—although they did not enter the same tournaments we did. We would often play three or four times a week. In fact, I found that if we did not play at least three times during a week we would lose our edge. The players were fascinating, a very different cross section of Americana.

It was interesting to see the intensity of emotions over the "game." In particular, long-term partners (often married) would have terrible arguments over perceived mistakes in bidding by a partner who had obviously failed to understand clear bidding signals. The intense players would also be quick to go after opponents if some breach of the rules, however minor, was observed. Thus, you would frequently hear someone shout out "director," signaling that a director should adjudicate a problem. When that was directed at you, it felt like being arrested for a serious offense. We were competitive, and it was a very involving experience, but a questionable use of discretionary time.

I moved into a street full of apartments which were collectively labeled as "sin-alley" because it was full of young people who liked to party. However, when I arrived it had seen its best days, and other complexes were much nicer. Nevertheless, there were neighborhood activities including pool, volleyball, and various parties that provided an outlet. One neighborhood group once spent a weekend in Galveston water skiing and crabbing (where crabs stupidly crawl into a trap). We caught and ate some fifty crabs that day.

There were a lot of single women in the neighborhood but very few that passed the appeal and availability screens. One women I was attracted to told me I was way too young for her. She emphasized "way." She and the times were not ready for a Demi Moore relationship.

I hooked up briefly with a society woman who got me into some very opulent debutant balls. There was a lot of oil and banking money in Houston, and the balls were an outlet. One had Lester Lanin, one of the top society bands, playing. I don't think I really fit into the lifestyle, and I eventually became a dumpee. Early on I recall I went skating with her and got her to describe in detail the River Oaks tennis tournament without telling her I had played in it. When I finally mentioned that I had played there, she failed to see the humor in my deception and instead thought that I was just duplicitous.

I dated a tall, attractive woman who was great fun and a source of companionship during the Precision days. I would arrange to meet her after my long Saturdays spent estimating jobs and doing accounting work. I enjoyed her company.

The Houston Scene

Houston is and was a cross between the Deep South and a cosmopolitan urban center. There were many people who were from all over, but there was also a hard core of Southerners with Southern accents, habits, and values. They were very gracious—always ending a conversation with "y'all come see us." Of course, when you would reply, "How about next Tuesday?" they would backtrack. There seemed to be a disproportionate number that were aligned with the University of Texas (UT), Austin. I always suspected that people that had graduated from Texas Tech or Baylor were claiming UT roots, but maybe I was imagining things. Anyway, at parties there would be some excuse for everyone to stop and hold the index and little finger in the air and shout "Hook 'em Horns!" which I guess was the Texas yell. It got really old.

Texas cuisine in those days started with Tex-Mex food and BBQs. Tex-Mex was very bland but hearty Mexican food that was everywhere. BBQ outlets served BBQ chopped-beef sandwiches, ribs, and chicken along with beans. For upscale dining, we could drive to the San Jacinto Inn where there were piles of shrimp.

Houston was and is a conservative town. But I fit right in. I voted for Goldwater in 1964, although he lost in a landslide to LBJ. I just liked his logic and was captivated by the Reagan pitch for the conservative cause. It was not until I got to graduate school and the Vietnam War opponents were Democrats that I changed.

A new (actually used) convertible sports car, a 1959 TR-3 Triumph with 20,000 miles in mint condition, replaced the old family Chevrolet. It was a terrific car with unique styling—the door had a dip in it so you could touch the ground while sitting in the driver's seat. The convertible part was great. Having the top down worked at night in the summer and during the day in the winter. I really enjoyed that car, but it actually was less successful than might be expected at attracting women. I guess I needed a stronger or more authentic personality statement, or maybe a better personality.

Houston is the land of hurricanes, and each year there were storms that threatened the coast—and some that hit. One of the biggest was Carla. Carla arrived on September 11, 1961, in Galveston with winds of 120 mph. Some areas got over sixteen inches of rain in a four-day period, and forty-three people lost their lives. The storm was a bit weaker in Houston but still had winds of over eighty mph. I had never been in a hurricane and went outside to see what it was like. I can tell you that it was difficult to stay on your feet in such high winds. With electrical lines down all over, it was really dumb to go outside. Judgment was never my strong suit.

There was an active theater in Houston. I recall attending the musical *Fantasticks* in April 1962 when my parents visited because I knew some of the people involved in its production. I fell in love with *Fantasticks*, as did many others, in part because of its marvelous lyrics. The musical, which actually opened on May 3, 1960, in New York and ran for 17,162 performances before it finally closed on January 13, 2002, was the longest-running New York show ever. I made sure that all my kids saw it once and took a very young Jolyn to a version playing in Oakland. It was my top musical until *Les Mis* arrived. The 1995 movie, set on a farm in the Midwest and starring Joel Grey as one of the fathers, is good, but the musical works better on stage, where you have to use your imagination.

The Fantasticks tells a story about two neighbors that plot to get their children to fall in love by creating a feud, building a wall, and telling them they cannot see each other. The plot works. However, as the plays says, "What is last night scenic may seem cynic by the day ... life never ends in the moonlit night ... the story is not ended until we have been burned a bit." The boy finds that love the next day is less compelling and decides to leave for adventure only to find his travels to be arduous, lonely, and full of pain. He returns and the couple reconciles. They're wiser now, but their dreams are a bit tarnished. The show has songs with wonderful lyrics like "Soon It's Gonna Rain," "Love, You Are Love," "Plant a Radish," and "Try to Remember," the signature song (and one of my all-time favorites) which starts the play with, "Try to remember the kind of September when life was slow and oh, so mellow," and ends with, "Deep in December, it's nice to remember the fire of September that made us mellow."

On November 20, 1963, I was coming back to the TI plant from lunch and learned that John F. Kennedy had been shot while in a motorcade in Dallas. I was stunned and felt that part of my infrastructure had collapsed. We anxiously listened to the radio and followed the confirmation of his death and the details of the incident. We were all in shock. The death of JFK was a defining moment for my generation, and virtually everyone can recall exactly where he or she was when the news hit.

I lived in assorted apartments for several years, usually with TI people. However, one non-TI roommate developed some mental problems that naive me took a long time to realize. The reality hit when the two of us drove to Aspen for a week of skiing. I recall his driving without all his facilities on one scary road between Denver and Aspen. I should have gotten out of the car, as I was scared out of my wits. We did make it to Aspen and back again. I changed roommates as soon as possible. He was definitely a danger to himself and others.

Sometime in 1962, I was invited to join Dick Schey, who had long leased a four-bedroom house with three roommates. It was a great concept, qualitatively better than a small apartment. I really enjoyed Dick and his group. We would all have a go at parties at our house and elsewhere with the idea of getting phone numbers. I have never tired of telling the story of how again and again I would hear Dick call a woman and hear something like the following: "Hello, this is Dick and I was wondering if you would be free next Friday." Big pause. "Dick," another pause, "Dick Schey." Another pause. "We met last month at the party at so and so's." Dick always acted surprised that the women didn't recall meeting him, even if it were weeks if not months in the past. We spent hours discussing girls we barely knew and plotting social strategies. We were the Seinfelds of the day.

Kay Arrives

In the spring of 1963 I arrived in LA as a "substitute" field salesman, knowing no one, but excited to be in California and experiencing a new lifestyle. One of my first adventures was to spend a weekend in San Francisco.

The one person I knew in the San Francisco area was Kay Andrist, the daughter of Mabel, a golfing buddy and friend of my mother. She was two years my junior and had grown up about four or so blocks from me in Fargo. Her father passed away when she was a child, and Mabel raised her while also running a farm near Casselton.

So I called Kay and arranged to see her on the weekend trip. We had an excellent time during that trip and it led to many more during the five or so months that I was stationed in LA. We played a lot of golf, and I felt it was terrific to find a woman that shared my interest in golf—it would have been better if she'd liked tennis, but you can't have everything. One course we enjoyed was Crystal Springs in the hills north of Palo Alto.

She also came to LA several times. We spent time with Fred Kayne, my tennis team friend from MIT, then a stockbroker, and with Kay's relatives, Eddie and Elizabeth Schesinger. They lived in the valley and were really into dogs. When I see *Best in Show*, the dog-show movie with colorful characters, I sometimes think of them. Their dog ate the best lamb chops cooked rare. Why? Simple: he refused to eat alternative meals. They were very supportive of our relationship and seemed to take some credit for it.

We got closer and closer. The romantic and glamorous setting of San Francisco was definitely a factor. The Tony Bennett song "I Left My Heart in San Francisco" became our song, and we danced to it many times. I recall driving into San Francesco on many occasions and always being blown away by the view of the city as you passed the final curve on 101.

Kay lived in Palo Alto where she taught fourth grade in the Barron Park elementary school. We shared Christmas for many years with one of her co-teachers, Bob Berry. With Kay any tradition dies hard. A student during her first year was Kathy Roe, the daughter of a minister. An inordinately sensitive and empathetic girl, she became a professor at San Jose State and gave a talk some forty years later at a party celebrating Kay's Orinda citizen-of-the-year award.

Kay lived in an apartment complex with Bonnie Jones, a nurse that came to California with her from Fargo. Bonnie was caring, fun, attractive, and had striking red hair. She was seeing two men; one was a construction worker with a great personality and an interest in golf—he and I played several times. I really resonated with him, and he was my choice by a huge margin. The other, a college graduate who was in my view not only a jerk but a boring jerk, was the choice of Kay and, more importantly, Bonnie. I was rather outspoken in my opinion—which was probably neither sought nor valued.

Bonnie's choice went on to get a PhD in education in Oregon and became an administrator at Moorhead State Teacher's College (across the river from Fargo). He felt the job was very important and an indicator of a successful career—I recall asking him about his publication efforts and managed to make the point subtlety that he was not exactly an academic star at Harvard. He was an avid racquetball player, and on a visit home I beat him despite never having played before—it was one of my most satisfying athletic accomplishments ever. He subsequently left Bonnie soon after she got brain cancer, and after that he killed his second wife and his two children before committing suicide. Normally Kay is a better judge of character than I—but not in this case. I never before or since have been proven to be so right.

Kay was the one for me. Our many romantic moments in magical San Francisco helped. We clicked, shared an interest in golf and bridge, had a common heritage, and did not have to worry about in-law problems. We had, by the standards of our three daughters, a short courting period. However, we have found common friends and activities, raised three great kids, and created a loving relationship that has grown over the last forty years. Kay has been largely responsible for my rewarding, stimulating, and comfortable life. So by the bottom-line measure it was a great choice. And it also got me out of the dating scene and cooking, both of which were getting old.

In the late summer of 1963, we shared a Fargo vacation. After a dinner at an upscale restaurant (given Fargo standards), I proposed. Kay's first reaction was to think through how she might leave the Palo Alto School District and her kids in midterm. But she quickly decided that it was feasible and said yes. The emotional response was there but, as often is the case with Kay, was a bit delayed. I did suggest that we delay telling our folks so as to reduce the distractions to the rest of our vacation. It was hard for Kay to keep the news from her mother, but she managed. When we did tell them, Mabel and my folks were literally dancing with happiness.

A few days later I took Kay to the Aaker lake cottage on Pelican, purchased after I'd left for college. We were sitting in a hammock in the night with the lights of the far shore on the horizon when I gave her a ring I had purchased from a jeweler recommended by the mother of my friend, David Scott. I think it was about one-third of a carat and cost under $400, about three weeks' salary. Times were different then. The wedding was scheduled for December 28. She would leave the wonderful Northern California area and a great job—definitely a sacrifice.

The days leading up to the wedding were emotional. There was Christmas, of course, which was shared between two families. Tragically, Kay's grandfather, a house painter in Moorhead, died on the 20th, so that became an occasion of reflection for Dorothy Dronen (Kay's aunt) and her family (husband Art, a high school biology teacher, and kids Jane, Don, and Nancy). Then there was the influx of visitors for the wedding.

The wedding was in the First Presbyterian Church, in which resided a stained glass window commemorating Kay's father, Don. The best man was Tom Wright, my friend from high school. The matron of honor was Muffy Tiede, Kay's college friend. We keep up with both. I recall that Tom gave us a toaster. When

Julene Grondahl, Bonnie Jones, Stephanie Fjestad, Jaynie Dronen, Muffy Teide, Tom Wright, Bud Acker, Roy Smillie, Larry Swenson, and Paul Acker

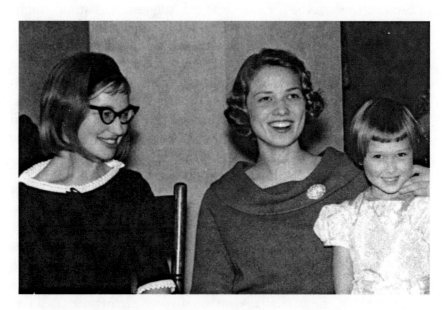

Margaret Nielsen, Karen Aaker, and Linda Nielsen
at the wedding

Kay joins the family

it broke after maybe fifteen years, I suggested that he might want to replace it, but he never followed up. In the wedding as well were my brother Paul, my cousin Bud Aaker, and my high school friends Larry Swenson and Roy Smillie. John Aaker, Bill Nielsen, and Bob Nielsen were ushers. The attendants included Bonnie, Cousin Jaynie, and several of Kay's high school friends. The reception was in the basement of the church, after which there was a gathering at my home for the relatives. Very low-key parties next to the weekend events that my daughters Jo and Jan had—and even when compared to the one-day affair of Jennifer's event. We spent two nights at a local hotel, and then we were off to Houston. Not exactly a glamorous start, but the times were different.

I had been assigned to rent an apartment for us in Houston. The major criteria were that it have a kitchen that looked out a window and that it not be above a pool. I found one that met the requirements. The catch-22 was that if you were off the pool you were in a walkway and the kitchen view was a wall. I learned that common sense would tell you that a wall view would be unaccept-able—it did not have to be a formal criterion. Walking into the new love pad (or carrying her over its threshold) therefore lost a lot of its specialness. So Kay arrived in a town with no friends, no job, and an apartment that was disappointing at best. We did have a modest social life (mainly with Steve and Sue Shaper), but there was a big hole to fill.

Kay did cook (I quickly gained ten pounds) and write thank-you notes (it never occurred to me to get involved in that project). But there was still time to fill, and then some. A first task was a new apartment. Houston was blessed with a ton of new apart-ment buildings all begging for tenants. One had Al Hirt, the famous Dixieland cornet player from New Orleans, play to get foot traffic. We found one on Memorial Drive that had some complexes with pools and others with fountains. The fountain one filled the criteria nicely, and we moved in. Two neighbors, a young couple and an older single woman, became good friends of Kay's—friends were needed at that point.

Three components of the new apartment were to stay with us through many moves and years. One was a door that, with four wrought-iron legs, became my desk. It was huge and functional but was hardly a fashion statement. Another was a used, green, four-piece sectional (without arms), a gift that had cost Oscar and Ida $100. Still another was a walnut, Danish, modern dining-room table with three leaves (also a $100 gift, this one from Mabel) that was part of our household for decades.

Another diversion for Kay was to sell the TR-3. Showing my generosity and my understanding of financial incentives, I offered to let Kay keep whatever she made over a certain amount. She "made" some $500 but had a lot of strange people come by, so it may not have been the best idea. We were a lot more naive then.

Kay decided early on that it was imperative for her sanity to get a teaching job at soon as possible. It turned out that in the suburb of Spring Branch there was a fifth grade class of thirty-eight or so students (Kay's classes now are around twenty) that had literally driven a teacher to a nervous breakdown. The students were out of control, and the parents and the principal were panicking. Kay took the job. Two days after starting, the class was under control, and Kay, incredibly, had a "back to school" night for parents. They were so relieved to meet a relaxed, confident Kay. Everyone, including me, was in awe of what Kay had done with that class.

During the following year, Kay switched to the third grade, had a good experience, and bonded with several teachers. The parents often invited us for dinner, meaning we could avoid cooking, have a social experience, and save some money in the bargain. I always liked the fact that Kay taught. It made her more interesting and stimulating to me because she had to address a variety of challenges in each class and setting. Also, it did not hurt in those days to have a little extra income.

Kay was and is a superb teacher (as is her daughter Jan). She is just a natural. I believe that teaching quality (like tennis or golf performance) is largely based on talent and that no amount of effort can alter significantly teaching ability (just as no amount of coaching can make a mediocre golfer shoot in the seventies). The best teachers like Kay were usually among the best in their first year. I thus do not subscribe to the theory that teaching quality can be noticeably improved by taking courses, receiving mentoring, and gaining experience, although such efforts may make small differences. As a result, I have suggested to Kay and her colleagues that merit pay for elementary school teachers is a sensible way to reward gifted teachers. However, I found that to a person, educators believe that it is impossible to evaluate teaching quality. Despite the fact that evaluation of professionals' performance in other fields is routinely done, I eventually gave up making the case, as it just seemed so hopeless. Entrenched attitudes and established norms are difficult to change.

We didn't get too many visitors in Houston; it is not exactly a Mecca for tourists. However, Ida and Mabel did drive down with our wedding presents soon after Kay arrived. They never saw the first apartment. Later, Oscar and Ida drove to Houston with Don and Virge Warren, and the six of us visited a Mexican border town. There is a great picture of all of us enjoying some Mexican cuisine.

We did not really have a honeymoon. Kay to this day claims that it was because of the Super Bowl that occurred a week or so after we arrived in Houston. But that seems far-fetched to me. I think the real reason was that I could not afford the time away from work and wanted to conserve vacation time. How dumb! So I thought a trip to Houston would be a nice substitute, at least initially. Dumb, dumb, dumb! It was one of my worst decisions, and I still regret it. However, we did have a nice trip to New Orleans a few months after we arrived. It was not exactly the same, but it was a special time. We ate at the famous spots and really soaked up the Dixieland music that we both liked. Kay thought that the dinner at Brennen's was the best meal she had ever had (remember, she grew up in Fargo).

Houston is extremely humid, especially in the summer. And Kay with some asthma problems suffered from the weather. At times it actually was a bit scary. She was a good sport but was definitely ready to move on.

Managing Finances

When Kay arrived, we had a detailed monthly budget and kept track of everything. The goal was to make our salaries cover the outflow and have some left over for saving. The frugality was just something that was natural for both of us. Over the years

Kay retained this frugality, whereas I found it easy to drift into a "spend whatever" attitude.

When Kay started teaching, her income, although modest, was a welcome addition. I thought that she deserved some money of her own so that she could "splurge" on hair and clothing. So we set up an arrangement where she would keep 10% of all she made (after taxes of course) for such uses. For several years she did use the money according to the plan. However, eventually she just banked it while still getting her hair done and buying clothes. Over the decades she accumulated a significant pile of "mad" money. Ironically, this generous arrangement has somehow been distorted into some sort of exploitative Scrooge situation implying that 10% was too low and, further, that later when the program gradually disappeared she unfairly got nothing. The spin concludes that that I am cheating her out of her hard-earned money.

I had taken investments at MIT and firmly believed that I could make a good nest egg—if not a fortune—with clever investing. With Fred Kayne, my MIT tennis friend, as my broker, I started investing aggressively in stocks. A major early investment was Open Road Industries, a maker of RVs. I thought the industry looked attractive as more money was being spent on vacations and the company had a good story. The stock just tanked and I lost nearly everything. That incident completely changed my orientation, and for decades after I emphasized bonds—I thus missed some big gains in stocks. Ironically, I became much more conservative than my father, who was mainly in AT&T. It was not until well into the 1980s that I ventured back into stocks and developed a belated respect for my father and his investment strategy.

Moving on

My years in Houston ended in June of 1965. By most measures it was a resounding failure. The effort to break out, to become a wealthy, successful, independent entrepreneur failed. My TI career never took off to say the least. Realistically, it was doomed from the start because I was in the wrong part of the wrong organization. I was a marketing person in an engineering and manufacturing company that had no clue about marketing or marketing people. Further, TI Houston was removed from Dallas in distance, organizational linkage, product line, and growth prospects. No Houston employee except for the general manager (one, Fred Bucy, became a TI CEO) had any Dallas visibility.

However, as I already noted, these twin failures were the best thing that ever happened to me. If I had a modicum of a success at either I might have still been there. If, for example, I had gotten a strategic planning job in Dallas with top management visibility, I very probably would have stayed at TI. Or if our business had developed a $200,000 sales rate instead of half that, I might have become a struggling small businessman. In either case, I then would not have enjoyed the terrific career and life that followed. The fact is that working at TI (and perhaps any high-tech firm) was (and maybe is) a tough life. I recall Fred Bucy popping pills during meetings, and Ed Hill (another general manager that made Dallas) saying during a Saturday golf outing that he felt guilty not working on Saturdays. The norm was to put in long hours whether they were productive or not. Theoretically, you then could take an afternoon off occasionally, but I recall that people gave me a guilt trip any time I would leave early. Running a small business, even a successful one, is not that much better. Neither represented the prospect of having an enjoyable, balanced, satisfying life.

In 1964 I sent out my resume looking for a job in strategic planning or sales. Except for the instrumentation industry, I did not have much to offer. A search firm person explained to me that my management degree at MIT was not all that impressive as he had resumes of people with EE degrees from MIT and MBAs from Harvard that were also on the market. I did not even get an interview.

It appeared the only escape would be to enter an MBA program. Toward that end I applied to Northwestern, Berkeley, and Stanford, the later two in part because they were in Northern California, which now looked very good to me. Berkeley somehow lost part of my application, so I never did hear from them. Stanford and Northwestern, however, said yes. Northwestern was the choice because, given my undergraduate business background,

I could complete the program in twelve months instead of two years.

So in May of 1965 Kay and I took off to Northwestern via the Smoky Mountains and New York City. We had a wonderful, relaxing trip and looked forward to a new page in our lives. We were both very happy to leave Houston; the suffocating humidity had become old for Kay, and I needed to change and jump-start my professional life.

5 The Stanford Years

I was ready for graduate school. It was good to escape from TI and face a new adventure. The prospect of taking courses in new areas was especially appealing. Exploring new subjects with books and projects had always been exhilarating to me. It really did not matter if it was statistics or organizational behavior or Shakespeare. I had in front of me many such experiences. I thought the MBA was a ticket to a new career, but it turned out to be a stepping-stone to Stanford.

Northwestern

We arrived at Evanston knowing no one but eager to start a new life. The first task was finding an apartment in a tight market. The choice was a one-bedroom walk-up next to the El—the local commuter line. The building shook when the train went by. Worse than the noise was the dust and weather. You could literally see the dust build up. Kay would clean every day at least once, and it did not help. The oppressive heat and humidity extended into the night. We would take cold baths in the middle of the night to survive. Can you imagine, cold baths at three in the morning? We finally shamed the landlord into adding a room air conditioner.

Everything was falling into place. We had moved our furniture from Houston, including the green sectional, the Danish modern dining-room table, and, most importantly, my "door" desk that had to be set up in the dining area off the kitchen. Kay started to look for a job. Remarkably, she was offered one right in Evanston, one of the top school districts. We were rolling.

Mabel, Kay's mother, came to visit, and we took her to the play *Barefoot in the Park* with Myrna Loy, a famous actress in the twilight of her career. I had never laughed so hard at a play before. Loy's comments on her daughter's less-than-ideal apartment were hilarious—we could empathize. The movie version with Jane Fonda and Robert Redford was good, but not as funny. We also did some exploring of Chicago, but I was a serious and motivated student. It was not hard to spend time on school, as I found the material fascinating, the classes fun, and the fellow students interesting and stimulating.

Northwestern was then a four-quarter MBA program if you had an undergrad degree in business as I did. This option has long since been eliminated at Northwestern and elsewhere, despite the fact that it makes eminent sense. A full two-year program, now the norm, was established because the top schools did not want to hassle with the variation in course work that was implied by two tracks and simply because they could. They were facing excess demand and did not have to bother tailoring a compact program for business degree holders. So they didn't.

There were four courses in the summer quarter. The first half of the summer session had statistics and organzational behavior, and the second had operations research and strategy. The quantitative courses had to be geared for students with little math in their undergrad program, not for an MIT-trained person. So those courses were easy for me, even though I was five years away from MIT. The other two courses, both of which used case discussions, put you in the decision contexts of a real manager. Working with cases was like living the most interesting time of a person with a great job. I loved the challenge of taking a position and then defending it in a group of smart, informed people.

Toward the end of the summer, I began to have doubts about the MBA. In the remaining three quarters, I would be taking courses not unlike those I'd had at MIT, although they would be more advanced and include electives I had not had before. Worse, I would be propelled into a business career. While I was confident that a position with another firm would result in more challenges and opportunities than I'd had at TI, it would also have similarities.

I would be in an organization hierarchy and subject to its policies and cultural norms. I would not be my own man, so to speak.

I also observed (and imagined) the lifestyle of the professors. It was clear they had enormous freedom to do what they wanted, when they wanted in both their private and professional life. They also clearly led a stimulating life with interesting research and consulting. Further, teaching looked like fun in addition to being something of an ego trip. This line of thinking led me to decide that I really wanted to get a PhD and become an academic. Once the PhD decision was made, it seemed like another year in the MBA program would be a waste of money (a significant amount even in those days) and, more importantly, a waste of time, a precious commodity to someone who had frittered away five years already.

How could I get into a PhD program a month before the fall term began and some six months or so since the PhD applications were due? And which one? Stanford seemed right. It was a prestigious school and was in Palo Alto, a city and area that was very appealing to both Kay and me.

It was a long shot, but I called the director of Stanford's PhD program, Harvey Wagner, one of the top people on operations research, and explained my situation. To my amazement, he said he would consider me and would look at my MBA application on file. The next day he called back to say he would admit me. This decision was made despite the fact that my GMAT barely qualified (at around 605 it may have been the lowest in the entering class and much lower than the other marketing students, several of which were in the high 700's) and my grade point average at MIT was marginal (a B average). The key was my MIT degree. It opened this door. Wow! He apologized that there were no scholarships available, but he did think he could deliver an RA (research assistantship), but he would have to confirm this with the marketing faculty.

There are no words to describe how incredible my luck was. I'm positive such an event never happened before or since at any top research university. It was predicated on so many things, including the facts that there must have been space in the PhD program and Harvey Wagner was particularly open and flexible. The stars were aligned.

So we got out of the lease, I dropped out of Northwestern, and Kay backed out of the Evanston job. The fact that we heard that I was admitted the day before Kay was to start teaching made it extremely awkward. The superintendent was disappointed but said, "Professionally I frown on this, personally God bless you." We again arranged the move and got into the car and drove west, leaving behind our hard-won air conditioner.

Life in Palo Alto

Another apartment in another tight market. The answer was a two-bedroom apartment in Palo Alto at 434 Addison; it was the upper-rear apartment in a three-plex set off the street about a mile from campus and a few blocks from downtown Palo Alto. I could and did bike to school. Stanford is a very flat, bike-friendly campus. On one occasion, however, I fell while riding at night and knocked myself out. No helmets in those days.

Realizing that the apartment would be our home for the next three or so years, we plunged in and painted rooms and even wallpapered the kitchen. I now can't imagine doing that. It had a balcony in the back where we cooked a lot of chicken. My "door" desk was again set up and the green sectional dutifully installed. The owner, a plumber, installed new fixtures. It was comfortable and home. An older couple living below us, Bill and Margarette Martens, were part of our support system.

The house in front contained a bearded statistician, Paul Switzer, who subsequently helped me with tough math proofs. Kay and I were Midwestern straight and he, his wife, and baby came off as being a bit hippie in terms of their appearance, eating preferences (vegetarian), and opinions. They were the first people we met who were opposed to the Vietnam War. I did not understand the war or their argument initially (and was a Goldwater Republican) but grew to share their opinions over time. They were great neighbors, nice, helpful, and broadening. We shared dinners, and Kay befriended a pregnant nanny that came to live with them.

Kay's job search began. The jobs in the best, close school districts were not available in late August. So she looked in the sub-prime areas and found one in a poor section of Sunnyvale. A new challenge faced Kay, one she'd never experienced before or since. Rather that her typical situation of parents that are way too involved, she had parents that lacked the time or interest to be involved at all. Not one of her fifth-graders had ever visited the public library until Kay developed a library visitation program. She came through as usual. Of all her teaching positions, she might have changed lives more in Sunnyvale than anywhere else.

The apartment became the center of our social life as we lacked money and time to venture out much. A typical event would be to cook up something and play bridge with another couple. We had a small set of standard meals that we used that were influenced by our Midwestern roots, such as chicken casserole (with mushroom soup), grilled marinated chicken, green bean casserole, and lemon meringue pie. Jim and Mimi Kinard were frequent companions. Jim was an accounting student and fit the prototype: precise and serious but with a wonderful dry wit (often aimed at Mimi's activities). We were with them when their baby arrived, a baby named Tim that clearly had problems from the outset. Ultimately he found a place in society, but not in the mainstream. It was definitely hard for them to deal with, even though they later had a second perfect baby, and the stress of the situation probably contributed to their ultimate separation. Jim spent his career as an accounting professor at Ohio State where he specialized in the human side of working with accounting information.

The big event at Addison was the arrival of Jennifer on January 15, 1967. The doctor had become a valued friend to Kay. She enjoyed going to his office even when there was a long wait. She shared her pregnancy experience with Mary Kadarauch, whose husband Bob was in the MBA program. Kay became impatient for the baby to arrive and, on her mother's advice, went for aggressive walks. Then, to Kay's great frustration, Mary had her baby, David, a bit early. But we went to the hospital the same night. We actually waited for thirty minutes so we would arrive after midnight and thus save a one-day lodging expense. Can you imagine? Jennifer arrived around seven the next morning, and Kay was set up in a room adjacent to Mary's. It was a Super Bowl Sunday, the first one in history—Bart Star led the Green Bay

Packers to a thirty-five to ten win over the Kansas City Chiefs. This was certainly the most meaningful Super Bowl for Jennifer.

The Kadarauch family has enjoyed an exotic lifestyle and enriched ours vicariously. Bob and Mary are both accomplished violinists and are always practicing or playing in a quartet. But their lifestyle—particularly after Bob retired from a successful management career at HP and another as a start-up CEO (he would be the adult on the team)—is out of the mainstream. They have a house at Sea Ranch, north of San Francisco, and a 500-year-old cottage near Henley, outside of London, but they still manage to rent homes in places like Ireland and Southern France where they golf and hang out. David, who played with Jennifer as a baby, graduated from Cambridge (England—Bob was then in charge of HP UK) and went into investment banking in Southeast Asia. He lived like a prince, made his fortune, and married a Polish girl in an Indian ceremony complete with elephants. Kay still regrets not attending the wedding. He then retired and moved to Poland where he began to dabble in real estate and play his violin. To his father's periodic suggestions that he get a job, he simply answered, "Why?" His sister, also an accomplished musician, played for symphonies in Europe and Australia. Very different from the Aakers.

Jennifer from the beginning was a model baby. She slept through the night after a week or two, was always happy, rarely cried, and was a delight to be around. The babysitter, an older German woman, would say again and again that this child was special, and since we had little perspective we probably neither realized nor appreciated what we had. She was right. Jennifer took over part of my office with a changing table. I once left her there for a few seconds, thinking she had no capacity to turn herself over, but Kay convinced me that this was a big mistake; who knows when that first time might occur? And this was an exceptional child who was likely to turn over early. This story has lingered. Another time we loaded our car with all the baby equipment and supplies (less compact than today's version—we used cloth diapers, for one thing) and took off for Santa Cruz—without Jennifer, who remained on the sidewalk. Four blocks later we realized that we had forgotten something. Jennifer survived.

Jennifer
arrives

Jennifer does
yard work for
the first and
last time

Jennifer was so much fun. She loved the jumper that we would attach to the doorframe; she could jump forever. When Jennifer was twenty-one months or so, in 1968, she figured out Halloween. She got the candy in her bag and raced to the next house. We then and there believed that Jennifer was an impressive child that would surely get into Stanford (we were thinking undergrad—to which she ultimately was denied—it never occurred to us that she would become a Stanford PhD student and, later, a chaired Stanford professor).

Kay did not teach the rest of the 1967 spring term. Rather she had a home-teaching client, a child of the owner of a restaurant chain. But the following fall she was at it again, this time in the third grade at Menlo Park, right next to the golf course at Stanford.

I was a disciplined student. It was very important to me to do well and especially important not to flunk out. I had chosen some tough courses and, like at MIT, was totally intimidated by my fellow students that were clearly much brighter than I. So I developed a policy of getting in a quality three hours of study each day at a minimum. I would usually study much more, but I made sure that three hours happened. I think that policy was an inspiration. Three hours is always doable, and it adds up. Plus after three hours are behind you, additional hours seem to be a bonus. The result is a feeling of accomplishment and an absence of guilt. I have since advised others to adapt this policy, but, with the possible exception of Jennifer, I don't think many took me up on it. Kay was supportive. In fact, she would make a list of things to discuss with me and save them for a study break. Our quality time was often doing dishes (no dishwashers in that place).

My recreation was limited because of time. My indulgence was a weekly tennis doubles match with Burke Jackson, a fellow operations research business student who was an exceptional athlete and a very fine player, and two marketing professors, Henry Claycamp (more later) and Harper Boyd. Harper was an older full professor who, while at Northwestern, had published a leading marketing research text, several influential books of readings, and some conceptual articles. He no longer fit the mold of the disciplined-based professors in the new Stanford. A debonair man (good with the ladies—maybe too good, as he left his wife for another and ultimately left Stanford for a school in Louisiana), he had a nice-looking but soft game. Henry was the opposite; his game could be described as effective but unattractive. Neither was close to either Burke or me in tennis ability. We must have played a year of lopsided tennis before we gently suggested that Burke and I split up. I felt funny calling them by their first names, so I went three years without using their names at all. It was "nice shot" or "your serve," but no names were involved. Burke married a wonderful Mormon girl, taught at BYU, and raised seven or so gifted athletes. He returned to Stanford in the early 1970s to finish his thesis, and I actually became a member of his PhD committee.

In my second year, I started to relax a bit and joined the Stanford table tennis club. We would play other schools, such as Davis and Berkeley. I recall a teammate that played with one leg. What an inspiration. In addition to playing table tennis very well he also skied. I recall that at one Davis match I brought two right-foot shoes and learned that wearing a shoe on the wrong foot does not work, even for a short time. It appears that my penchant for making such mistakes has been around for a while.

Being an RA

My first introduction to Stanford was to meet the professors that I was to help as an RA. I was assigned to Bill Massy and Henry Claycamp. Bill, eventually my thesis advisor, was one of the stars in quantitative marketing, along with John Little of MIT, Paul Green of Wharton, and Frank Bass of Purdue, one of the hot areas of research. Henry was a solid researcher, but Bill was the star for sure. He was a MIT-trained econometrician and was perceived by

Entering Stanford—1965

the academic marketing community to be an awesome statistical modeler.

Both were contributors to the 1966 symposium on the applications of the sciences in marketing management that was a watershed event in marketing, marking the growth in influence of the scientific disciplines on the research in marketing. The symposium resulted in a book in which both had chapters.

Both left academia. Bill became the provost of Stanford. After getting caught up in a controversy about how you charge overhead for government contracts, he moved to Jackson, Wyoming, where he became an influential researcher and consultant on academic institution management. Henry joined International Harvester in 1973 as VP of corporate marketing, where he implemented a planning system he named MOSAIX. He later helped lead a successful turnaround of the Allis Chalmers company and, still later, became a consultant focusing on strategy and planning.

I recall my first meeting with Bill. He was impressed that I had done a statistical thesis at MIT until he heard the title and realized that all I had done was create tables of an obscure probability distribution—at best a minor computer programming exercise—and that I had no training in statistics. To his credit he avoided letting on how trivial and irrelevant my thesis had been.

Bill had a substantial stream of articles and books, many with Ron Frank (who later became a successful business school dean), that were impressive in terms of their number, complexity, and use of powerful statistical methodology. One involved a simulation model that allowed marketers to test promotional programs on an artificial computer-based test market (Bill later developed simulations that allowed users to practice being university administrators). As I arrived he was engaged in exploring a gigantic database in order to determine what caused people to buy and rebuy packaged-good brands. The resulting insight was limited—the final report noted that a cannon (in terms of data and statistical sophistication) was used to hit a mouse (the relationship found). But then, like now, academic researchers were not as concerned with insight as much as the defensibility and sophistication of the methodology used.

Henry addressed interesting issues but tended to use familiar methodologies and commonsense models. He did an analysis of new product success and showed that new product awareness depended on advertising, but the trial and repeat purchase was influenced by how different the product was. The insight into why me-too new products are likely to fail was both insightful and useful.

I had a desk in Henry's office and labored to enter and arrange data and run programs. In those days you had to create a punched card deck for every statistical model you ran, whether it was regression, factor analysis, or whatever. The data itself was also on punched cards or on large spools of magnetic tape. In any case, there was a lot of lugging boxes to the computer center and waiting for reams of hard copy to come out—a thin output meant a coding error. It was very useful to see two good researchers up close, especially two with such different skills and styles.

An RA's job description was to work twenty hours per week to support the research of a professor. In many cases it was a nominal job where the student put in essentially no time. There had never been an RA anywhere who actually worked the full twenty hours. Until I came along. I figured that twenty hours was twenty hours, and I religiously put in the time. I'm sure that Bill and Henry would have liked me to be less underfoot.

The Course Program

I decided to gain a depth of knowledge in probability and statistics. Bill, in particular, had knowledge of statistics that was clearly impressive and an asset. About this time I developed the "intimidation model" based on the level of math and statistics a person knew. Some in the field with little knowledge and fluency were easily intimidated. Others could keep up, but the real stars were able to intimidate—using concepts, vocabulary, and methods that others could not follow. I wanted to be, like Bill, in that group. That route has two downsides, which I did not appreciate. First, you might become a "have method, will apply" (named after a TV Western show, *Have Gun, Will Travel*) researcher doing uninteresting research with inappropriate methods. Second, you might become a methodologist that was always considered somewhat boring. The trick was to use powerful methodology to do interesting things—not always so easy. Nevertheless, I had a direction.

In addition to Bill, two of his former students who were labeled hot prospects by our field, namely David Montgomery and Don Morrison (also an MIT undergraduate, and someone who still has and wears his beaver ring), influenced me. Each had built stochastic (probability) models of consumer choice (as had Bill) based on panel data (where consumers record all their purchases and the model goal is to predict the next purchase based on past purchase and perhaps demographic information). Dave, who left for MIT as I arrived, returned to Stanford about six years later and became a leading model builder attacking a variety of problems. Don, who had already left for Columbia when I had arrived and later moved to UCLA, maintained an interest in probability theory though his career. He once calculated when you should pull a goalie during a hockey game. I decided that I would also try to build a stochastic model. I distinctly remember Dave telling me that I should rather look to other quantitative model traditions, but I was not listening. In retrospect, a big mistake, but one that did not hurt my academic career.

To prepare for the quantitative route, I wanted an academic background that was comparable to Bill, Dave, and Don. As a result, I embarked on a course program of statistics and operations research that extended for two years, resulting in a master's degree in statistics. During the two years, I took a series of courses in probability theory (including finite sampling, in which I learned to design large-scale sampling plans), in statistics (including a series of courses on econometrics and multivariate analysis), and operations research (including a course on linear programming from Professor Dantsig, the pioneer in the area and not a good teacher). Nearly all my grades were A's, but I was proudest of the B's I received in two theoretical math undergrad courses (in linear algebra and real analysis) that I took with math majors. My neighbor Paul Switzer was indispensable in helping me through the homework. Theoretical math is justifiably at the top of the academic food chain, as it requires creativity and intellectual horsepower. I was over my head for sure. But the courses put me up another step in the quantitative intimidation ladder.

I took only four courses in the business school, required PhD seminars in macroeconomics, microeconomics, and organizational behavior, as well as the MBA marketing-models course taught by Bill. I recall one time in Bill's course that some cold calls revealed that the class had not prepared the case of the day, and he simply walked out of the room. The class was stunned. I would never have the guts to do that. The micro seminar was taught by one of the important researchers in applying linear programming to problems of developing nations, but he was not a gifted teacher. He once spent a full hour on a four-line proof and had to leave the end to homework. The third was organizational behavior, taught by a young professor that always brought a Coke to class. He introduced me to influential writers on organizations including Herbert Simon (a pioneer in organizational theory and a Nobel Prize winner) and Cyert and March (who wrote a book that had a host of hypotheses about organization and how they behave). I was intrigued by the subject matter and the fact that so much was known about it. I have since developed a fascination about how certain people can excel at motivation, leadership, and in making organizations effective. The macro seminar was taught by Jim Howell, a marvelous teacher.

Howell was the coauthor of the 1959 Gordon-Howell report (Gordon was a Berkeley professor) that assessed the state of business school education and created nothing less than a revolution in business education. They found that schools of the day were basically trade schools run by poorly trained faculty using simplistic teaching and research methods and attracting inferior students. The marketing faculty of the fifties, for example, would do descriptive studies of distribution systems, charting the use of wholesalers and distributors. As a result of the report, business schools rather abruptly began to recruit people trained in economics, psychology, sociology, political science, or quantitative methods. These recruits were expected to find a home in marketing, finance, organizational behavior, operations, accounting, or business economics, but the fact that they had an underlying discipline was the signal that their research was academically respectable.

This change in business school orientation had the beneficial result of introducing academic and scientific rigor into the research efforts of business school professors. However, this emphasis on basic disciplines, which has grown more extreme over the years, has a downside as well. It has encouraged research that is abstract, theoretical, specialized, and with little concern for any link to meaningful managerial problems. Some observers believe that this research direction has contributed to the fact that much business school training is not relevant to business and does not serve to train effective mangers who must engage in cross-discipline problem solving.

In a quest to gain familiarity with psychology, one of the core disciplines for a marketing researcher, I unofficially took a fifth business school course, a behavioral science reading course from Michael Ray. Michael, trained at Northwestern, was one of the first psychologists to be hired by a marketing group within a business school. Extremely current, knowledgeable, and talented, he took me through a rather comprehensive reading list of articles and texts. I absorbed Hall and Lindzey's *Theories of Personality*, learning about the ideas of Freud, Jung, Adler, Murry, Lewin, Allport, and Roger, plus factor and stimulus-response theories. An attitude-change book by Kiesler of Yale and others introduced me to dissonance, consistency, social judgment, and functional and behaviorist theories of attitude change. A methodology book by Campbell and Fiske introduced me to theory testing. All were not only fascinating in their own right but were also clearly applicable to the study of buyer behavior. It was perhaps the best course I ever took anywhere because it got me into the behavioral theory and methodology that I drew upon in my subsequent research in advertising and branding. Michael had a long productive career at Stanford, although in the last decade or so he moved away from marketing into creative thinking using elements of Eastern religions and meditation. Some believe, then and now, that creative thinking is what business schools should teach, but it is the type of practical course that needs to fight for academic respectability.

The Exams

Although I did not have to take any MBA courses in business, I did have to pass an internal and external examination. These two exams were for me worthwhile because the knowledge gained was put to good use in my subsequent research and writing. The exams have long since been dropped as students get more and more specialized. I joke about my daughter Jennifer's graduate education in marketing at Stanford some thirty or so years later because she learned nothing about business disciplines beyond marketing, and in fact even her marketing training lacked breadth, as the discipline specialization, in her case psychology, was the focus of Stanford's PhD program in the 1990s.

The internal exam covered microeconomics, accounting, finance, marketing, and organizational behavior. The external exam included the social and economic environment of business. For each I studied with incredible discipline. I found a set of basic texts in each area and supplemented them with a few other books and articles. I then created notes about the major concepts. I finally reduced those notes to a compact page divided into two to six sections with a lot of small writing. I ended up with some twenty pages for each exam. I then memorized each page. It would be hard to write a question for which I would not have some content to bring to the party.

My fellow students and I would work together to take exams from prior years under exam conditions: four hours and no notes. The danger of being too prepared (that was me) was that you would be tempted to do a memory dump and include material that really did not address the question at hand. The result could be a failed answer, filled with tangentially related material. So part of the practice was to focus on answering the question. A reasonable strategy, which seemed risky to me, was to be prepared at a superficial level, perhaps reading some introductory texts. You would then have no stored information bank to dump, and you would find it easy to address the question.

The exams contained five or six questions, some of which were required and others you could select one of two. One question from an internal exam, for example, asked to discuss the problems measuring opportunity costs and making them a part of the accounting systems. Another required you to explore the major organization problems and centralization/decentralization issues facing a firm with 35,000 employees and 112 plants in 32 states and 13 countries making machinery, chemicals, fibers, films, and defense products. Still another asked to evaluate the pricing policy of Buick with particular focus on the conditions under which price leadership may exist.

To my great relief, I passed both exams, which were given a few weeks apart in the fall of my second year. One of my contemporaries, a business economics major (which I always felt was a contradiction in terms since economics to me was unrelated to business) froze on the exam and could not finish. I think he never did get through this barrier. Certainly an exam that has so much at stake can create stress-related performance that is unintended. Such a tragic event makes you wonder about the whole exam process and what exactly it measures.

The final barriers were a field exam, an oral exam, and the thesis. I was actually not in marketing but in an operations research major because of my course work. I easily passed the OR exam, which was based on the course work, and prepared to take the orals.

On the five-person orals committee were Henry, Bill, and three OR people, including a heavy-set professor named Ron Howard who had given me an A+ in his decision theory course. I went in confident because of my course work and my performance on the field exam. My OR courses were all based on understanding the methods and how to solve problems and never addressed, in any non-trivial way, how to formulate a programming problem. The first exam question asked something like how would you set up a model to maximize the efficiency of an oil field in India or something equally real-world. I was stumped. I had never addressed such a problem, and in the end my knowledge of programming was limited to textbook exercises. All the course work was focused on solving problems already set up. There were no business school "case" discussions on problem formulation. A similar question about queuing theory had a similar result. I was over my head. Although Henry and Bill argued to pass me on the basis of my course work and promise, it was clear that I had failed and the others did their duty and flunked me.

I was shocked and devastated. However, after having a postmortem with Bill, the consensus was that this was a fluke given my qualifications. I should simply review some more, get more comfortable with setting up the models as well as solving them, and take it again with the same committee. I did and showed that the first one was no fluke. I again flunked. This time I was really stressed and upset. I thought that there was a good chance my dream would be sidetracked. I recall attempting to go for a long run to shake it off—with no luck. Several times during the next decade when my research was going well at Berkeley, I was tempted to contact the professors that failed me so we could compare careers, but I never did.

I clearly had to give up the OR major and this committee, whatever the effort. The best course was to switch into marketing, which meant taking another field exam and a marketing oral. So I studied for the marketing field exam like I did for the internal and external. I created about ten categories, found books, outlined them, condensed the outlines to a few dozen pages, and memorized the pages. I again had to discipline myself to answer the questions. I passed.

The marketing oral was not taken until the fall of 1969 when I was living in Orinda. So I was concerned about the drive for an early exam. The group now had three marketing professors and two other "friendlies" from the business school. Further, my thesis was done and solid, and the exam was likely to spend much of the time on that. I was not even stressed. As predicted, the exam emphasized the thesis and I had no trouble at all. It was still a big relief! I was done except for polishing some thesis chapters. It was a good feeling.

My Research

My thesis was going to be a stochastic model of buyer behavior because that was what Bill, David, and Don had done, and their work was well received. I did not really attempt to find alternate topics. However, I had to find a reason to extend their models or to create another one. Of course, the world did not need another model; in fact, there were several too many the way it was. Bill, David, and Don had explored in detail a wide variety of descriptive models of brand choice with unclear implications. And Frank Bass had created "the" model for predicting the demand from a new product—a model that was elegant and stimulated a lot of research. However, I was not a Frank Bass student and actually was not at that time familiar with it. Nevertheless I plunged on ahead with no sense of direction.

My take was to provide a new approach to the evaluation of sales promotions (cents-off coupons and other stimulants to buy). Heretofore, the basic measure was the increase in sales they might generate. However, I reasoned that their real value was attracting a new trier to the brand, a customer who had never purchased the brand before (or whose last purchase was a long time ago) and who would, because of his or her future purchases, be worth a lot over and above the short-term sales bump. To evaluate a promotion, there was a need to determine in addition to the sales bump from existing customers the number of new triers attracted and their acceptance of the brand, given they tried it. My thesis was entitled *The Long-Term Value of Temporary Price Reductions*—creating titles has never been my long suit.

The core of the thesis was a predictive model, termed the New Trier Model—another less-than-punchy name. The model task was to observe the first few purchases after the trial purchase and predict the eventual loyalty level of the new trier. The model was complex. It assumed that a certain number of new triers would reject the brand and that this percentage would grow over time toward some final level. The rest were assumed to have a brand-repeat purchase probability that would be between zero and one and follow a defined probability distribution.

Three variants of the model were tested using three years of liquid detergent panel data (where panel participants recorded their purchases) involving some 135,000 purchases of 8,000 families of which some 3,000 were new triers of one of four brands (a new trier had not purchased the brand for at least a year). The model parameters (such as the final rejection level) were estimated by finding parameters such that the model would best fit the purchase pattern of the new trier group over their next five purchases. The purchases were coded as one (the brand was purchased) or zero. There were thus thirty-two possible such patterns (00000 would indicate that the new trier failed to rebuy the brand at all, 10000 would indicate that the brand was repurchased only at the first repurchase opportunity, and 01000 would indicate that the brand was purchased only on the second opportunity, and so on).

The new trier model required two enormous computer programs. One was simply to prepare the data. The purchase history of each person had to be distilled from three separate tapes representing three years of data. The other was the parameter estimation program. The probability expression alone required three pages of equations in my thesis to record. I would have to run my programs at two in the morning to get computer time. They would run for over an hour and I would be there observing so that if they went into a loop I could abort them. If I had known the effort involved and was rational, I never would have undertaken such a project. But then it was one step at a time—I never doubted I could do it. I enjoyed programming and the problem solving that went with it. Anyway, it did finally work. The new trier model results were published in *Management Science* in April of 1971.

A clever part of the thesis exploited the fact that I could generate a measure of new trier acceptance for each of the thirty-two groups defined by their purchase pattern after the trial purchase. This measure could then be correlated with the characteristics of the group, their average product class purchase volume, their tendency toward brand loyalty prior to their initial purchase, the percentage of new triers whose initial purchase was associated with a promotion, and the average promotion size. The results showed that new trier ultimate loyalty toward the brand would tend to be higher if that person had a proclivity toward being brand loyal and if the size of the promotion was small. Clever and interesting but hardly shocking or "stop-the-presses" useful, although the suggestion that large promotions, used then and now by firms to hype sales, have a downside might have been helpful had it been visible to practitioners. It was, however, a solid *Journal of Marketing Research* (*JMR*) article published in May of 1972.

My thesis resulted in three more articles. The basic promotional decision model (when and to whom should you promote) was published in *Management Science* in February of 1973. Two others were less clever and interesting (if that is possible). A methodology article suggesting that a model should be evaluated on its ability to predict rather that fit historical data (the new trier model was compared to a competitor) was published in August 1972 in *JMR*. An overview article on how you can use buyer behavior models to improve marketing decisions was published in the *Journal of Marketing (JM)* in July of 1970. In addition, there was a sixth related article in *JMR* on applying buyer behavior models (the linear learning model was used) to store choice rather than brand choice.

Post mortem. At one level my thesis was an incredible academic success at least in the short run. It was for its time an extremely advanced, sophisticated, solid, impressive piece of academic research. It resulted in a staggering number of articles. Five articles in A-level journals (although *JM* is perceived by some as A-) right out of the thesis. The most common result, in contrast, is to get one article in a major journal out of a thesis, and some don't even get that. The work established my reputation as one of the young stars, helped get me get job offers, and made my early tenure decision an easy one.

However, with respect to impact the thesis research was a big zero. It had no practical value to managers at all. The new trier model had five parameters, and it was thus impractical to estimate in the real world given the state of computing. Further, Bill, Don, and Dave plus Frank Bass and others had exhausted whatever limited interest there was for practitioners. Worse, it really had no lasting impact on academics. Few read what I did, and it certainly did not stimulate follow-on research. I had joined a movement that was on its last legs. Over the years, some have observed that I tended to be ahead of the field. Not so here. My basic idea that new triers were really the key to strategic promotions was independently discovered about two decades later (when, not coincidentally, computers were far more advanced) after my work had been forgotten. I had attacked a minor problem with tired models at a time when the computer systems were inadequate.

As a Stanford student, I also developed a model to make media decisions—how should you allocate your advertising budget over magazines or TV programs. It was a complex model that really was not practical. Further, it was handicapped by a horrible name: POMSIS (Probabilistically Optimizing Model to Select Insertion Schedules). It was so complicated that Bill Massy in reading early drafts misinterpreted it—I got impatient but then realized that at a minimum my paper should at least be coherent to Bill. At the same time my contemporary, Len Lodish of MIT, was coming out (with his professor, John Little) with an elegant media model with a wonderful name, MEDIAC. I was trumped. Nevertheless, the article was published in the *Journal of Advertising Research* (*JAR*) in September 1968. Few students get into print with a sole-authored article.

My Fellow Students

We had some impressive students in my class. I ran into one, Hank McKinnell, in 2001 (at a cocktail party at the World Economic Forum) and was stunned to learn he was about to become CEO of Pfizer, a major global pharmaceutical company. Bob Joss, a finance major, went into banking and became CEO of a major Australian bank and then dean of Stanford's GSB (Graduate School of Business). Several have had successful academic careers; the most illustrious of which may be Steven Wheelright, who has been a leading writer on operations, innovation, and technology at Harvard. I have been closest to George Parker, a finance student with a great sense of humor, who became, I believe, the only professor to get tenure at Stanford based on teaching and administration, two key skills at which he was gifted. While a student he drew upon me for statistics help, but later, ironically, he wrote an article for *Harvard Business Review* (*HBR*) on how to use regression. Two other finance majors, Jack McDonald and Bob Higgins, have had successful academic careers at Stanford and Washington, respectively.

In marketing my cohort has a mixed record. One never finished, and another became a professor at a teaching school and never published to speak of—I'll note that both had extremely high GMAT scores. Alan Sawyer became a respected behavioral researcher at Florida but did much of his writing at his Maine summer place. The most impactful was Bill Wilkie, who was a well-trained (by Mike Ray) behavioral science researcher who made his mark on public policy issues. Bill never tires of telling of golfing with me at Stanford and getting beat and then retiring from the game. He also might have left golf because he could not face the heat in Florida (where he was for many years before moving to Notre Dame) or because he just spent too much time doing research.

Journey for Perspective

During my first year at Stanford I was accepted for the June/July 1966 Journey for Perspective, a three-week tour of England, France, Russia, Poland, and Germany with three graduate business students and deans from five West Coast schools (among the deans was Jim Howell of Stanford, my future econ professor). My major qualification was being among a small set of students that had never before been to Europe. We talked to some thirty government and business leaders about major issues of the day. It was an incredible experience that I chronicled with detailed letters, portions of which follow:

> Three general observations emerge from the England portion of the trip. I feel that the English are living the good life as exemplified by the Beatles, "mini skirts," gracious luncheons and dinners, and the wonderful traditions—in London, 1776 is not considered old. Second, the political leaders show a sophisticated expertness in foreign affairs based on decades of experience. One made the observation that you cannot have a base in a country in which sentiment is against you, and thus England was pulling out of the Middle East. (Such wisdom might apply to our Vietnam and Iraq experiences.) They are very loyal to the U.S. in the face of the unpredictable threat of Russia. Third, the country faces economic difficulties based on a lack of efficiency and restrictive unions. A building in UK costs about 20% more than a comparable one in the U.S., despite the fact that workers are paid five times less.
>
> The highlight of the trip was a visit with J. Paul Getty, then the richest man in the world, at his Sutton Place, an

Comparing notes with J. Paul Getty—1967

estate built in 1526 by a close friend of Henry VII. Getty gave us a tour pointing out the artwork, the fifteenth-century furniture, the fifty-yard party room, the indoor and outdoor pools (truly a rarity in England), and the kennel housing the big dogs that ran free at night. Over seventy-five years old, he still worked fifty-five hours per week. Although he walked with a slow shuffle, he was alert, witty, intelligent, and gracious. During the Q&A session over tea, in response to a question of mine, he said that British businesses tend to milk their companies but are also less volatile than those in the U.S. because they are less aggressive. He noted that everything in the U.S. is overproduced except good statesmanship.

My tourist life in London was an experience of a lifetime. I was wide-eyed as I visited Parliament (where we lunched with several MPs), Windsor Castle, St. Paul's, Westminster Abbey, the portrait gallery, and more. The crowds in the pubs caught my eye, particularly the Prospect in the East End. A person would come from the bar with eight mugs pushing his way through an absolutely

packed room spilling beer over everyone. Songs were
sung at the top of their lungs and seemed to have several
versions. It managed to be quaint and charming in the
face of incredible energy. To this day London is, with
Tokyo, one of my two favorite cities.

Paris is very different than London. To me the city
and its building lacks the charm of London, and the
people seem less familiar and friendly. We visited the
Lido club with its figure skating, waterfalls, and horseback riding all on a small stage. As a volunteer for a
comedian/pickpocket show, I and two others got to go
backstage and mingle amongst the topless dancers, where
I behaved professionally. I was impressed when a dean
ordered two bottles of champagne for our table at a cost
of $39.

The French have a "new mood" based on the belief
that the cold war and the Russian threat is over, and that
Europe must be independent of the U.S. and address
their problems in their own way. The French believe
that the U.S. has presumptuously and even irresponsibly
taken on a Vietnam situation that, in their view, was a
disaster (the French, of course, lost their own Vietnam
War before the U.S. got involved). It was even suggested
that the U.S., through NATO, might trigger a nuclear
war by a misstep in Germany. (These reflections in 1966
are eerily similar to the French position on the Bush Iraq
war in 2003.)

Russia is drab with oppressive sameness. The Moscow
subway, an extravagant but beautiful system, is an exception. Moscow has block after block of gray apartment
buildings of shoddy construction providing cramped,
backward quarters. Leningrad (now St. Petersburg) is
not much better, but it does have an impressive river
and palaces from the time of the czars. In Leningrad
I visited the apartment of a student I'd met over table
tennis. We walked up five flights, as the lift was "as usual"
not working, to a five-room apartment shared by three
families. Each family had a single room around eight by

sixteen feet and shared a common kitchen. There are few cars, air traffic, or nighttime entertainment. Despite this oppressive atmosphere the people seem satisfied with their lot (which may say something about their past and their expectations) and are extremely friendly. The country is struggling to introduce free market concepts into their system such as profits, profit sharing, and sales (rather than production) goals.

The contrast between the East vs. West is more dramatic in Berlin. The wall, a line of real confrontation, creates an artificial, unreal *Alice in Wonderland* experience. Brothers three blocks apart must wait six hours for a telephone connection to be made through Frankfurt. East German guards control entry but are not recognized by allied personnel, who pass periodically through the gates without stopping. The contrast in the two Berlins is staggering. West Berlin is active and full of life while the Eastern Sector seems drab, dull, and lethargic.

The Wall is also a symbol of the solidarity of the West and a monument to the great eleven-month airlift that saved the town when East Germany closed the ground link to the city. Berliners still talk of Kennedy's visit and his announcement in German at the wall, "I am a Berliner." The Berliners are thus extremely appreciative of the U.S. and are among the few in Europe that are sympathetic toward our struggle in Vietnam.

The Doctoral Consortium

The AMA (American Marketing Association) doctoral consortium has been held every year since 1967. It is a four-day event in which leading professors come together to lead seminars for and interact with doctoral students, one each from any institution offering a PhD in marketing. It has been an incredible success from all points of view, and students and faculty prize invitations. I was nominated by Stanford to go to the first consortium but turned it down believing that I could not spare so much time from my research. How dumb was that? The decision reflected my (probably unhealthy) over-the-top discipline and goal-directed behavior (which had also been in evidence in Houston). Luckily, Stanford nominated me in 1968 for the second consortium held at Penn State, and, luckily still, I did not turn that one down.

The consortium is really incredible. You get exposed professionally and socially to all the big names—people whose work you have been studying—and you can also interact with them socially. You get to meet students not only from the top research schools but also from lesser schools; you quickly learn that the world is bigger than you thought, and that maybe you should not be so elitist.

I hooked up with three other students. One was Michael Etzel from Colorado, who went on to have a productive career doing research in public policy, writing several texts and engaging in several administrative posts at Notre Dame. Another was Orv Walker from Wisconsin, who added dry humor to the mix and went on to be a prominent researcher emphasizing selling and sales force management at the University of Minnesota. The other, Shelby Hunt from Michigan State (whose picture can be found in chapter nine), was particularly fun because of his irreverent, biting humor (his style has softened over the years), and his awesome intellect. Shelby, a prolific writer of books and articles on marketing theory, has been and is one of the leading philosophers in marketing. He and his work have received numerous awards.

As young PhD students, we should have treated these established professors, several of whom were already legends, with awe and respect. Instead we looked for shortcomings that would be vehicles for our incredible wit (we would not be described as modest, unassuming, and understated). We also rebelled at an effort to form task forces to come up with research ideas around topic areas, arguing that such a task required research for which we had no time. There were some awkward moments, but the rebellion basically won the day and the consortium format going forward owes a debt to our assertive group.

One professor was engaged in a huge study to predict the brand that a person would buy in a grocery store based on dozens of variables. The goal was to maximize r^2, which is a measure of the predictive power of the input variables. There was no theory or interesting hypotheses to guide him. (Actually, it was not unlike some of Bill Massy's research but with far less sophisticated statistical methods). His main finding was that a person's preference for a brand was a good predictor of what he or she would buy—not too insightful, we all thought. Shelby held up his hand and suggested that the researcher add the "shopping cart" variable obtained by inventorying the shopping cart just before checkout. He opined that the prediction of the model would improve even more. The sad part is that the researcher never did realize that he was being set up.

An eminent professor, John Howard of Columbia, with his student, Jag Sheth, had just published an ambitious, comprehensive book titled *The Theory of Consumer Behavior*, summarizing what we know about consumer behavior and attempting to provide a theoretical structure bringing together the constructs and empirical findings. This was an important and impressive work by respected and competent people. However, in the forward they warned that their effort "may seem presumptuous to the reader." They were right. The basic model had some twenty constructs and forty arrows, yet some of the constructs (like Overt Search and Choice Criteria) were themselves complex and their causation chain was incomplete (attitude influenced behavior only by affecting intentions, for example) and simplistic (the conditions under which relationships would hold were not modeled).

The fact is that a definitive, complete model of consumer behavior will never happen because it is just too complex and varied. But that did not deter John. I asked him if they were serious about calling the model "The Theory" as opposed to "A Theory." He replied that the title was correct—they had nailed it. We had a ball with that comment. Academics often avoid making definitive statements that will leave them vulnerable to having their conclusions altered by future research—so it is for good reason that you find qualifying phrases in academic work. John wanted to make a statement with the book title, but in the end it detracted from a nice piece of work by an eminent scholar.

Jag went on to be first an impactful, respected consumer behavior researcher and later a management strategist who wrote dozens of books aimed at managers. He was also a gifted speaker, generating talks often based on a two-by-two matrix that would mesmerize his audiences. He was always on the plane to somewhere in the world to give talks and seminars and has since shared his wealth—he donated a substantial sum to the AMA in 1997 to support what is now called the AMA-Sheth Foundation Doctoral Consortium.

Jag participated in a famous debate during the 1976 AMA doctoral consortium in which he argued that consumer behavior is deterministic and you can describe and predict with certainty how and why consumer decisions get made—as long as you have enough information. His position was in keeping with his ambitious book with John Howard, but it was also representative of the premise of the behavioral scientists of our field. His opponent was Frank Bass, already introduced as a premier modeler and the author of the most influential stochastic model of the day, who argued that consumer decision-making is stochastic (uncertain, probabilistic), and that in the end you cannot predict with certainty much of anything consumers do. He asserted that consumers might be influenced by the weather, their mood, a casual interaction, and other factors so detailed and varied that trying to model consumer decisions deterministically is hopeless and delusionary. It really got to the core of the differences between the behavioral scientists and the quantitative modelers, who even then had very divergent views of research. It was easily the most stimulating session I have heard at any of the dozen or so consortiums I have attended.

The Job Search

In my third year I decided to interview for jobs, meaning that I would have a three-year program rather than four. The life of a subsidized student is about as good as it gets because he or she can do research without the distraction of teaching. But I was ready to move on, to make up for lost time, and three years (ultimately it became three plus a quarter) was enough.

The process starts in the late summer with the AMA meeting where you sit for one-hour interviews with schools with openings. The first challenge is to get interviews, and the second is to get invitations to visit. I was considered, with Len Lodish of MIT, among the quantitative students with high potential, in part because of our association with prestigious advisors. I visited Berkeley, Indiana, Columbia, Carnegie, and MIT. My MIT visit was a great time to hang with John Little and Dave Montgomery, but they really did not have an opening. Columbia with Don Morrison was interesting but slow to process an offer. Indiana was an involving place with a pleasant faculty but too much like Fargo. Carnegie was prestigious with a strong, though small, marketing faculty, and it was the school favored by Bill Massy. However, Berkeley was in Northern California and promised a great lifestyle with year-round tennis and golf plus access to San Francisco and the mountains. I knew that it was the place for me. Carnegie was expecting to get both Len and I, but they got neither when he selected Wharton. I began on January 1969 and received a salary of $11,500.

During the decision process, Al Shocker, one of the most wired-in people in our field, advised me. An inveterate traveler who is always looking for the next venue, he has had positions at Cornell, Berkeley, Vanderbilt, Washington, Minnesota, and San Francisco State and has visited countless other schools including some in China and Hong Kong. Everyone has Al stories. Once we stayed with him at Vanderbilt and learned that he has huge collections of items like pens and toothbrushes. He can't resist a bargain and is willing to buy in quantity. Al has family in the Bay Area and would often join us for Thanksgiving and other holidays. When Jennifer and Jan were young, Uncle Al took them to Disneyland.

I actually officially graduated in the spring of 1969. I missed the ceremony because I did not think it worth a half day, and my parents did not press me. I regret not doing that. What was I thinking?

6   The Seventies

The seventies ushered in a new phase in our lives. Another home, a growing family, new friends, a Japan connection, and a new career were upon us.

Berkeley

I arrived in January of 1969 and entered Barrow's Hall, an unassuming (ugly might be a better descriptor) brown building which was to be my home until the new Haas Building was built in 1995. Barrows was built with cost control in mind under the false assumption of then-Dean E. T. Grether that if you housed the social sciences (economics, sociology, political science, and business) in the same building they would interact. Not so. Academics in these disciplines lack the motivation and interest to interact. They have nothing in common. Further, even if the desire was there, the rectangular building was designed to inhibit interaction within floors, to say nothing of between floors. The classrooms were also built on a budget, had limited board space, had awkward shapes, lacked tiered seating, and often didn't even have a stage. I envied professors at schools with exceptional classrooms and teaching resources like Harvard and INSEAD (outside of Paris).

My office was at the end of the sixth floor next to the elevator, which meant I did not have to walk down the depressing corridor. Walking up the six floors was an exercise option that I was sometimes shamed into by Dean Grether, then well into his seventies, who made walking the stairs a regular practice. The office was a touch larger than others and afforded a nice view of a wooded area, so it was not bad once you got there. I decorated the office with a print of Gustave Callebotte's *Paris Street, Rainy Day*, a featured painting at the Art Institute in Chicago, one of my favorite paintings. It creates a marvelous mood and provides a glimpse of life in Paris in the nineteenth century. The administration on the third floor was spartan in the extreme, reflecting an infrastructure and support that was dramatically less than Stanford and even UCLA. The only way to cope was to try not to think about it.

At most research universities the professors tend to work alone, often at home. Berkeley was not an exception. On the upside, you did not have people in your face about your teaching or research, but it could also get lonely. I recall observing that in my first two years only once did I have any kind of administrator stop by to ask how I was doing—and that was the faculty head of management science. It just wasn't the Berkeley way.

My first years were at the height of the protest against the Vietnam War, and Berkeley was one of the hotbeds. Barrows Hall was in the middle of the action. We had a front row seat to watch the helicopters spray tear gas over protestors. The business school, thought to be excessively establishment, was viewed with suspicion by the rest of the campus. But the students and faculty wanted to make their statement as well. One effort, in which I was an active participant, was to stand on street corners in the San Francisco financial district and hand out anti-war leaflets. I'm sure it was monumentally ineffective, but it was an outlet. It was the first and last time that I actively protested. I always felt there were more effective avenues of expression, such as donating money to like-minded candidates.

The marketing faculty was a big part of my Berkeley experience. When I arrived, there were several senior professors. Fred Balderston, with a wonderful, generous personality and lively mind, was a good teacher and active researcher. Dick Holton, who wrote a famous 1950s *Journal of Marketing* article on categorizing products, was my first dean and created the evening MBA program. David Revsen, about to retire, was a crusty, almost bitter man who resented the fact that the modern business schools ignored his descriptive research, which had been respected decades before.

Four younger professors were to be my colleagues and the core of the marketing faculty for decades. John Myers, a Northwestern graduate, well trained in behavioral science, was an extremely likable person and easy to be with. He and his wife Arlyn made coming to Berkeley a soft landing. They built a home in the Berkeley hills with an incredible view of the Bay; we often entertained recruits there. They were a driving force behind our Thanksgiving get-togethers with the marketing group, a tradition that continued through much of the 70s and 80s. The event, often at the Myers home, would always feature memorable pies baked by Arlyn. The Berkeley faculty members who attended recall these dinners as real bonding times. John and Arlyn raised three bright, musically talented kids. In fact, my girls would joke about how we needed to avoid making comparisons. Two of them went on to become important researchers in the fight against cancer.

John & Arlyn Myers

Pete Bucklin (whose picture appears in chapter eight) was a "star" (with another friend, Lou Stern of Northwestern) in the area of channels of distribution. He wrote several books on channels from an economics perspective (while Lou looked at it from a behavioral perspective, considering such questions as how manufacturers handled their relationships with retailers) and in 1984 won the Converse Award for career contributions. Pete's problem was that few researchers pursued his area and, consequently, he was a big fish in a small pond. He was a very conscientious and effective teacher, particularly with PhD students. In comparison, I let students be more on their own as my advisor had done for me. Pete's son, Randy, like Jennifer, became a Stanford PhD and a UCLA professor. So Pete and I shared a rather unique status—having kids who became successful marketing professors.

Pete was (and is) a bright, delightful, thoughtful person, but one whose interests rarely overlapped mine. Once, however, we got involved in a consulting assignment to conduct research on the attitudes toward private labels (store brands) by consumers and the opinions about private label strategies and trends by retailers. The result was a fascinating, informative look at an important issue. We thought the resulting reports would take tens of thousands to replicate and firms would surely be willing to pay $500 to have a copy. Accordingly, we formed a "firm" and communicated our "product" through direct mail and advertising. It was a big effort and resulted in only a few sales. We did not turn out to be successful marketers—no surprise there.

Jim Carman was a Michigan grad who was bright and a good contributor to seminars and discussions. Jim was interested in marketing theory and in the management of service organizations, especially in the medical area. He has done some influential writing and consulting toward making the medical system adapt marketing methods and concepts. An excellent listener, he had the patience during our frequent marketing faculty meetings to wait until the end before expressing himself on the issue of the day. I, in contrast, spoke early and often. As a result Jim had five times as much influence as I while talking about ten times less. Very frustrating.

Jim, who died in 2004 from side effects of chemotherapy treatment, was an outdoorsman who hiked all through the Sierras often on a quest to chart the trails used by the old 49ers. One weekend we joined him and his wife, Carol, at their cabin at Kirkwood, a ski resort near Lake Tahoe, to do some cross-country skiing. On our trip home we got in a blizzard that was so bad that it took us twelve hours to make the three-hour drive. But we were the lucky ones—others who left shortly after we did spent four days snowed in. With global warming such storms are less frequent, but delays on the highway are still common.

Franco Nicosia was a colorful Italian with a reputation based on his innovative effort to model quantitatively consumer behavior using some models from systems engineering. People were impressed by his approach, but few read the book carefully. Always eccentric and creative, he drove a sports car, had a big dog that would sit in his office, had a short-lived marriage to a former student, and challenged his students with rambling philosophical expositions (that some found stimulating and others just confusing). Over time, he became increasingly mentally unstable until he became sick and retired around 1990. I successfully stayed out of his way during this period. He and his reputation would have been better served had retirement come earlier.

During the 70s we struggled to hire and retain people in part because of our limited salaries and resources. Each year we would agonize as to who were the top two or three people, only to learn that we had no chance at any of them. One year we hired three that were not in that group. All three failed to beat the six-year tenure clock, although one came close and had my support. In any research university the promotion process is brutal. In marketing, an applied discipline, it also involves having top economists and psychologists within the broader Berkeley family apply their own standards.

We finally did hire a star, Rick Bagozzi, in the mid 1970s. After one or two years, however, he had some personality issues with Franco and was attracted away by Stanford, which had more resources than Berkeley. Very discouraging.

Teaching

Teaching was a blast for me. Having a captive audience who would appreciate well-organized lectures and respond to my efforts to be a humorist was a kick. My main teaching effort through the 70s was statistics and marketing management, although I did teach a seminar on consumerism and co-taught an advertising course with John Myers. Students generally liked my courses—especially my statistics course, where the alternative teachers were not highly regarded.

Although I liked to teach, I wanted it to be efficient so I would have more time for research and writing. That meant selecting courses that involved multiple sections so the preparation could be spread over more than one class (both marketing and statistics qualified) and minimal preparation (statistics was definitely in this category). I wanted to develop interesting, relevant material that could be reused year after year. The teaching deal was four and a half courses per year. Thus, you could teach five courses one year and four the next. However, with credit from PhD advising and other activities—and a modicum of planning—you never had to teach all three quarters in one year.

Statistics was cool, monumentally efficient, and leveraged my master's in statistics from Stanford and my knowledge of statistical models in marketing. Once the lecture set was complete (with realistic examples and humorous stories) and the tests created (students returned tests, so they were not circulated), I was on automatic pilot. At least twice, I taught three sections of statistics in the same quarter. The teaching preparation for the first class would be minimal, and it would fall to zero for the second and third. By the third class, I often felt a bit stale and sometimes could not remember whether I had told a joke or not—it seemed spacey to ask the class if I was repeating a humorous story. So the student ratings would be up for the second class when the session could be fine-tuned a bit, and down for the third.

One of my priorities was to teach students the hypothesis-testing concept. The logic is as follows: suppose brand users had the same opinion of a brand on a seven-point scale as brand nonusers. If we take a sample of size one hundred from each group, there will likely be a difference because we are dealing with samples and not the total population. The statistical question is whether this difference was statistically significant (not whether that difference is managerially meaningful)—whether it appears large given the variation we would expect from the sampling process. I got students, when confronted with some data, to always say, "Wait a minute, what is the probability that the two groups would exhibit this much difference by accident because of who got selected to be in the sample, if the two groups actually were not different." If the probability (p-level) was small, then it was unlikely that it was an accident caused by sampling. Some twenty years after taking the course, more than a few students have told me that what they

recalled best from their MBA program was "Wait a minute ..."
Some have said that it was one of their best courses. I know—
they should get a life.

The other point I drove home is omitted variable bias in
multiple regression. The classic example is that towns with
many churches tend also to have many saloons, which supports
the hypothesis that the addition of saloons will cause more
churches to be built. In fact, the number of churches and saloons
are related only because they both reflect an omitted variable,
namely population size, not because there is a causal link between
building more churches and opening saloons.

My other core course was marketing management, where I
could teach at both the undergrad and grad level. My discussion
style was interactive, with discussions based on substantial HBS
cases, minicases, or on provocative questions I would put forth. I
was demanding. Most answers to a question would be challenged
with "Why?" I would often rephrase the answer, distorting it so
that the student was defending an extreme position. The student
would thus be forced to think through what had seemed like a
flip, safe answer. Mini-lectures (from two to fifteen minutes),
representing useful points generally with an illustrative example,
would be sprinkled through the quarter. At the end of the course,
I created clarity and a sense of substance to the course by identifying the top twenty concepts and tools to be remembered. This
lecture added substantially to the course ratings. I know because
on one occasion when I arrived to the last class I found that an
eager-beaver student had already passed out the rating forms; the
course ratings were sharply lower. I never arrived late for the last
class again.

Teaching marketing wasn't always a walk in the park. I had
two recurring problems. First, I would be stimulated to make
a point even if it was tangential to the main thrust of the discussion. The discussion would always come back to the point,
but sometimes it could take a while. A few students each term,
reacting to an apparently ill-structured class, would complain that
I did not prepare adequately—in reality, I prepared extensively
for the marketing case discussions, even when I had taught the
case many times before.

Second, much of my humor was based on ridiculing people or their ideas, again, often by extrapolating their answer to a ridiculous extreme. I would always try to pick on someone that was verbal, confident, witty, and enjoyed attention. Even when that was achieved, one or two in the class would become uncomfortable with that style, a discomfort that was reflected in their course opinion and in a reluctance to speak. I did tone down my style, but the problem never went away.

The marketing class grade was primarily based on classroom discussion, and was graded subjectively. Hiro Takeuchi, a friend and Harvard professor (more on him shortly), told me that after every class he recorded and graded each comment by every one of his ninety students. So I did the same. I prepared for each student a five-by-seven card with his or her picture pasted in the upper corner (at Harvard, of course, the cards were prepared for the professors). After each class I made a notation for each time a student spoke—either an E (excellent), G (good), check (neutral), or – (did not advance the discussion). At the end of the term, these notes formed the basis for a valid and reliable grade. One time I lost the cards and went back to overall impressions. When the cards were found, I learned that grades based on gut feelings were highly unreliable.

On the average, I was in the top 25% of teacher's ratings— occasionally near the top and several times a finalist (but never a winner) of a best-teacher award, but I was not one of the three or four elite teachers, like Andy Shogan or Richard Lyons. Richard had an adjacent office in Barrows Hall and would forever be tutoring students. I accused him of manipulating teacher ratings by wearing a tie and being interested in students. Unfair. He has proved to be not only an outstanding teacher, but an excellent dean.

Research

To describe my research and writing in the 1970s, I need to introduce George Day. He and I had a wonderful collaboration that ultimately involved two books and five articles, three of which were published in the 1970s. Perhaps coincidentally (and perhaps not), we both eventually became interested in strategy

(George before I)—but that was
much later. Our successful partnership was due to several factors.
We respected each other's writing
ability and had no trouble allowing
the other to have his say in the
material. We were comfortable in
dividing up the space and working
with each other's drafts. I felt
George excelled at creating structure and flow, which he could
often represent with simple,
clever visual models. Further, we
complemented each other well. I
had a background in statistics and
model building, and George had a
background in behavioral science
and survey research.

George Day,
teaching executives
in the 90s

We were also very good friends, an observation that applies
to all my major coauthor relationships. I made it a point to work
with people whose company I enjoyed. Over the years we skied,
biked, and socialized together. One skiing adventure in 1968 or so
was particularly memorable. We arrived at Alpine Meadows, next
to Squaw, for a ski weekend, only to find that a snowstorm had
closed the lifts. No skiing—we were lucky to get back. We were
clueless when it came to weather and the outdoors—of course,
there was no Internet weather channel in those days.

George has had a remarkable career, becoming, in my view,
the leading writer on strategy in marketing. He has had numerous
award-winning, home-run articles and several influential books,
including *Strategic Market Planning* (1984), *Market-Driven Strategy*
(1990), and *The Market-Driven Organization* (1999). Several of his
articles set forth the limitations of popular concepts of the day
such as the Shareholder Value Model. Others advanced new
ideas such as the concept that customer choice sets related to use
occasions should logically define markets, or that market-driven
organizations have core capabilities that lead to competitive
advantage. George, who left Stanford for Toronto in 1974 and has

been at Wharton since 1991, has won nearly every available award in marketing.

Consumerism
Search for the Consumer Interest

David A. Aaker
George S. Day

Misleading Advertising **Product Safety**
Promotions Warranties and Service
Deceptive Selling Practices
Packaging **The Ghetto Consumer**

When George joined Stanford in 1967, he was an attitude researcher trained by John Howard of Columbia with a latent interest in public policy and survey research methods. His strategy work was at least a decade in the future. Our first collaboration was in creating a *Consumerism* readings book that was published in 1970 by the Free Press, with subsequent editions published in 1974, 1978, and 1982. Our editor at the Free Press was Bob Wallace, a real professional. Remarkably, he was still in place during the 90s and was my editor during my four branding books of that era.

Edited books of readings were influential in the fifties and sixties. An editor would bring together the best articles into a book, which could be used to support a course. To me it was magic—a book on the shelf and others did the writing. As the 70s came and Xerox machines improved, readings books declined in viability but still had a role to open up a new area.

The sixties were a time of agitation, even beyond the Vietnam War protests. In the mid-sixties there was a consumer movement that fit the times. It was triggered by President Kennedy's 1963 statement of consumer rights, by Ralph Naders's auto safety investigation, by the increased visibility of low-income consumers, and by LBJ's activist government. Most companies were forming or upgrading their consumer affairs department. By the late 1960s "consumerism" had become a hot topic.

With George's help, I reviewed articles relevant to the topic for my marketing field exam, drawing on a wide variety of sources including law, nutrition and product safety, as well as marketing. In doing so, I visited several campus libraries for the first and last time. With this set as a base, we decided to create a book that could be used by professors starting to teach in the area. We organized articles and excerpts of articles into those affecting pre-purchase (e.g. misleading advertising), purchase (e.g. selling practices), post-purchase (e.g. product safely), and problems facing the low-income consumer. We were at the right place at the right time, and the book did well, ultimately selling nearly 50,000 books over the next decade.

We also wrote an introduction that became a *Journal of Marketing* article that set forth the scope and causes of the movement. This article was one of the most cited articles that either of us ever published because there was enormous academic interest in the area, and all researchers needed to cite the initial work. It was reprinted in some thirteen other books of readings, including one titled *The Great Writings of Marketing*.

George and I looked at consumerism through managerial eyes rather than through those of an activist. Accordingly, we wrote for *Harvard Business Review* (*HBR*) in 1972 an article discussing how organizations should respond to consumerism pressures. We reviewed some innovative programs such as Whirlpool's "cool line" whereby consumers could contact Whirlpool's service consultants directly, Ford's product purchase educational programs, and the product screening done by Giant Food. We suggested that effective programs will emerge if firms understand real problems as opposed to visible symptoms, adjust organizational decision making processes and reward structures, and, finally, make sure that consumer programs are well designed and executed.

I was (and am) proud of an article with George that explored the influence relationships among advertising, brand awareness, attitudes, and behavior (market share). The accepted model of the day, the hierarchy of effects model, suggested that a person needed to become aware of a brand, then develop a positive attitude toward it, and finally purchase it. Brand success in the form of market share would therefore be preceded by first awareness (the percentage of people aware of the brand) and attitude (the extent to which those people liked the brand). The role of advertising was to affect awareness and attitude. Using George's data on six instant coffee brands, we explored the influence links (what influenced what). To sort out reverse causality (a relationship between advertising and market share, for example, could be created because successful brands can afford to advertise more), we used the fact (employing a recursive model) that current market share or other variable could not cause advertising or other variable in a prior period.

George and I did find that advertising influences both awareness and attitude and that each influences behavior. However, interestingly, we also found that the influence of awareness to behavior was direct. It did not go through attitude, as many had supposed. So a brand program could be based on awareness. This research helps explain the success of a brand like Intel Inside, which was built on creating awareness and not on influencing attitudes.

This modeling approach ("let the data tell you what is happening") was very different from that espoused by Frank Bass of Purdue (and his many students, such as Don Lehman of Columbia). Bass argued that you should first form a theory about the relationships among your variables—that the job of statistics was to test whether the predicted relationships actually appeared in the data (rather than simply observe whether any relationships existed). Frank, as noted earlier, was (along with Bill Massy) one of the top quantitative researchers of the day. I enjoyed defending the paper and the approach at a conference with Frank and about four of his students, who were all either on the panel or in the audience. Unfortunately, their beliefs caused the paper to be rejected by *Journal of Marketing Research* (a big *JMR* mistake, but I am not the first author to have such feelings), so we published it in *Journal of Applied Psychology*.

As the consumerism book was underway, I realized that there was also a need for a readings book on multivariate analysis in marketing; it was becoming a hot topic, and there was no single source that could explain the various techniques and illustrate how they could be applied. As part of my study for the marketing field exam I had done an extensive review of the field and thus had a good start to a book. The result was another edited book,

entitled *Multivariate Analysis in Marketing*, which was published in 1971 (with a revision published in 1981). It covered such topics as regression, factor analysis, discriminate analysis, and multidimensional scaling. I ended up writing several of the chapters to fill in some gaps—chapters that eventually found their way into a marketing research book. The book sold under 5,000 copies, but I occasionally run into a reader that found it helpful.

Around 1976, George and I decided to write a marketing research text. We perceived marking research teachers had two unmet needs. The first was for a text that covered multivariate analysis topics. My background in statistics, the multivariate readings book, and my statistics course material all suggested that I could write such material. It turned out that others—such as Tom Kinnear and Jim Taylor from Michigan and Gil Churchill from Wisconsin—had made the same observation and were also writing such a book—but we didn't know that. Second, we sensed (and exaggerated) an interest in introducing public policy issues relating to consumerism into the market research class. Thus a book that used not-for-profit cases and examples would be welcome. Thus, we were off.

The book, entitled *Marketing Research* and published in 1980 (with subsequent editions published every three or four years), was organized around a marketing research process model that emphasized that research should be stimulated by, and eventually influence, a decision in order to be useful. The model later became the basis for an article published in the *California Management Review (CMR)*. We divided up the work: George wrote the survey research chapters, and I wrote the sampling, statistics, and multivariate analysis chapters. We split a set of application chapters. Even though the workload was shared, it was still a 600-page book with some fifty cases—a nontrivial project. The book captured a reasonable share of the market, but it did not oust the leading book by Gil Churchill that had (in our view) readability problems but enormous market momentum—an instructor needs a good reason to change. The Kinnear and Talyor book, with no momentum, also sold more.

Revising a marketing research book is not onerous because, unlike advertising, the basics do not change that much. Nevertheless, after the fourth edition in 1990, George said that if the next edition took only two hours that was too much for him. I agreed, and we recruited V. Kumar, a professor then at the University of Houston (now at the University of Connecticut),
to take over the revision task, so the book still lives under his capable hands (as does a spin-off book for undergraduates—*Essentials of Marketing Research*). In 2004 the eighth edition came out. The total cumulative sales have been over 120,000 in English, and it has been translated into five languages.

There was another book that took a good chunk of the mid 1970s. Written with John Myers, this one was on advertising management and was started soon after I arrived at

Berkeley. The first edition was published in 1975. John was a behavioral scientist who specialized in attitudes and communication theory, and was familiar with theories and research from psychology and sociology. The existing texts lacked links to this body of knowledge and generally had no quantitative modeling. Our vision would be to write a managerial advertising text that integrated both behavioral and quantitative modeling.

We accomplished our vision, and the book was well accepted by the top schools (which turned out to be a modest market) and was generally respected for what it was. The partnership with John, who is a wonderful person and friend, was difficult in part because I proved to be a forceful personality in this context, and it was difficult to divide up the subject matter. I was very interested in perception, attitude change, and the public policy aspects of advertising. As a result, I would get involved in sections that should have been left to John. Nevertheless, we went through three editions and remained friends. For the fourth edition we turned over the book to Rajeev Batra of Michigan, who did two more until the publisher pulled the plug. Overall it sold something like 70,000 copies in English and was translated into two languages.

I wrote a section on deceptive advertising that was originally included in the advertising book and was later reprinted in the consumerism book. The section was widely quoted, as there were no other definitions that had been established. My definition emphasized that deception occurs when the output of the audience member's perceptual process differs from the reality of the situation (even if the claim is literally true), and when it affects behavior (if there is no impact on action, then there is no deception). The important point was to introduce the psychological concept of the perceptual process into the realm of deceptive advertising.

Two other articles published in the 1970s were noteworthy. One was a comprehensive advertising decision model called ADMOD, which was published in *JMR* in February 1975. ADMOD not only addressed the media selection decision (in which media vehicles should you place advertising) but also the media budget decision (how much should you spend on advertising) and the copy decision (what types of advertising should be run). It required knowledge of the value of successive exposures to the advertising. The model was the ultimate quantitative advertising model, but, like its predecessor POMSIS (my 1968 media model), it was not practical given the computer demands and the inputs required. Nevertheless, one Japanese agency, Hakuhodo, did implement a version of it—more on Hakuhodo later.

The second was one of the first methodological articles introducing structural equation models into the literature, a methodology that was to become widely used during the next two decades. Published in *JMR* (May 1979), it was coauthored by Richard Bagozzi, our hot recruit, during his short tenure at Berkeley. Rick was (and is) the most academically pure person I know. He was deep into the philosophy of science and its implications for how you conduct research and how you interpret results. In fact, he wrote a series of "heavy" articles in that area and in doing so became, with Shelby Hunt (my 1968 consortium friend), an important force in applying philosophy to research in marketing. He was also a talented runner and a nice, considerate person. During our lunchtime track outings, he would patiently run with me until the time came to "stretch his legs," at which time he would accelerate. While I was an eight-minute miler when sprinting (which was not often), he was more in the five to six-minute category.

The decade for me was largely about putting out four textbooks. The books stuck in terms of sales and an ability to support revisions. However, books, even books that break new ground, are not perceived as academically impressive or even, in some people's eyes, respectable—a text-writer label is a pejorative.

Why write books then? First, I was highly motivated to gain a comprehensive knowledge of each of these four areas. I felt that writing or even editing a book was the ultimate way of doing that, even if it was inefficient. That same drive made my detailed preparation for my exams at Stanford rewarding if not fun. Second, at the time I thought there was something that needed saying in each case. My value add was undoubtedly overestimated, but it did motivate. Third, the prospect of putting the output on a shelf in my office and in my parents' home was appealing—not that my

parents read any of them. Fourth, books would serve to supplement my salary and would be more productive than consulting or
executive education. Finally, I felt that writing texts was relevant
to the teaching front. At Berkeley and other research schools,
teaching was a separate, albeit lesser, dimension of faculty contribution. Although I did not know it at the time, these book activities provided me with both the writing stills and the knowledge
that led to future books that would be much more worthwhile
from all perspectives.

I'd had a home run in the consumerism article with George,
along with several solid, visible articles that were related to the
modeling area with which I was associated, namely the thesis
articles, the *JAP* article on awareness, attitude, and behavior, the
ADMOD article, and the Bagozzi article. However, with respect
to articles, my output in the second half of the 1970s was light
in terms of both quantity and impact because the books had
diverted my time and energy. Worse, I was clearly undisciplined,
all over the map.

My work on consumerism was off-brand in the sense that it
was removed from modeling. Except for one minor article, I basically dropped my thesis research area of stochastic models. The
substantive area of advertising was not defining in part because it
was broad and most researchers did work that involved advertising. There was really no focal point to my research. I basically
did what was interesting and convenient. Being eclectic may be
fun, but it is a liability in academia. This ill-defined image was to
continue until I hit on brand strategy in the late 1980s.

Despite my fuzzy image and weak output in the second half
of the 1970s, I was still considered at the top of my cohort as a
modeler throughout the decade. I got promoted to associate professor with tenure effective July 1972 after four years (although
because I delayed my start it was really three and a half years);
four years later, July 1976, I became a full professor. Most have
six or seven years and sometimes more (but who is counting?)
at each level and find the process extremely stressful. In fact, I
suspect that over the last forty years, very few people at Berkeley
got tenure in under five years. I got named to the editorial board
of *JMR*, the top quantitative marketing journal, in 1969, within

a year of getting to Berkeley. I was invited to write a paper on the state of the art of management science in marketing for the 1972 AMA (American Marketing Association) conference. I was invited (by Jag Sheth) as a faculty participant in the doctoral consortium in 1971, exceptional for a second-year faulty member in those days. And, incredibly, I was named one of the thirty top perceived leaders in marketing thought in a survey of some 250 academics in 1975.

Why did I have a lingering reputation that was not justified for sure by my actual output? In my view, it was largely based on the strong first impression that I made on the field because of my academic credentials, the rush of articles that emerged from my thesis (never mind that they had little lasting impact, they were in the best journals and there were a lot of them—few reviewers were interested in or capable of judging the ultimate impact), my presentations at meetings, and that fact that I was visible to the right people. People in the field were impressed that I was a student of Bill Massy (and thus associated with his "hot" students, Dave Montgomery and Don Morrison) and had a master's in statistics from Stanford. Academics are snobbish. I benefited from the fact that having the right credentials is important, and a strong first impression is not easily changed.

The Academic Review Process

To understand academics, you need to know about how professors are appraised and the role of the journal reviewing process. Articles in major journals are the key to promotions and reputation. The number of articles and the prestige of the journal in which they appear are important, but the impact of the articles is even more so. To evaluate a professor's work at hiring or promotion time, a school will ask as many as ten leaders in the field to write letters appraising a candidate's principal articles and relative achievements as compared to peers. If a person has a narrow research scope, it will be easier to get letters saying that he or she is in the top of the cohort—the Holy Grail. It is more difficult to make such statements for a person with broad research interests. Interpreting the letters is an art—it is necessary to read between the lines for the absence of superlatives.

Getting research into the top journals is thus crucial. Understanding and dealing with the review process becomes an important skill. For most top journals (like *JMR*, *JM*, *Journal of Consumer Research*, *Marketing Science*, *Management Science*), there is an editor who assigns a submitted paper to two or three reviewers from those on the editorial board, plus a set of ad hoc reviewers. Each reviewer evaluates the paper's potential impact and looks for faults—mainly the latter. Faults can come in a variety of forms, including experimental design flaws, conceptual weaknesses, or the absences of "theory."

The tone of most reviews is overwhelmingly and unrelentingly negative. If the reviewer actually likes the paper there will be a few sentences in the front end about "showing promise if substantially improved" along with pages of criticism. An offer by the editor to invite a revision will be generally accompanied with the qualification that much work needs to be done to overcome serious flaws, and the chances of eventual acceptance are uncertain. Such an offer is greeted with celebration by seasoned, confident authors and disappointment by novices or insecure or exhausted authors.

The revision then becomes less a vehicle to promote an exciting idea and more about "getting it through." There is an art to knowing when and how to fight an unreasonable or stupid reviewer's demand and when to praise (butter up) a reviewer by expressing thanks for an "insightful suggestion that will dramatically improve the paper." The revision will be accompanied with a letter to the reviewers that can be longer that the paper itself. An acceptance of an article in a major marketing journal provides a sense of satisfaction for not only getting an acceptance of worthy ideas and findings but also to have "won the game." There are professors who do good work that never get an article through because they lack the perseverance, writing skills, and process tactics needed. Many more get one through and then quit trying.

As a result of this process, published articles tend to be competent, scholarly efforts; a sloppy, verbose paper just does not get through. However, there is a bias against significant papers because they often contain visible faults. Papers that break new ground are more likely to have technical issues. Further, there is a bias away from conceptual works that structure, evaluate, and prioritize an area of thinking and research because they are vulnerable to criticism that the conceptualization is inaccurate. Each decade has seen fewer papers of this type, and now they have just about disappeared.

When a group of professors gather, there is general agreement that the reviewing process is too negative, too nit-picky, and biased against breakthrough research, conceptual articles, and articles that deal with real issues of concern to executives. The irony is that these same professors are the editors and reviewers. They complain about the "other" reviewers. Like the title character in the comic strip *Pogo* once said, "We have met the enemy, and he is us."

I, like others, complain about the process but also contribute to it, as I have been an active reviewer over the years. I was on the editorial board of *JMR* 1969–1979, *Management Science* 1977–1989, *Journal of Marketing* 1978-1995 (and section editor from 1981–1984), *Marketing Science* 1980-1995, and *Strategic Management Journal* 1985–1992, in addition to an assortment of less academic journals. I have felt guilty about avoiding becoming an editor, a job that is onerous and time consuming but essential to making the academic system work. It always just seemed so "not fun."

Being on the editorial board requires a significant reviewing commitment. Reviewing a single paper can take as much as seven or eight hours and rarely takes less than three or four. It is also a significant recognition. Being named to the editorial board of *JMR* in 1969 during my first year as an academic was a huge honor. I joined a select list of twenty-two people including Bill Massy, Paul Green of Wharton, Don Morrison of Columbia, and some eight practitioners (mostly marketing research executives). Being on the *JMR* board was heady stuff but required me to review about three often-dense articles a month. Today the *JMR* editorial board contains over sixty people supplemented by dozens of ad hoc reviewers, so the workload is reduced. Interestingly, there are now no practitioners on the *JMR* board, reflecting the fact that articles have increasingly become abstract and theoretical.

Japan

Japan is now a second home for Kay and me. I have been there nearly thirty times, and Kay has joined me for many of these trips, including every one of the first fifteen or so. During the 1975 to 2000 period, I would go nearly every other year. From 2000 and beyond, I went much more frequently as I became an advisor to Dentsu, a major advertising agency, a story recounted in chapter nine. Japan for us is now familiar, comfortable, and home to many good friends.

Our first trip in 1975, full of newness and adventure, was one of the most memorable events of the 70s for both of us. The next two, in 1977 and 1979, were not far behind. A new, very different culture was experienced from the inside out because we got to know and work with people. We were pampered and spoiled. It was so much fun. Our Japanese story starts with Hiro and Jiro.

Hiro Takeuchi received his PhD from Berkeley (under Pete Bucklin) as I was arriving. After spending six years teaching distribution strategy at Harvard, where he was an outstanding teacher, Hiro was attracted back to Hitotsubashi University (by Jiro). Leveraging his Harvard experience and his personality, he developed a link to the business community and its senior executives. His Hitotsubashi students both past and present regarded him as a second father. He would take them on outings and become their mentor before and after their graduation. Each year, his birthday was an occasion for a special event for his student family. Always ahead of the fashion of the day, Hiro's wardrobe was so noteworthy that he would periodically auction items off for charity.

Very visible in Japan, Hiro's writings on new product development and knowledge gave him worldwide exposure. His award-winning book *The Knowledge Creating Company* (with Jiro), published in 1995, was one of the most influential business books of the nineties. He became a fixture at Davos (the World Economic Forum in Davos, Switzerland) where the CEO of Sony got him to MC the prestigious Davos Japanese dinner. *Business Week* put him on the cover in the late 1990s along with two-dozen others they identified as the rising stars of Asia. In 1996, *Fortune* introduced Professor Takeuchi as " ... among the intellectual leaders of the younger, globally-minded generation that is coming to power in Japan." He was the founding dean of the Hitostubashi MBA program in downtown Tokyo that is already considered the most prestigious in Japan. His wife, Nobu, and his children, Ko (a promising actor

Jiro Nonaka, Dave, Hiro Takeuchi

Adapting the ADMOD media model at Hakuhodo—1977

and musician) and Yume (now studying Eastern medicine in San Francisco), grew up in English schools and are more Western than Japanese. Yume joins us for special events. We consider the Takeuchis to be part of our family.

Jiro Nonaka also received his PhD from Berkeley in the late 1960s (under Franco Nicosia). Joining Hitotsubashi University, he became the leading business professor in Japan—and certainly one of the most visible worldwide—because of his pioneering work on the knowledge organization. He started out studying the organizational dynamics of the Japanese navy during WWII. He moved to the study of evolutional management, new product development, and knowledge creation, for which he is best known.

At retirement age (young in Japan), Jiro left Hitotsubashi to be the founding dean of the first Graduate School of Knowledge in Tatsunokuchi, a new campus on the Sea of Japan, west of Tokyo. We visited the new school and can confirm that it is an isolated outpost. He recruited faculty and oversaw the start of an academic and research program around knowledge. After several years of commuting from Tokyo, he was enticed back to join Hiro's new MBA program. Since 1997, he has spent some time each fall as the prestigious Xerox Distinguished Professor in Knowledge at Berkeley. Jiro, older and much more academic and Japanese than Hiro, is considered by all to be the senior partner intellectually. Both have great loyalty to Berkeley.

Hiro was not back in Japan long before he arranged my first trip in 1975. The core purpose was to consult to the quantitative model group of Hakuhodo, the second largest advertising agency in Japan. My assignment was to give a three-day in-house seminar on advertising models plus some public talks. My second and third trips, in 1977 and 1979, also had Hakuhodo as the primary sponsor. In 1977, I spent five days developing for them a commercial version of my ADMOD media model. In 1979, I helped them develop a new product model drawn on some MIT work. The group I was working with was capable but had limited resources and political clout within Hakuhodo, so the new product model, which required funding, was never implemented, despite the fact that it was far more potentially impactful than the unwieldy ADMOD model.

The first two trips found us at the Takanawa Prince Hotel, an out-of-the-way but charming place with a spectacular Japanese garden. It came with a substantial discount because one of Hiro's friends was a consultant to the parent Prince hotel chain. It was coincidentally the hotel where Hiro's wedding to Nobu took place. The Hotel's French restaurant, the Trianon Room, was special to us. We would have salad and chocolate soufflé while listening to a harpist. We returned many times to that place over the years, and the maitre d' would always remember us by name. Incredible. The Takanawa Prince was also one of the two hotels in which we experienced our room swaying from an earthquake. To the Japanese at the desk it was barely newsworthy, but it was a major event to us. The Takanawa Prince added a new tower and thus, for us, lost some of its charm.

I gave several talks on each trip. In 1975, *Nikkei*, the *Business Week* of Japan, sponsored a talk in Osaka and Tokyo. I had no basis of credibility as a speaker or interviewee except that I was from the U.S., and I guess people assumed that anyone that came that far and was sponsored by *Nikkei* must be worth hearing. In 1977, the Japanese translation of my advertising book came out (translated by Jiro, who also translated my earlier consumerism book), but in 1975 there was really nothing to create any Aaker reputation in the Japanese business community.

My *Nikkei* host, an older gentleman named Onishi-san, had a high school friend named Suzuki in Kyoto whom we visited on our way to Osaka. The Suzukis adopted our family and even sent their kids to spend a week with us. I recall our first visit when they were seeing us off at the train station. Kay, to make small talk, told Mrs. Suzuki that her purse was pretty. Immediately, she emptied the purse and handed it to Kay. This made small talk even harder. They were wonderful, charming people but difficult to communicate with because they knew no English, and our Japanese consisted of around five words. Actually, I tried to learn Japanese by taking a quarter course at Berkeley in the late 1970s. It was tough because I was not good at languages, and reading was not feasible because the Kanji characters were simply impossible for me. So I gave up. Another effort some thirty years later led to the same result, although I did get good enough to engage in some simple street conversation.

Hisahi Ikegami, my sponsor and the head of the models group at Hakuhodo, knew nothing about models but was a great host. There are many senior executives in Japan whose prime skills revolve around relationships and organization, and he was in that group. He took us to discos (where the song "YMCA" was popular), various dinners, bars, and his vacation house in Hakone, a mountain setting not far from Tokyo. At the disco, I developed the sensei (professor in Japanese) move (which involved pretend-

The 1979 Hakone Seminar badge

ing to write on a board) to the delight of all who enjoyed seeing me look ridiculous. Ikegami's role as host was impeccable.

During every Japan visit, I would give talks. It was always a trip to see my name in lights, so to speak (sometimes quite literally), and to realize that people were actually coming to hear me. I had to adjust to simultaneous translation (key insight: you need to slow down) and the fact that humor usually doesn't translate.

On occasion the laughs would come only after the translator told the audience to laugh. Often there would be an opulent reception as well.

In the 1979 trip there was a special event (organized by Jiro). The David A. Aaker '79 Hakone Seminar came complete with a four-inch-diameter red and white heavy plastic badge. It was held in the hundred-year-old Fujiya Hotel (named after Mt. Fuji), a famous old hotel in Hakone. Kay and I stayed in a room that then cost $350 (probably $1,500 a night in today's money) that had recently housed the Queen of England. Two people from Hakuhodo came up from Tokyo just so I would have a tennis game. The event, "Redesigning Marketing Strategy," was for senior executives and had two other speakers. One was Jiro, always an attraction in Japan. The other was Isao Nakauchi, a visible and outspoken Japanese executive who owned Daiei, one of the largest retail chains in Japan.

Having dinner with Nakauchi was a thrill for me. Over the years, I came to realize that, in Japan, I would have remarkable access to CEOs—access that would never happen in the U.S. Such access is due in part to the relationships that Hiro and Jiro enjoyed, but the respect professors have in Japan and the fact that the Japanese CEOs tend to be less hands-on than in the U.S. also play a role. I have had numerous sessions with CEOs of major Japanese firms and am always puzzled but honored that they would be interested in spending time with me. The discussions have always been fascinating.

Many years later, my work and I became widely known in Japan. As a result, it was easy to conclude that attendance at my talks and my treatment (which often included a car and driver) was due to a deserved reputation. However, the fact that my reception in the 90s was similar to that of the 1970s when I had zero reputation suggests that the driver of my acceptance is in large part due to the Japanese tendency to be polite, coupled with respect toward Hiro and Jiro.

Jiro was a particularly generous host during each trip. During our first trip, he showed us Nagoya and its marvelous castle. During our second trip, he took us to our first ryokan (Japanese inn). It was such a cultural experience—sleeping on tatami mats, dining in our room, using a "public" bath, enjoying the gracious and attentive staff, and experiencing a Japanese breakfast complete with fish and pickles. The service was particularly good and unobtrusive (no waiters hovering around). We were wide-eyed. We visited Pearl Island where we saw the cultivation, harvesting, and processing of pearls. We looked at Mikimoto products differently from then on.

Just getting to Japan was an adventure during our first trip. To save money we flew Air Siam, which was a significant step down in services, competence, and, I'm sure, safety. They failed to check to see if Kay had a current passport. She uncovered the problem on the first Hawaii leg, got off, and spent a day getting a new passport and visa before continuing. Since then we make it a point to make sure our passports are up-to-date (although on a recent trip I had to be bailed out by our neighbor, Barbara Meyers, when I brought an expired passport to the airport). Because I had commitments in Japan, I had to fly out of Hawaii without Kay. One of my happiest moments was seeing her a day later because I had no idea what trouble she was having. It turns out she enjoyed a day on the beach and the U.S. authorities efficiently got her another passport—but I didn't know that. Another was when Hiro was able to change our return from Air Siam to Pan Am. What a relief. Jet lag in these early trips was an issue. Kay and I spent a lot of time at three in the morning playing games or reading.

We did a ton of must-sees and must-dos during those first trips in case we never got to come back. Kay, nearly always armed with a car and translator courtesy of someone, would do flower arranging, experience tea ceremonies, watch Cloisonné-making, learn origami, visit a chocolate factory, see glass being blown, learn how Japanese dolls are created (often in homes), observe paper artwork, and more. Then there was sightseeing. In Kyoto I recall getting in a taxi one day and visiting seven Kyoto gardens, including the Golden Pavilion, the Moss Garden, and the Katsura Imperial Villa (requiring special permission), before finally stopping in exhaustion. On the last stop Kay stayed in the car. We learned later that there were four other gardens and shrines left on the plan for the day. Our guides had a checklist, and lingering at a site got in the way. One of the most interesting historical sites, visited another day, was a building that was made with squeaky boards around the exterior so that the occupants of the 1600s would not be surprised by bad guys sneaking up on them.

My favorite site in Kyoto was the rock and sand garden in the Ryoanji Zen Temple. Constructed around 1500, it consists of fifteen rocks placed on a bed of sand that is raked each night. The rocks are positioned in five groupings and arranged in such a way that you can never see all fifteen no matter what angle is chosen. About thirty by ten yards, it is peaceful and intriguing—a place to contemplate the mysteries of Zen. The longer you sit the more that you see. To me, it has the same appeal as a fine contemporary art piece.

Kay especially enjoyed seeing schools. She once saw one hundred pairs of sandals all outside the school door and could

Kay teaching in Japan

The rock and sand garden at Ryoanji Temple in Kyoto

not understand how each child could find their own. She was amazed at the cleaning period where everyone washed the floors together. The children in one school had colored hats coded as to their grade. What a good idea—creating class spirit and a way to identify kids in one visual. Not just a spectator, she would usually get involved with the class, answering questions.

We always tried to see homes—nontrivial because Japanese people have small homes and are used to entertaining in restaurants. But those with whom we interacted were so accommodating that we always seemed to visit one each trip. We were struck by the small size of the homes and the use of multiple purpose rooms—a single room would be a dining room, a living room, and a bedroom depending on the time of day. Visits in the home would usually come with Japanese sweets that take some getting used to.

The subways were a twenty-five-cent cultural experience in the 70s, and we took pride in being able to navigate the system. The ability to stuff people (some with hour-and-a-half commutes) in during rush hour was particularly interesting. The subway system is a good way to learn the various parts of Tokyo, but some stations like Tokyo Station or Shinjuku will always be mazes with a bewildering set of trains and subways to choose among. Just getting out of Tokyo Station after a train ride from the airport still requires me to ask at least two people for directions.

Eating is an adventure. There must be a million restaurants. Most, especially the very best, specialize—they are sushi, tempura, eel, or whatever. People will travel a half hour to a favorite place, passing thousands of others in the process. The prices at the high end are outrageous—around three times that of the U.S.. However, the noodle shops at the low end are not that much more. My favorite food is eel, and I try to get one eel meal in each trip. Although there must be hundreds of eel restaurants, I am always taken to a few "authentic" places.

I have become a sumo devotee. My love affair with sumo began when Jiro took us to one day of the Nagoya fifteen-day sumo tournament (or Basho) in July of 1975. Since then I have attended eight or nine more (six are held each year) and seen many more on TV. Sumo involves two fighters that attempt to push or maneuver an opponent outside a ring or to the floor. Each wrestler is assigned a closely watched ranking, one of nineteen levels that are dictated by performance. The wrestler will move up or down depending on his record during the Basho. Winning eight or more of the fifteen matches will result in an upward move, and fewer wins a downward one. Only those that can win several Bashos become grand champions or Yokusunas, the top rung. During the 90s, the Yokusunas included Takanohana (a strong, quick 350-pound fighter) and Akebona (a tall 500-pound American, in fact the first American Yokusuna), both of whom were popular with the fans. Currently, the interest in sumo is low in part because there is only one Yokusuna, a Mongolian with a poor public personality. Like all professional sports, a star system is in play.

I like sumo on several levels. The wrestlers are a sight to behold. They are rarely less than 300 pounds, and most are over 400 pounds; the Hawaiian Konishki, who fought in the 90s but never made Yokusuna, was over 600 pounds (a colorful character, he had a short marriage to a tiny model and now has cut a CD as a balladeer). They lumber down the aisle toward the ring and then show extreme flexibility by squatting prior to the match. In the ring they exhibit incredible strength, quickness, and technique. On several occasions, I have seen Konishki beaten by an opponent half his weight who simply stepped aside and watched him fall forward. There is a ceremony and rhythm to sumo that has a cultural charm. Before each fight, each wrestler passes water to the last fighter, conducts a ceremony involving raising each leg in turn, and after squatting and staring at his opponent retreats to pick up some salt to throw into the ring. After the fight the fighters bow to each other.

I always tried to schedule a trip to Japan to coincide with a sumo tournament. Even if I did not go to see the match in person, the TV coverage of the fifteen-day event provides something to watch on TV late in the day. In addition to live coverage with English commentators, there is a thirty-minute sumo digest that shows the matches in the late evening. On our second trip, I got to watch the final match of the fifteenth day while at the airport—Wajima, the hero of the day, won. Wajima has since fallen into disrepute because he turned to commercial wrestling to recover from financial difficulties. However, at that time he was a strong, gifted, and popular competitor. On our third trip, I got to get an insider's perspective by going to see a sumo practice session.

Of all the sections of Tokyo, I am drawn to the Ginza, which has energy, lights, shopping, the fish market, the Takaruzuka Revue, the Kabuki Theater, and Denstu's high-rise building. On recent trips, I have rarely strayed outside of this area except for a talk or client visit.

The heart of the Ginza is the Mitsukoshi department store, which has a sign that to my eye is larger and more colorful than anything in Times Square. Across the street is the Nissan showroom in which knowledgeable, attractive ladies guide patrons to two of their models. Down the Ginza Dori (street) from Mistukoshi are two other department stores, Matsuya and Matsuzakaya (Kay's favorite—and she should know). Each department store contains two basement levels with food displayed as if it were an art gallery. Only perfect produce is available, including the famous $100 (in current dollars) melons. I always browse there to capture the sights and smells and to enjoy tasting unusual items.

The level of service in all of Japan is remarkable, not only in quality but quantity. Nowhere is the number of staff more visible than in these department stores. Even with sections of the store that are heavy with shoppers, there are always an excess of clerks. Puzzled over this, I did a study in the mid-eighties (published in the *California Management Review*, Fall 1990) in which I interviewed mangers of banks, hotels, and retailers that operated both in California and Japan. I learned that they had no desire to deliver Japan-level service in California because it was too costly. Further, it would not be feasible because the American employees would not accept the organizational culture that makes Japanese service possible. Can you see Macy's clerks arriving early to sing the company song?

The Ginza is paradise for an upscale shopper. All the prestige Western brands from Tiffany to Gucci to Vuitton appear on or near the Ginza Dori—but there is more. The five-story toy store, Hakuhinnan, features several people outside the store demonstrating the latest toy on the street. Two doors down is a foot-massage emporium right on the street with five operators providing flexology services. It is so convenient that we have learned to make it a post-dinner stop. For me a highlight of the Ginza is a tiny store that sells warm fresh waffles (with or without chocolate topping) that you eat as you are walking. I am an excellent customer.

During a visit in the mid-eighties, Hiro steered us to the fish (tsukiji) market, which is a cultural and sensory experience. The flash-frozen tuna (caught around the world) are auctioned off with active and loud bidding (the auctions are held early, but with jet lag early becomes feasible). People are furiously sawing up the tuna and cleaning a bewildering variety of other fish. Countless numbers of Styrofoam containers with hundreds of different types of sea creatures are laid out for blocks. Eels are particularly plentiful. The energy is palpable, and just walking around is an educational experience. Contributing to the energy are motorized wagons that are everywhere. About four by eight feet, they have a short turning radius, a steering wheel that doubles as an accelerator, and a standing driver who is used to going full blast. Next to the fish market is a vegetable market with only a bit less vitality. I once saw the auction of sets of melons there and was struck by the knowledge it must take to participate. I have since visited the market dozens of times. Sometime around 2002, I stayed at a hotel during several of my trips about three blocks away. Each morning I would go for a run along the river and end up in the market, providing an energy pick-me-up to start the day.

On a recent trip, Kay and I got to attend the Takarazuku Revue, which turned out to be a spectacular musical with a storyline followed by a singing and dancing revue. The most unique aspect of the show was that the entire cast consisted of women, which meant that women were playing the male roles. The music and dancing was lively and the costumes and sets were out of this world. The costumes of the leads reportedly cost over $10,000—and looked it. The leads had powerful alto voices that were as good as any I have heard on the stage. It was an experience I plan to repeat often—sumo has a competitor.

Takarazuku Revue traces its roots back to 1913, when a railroad (now named Hankyu) thought that some entertainment would attract people to Takarazuka, their destination city. In 1916, they opened their music and dance school for young women. Today a thousand women audition for the few spots in the two-year school where one incentive is to graduate into becoming performers in the revue. In 1918, the first revue performance was held in Tokyo. Since then, they have performed many Western musicals, but have also created a host of original pieces such as the musical version of *Gone With the Wind*. When the lead singers get married (and then become ineligible for the review) or leave, they often become movie/TV stars or marry rich men—or both.

The most unique aspect of the revue is the audience, which I estimated to be 98% female—and mostly older females at that. These women are devoted to Takarazuka, going to many performances and learning whatever they can about the star's private lives. Fan clubs have their tables outside the theater, and fans wait before and after for a glimpse of their heroes. The wife of one of my good friends goes with her mother about thirty-six times a year (while he has never attended a performance). As a result of this cadre of fans, all the performances are sold out. I got seats in the 2,000-seat theater only because the producers wanted to discuss some brand issues they were facing. Some of the devotees are not proud of their intense obsession because there is a perception that the Takarazuka followers are not attractive enough to have an active social life of their own. Only in Japan.

Another Ginza attraction is the Kabuki Theater. With its classic, exotic appearance, it stands out in the middle of Ginza modernity. Kabuki goes back to the Edo Era (1600-1868), and its plays are often set in that period. Products of the merchant class, the plays were in part a vehicle to express emotions and frustrations with the feudal system of the day. While the Takarazuka is lively with a female cast, Kabuki is usually slow and serious with an all-male cast with some actors specializing in playing female, or onnagata, roles using elaborate costumes and heavy make-up. The movements of the actors are very stylized. A pose, a glare, and a subtle hand movement, for example, can represent a violent fight. The dialogue, often involving long speeches, is in a monotone and can sometimes sound like wailing or moaning to the Western ear. Classical music using a three-string instrument called a shamisen sets the tone as well as entertains. The audience gets involved by yelling out the name of a favorite actor (an action labeled "kakegoe"), so you sometimes feel that you are, incongruously, at a basketball game. The enthralled audience can identify the fine points of a performance, but for a Westerner it is a matter of catching mood and feelings.

Being in Japan is simply a mind-bending cultural experience. The little things stand out. The lights at Shinjaku, Raponggi, and Ginza. Random people who would take time out to make sure you got to where you were going even if they had to walk blocks out of their way. Observing those directing traffic or operating elevators taking their job so seriously. I love to watch a doorman carefully show a taxi just where to stop, as if the driver did not know—and as if it mattered. You don't know whether to laugh or be impressed. Taxi drivers polishing their cars. Drivers waiting for hours to provide return trips. On-time, comfortable bullet trains. Delicate flowers in a niche at a restaurant. Tatami mats adding peace and class to a simple house or restaurant. Showing respect by removing shoes and bowing. Mt. Fuji from a train going to the mountains. Schoolchildren in uniforms. Female caddies controlling four bags with automated carts. Pachinko, a sort of vertical pinball game set up to look like a bunch of Las Vegas slots. The homes and lifestyles. These touches contribute to the Japan experience that has resulted in a love affair with the country and its people.

18 Eastwood

Starting a new life begins with the basics: finding a house. We wanted a neighborhood feeling, and the Orinda/Moraga area felt right. So in the fall of 1968 we bought a small 1,700-square-foot, four-bedroom home in the Ivy Drive area, within walking distance to three excellent schools and only a mile to a wonderful tennis and golf club. We paid something like $35,000, which was just over three times my salary at the time—few could do that today. My father thought we were out of our minds to pay so much at a time when I still did not even have my degree. What did we know?

18 Eastwood Drive

In 1974, we decided to expand the home. We created a formal dining room, converted the master bedroom to a TV/guest room, installed an intercom, and added above the garage a new master bedroom with fireplace and Jacuzzi and a small nursery (which was eventually turned into my office). The process was cool. Each day I would see progress and often make suggestions, such as adding a foot to the bedroom, recessing a chest, adding a built-in cabinet, or changing a door. The end result was a children's wing on the opposite side of the house from our new master bedroom. The intercom was critical to make the arrangement work.

Over the years we have resisted moving because we liked the location and features we added, plus the transaction costs were high. In 1983 we added again. This time it was a large room that housed a pool table, exercise area, large TV set, sectional, and library. Kay claims that the room was intended to have a sewing area but I lack a good recollection of such a goal. Later we added a hot tub and deck, plus we turned the backyard into a garden with a ton of rocks and a host of trees, bushes, and flowers. It gives my office a terrific view and provides Kay with a great deal of satisfaction and pleasure. The house is very livable and full of precious memories. So we stayed.

The Girls

Jan was born on March 29, 1969, joining her two-year-old sister. Kay shared a room with Charmian Dobell. Her husband, Dick, an architect, brought flowers, which made him appear more romantic and thoughtful than I. It turns out that perceptions are important. In contrast, I appeared with a milkshake that was highly appreciated but less romantic. Dick was quick to promise things like trips to Mexico that I accused him of never planning to deliver. I was always amazed how much mileage he got from impressive promises. Several years later I gave Kay on two successive birthdays a flower box that was never built. There is something to be said for impressive promises

Jolyn arrived on June 2, 1974. I missed taking Kay to the hospital as I was playing in the final of a tennis club championship at the Sleepy Hollow club. After I left for the courts with no hint that the baby was close, the contractions started and Kay got our neighbor John Hallisey to drive her to the hospital. When I got

Jennifer, Jolyn, Jan

home and got the news, I rushed to the hospital in plenty of time to see the birth of Jolyn, a magical experience for sure. Any objective observer would realize that I was blameless in this incident, but the story is told (and retold) with the implication that I chose tennis over the birth of a child. So unfair.

When 1980 arrived Jennifer was thirteen, Jan eleven, and Jolyn six. The 70s were an eventful time for all three.

Jennifer was empathetic, artistic, and organized. A moment that is etched in our memory is when, after her third birthday party, she looked up and said with such complete sincerity, "Thank you for the party." We were blown away. Her empathy and consideration can also be found in her poetry. Her most famous (within the family) poem was written when she was twelve years old and reads in part:

Life is so fragile so handle with care
Do not hurt it, don't you dare.

and

Life is happy so give, give, give,
Be happy in life so live, live, live

She rolls her eyes when it gets read at gatherings.

Jennifer was also hyper-organized. There is the image of her tiny shoes all lined up in the closet (in contrast to Jan's shoes, which were in a pile) and, later, the fact that she kept track of what outfit she wore for which day. On Saturdays, for fun, Jennifer would re-organize her room. She recalls me teasing her by saying she needed to clean up her messy closet. Her anal personality has not changed. Her office is always perfect. If there is a pile of papers, it is only one pile and it is active. I once surreptitiously turned a vase in her office a quarter turn as a test. As Jennifer swept out of the room, she turned it back.

Jan lacked any drive toward neatness but had exceptional skills at pouting, smiling, and having fun. Her pout was something to behold, very expressive and determined. During a serious pouting session I would tell her not to smile. It would infuriate her when she would break up laughing. Once when she was placed in her room to pout she cut a white vinyl kids' couch that had been in the family for years. She was not to be fooled with. But she could also turn on the smile—it was dazzling. And Jan was into having fun. "Go for it" was her mantra. Whatever, she was game. Her ability to be disorganized has eroded over time (with three kids and a job, having a schedule is an imperative), although she is still no Jennifer on this dimension.

Jennifer and Jan were raised strictly. Everyone still recalls the evening when Jan complained that she did not get enough ice cream I took the dish away, and she got nothing. It was one of my finest moments as a father. Over time, however, I drifted toward a more permissive, supportive view of parenting. It was, for me, easier, more natural, and a defensible (if not optimal) philosophy of raising kids.

Jolyn was thus not subject to the same set of rules that Jennifer and Jan had lived by, a fact that they frequently brought up. So Jolyn, the third child, was more on her own; she was not micromanaged. We all assumed that she would turn out OK. She was a bit shy, but she usually had an extra friend and playmate in Jan and an extra mother in Jennifer. I was involved in her life from the beginning. I recall driving her to the Montessori nursery school in our red VW convertible (without seatbelts—it was a different era), teaching her the ABC song. She did fine but always forgot "Mr. J" so we had something to work on. Her school featured "works" that allowed the student to explore and advance at their own pace. She learned to only have one "work" going at a time and to put it away. So there was some discipline in her life.

I was so involved in tennis that I did not get organized to get Jennifer and Jan into sports (except tennis of course). Soccer and softball would often arrive and I would realize that I was supposed to have signed them up months before. I did get them into basketball and coached two years. I pushed (gently, by my judgment) them into tennis, but they were not as enthused as I would have liked even though each had some talent. I recall Jennifer was a member of Geronimo's Juniors as a pre-teen and was taught to spread her arms out like an airplane in order to learn to rotate her shoulders. It was only partially successful. I would try to get Jennifer on the practice court with some of her fellow students, but she had little patience. Jan, on the other hand, was eager to be out there but at that time was a bit young to actually develop groundstrokes.

We belonged to a neighborhood swim and tennis club, and Jennifer and Jan both learned to swim there. To be allowed to swim in the deep end you needed to qualify for a blue badge by swimming the length of the pool and treading water. Jennifer, who had good strokes, was going to take the test although she was not excited about doing so. Jan was not about to have Jennifer gain such a status and leave her behind. So Jan took the test and passed it despite the fact that she could only dog paddle a few strokes. I always felt that Jan's passing of that test was one of the greatest athletic achievements that I have ever witnessed. (I can see Maile, Jan's second girl, having similar characteristics). Of my three girls, whatever the sport (or activity), Jan was not always the most talented (skiing was the exception), but always the most willing and committed.

Skiing was an important part of our lives. Several times a year, I would wake them at five and say no school today we are going skiing. Jan, no early morning riser, jumped up immediately grabbed her boots and was out the door. Jennifer had to review her school schedule at length to decide whether she should go. She always joined us, but it was not an automatic decision. Those trips were the best. Once we went to Bear Valley. Little did I realize then that some thirty years later we would get a vacation home near there. Jolyn learned much earlier than the other girls. The initial trip for Jolyn was to Boreal Ridge in a snowstorm. Joyln was so excited when she could get off the chair by herself and turn on purpose. She must have been four.

When Jennifer and Jan were about three and five, I started bringing them to the *Nutcracker* ballet in San Francisco. We would typically go on Christmas Eve at eleven in the morning. During the 70s people dressed for the theater. Before the performance and during intermission we would search for our nominee for the best dressed among the women and girls. We would always have our picture taken. Jolyn joined as soon as she hit three. Over time the group has expanded to include Paul, Ida, and occasionally Kay. It has been a very special event for me during the last thirty-plus years. The new generation is now joining the group.

The girls loved to visit Oscar and Ida in Sun City where they would play miniature golf and ride in the golf cart (being careful to avoid breaking the many Sun City rules designed to regulate the activities of children). They also, in 1975, traveled to their roots in Minnesota. The family visited Bjarne's Child Lake, site of the Aaker family reunion, stayed at Fairhill's (the resort that Kay had vacationed at every summer growing up), and spent time with Kay's relatives on Lake Cotton.

Special Days with the Girls

I always felt that it was important to spend quality individual time with each of the girls. When two or more were together they would relate to each other, but when there was just one girl their only option was to relate to Dad. I probably did around eight or nine per year. Kay claims that it was her idea in the first place, but, even so, I still get some credit for running with the idea.

The first special day was with Jennifer, then about four, when we went for a walk in the Berkeley Hills and picked some poppies for mom—which turned out to be illegal. But the thought was there. A few years later, I took Jennifer in a party dress and a special hairstyle to a fancy restaurant where we played grown-up, an event she still vividly recalls. Recounting her trip to her mom she observed that it was "a lot different than McDonald's." Another time we went out to the Berkeley pier and watch the fishing and the view. We flew kites, went to the zoo, bicycled, and went hiking. We saw a lot of Cal basketball games where eating cotton candy, talking to Oski, having frozen yogurt, waving pom-poms, and parking the VW Bug were important parts of the experience. We had a VW red convertible, and Jennifer recalls thinking how creative and daring I was to drive it on a sidewalk to park beside Barrows Hall on game days. Decades later, in 2002, Jennifer wrote how memorable, fun, and bonding the special days were.

The most spectacular special day for Jan occurred in 1978 when she was around nine. The family brought me to the airport for a trip to the Aaker family reunion in Minnesota. When we got to the airport, Jan's suitcase appeared and she came along. She was thrilled. Jan was (and is) always up for anything. We went to

Bjarne's cabin at Child Lake where we canoed, swam, dealt with foot injuries, hung out with the relatives, and represented our family at one of the reunions.

The most spectacular special day for Jolyn was when we went for a helicopter ride in San Francisco. Entering the helicopter was an event for a little girl. Ice-skating was another regular event for Jo and me. We would often "coincidently" meet my friend Tom and his daughter Nicole. As a result the word "coincidence" became part of the vocabulary. After a while, there was some suspicion as to whether the coincidences were really happenstance.

A staple was going to the bookstore. I developed a practice at an early age of always letting each girl buy a book any time we visited a bookstore. One motivation was to help them develop a love and appreciation for books. Another was to make sure they liked me. Bribery was not necessary, of course, but I felt it could not hurt. To this day they look forward to going to a bookstore knowing that I will spring for books.

The DeJonghes

The DeJonghe family has been a part of our lives since the 1970s. We are like a blended family. Around 1971, Kay and Marty Bruno were teachers during the opening of the Wagner Ranch School, which had classrooms in a circle around a central pod. There was a lot of room for energy and innovation. Marty married Tom DeJonghe, a Chevron patent lawyer and real estate entrepreneur, on New Years' Eve in 1973. We connected. Tom was the friend I was looking for. He had lots of interests and opinions, and he skied at about my ability. It is not easy to find skiing partners. We began skiing and, soon after, began playing tennis and backgammon as well. We also began an evolving discussion of economics and politics. So we enjoyed being together, as did Marty and Kay. Tom wrote in a note in the mid 80s that our friendship has been one of the main enduring joys of his life. I dedicated my book *Brand Portfolio Strategy* in 2004 to Tom, describing him as a real friend who enhances my life with his remarkable ability to be stimulating, adventurous, enthusiastic, humorous, and fun.

Tom is relentlessly positive, a trait that I admire, enjoy, and envy. He has characterized missing a plane in Paris as the best

Child Lake—Bjarnie, Jan, Dave

Jan is surprised

thing because he got to visit Claude Monet's gardens in Giverny. Asking how Tom liked a trip, a bike ride, or a golf course is a waste of time because the answer is so predictable. His attitude is so over-the-top that it is an ongoing source of amusement—and sometimes gets in the way of some healthy grumbling when the day is too hot or the hill is too steep. However, on balance, a positive approach to life adds to the events of the day.

In contrast, although I would like to have Tom's optimism, I am an ingrained pessimist. I try to turn this pessimism into a way to cope with stress by adopting one of the rules of Dale Carnegie's classic book (which has sold over six million copies), "How to Stop Worrying and Start Living." His second rule is to consider the worst thing that could happen, accept it, and try to improve on it. I recall when I was playing competitive tennis in college; I would assume that I would not win a single game. Then the pressure would disappear and I could play relaxed. Most top players would take the opposite course and assume they could win every point. But it seemed to work for me.

Kay and I have always led lives focused around families. Growing up, family and relatives were important for both of us. During the last thirty years and more, our family has involved the Aaker/ DeJonghe extended family. Having a close family is not for everyone. Some find it confining, forced, and even stressful and

Kay & Marty

unpleasant. Others anchor their lives around activities and friends. But having a family center has for us provided a sense of belonging, continuity, companionship, and an ability to share events, activities, and memories. And it works. A friend expressed amazement recently that seventeen people from the extended Aaker/DeJonghe clans could thrive in a confined setting for a week in Maui in 2004 without some interpersonal problems. We just take it for granted. I feel blessed.

Mark DeJonghe arrived a year before Jolyn, and Nicole DeJonghe one year after. With the kids in tow, we began the habit of having Sunday dinner together, a habit which has lasted for many years. We also began to share Christmas, New Year's Eve, and vacations in both the winter and in the summer.

The Aaker/DeJonghe family found the summer camp at the University of Santa Barbara in 1977 and made it a centerpiece of the summer for five years. We stayed in the dorms and ate in the cafeteria just like students. There was organized play for every age group including square dancing, crafts, tennis tournaments, and meditation (where I promptly went to sleep, which kind of missed the point) for the adults. The

Jolyn, Mark, Nicole setting swim records—not

beach was an attraction but required an oil removal process because of the oil wells out in the ocean. We biked and roller bladed all over the campus—it was cool. A memorable picture is Tom transacting some real estate business on a pay phone with his helmet and knee and elbow protectors on. He never stopped.

Tennis was an important part of Santa Barbara for Tom and me. One year we were on the courts when there was a huge earthquake with the light poles and building swaying and the ground shaking. We waited it out and kept on playing. We called it being composed, but the rest of our family called it being insensitive to their potential danger. It turned out that getting Jolyn down from a nap on the fifth floor of a dorm was somewhat frightening. But we played on.

Tom and I were into playing backgammon—ultimately we have played well over 30,000 games and still counting. Tom leads despite inferior skills. My theory is that he thinks through things so much that I get frustrated and play hastily. Our most memorable game occurred on a bluff overlooking the ocean at Santa Barbara with the sunset in front of us. The doubling cube went back and forth until it got up to thirty-two (it rarely reaches four, and I can't recall another time it got over 8), and Tom rolled a large doubles at the last minute to win.

In the winter we would get a cabin at Squaw Valley and enjoy evening fires and Squaw skiing during the day. It was always special to be in the mountains during the winter, especially after a snowfall. The kids loved it as long as they didn't get too cold. One of my jobs was to get their hands warm during the chairlift when it was windy. When learning to ski, Jennifer would take instruction and became a beautiful, if somewhat mechanical, skier. Jan, in contrast, would not process any tips but would instead bomb down the hill in her snowplow (often with Mark DeJonghe) having the best time. I would explain to her that having fun is secondary to learning to turn (the logic seemed a bit off), but it didn't work. Ultimately Jan turned out to be a natural, beautiful skier but never could articulate how—she just did. My many tips had nothing to do with it.

Mystery Weekends

In the spring of 1978, Tom and Marty DeJonghe, Charmian and Dick Dobell, and Kay and I inaugurated mystery weekends. One couple would design a weekend and give the others minimal guidance as to what to bring. The weekend would unfold as one surprise after another. We did about two of these a year for nearly ten years. Occasionally Mark (a fellow professor and neighbor) and Barbara Garman would substitute. Dick was artistic (an architect by profession) and he would give us a different perspective.

These weekends were a kick. They got us out doing accessible but unusual activities that exploited the rich Northern California area. Sprinkled in were activities that we would never have done without this type of organization and commitment. The first one was a boat outing on the Delta that included rooms at the Ryde

The Mystery Weekend group:
Kay, Dave, Marty, Tom, Charmian, and Dick Dobell

Hotel, a place with considerable nineteenth-century charm. We considered buying an old run-down mansion complete with a bowling alley, but we lacked the imagination, time, and money to go for it. Among the other weekends were:

- A wine country outing complete with mud baths, a glider ride, and meals at the French Laundry and Domaine Chandon
- Gold Country's Murphy's Hotel (near our current vacation home) and rafting on the Stanislaus River
- Canoeing on the Russian River and a visit to Jack London's home
- A limo to San Francisco's Fairmont, sailing on the bay, and the theater

- Hang gliding, cycling, and Highland's Inn in Monterrey
- Deep sea fishing in Mendocino
- Ballooning in the wine country
- Nordic skiing at Bear Valley
- A weekend at an island lighthouse

There were many memorable moments. I recall that Dick was taking a course on photography, and one assignment was to take interesting pictures of fences. It made you look at the landscape very differently. After a rafting trip, we had some extra time and no backgammon set so Tom and I fashioned one out of rocks and had others think of a number between one and six to simulate dice. We were over the top in terms of our inability to just mellow out. Another was our difficulty with hang gliding. We did well to get a foot off the ground. I assume it would be easier if you had the courage to step off a high cliff.

Tennis and Other Activities

Tennis was a big deal for me during the 70s and 80s. It was mostly doubles, in part because I was used to playing doubles from my Stanford days and in part because there were others that set up the games and all I had to do was say yes.

One tennis organizer was Ed Cross, who had his own court in Lafayette and several regulars. One was Jay Rubinow, a short left-

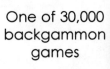
One of 30,000 backgammon games

Jorg Reinholt, Bob Witman, Ed Cross, Dave, Dave Moffet

Dave Moffet, Joyce
Hawkins, Dave, and Judy
McKeegon

Many will be surprised
to see evidence that I
can get air

handed player with a great sense of humor. He ultimately moved to Pennsylvania, developed a successful building alarm firm, and switched from tennis to big-time road biking. John Thomas, another regular, was a Stanford MBA who was unhappy as a San Francisco investment banker. So he dropped out and became a successful tennis pro in San Mateo. Another was Bob Whitman, a commercial real estate broker who was a small cut above the rest of us. The Cross group would have an annual tournament and dinner each year.

Another Cross regular was Jorg Reinholt. An interesting, likable Norwegian, Jorg always had opinions, but most were somewhere to the right of Attila the Hun. However, he had a knack of expressing his views in a way that was not excessively annoying. Jorg and I also played in a lot of the local tournaments. We had an unorthodox game. He would stay back and hit frustrating lobs and blazing passing shots, especially from the forehand side. We were not above using some guile. Playing at Sleepy Hollow, we once beat Mike Bauer (who became a world ranked player—more on him later—but was then barely a teenager) and his father by hitting soft balls to Mike. We played the regional circuit when we hit forty-five in 1983 and did well, achieving a doubles ranking of three in the forty-five age group in Northern California.

Jorg did not handle bad calls well. On several occasions during important tournament matches or in a Cross match, he would simply start hitting balls out in protest. Luckily the Cross group was patient and usually could see the humor in the situation. Others were not so tolerant of Jorg's unique way of making a point.

Jorg was also an avid bridge player, and Kay and I played a lot of bridge with Jorg and his lovely wife Lisa. They invited us to join a four-couple bridge/dinner club, a group that has survived (although with a changing cast of characters) for twenty-five-plus years. A picture of the group appears in chapter eight. Jorg and Lisa were also regulars at our Christmas events—they would always bring a traditional Norwegian dessert. In the mid 90s, Jorg and Lisa moved to Orcus Island, outside of Seattle, to enjoy retirement and boating. They take their powerboat out for an extended trip each summer. Their idyllic home is right on the water. Not a bad life.

A Cross semi-regular was Dave Moffett, who also had his own court. Dave left in the late 70s to go to Seattle to take over the Snowqualimie ski area started by his father in the 30s. Dave was an entrepreneur, and we enjoyed talking about ventures. I still had some entrepreneurial interest left over from my Houston days. Any idea was fair game, and for a while Dave was in the business of starting companies. We have kept in contact, and in fact he has joined me in backing Annie Chun's, an Asian food business run by Steve Broad, the brother of my son-in-law, with his wife, Annie Chun. Once we had a family vacation planned to Sun Valley, but at the last minute we found there was no snow there so we went to Dave's place and stayed in their condo and had a great time. Dave and I were both into mixed doubles and have played a lot of tennis socially and in tournaments, with or against Joyce Hawkins (who became Orinda's mayor, but not because of her excellent tennis) and Judy McKeegon, a fun woman with classic strokes (except with an unaccountable tendency to look at the ground as she served). The play continued even after Dave moved, because he had frequent occasion to visit.

Ed Cross and his family (including his wife, Sue, and his two kids, Wendy and Scott) joined us for some family vacations at Tahoe and some holiday meals as well. Ed and I had three other connections. First, an avid ski patrolman and expert skier, he once made my skiing much better by telling me to pretend my hands were on a steering wheel. It made all the difference. Second, in 1975, Ed and I got tickets for the Rick Barry-led San Francisco Warriors playoff games, the year they won the championship. It was a trip. Third, a broker for Dean Witter, he helped me manage my mother's portfolio after my father died in 1982. We did not get a lot of thanks from my mother, who'd always dreamed of having a broker she could visit nearby. But she never took up our offer to step down.

Dick Holliday, who lived in Lafayette, had a court and would often organize games with good local players. I was in his group. Through him I got to know another person in Danville who also had his own court and was looking for good players, so I had a fairly wide exposure to the local elite—it is all relative, as we are talking about a five or six-town area. Nevertheless, the play was relatively good and my doubles play improved (within the limits of my serve). I was able to refine my service return and net play. I was particularly good at half volleys where you take the ball at a short hop—because of my weak serve and slowness, I could never get close to the net after my serve and had a lot of practice hitting half-volleys.

I was also active in the active local tournament scene at both the Sleepy Hollow Club where we belonged and the Orinda Tennis Cub (OTC), a group of 200 or so players that had access to a dozen or so private courts that supplemented a central location. As a result you would play on courts at fabulous homes. One had its own lake with canoes and birds. The interest was high and the draws large. The finals would often get from 60 to 200 people watching. I always felt pressure in the early rounds because I wanted to keep playing. However, when the finals arrived, the pressure dropped away because there were no more matches to miss should I lose. Further, I was then warmed up and in a groove. Playing in the finals and having some good shots was exhilarating.

I specialized in mixed doubles. My serve was not a strength. I just lacked a natural throwing motion. As noted in earlier chapters, as a young catcher I could only get the ball to second on one hop, and as an intramural quarterback at MIT the passing routes could not exceed fifteen yards. I once had a top pro get me to serve well, but when I used his suggested motion my arm would give out after a few sets. So I had a serve that was somewhere from weak to pathetic depending on the frame of reference. However, in mixed doubles a serve is not that important and my service return and net game, complete with head feints, were huge advantages.

During the 70s I won a host of club tournaments. At one point I won the OTC mixed doubles tournament five years in a row, most of them with Joyce Hawkins (I was excellent at selecting partners). And I was often a finalist, losing to some good players. Robbie Olson, a former star basketball player at Cal who later won the national thirty-five doubles when he was forty-five, beat me in a host of finals. Robbie was not the only competitor that did well in age groups regionally and nationally. I also had trouble with Hank Lancaster and Clark Wallace, a pair who became national ranked players in the fifty-five and older group. Rollie Odell was a Sleepy Hollow competitor, and he is now one of the top national players in the older age groups.

There were a fair number of social tournaments as well. One annual affair was the Sleepy Hollow Fall Calcutta tournament that featured a huge party at which the teams would be auctioned off. The bidding for the teams, which paired a high-ranking man with a lower-ranked woman and vice versa, would be spirited. The financial return would be based on how well their team did in the tournament, so interest in the finals would be high. I was really good in such settings and usually won even when my opponent would be given as much as eight free points to be used during a set. My net play was one of the reasons. Another was that I was very good at building my partners up with encouragement. I would also give them a short lesson on how to lob as we warmed up for the first match. As a result, women in generally loved to play with me and played at the top of their games.

For the first few years of the 70s I also played serious table tennis. There were open, A, B, C, D, and novice classes for both singles and doubles. I became a B player, which is much better than it sounds. You could play up so it was not uncommon to enter three or four tournaments and get a real workout. As I noted in chapter three, table tennis is a sport that fitted me best, as it required hand-eye coordination and reflexes and not foot speed or a throwing motion. However, I observed that table tennis was played in black clothing in industrial areas while tennis was played in white (in those days) in nice country clubs. Tennis won out.

Cal Bears

I have always been a huge Cal fan in basketball, football, and tennis, mostly in the face of disappointments. I have always looked with envy at UCLA, Michigan, and Duke. Why wasn't Berkeley blessed with such teams? But Berkeley gets in your blood.

The 70s were the era of UCLA in basketball, and Cal was a perennial also ran. We were at the bottom of the then Pac Eight most of the time. Only twice did we get in the top half, and the best of these was third. The team that finished third had four players who went on to the pros and a fifth that still holds scoring and rebounding records at Cal. Yet that year we lost both games to UCLA by over twenty points despite having better talent. That Cal team simply never passed the ball. Whoever in-bounded the ball usually took the shot. There were some bright spots during the 70s. It was a pleasure to watch John Caselli who was the most fundamentally sound defensive player (on a terrible team) I have seen. And there was Gene Ransom, an exciting guard that played 63.5 minutes in one of the most remarkable games I have seen, a five-overtime win over Oregon.

My interest in basketball led me to a project with Tom Reynolds, a colorful quantitative psychologist that was visiting Berkeley in the mid 1970s (a world-class beer drinker, he knew an amazing array of barmaids). We attempted to statistically determine the best measures of team defense by modeling the ability of each measure to predict game outcomes. The winning measure was the opponent's points per possession. We had fun.

When I arrived, Cal football was both bad and boring while Stanford had Jim Plunkett and Rose Bowl teams. So for a few years I retained my allegiance to Stanford. But things at Cal perked up, and I became a Bear. We got players like quarterbacks Steve Bartkowski and Joe Roth, end Wesley Walker, and power running back Chuck Muncie, and the fortunes turned from embarrassing to mediocre. The high point was in 1975 when Roth, Muncie, and Walker led us to an eight and three record and a tie for the conference title, but (only at Berkeley) we lost the tie-breaker and did not go to the Rose Bowl. The quarterback that year was Joe Roth, a gifted athlete that tragically died of cancer not long after his terrific season.

Cal tennis was also fun to watch and more competitive than the other sports. The format was great—six singles going at the same time and then three doubles matches. One of the nice elements was going to Wimbledon where, during the first week, you could always see Cal players in doubles. Mike Bauer, one of

Cal's best number-one players, started playing at the age of twelve (late for tennis), at which point I beat him at Sleepy Hollow. He later achieved a world singles ranking of twenty-nine and once beat Jimmy Conners. An excellent doubles player, he reached the quarters at both the 1983 Wimbledon and the 1984 U.S. Open. I twice saw him play at Wimbledon. Had he a better second serve he would have done even better. I recall watching Mike play UCLA and be down 0-3 in a key game (where each game was decided by the first to four points) when he served four straight aces, each placed in a corner. My first reaction is what luck, but my second was that there was some skill there.

The 70s

The 70s provided a great platform. I advanced to tenure and full professor, which meant that I was established at Berkeley and in academic marketing. I got started on a career that was just about perfect. The three girls grew from being unbelievably cute to active young women. And I was part of the process, which was both fun and rewarding. The Aaker/DeJohgne extended family was off to a good start as well. Tennis, skiing, and coaching filled in the edges. I looked forward to the 1980s.

7 The Eighties

The decade of the eighties was a time of growth and transition, both at Berkeley and in our family life.

Research

The eighties were much more productive and defined than the seventies. My research involved advertising, the "warmth" emotion, strategy, and brand extensions. Don Bruzzone, Doug Stayman, and Bob Jacobson played important roles (as did Kevin Keller, but his role is described in chapter eight). Three home-run articles emerged, and several others were significant. Another text, this one on business strategy, was written. And, most important, the stage was set for my work on brands and brand strategy, which served, finally, to define my writing and me.

Advertising

Don Bruzzone is one of my favorite people. He has, since the early 70s, run a marketing research company in Alameda, an island town next to Oakland. He is an insightful, seasoned, bright, clever researcher with a great sense of humor and a small committed staff. When I call Don, I usually ask his staff if he is awake. We go from there.

Over the years I have cultivated a small number of industry people who are especially stimulating, insightful,

Don Bruzzone

and fun to be with. I would manage to spend a few hours with each exchanging brand stories and insights whenever it was convenient. For me, that was as fun as it gets. In the eighties this group included Don and also Bill Wells and Stuart Agres.

Bill Wells, a research guru at Needham (who finished his career as a University of Minnesota professor), did the pioneering early work on lifestyles and developed the concept of transformational advertising—advertising that transforms the use experience. I would spend time with Bill whenever I was in Chicago or when we both were at a conference. Once Brian Sternthal, a brilliant Northwestern behavioral science professor, and I decided that we would get a half dozen advertising researchers to listen to some top creatives (people that create advertising) and see if we could get insights and even model their thought process. Bill contributed the creative team that had done Betty Crocker cake and frosting products, and they described their process of generating advertisements. One of the academics asked why one of the creatives had done a close-up of the frosting. The reply was that "I always do close-ups." So much for learning how creatives think. We realized for sure that we lived in a different world.

Another guru friend was Stuart Agres, whom I met at an advertising conference attended by about forty people, half of whom were academics. I quickly decided to spend my time with Stuart, who had stories and ideas that would not quit. We spent hours talking about society trends and how they were impacting audience response. This was the first of many such conversations. Widely read and creative, he always had a different take on a wide variety of topics relating to advertising. When Jennifer graduated from Berkeley it was Stuart, then at Lowe and Partners, who hired her as a researcher. He (and Jennifer) claimed it was on merit, but my position was that my contact did the job. He subsequently developed the huge Y&R (a major advertising agency) brand database in the 90s (thirty-five countries, thousands of brands, over fifty measures) and was a regular presenter at my classes and, later, at the classes of both Jennifer and UCLA's Aimee Drolet (Jennifer's friend, Stanford classmate, and UCLA colleague).

Don Bruzzone's main business was to test audience response to television commercials by mail. A few scenes from a commercial would be presented in his questionnaire and respondents would answer questions involving commercial recognition, brand name recognition, and product use. They were also asked to check any of twenty alphabetically listed adjectives they felt described the commercial. In a study published October 1981 in *Journal of Advertising Research*, we conducted a factor analysis (a method used to group adjectives that are correlated across commercials) of 524 ads from his database. We found that there were four general dimensions that describe how commercials are perceived: entertaining, informative, warm, and irritating. This study, which in my view lacked the visibility it deserved, provided not only insight into advertising and how to make it effective but also a platform for a series of research studies that attempted to explain what made an ad irritating or warm.

In a study to understand the causes of irritation in advertising reported in *Journal of Marketing* in 1985, Don and I found a strong product effect. People were uncomfortable about products that were embarrassing or were associated with discomfort, such as feminine hygiene products, hemorrhoid treatments, laxatives, women's underwear, mouthwash, and antacids. Then we (at Don's suggestion) found twenty pairs of ads that differed markedly on irritating but were from the same product category and often the same brand.

Some provocative findings emerged from the paired ads. The product effect was magnified when the product and use were made explicit (e.g., a graphic illustration of the pain of hemorrhoids). Ads that were contrived, phony, unbelievable, or over dramatized tended to be irritating (a battery commercial showed an actor roaring up on a motorcycle, daring the viewer to knock a battery off his shoulder). The relationship between the people portrayed in the ads was important. When a person was being put down with respect to appearance ("Your awful hands") or knowledge ("Don't you know ...") the ad will likely be more irritating. A dramatic example for me was two nearly identical ads with very different irritation levels. A smiling wife telling her husband about the need for the dandruff removal action of Head and Shoulders was much less irritating than a husband giving the same message to his wife—which came off as judgmental. The source of identical advice using identical words changed the audience reaction—the subtlety of advertising was never more apparent.

Another dimension, warmth, was ripe for exploration. Doug Stayman and I embarked on a research program to understand warmth in advertising and its impact on audiences.

Warmth

I have been monumentally unimpressive as a PhD advisor. Over the years I have had only a handful of students and, of those, I can't say that I contributed much to their program. One of my most successful students, Toshi Akustu, for example, became a leading brand researcher in Japan, but Jennifer had more influence on his thesis than I did. Another, Andrew Mitchell, now at the University of Toronto, had a successful research career that was far removed from his thesis research. Most of the others never surfaced in major research universities. I felt that the average PhD student would just take a lot of time and patience, and I was not blessed with either. Further, others were good at supervising PhD students and enjoyed it, so there was no need for me to get more involved. I enjoyed teaching but felt my skills and interests were better suited for undergrads and MBA's. Doug Stayman was the exception.

Doug Stayman

Doug Stayman was a laid-back, curious, bright PhD student who was interesting and likable. We hit it off personally and professionally. Because of the work with Don, I realized that warmth was an important route to successful advertising and nobody in marketing had looked at it. Doug was immediately interested. Further, Doug was a behavioral scientist, which meant that the literature relevant to emotions was easy for him to access. He was also an experimentalist. He could design experiments and, more important to me, he could implement them by actually creating laboratory settings, recruiting subjects, and running studies. I lacked not only the skills but also the motivation and the time (in part because I was a bit lazy), so we made a great team.

Doug was and is an outdoorsman. He loved to hike in Yosemite around Tuolumne Falls. After a stint at Texas, he moved to Cornell, where he could indulge his outdoor interests. He moved into administration during the 90s and had less time for research but was and is highly regarded in the field. A good athlete, Doug liked tennis but never devoted the time to be proficient. When he was in Texas I went down to finish some research projects one summer and recall playing tennis in what seemed like 110-degree heat. It was brutal.

Doug and I wrote nine articles during or shortly after the three or four years he was getting his PhD; it was an incredibly productive time for both of us. The key article, "Warmth in Advertising: Measurement, Impact, and Sequence Effects," published in *Journal of Consumer Research* (*JCR*) in 1986 was a home run. My colleague, Mike Hagerty, was a coauthor as well but made only modest contributions. I always felt that being generous with coauthor credit resulted in a lot of good will. In this case, Mike made me a coauthor in a *Marketing Science* article for which my contributions was modest, so the credit was balanced. The warmth article was named one of the top ten most cited articles in the first fifteen years of *JCR* and created interest, controversy, and follow-on research. As a result of this stream of research, I was known as Mr. Warmth, a label made famous by Don Rickles, a comedian whose style was to ridicule others.

In this article, we defined warmth as a positive, mild, volatile emotion involving physiological arousal and precipitated by experiencing directly or vicariously a love, family, or friendship relationship. Each word and phrase was deliberately selected. The definition was notable because warmth had never been rigorously defined before, and because it precipitated a healthy debate that included the question as to whether warmth was an emotion at all.

We designed a series of studies that utilized a measurement device we created and termed a warmth monitor. A respondent would record the level of warmth they were feeling (absence of warmth, neutral, warm-hearted/tender, emotional/moist eyes) as they watched a television commercial. Test showed that it was reliable (generating a similar pattern with repeat trials), sensitive, and correlated with the physiological measure of skin response (GSR). In our study, respondents were exposed to one of four-test ads: two warm ads (McDonald's and Gallo), a humorous ad, and an irritating ad. Preceding the test ads was either a warm, humorous, or irritating ad. In addition to the warmth monitor we measured the post-exposure ad liking, purchase likelihood, and recall of copy points.

The findings were fascinating. First, the warmth monitor, in one of the few efforts to measure the dynamics of reactions to TV commercials, showed that the warmth emotion was volatile as substantial changes were evident over time. The judgment that a commercial was warm (or humorous or informative) does not capture that dynamic—the pattern such as a steady rise or a rise and fall could easily affect the impact. Second, the warmth monitor endpoint (and change) was correlated with purchase likelihood. For the first time, the self-reported emotional response was shown to be related to a relevant advertising goal: to increase loyalty. Third, there was a large and unexpected sequence effect. With respect to ad liking, recall, and purchase likelihood, it was actually better to be preceded by a contrasting ad (having a humorous rather than a warm ad preceding a warm ad). We (and others) had expected that a warm ad would best be preceded by other warm ads. With this article, warmth, always part of the advertising practitioners vocabulary, entered the academic research arena.

Most of the other articles with Doug supported and extended the warmth research. One in *Psychology and Marketing*, 1988, showed that there are thirty-one clusters of emotions associated with TV commercials, including relaxed, excited, contemplative, sad, and bored in addition to warmth. Another in *JAR* in 1990 estimated that 19% of all ads are warm and 1.5% are very warm. Still another *JAR* article, also in 1990, showed that both ad liking and tendency to buy were affected by the ad characteristics with informativeness having the most pervasive impact. Finally, a 1988 *JCR* article showed that feelings engendered by both warm and humorous ads had an impact on brand attitudes over and above that due to the liking of the ad, thus dispelling the notion that we were only capturing the well-traveled "ad liking" construct. The two other articles explored the validity of the warmth monitor and discussed why a dynamic measure of a commercial provides useful information.

In another article, published in *Psychology and Marketing* in 1992, Doug and I explored whether Bill Wells's intriguing concept of transformational advertising actually occurs. We showed that when placed in a hiking/campfire context, the experience of drinking Coors was perceived to elicit much stronger feelings of being refreshed and healthy than if the setting was a barbecue with friends, a difference that did not appear if Lowenbrau was the beer involved. In contrast, for Lowenbrau, feelings of warmth were higher if the use context was a barbecue with friends rather than a hiking/campfire setting, a difference that was much less pronounced for Coors. Although exploratory, this study suggested that the past advertising of Lowenbrau and Coors did transform the use experience.

This was an exciting and creative time for my research. Research ideas based on the work Doug and I were doing just seemed to tumble out. At one point I had around seventeen studies just starting, under way, or being written up, nearly half of which involved Doug. We had clearly stumbled on a rich vein of gold with warmth, and more generally, emotion in advertising. Further, our experimentation was a powerful vehicle to generate and test ideas. This research activity, which lasted only three or so years, did not survive Doug's move to Austin and then to Cornell, for two reasons. First, instead of being able to devote full time to research, Doug had the time demands of a teaching professor. Second, there was pressure on him to demonstrate that he could do research that did not involve me. I really believed that had Doug been able to stay a graduate student at Berkeley, we could have continued the stream with an emphasis on transformational advertising. However, it was a great run while it lasted. Further, Doug ended up with an excellent education because he was able to access some great courses and professors in psychology and couple that with hands-on research.

During the mid-80s, I also developed a research stream on business strategy, in part with Bob Jacobson, that in some ways was even more productive.

Modeling Business Profitability—Bob Jacobson

Bob Jacobson is one of the wittiest people in marketing and one of the brightest and well trained. He got his PhD from

the Berkeley economics program with an interest in econometrics (statistical modeling) in 1981 and worked for a time at the Federal Reserve Bank of San Francisco. I take some credit for exploiting his boredom with economics and enticing him to teach marketing for us and start some research in our area. He subsequently became a professor at the University of Washington.

Bob's interest in marketing was solidified by our first study (with Jim Carman) published in *Journal of Marketing Research* in 1982. We found

Bob Jacobson

that there was little evidence of any advertising to sales influence in a database involving six cereal brands. We also showed that that there was also little evidence of any sales to advertising influence either (increased sales sometimes leads to increased advertising budgets). This finding stimulated Jim and me to examine the evidence that advertising may have less impact on sales than is commonly assumed and, as a result, overadvertising might be widespread.

The 1982 article in *JAR* by Jim and me (titled "Are You Overadvertising?") reviewed sixty field experiments in which advertising expenditures were raised or reduced and some seventy statistical studies of the relationship between advertising expenditures and sales. One conclusion was that in many contexts sales would not be affected even if advertising was sharply increased or decreased, suggesting that overadvertising was prevalent. The article also chronicled the difficulties of such research. Statistical studies, for example, suffer because there is usually not enough variation in advertising to trigger a sales response. For some reason John Little of MIT (there was once serious talk about putting him up as the marketing candidate for a Nobel Prize) picked up on this paper and frequently mentioned it. Who reads your articles is important, and John represented the highest audience quality there could be in my world.

Of my tennis-playing coauthors, Bob was by far the best, having played for Cal, one of the strongest college teams. I once beat him when I played a perfect game and he was off. But he was just better than me. He had an awesome forehand and serve. Tactically, I would play a whole match and never hit to his forehand. The problem was that after hitting 200 straight backhands, that stroke would start to get good as well. I also engaged in psychological ploys. Trying to make him self conscious, I would describe his forehand as the frog shot because he would face the net and jump as he hit the ball (ironically, most of the top players like Roddick now also appear to hit forehands in the same way). To attempt to get him to the net where he was vulnerable I would challenge his masculinity or compliment him whenever he ventured up. Nothing really helped.

The best thing about working with Bob was that he would handle the data analysis and use the most suitable and sophisticated models with precision. The worst thing was that he was a great writer, which neutralized my best potential contribution. So my usual role was to obtain data, conceptualize the research direction, act as a sounding board to his ideas, and write letters to the editor and reviewers responding to their criticism (which was usually extensive) and suggestions, protecting them from Bob's impatient and intemperate comments. I recall his being particularly incensed about a reviewer that did not understand a basic statistical concept (multicollinearity does not cause bias—believe me, it is not worth explaining). I had to reword the rather patronizing tutorial he wrote. Another time, when confronted with a less trivial challenge, he asked the *JMR* editor (then at Wisconsin) to ask a top time series expert in the

Wisconsin statistics department to adjudicate the issue—we won the day. He could not resist exposing incompetence and was not always diplomatic about it.

We coauthored a total of ten articles to date, all of which employed statistical analysis of time series data to uncover relationships between variables. Two involved the relationship between brand equity and stock return and will be discussed in the next chapter. One explored the role of risk as defined by the finance community on financial return, and another showed that Japanese investors seemed better informed about accounting information than their U.S. counterparts. We learned from these two efforts that finance researchers are not looking to marketers for insight into their world, especially when some of their models and beliefs are challenged. Among this group of ten articles, two from the 1980s were home runs. Both won the best article award for the *Journal of Marketing* and influenced research and ideas of the day.

The 1985 *JM* article entitled "Is Market Share All That It's Cracked Up to Be?" was a bombshell because it challenged one of the most influential tenets of business strategy and one of the most impressive and accepted empirical findings in our literature. This established finding, that a 1-percent increase in market share would result in a 0.5-percent increase in ROI (Return on Investment), was based on analyses done on the PIMS database. PIMS data, used extensively by academics, contained dozens of variables from over 2,000 businesses that reported annual data over an extended time period. This relationship between market share and profitability and its implications, reported in *HBR* in 1975 by Professor Bob Buzzell of Harvard and some colleagues and in a subsequent book in 1985 by Buzzell and Bradley Gale called *The PIMS Principles*, supported a business strategy model that argued that increasing market share would lead to reduced costs (because of scale and experience effects) and should be a strategic objective.

Bob and I explored the hypothesis that market share and profitability may be jointly caused by other factors such as management skill or luck. If so, the interpretation that the observed relationship between market share and profitability was created by a causal link between the variables would be placed into question. Using the same PIMS database, we controlled for other factors by subtracting the effect represented by the last year's ROI (which should represent management quality since the same management was probably in place during the prior time period), the effect of other variables like advertising and quality, and the short term random changes in market share (that should represent a lucky event that would affect both market share and ROI). We then concluded that the real causal relationship between market share and ROI is more like 0.1% instead of 0.5%—five times less.

The article raised a furor. We got overflow audiences when we presented at conferences and a host of formal and ad hoc criticism from the "owners" of the market share truth. Bob was both clear and humorous when presenting the results. At one point Bob observed that "Buzzell and Gale write that they *are* at a loss to understand the Aaker and Jacobson findings. I agree. They are at a loss to understand our findings." He went on to explain our findings in a clear manner that was in no way hard to understand.

I actually had a great relationship with Professor Buzzell, even back when I was still a graduate student, in part because we were both statisticians. I always respected one of his early papers that showed using ad testing data and a clever analysis that the quality of the ad is four times more important than how much was spent buying space for that ad. He had an illustrious career as a teacher and researcher. However, after our paper appeared, I noticed that Professor Buzzell was distinctly cool to me. I always tried to avoid such tensions. However, he had developed an empirical conclusion using inadequate methodology and ended up committed to a conclusion that was simply untrue and that encouraged executives to make unwise strategy choices. In essence he argued that because large market share companies were more profitable than smaller ones, every firm would benefit by adding share, a conclusion that was naive and deceptive.

The second *JM* article published in 1987 and also based on PIMS data was entitled "The Strategic Role of Product Quality." The quality movement was the hot strategic idea of the 80s. Yet it was understudied in marketing, as were other important strategic, real-world issues. Nobody had really showed that quality investments would pay off and, if so, how. Was it, for example, by supporting higher prices or higher market share? To explore the impact of quality, we proposed using a model (termed the vector autoregressive model) that looked at the causal effects among a set of variables based on the premise that last period's results will influence this period's and not the reverse. Thus, the impact of lagged perceived quality (the perceived quality during the prior time period), lagged share, lagged perceived price level, lagged cost, and lagged ROI on ROI was modeled. The impact of these same five lagged variables on perceived quality, market share, and perceived price level were also examined. As a result we could learn, for example, the impact of perceived quality on ROI.

The research showed that perceived quality does, on average, affect ROI. It further suggests that the enhanced ROI is in part due to a price premium obtained by the higher perceived quality. There was no relationship between perceived quality and market share; on average, perceived quality does not lead to higher market share. This article did not create controversy because, in contrast to the market share paper, there was not an accepted finding in the literature with which it took issue. However, it did fill a significant hole in quality research, an area recognized as important. It also introduced a powerful methodology (the vector autoregressive model) that was actually identical to that used in the Aaker/Day article of 1972 (then termed the recursive model). Bob was more capable of describing and defending it then I had been and the Frank Bass-led detractors had mellowed.

Strategy

When I was at TI, I was interested in business strategy. Setting the business direction and evaluating acquisitions seemed like the ideal job. I always thought in the back of my mind that I would get into strategy, but it was clear that the route to a dissertation and to publishing in the top academic journals did not lead in that direction. A more specialized focused research thrust around marketing was the way to go. However, in the early eighties I had a "spare" research direction and decided to explore strategy. When entering a new area, most would start with a modest research effort. I started by teaching a course and writing a book.

The book, which was published in 1984, came out with two titles. The soft cover was *Strategic Market Management* (*SMM*) and was aimed at the college text market. The hard cover, called *Developing Business Strategies* (*DBS*), targeted the business bookstore market. They were the same book. The two-book strategy was the brainchild of Rich Esposito, the then editor of John Wiley. The two markets involve different sales teams and require different discount rates (the college discount is typically 20% where the business market needs much more). It was only in the seventh edition published in 2004 that finally an effort was made to create some cases for the *SMM* book to differentiate it and to justify what had become a much higher price.

The book contributed a host of concepts, structures, and methods to address five strategic challenges—namely how to:

- Conduct an external analysis of the customer, competition, market trends, and technological, cultural, and economic forces.

- Develop sustainable competitive advantages based on assets (such as brand equities or presence in key markets) and competencies (such as skills in product development) that will be relevant over time as the business changes to respond to market trends.

- Create customer-oriented business strategies that involve a customer value proposition that is relevant, meaningful, and sustainable.

- Make sound investment and disinvestment decisions among existing product-market business areas and chart growth directions involving product expansion, market expansion, or diversification.

- Create organizational structures, systems, people, and cultures that will enable the business strategy to succeed.

This book, like my others, had two or three relevant quotes preceding each chapter. It is surprisingly hard (but rewarding) to find good quotes. My favorites from the *SMM* book include:

Plans are nothing, planning is everything.
—Dwight D. Eisenhower

If you don't know where you're going, you might end up somewhere else.
—Casey Stengel

There is nothing more exhilarating than to be shot at without result.
—Winston Churchill

If you don't have a competitive advantage, don't compete.
—Jack Welch

Results are gained by exploiting opportunities, not by solving problems.
—Peter Drucker

There is a tide in the affairs of man which, taken at the flood, leads on to fortune; omitted, all the voyage of their lives is bound in shallows and in miseries. On such a full sea are we now afloat, and we must take the current when it serves, or lose our ventures. [I love this quote, which comes from my favorite play; it is thought-provoking and the wording is simply perfection.]
—William Shakespeare, *Julius Caesar*

I wrote the book because I wanted to write the book. It gave me an excuse to absorb and integrate the writings on strategy from all the disciplines: finance, accounting, organizational behavior, and economics, as well as marketing and strategy itself. There was no thought as to potential market or impact on my already confused academic image. However, it hit just at the right time. The marketing curriculum needed a strategy course and *SMM* filled a need for a supporting book. During succeeding years, several prominent academics have written competitive books that failed to gain traction. Recent editions gained an outstanding teacher's manual by Jim Prost, a gifted strategy teacher. The seven editions have sold over 220,000 copies in English, and there have been around thirteen translations. Sales of translations are difficult to determine, but it is known that the Japanese translation sold over 22,000 books. Each edition changes about 20%, so the seventh is very different from the first

In addition to the articles with Bob Jacobson, I wrote eight additional strategy articles, two of which are notable. One, written with George Day, was entitled "The Perils of High-Growth Markets" and was published in *Strategic Management Journal* in 1986. The conventional wisdom is that businesses should invest in growth markets because share gain will be easier and be worth more as the growth materializes. During a break in a conference, George and I got together and simply asked what was wrong with these assertions. We ended up challenging the assumptions and identifying risks, such as competition may be more intense than expected, distribution may be unavailable, resources may not support a high growth rate, technology may change, or the growth simply might not happen. We essentially wrote this paper in under two hours, while most papers require many months if not years to create. We subsequently tried to duplicate this feat but never did.

The other notable paper, entitled "Managing Assets and Skills: The Key to a SCA (Sustainable Competitive Advantage)," which appeared in *California Management Review* (*CMR*) 1989, was extremely influential in directing the next phase of my research. My work in business strategy led me to the belief that executives were too short-term oriented, driven by the pressure to deliver immediate profits in part to satisfy stock market investors who rely on quarterly earnings (and usually lack information about strategy) and in part to gain personal advancement by showing profit gains. What should be done about this short-term orientation? My answer: executives need to take a strategic perspective, improve their motivation and ability to create and manage assets and competencies that will be the basis for future success, and reduce their preoccupation with short-term financials. I wanted to participate in this direction. But what assets and competencies? And how should they be managed and measured?

In my *CMR* article, some 250 executives, interviewed by students in my strategy class, were asked to identify their SCA. Of the thirty-two or so SCA's mentioned, the number one most identified was "reputation for quality," number three was "name recognition," and number ten was "customer base." All these were elements of a brand. Since I had no background or competence to study customer service, good management, cost control, or any of the other SCA's on the list, I decided to advance the cause of moving managers from a short-term to strategic orientation by focusing on brands. I was committed to help executives understand why brand assets should be developed—and to show them how to do it.

In summary, the 80s were much more productive than the 70s. The research resulted in thirty-two articles, of which thirteen were in "A" academic journals and three were qualified as home-run articles based on the attention they received. In contrast, in the 70s I published seventeen articles, twelve of which were in "A" academic journals—and five of those were published in the early years of the decade from my thesis. There was one home-run article, and that was the one on consumerism that was "off-brand" because it did not support my image as a quantitative model builder. The strategy text of the 80s was more innovative and successful than the readings books and the advertising and marketing research texts of the 70s.

However, I was still not well defined. From my base of quantitative modeling I had veered off to being something of an experimental psychologist with the work on warmth. The behavioral group in marketing never accepted me; I felt like the outsider when I was at their ACR conference meetings. I never got invited to go to dinner with the "in-group." Bob and I ventured into finance theory and were definitely on the outside looking in. Two worthwhile (in my view) articles were ignored by the finance community and were unknown in marketing. Further, the strategy research and writing were other very off-brand departures. So I had yet to put it together, but on the horizon was the brand equity umbrella that would finally do just that.

Talks, Seminars, and Consulting

The 80s involved four more trips to Japan. My core sponsor on each trip was now a marketing research firm that arranged an open lecture for me and involved me in some of their client work. In addition, each trip Hiro and Jiro would arrange some four to six company lectures as well. It was great for the ego. I would be treated as a rock star in part because they are just such good hosts and in part because my talks would be built up. And my name was starting to mean something in Japan (unlike the U.S. and the rest of the world) because well-known people (namely teams headed by Jiro) translated all my books. It was really a trip living the star life, if only for a few days.

I was invited to give a series of lectures on strategy (based on my book) in New Zealand by a large firm that made cement and other products. I flew to a remote northern island in a small plane and bombed; it was one of the few times that my presentation just fell flat. There was no energy in the audience, and nobody came up afterward to say how helpful it was. My material on strategy was fairly pedestrian (although fine for students), and my ability to link my models and processes to what was really troubling them was limited. My executive teaching at that point was simply not very refined (it would improve in the 90s). Further, I followed one of the foremost strategic writers and lecturers in the world, C. K. Prahaled. He apparently was so inspiring that they got emotional. I did not look good by comparison. Ironically, around fifteen years later, when I was talking brands, I again followed C.K. and this time had indicators that my material was received better than his. But that was not the case in New Zealand. I was glad to have that behind me.

I was joined in New Zealand by Jan and Kay. A trip highlight was when Jan and I got to helicopter ski in the South Island, our first time. The helicopter would surge toward a ridge beyond which there would be a gorge hundreds of yards or more below. The feeling was akin to being in a roller coaster, except with fantastic vistas. Jan skied well even when she broke a ski and had to make a run on one ski. The trip also featured a ride on a flat-bottom speedboat, which gave you the illusion that you were going to hit huge rocks. We bypassed bungee jumping although Jan was tempted, but we did visit by plane the fjords of New Zealand, flying over the famous five-day Milford Track hiking trail. The setting of Milford has Norwegian-quality fjords next to rainforest beaches. Incredible.

One nice thing about being an academic is that you can go to conferences anywhere in the world. I rarely availed myself of that opportunity because it always seemed to be justified only if you wanted a tourist experience. But I did go in 1989 to Athens to speak at the European Marketing Conference, which is always noted for having an event or dinner that each host city tries to make special. Kay and I took a few days to see Greece, and I recall that the driving was scary (oncoming cars seemed to want to span the middle line), the food (Greek salad) was good, and the antiquities were breathtaking. I ran in the same venue as the ancient Olympics, although much slower.

From 1975 to 1985 I was an expert witness for a legal case or two each year. The cases were universally interesting and financially rewarding because the cost of an expert was usually small in the context of the case. My last case involved a firm that had invented a new golf ball that had been ruled illegal by the USGA. My task was to design a survey of golf pros to support an estimate of what sales would have been had the ball been approved. My testimony helped trigger a substantial award and a celebration that turned out to be short-lived, as the verdict was overturned by the judge the next day.

Some enjoy the give and take of being on the stand, but I was not among this group. I was bothered by the fact the the lawyers were not interested in the truth but only in tripping me up. And I really hated the uncertainty as to what would be asked. I would rehearse possible questions and my answers again and again. I engaged in what is called obsessive thinking. After it was over, I was surprised to find that a residue of the anxiety and stress lingered for months. I decided that, for me, it was not worth it and retired from the expert testimony field.

I became part of an advisor team for a small software company called Mondrian (after the famous modern art painter) that made a windows software product that was superior to that of Microsoft. It was smaller in terms of memory space and more powerful in that it could manage more windows at the same time. Nathan Myrvold, a brilliant physicist, started the firm with some colleagues that had been studying black holes at Princeton and thus were called the "black-hole gang," a term made famous by the movie *Butch Cassidy and the Sundance Kid* with Robert Redford and Paul Newman. It was challenging and interesting to meet with the team and the advisors, a group of bright and interesting people. We met in a run-down house in Oakland that had wires and monitors in every room. We tried to get computer firms to adopt our product with, ultimately, no success. So the firm was sold to Microsoft, which was motivated to acquire Nathan (who went on to become the guru of Bill Gates), his team, and the product, which, I believe, became the basis for the next generation of Windows. I gave the stock to my girls and had them sell it so the proceeds got taxed at their low rate. If I had retained the stock it would be worth millions today. I wish I had not been so clever.

Berkeley

In 1981 I was named the J. Gary Shansby Professor of Marketing Strategy. In all my years at Berkeley I only considered exploring another school once although I did get overtures from Northwestern, Harvard, Wharton, MIT, and others. I just never felt comfortable getting offers when I was so attached to Berkeley, even though I knew that an external offer was the only way to gain a competitive salary. In the fall of 1981, I was approached by Minnesota about the Carlson Chair. In those days chairs were not common; there were only two chair holders at the Berkeley Business School, and few in the rest of the campus. I had

fond memories of life in Minnesota—lake life in the summer and
white Christmases and skiing in the winter. Summer mosquitoes
and humidity and the long, cold winters sort of faded in my mind.
Further, I had friends and relatives in Minneapolis. So I was
prepared, with Kay's support, to visit Minneapolis and seriously
explore the job.

Before I actually made the trip, Dean Budd Cheit called me
into his office (that in itself was a novel event) and said that the
committee to name a marketing professor to the newly formed
Shansby chair had unanimously and enthusiastically concluded
that I was the best choice. I was stunned because I assumed that
I would be third or fourth in line for the chair behind my more
senior colleagues. I had absolutely no expectation that I, as the
junior person, would be the choice. I could not very well pursue
the Minnesota job after this honor was thrust upon me. The
chair, in addition to the honor, had an income that allowed me to
have one or two month's summer salary, to hire a research assistant, and to buy assorted equipment like computers.

Most chair donors have no link to the chairholders (indeed,
many are deceased), but I got to know Gary Shansby, then an
executive with Shakley, a vitamin supplement firm, and later a
venture capitalist specializing in consumer products firms (he
bought and turned around Famous Amos Cookies). He was both
interesting and stimulating, and I enjoyed having periodic lunches
with him through the years. His huge Shakley office, tastefully
furnished with antiques, just blew me away. I'm not sure I have
seen another more impressive. A black-tie dinner came with the
chair, and it was clearly designed to impress the donor and other
school benefactors, not the chairholder. My talk was short, but I
did suggest that vitamins were a part of any success I might have
achieved.

An aside about Budd Cheit ... during my tenure at Berkeley
I had a series of good deans who made progress toward important goals in the face of a formidable campus bureaucracy that
was biased against the business school because they resented our
high salaries (compared to the campus, not our competition) and
because they believed (with some reason) that our faculty was
not up to Berkeley standards. Budd Cheit, the dean from 1976

to 1982 and again from 1990 to 1991, was a cut above, a top 1% executive. He could do it all—set priorities, establish goals, get buy-in, stimulate progress, get things accomplished, measure results, raise money, inspire, and give wonderful talks. It was such a pleasure to see him in action. And he was humorous. He once observed that economics professors who understood why they should make more than English professors sometimes had a hard time understanding why finance professors earned more than they did. When he took over the athletic department in 1993 for a year, the people there said that more was accomplished in his first four months than in the prior four years. I have since been a student of leadership and have never ceased to be amazed what a difference it makes when you have a leader that is exceptionally strong or weak.

Although my salary was chronically behind my peers at other schools, I did progress. I moved to step V full professor in 1981, the final step for many professors. In 1982 I took a turn at being the head of the somewhat dysfunctional (because of Franco's unpredictable behavior) marketing group. Not much was accomplished under my leadership, but we did have efficient meetings. In 1984 I was advanced to Step VI, which required evidence of international stature from top scholars. In 1987 I advanced to step VII, then the highest academic level at Berkeley. A step VIII was subsequently added, and I was promoted to that level in 1995.

In 1984, I started teaching a course in strategy around the *Strategic Market Management* book. It was basically a business strategy course dealing in top-level issues such as selecting new product markets to enter and developing assets and skills to be the basis of sustainable competitive advantages. But it viewed strategy as being driven by the external marketplace so it had a marketing perspective, unlike strategy courses in finance, organizational behavior, or economics. It was well received and always oversubscribed, in part because I limited enrollment to thirty-five students and only offered two sections.

As I was developing the strategy course I decided that I would have group projects and devote two days to their presentation. My motivation was to save work because that would be two days that I would not have to prepare a class. I was stunned to learn that the projects were the most effective part of the class, better than lectures, cases, or guests. This experience was a good lesson about the power of learning by doing and the pedagogical value of having social stimulation and support.

The marketing faculty situation at Berkeley did not improve in the early 1980s. We did make another excellent hire in 1986, Kevin Keller, but he, like Rick Bagozzi a few years earlier, was enticed away by Stanford. Kevin stayed only one year. Kevin's leaving coupled with the failure of any assistant professor to gain tenure since my elevation in 1972 caused the school in the spring of 1987 to ask a three-person outside review team to evaluate the marketing group. They concluded that it was bankrupt and in need of a savior, someone from the outside who would be able to stabilize the group and lead the recruiting.

That savior was found in the form of Russ Winer, who arrived in the fall of 1988 (a picture of Russ appears in the next chapter). I was instrumental in getting Russ so have always taken indirect credit for his success. He was not a research superstar, although he had solid articles under his belt, but he was clearly an institution builder. After Russ arrived, we started our upward climb and ultimately created and maintained a strong market-ing faculty. Actually, our first "rebuild" hire came in the fall of 1987 just before Russ arrived in the form of Itamar Simonson, a promising consumer behavior experimentalist. Itamar proved to be an exceptionally successful researcher and was hired away by Stanford, but not until 1993. We hired Rashi Glazer from Columbia (an innovative thinker with several important articles to his credit and a great teacher) in 1989, Miqual Villas-Boas (a top quantitative economist) in 1991, and Tülin Erdem (who has turned out to be a research star, an excellent teacher, and a gifted administrator) in 1993. All three were sought after and all have stayed. Actually, maintaining is much easier than creating because momentum is so important and people want to join a quality group that is going the right direction.

Germany

One of the great things about being a professor is that you can pretty much go anywhere in the world for any length of time as a visitor. Many of my friends regularly spend a year at some other school. I have always been of the opinion that life in Northern California is just too good. I was involved in the kids' activities, Cal football and basketball, and my tennis events. Life was good and a sojourn abroad would be risky—what if it was boring and lonely? So I stayed home. There were two exceptions.

I became a visiting professor in Aoyama Gakuin University in Tokyo in 1991, where I taught a course on strategic management that was received well by the students. Kay and I moved into an apartment and became part of the community—shopping at the local grocery, jogging around the Aoyama district (where the small office buildings were architectural gems; the land was so expensive that a lot of money went into the buildings), visiting the local modern art gallery, and doing some upscale shopping where simple house dresses were going for $700. But that was only for two weeks or so. My visit to Germany was more substantial.

I became the Chamber of Commerce Visiting Professor at Goethe University in Frankfurt for six weeks in the spring of 1987. The experience was an effort, but it was also memorable and worthwhile. I always felt I should have done more visiting gigs.

We rented a home in Eppenhain, one of many quaint villages outside of Frankfurt. In commuting, it was a challenge to cope with the realization that 100 mph can be considered slow and to navigate the traffic circles—once in one it was not clear how to get off. The home, charming and cozy, was next to a large open space where we played a lot of Frisbee. Life in the suburbs was pleasant and very German—it was a kick to drive a few minutes to an old castle. We acclimated to German food but never fell in love with it—we craved a simple green salad. Frankfurt had a wonderful art gallery on the river, an English-speaking play-house, and many good restaurants. The most charming aspect of Frankfurt was the many small towns like Eppenhaim nestled in rolling hills that were sometimes only a few miles apart.

At the university, I had a nice office in which I worked productively on the second edition of my strategy book. It was fascinating to get to know one of two marketing professors, Klaus Kaas. Klaus was doing the work of what would require three or four professors in Berkeley. In most German universities, there are

Prof. Klaus Kaas,
Goethe University

only a few professors, each managing a team of assistants that do much of the teaching. I could not believe his teaching and administrative workload. He had a nearby flat that was nice but a bit austere. My teaching was fun, but over half of the students had trouble with English that inhibited interaction. The chamber got some value as I gave a businessperson talk as well. Kay, the kids, and I got to see how the diplomatic core entertained when an elegant dinner for us was hosted by the U.S. Consul General. We learned a bit about Goethe (who has been termed the Shakespeare of Germany) and were presented with his bust at my going-away party.

Life on the weekend was side trips. We went to Munich, Heidelberg, Tier, Rothenburg, and Cologne. We saw old medieval towns, visited cathedrals, partied at beer halls, and, most of all experienced a more relaxing culture and lifestyle. On one of our most memorable trips, not far from Frankfurt, we visited some elaborate baths with a huge swimming pool, steam rooms, and on and on. The unique part was that everyone was nude. It took some getting used to—walking around and pretending not to stare. We learned that not everyone looks good nude, and that covering up is not that critical after an acclimation period.

One side trip was to the Alsace area where we had a four-hour-plus lunch with a researcher, Werner Kroeber-Riel, whom I respected a lot. I'm not sure that I ever in my life had a lunch half that long. The courses and conversation kept coming. There is much to be said for that lifestyle—where efficiency takes back seat to savoring the experience. His take on vacations was interesting. Once he spent three weeks in the middle of the Sahara Desert. Another time he vacationed in Antarctica. Nothing like our vacations. Kroeber-Riel was one of the early proponents of physiological measures of audience response. He argued that consumers can't and/or won't tell what really motivates them to buy.

IHK-GASTPROFESSUR

AMERICAN MANAGEMENT
Prof. Dr. David A. Aaker

University of California, Berkeley

Seminar on:	Vom Mittwoch, dem 15.4.1987 bis Mittwoch, den
Strategic	20.5.1987, 14.00 – 16.00 Uhr, Raum 430B, Haupt-
Market Management	gebäude (Teilnahme nach persönlicher Anmel-
	dung)

Dave is teaching strategy

In one of his studies he showed that if a brand is connected in an ad that engenders an emotional response like eroticism (triggered by pictures of nudes), the next day exposure to the brand name alone could precipitate an emotional response.

The castles were fun, especially when they had a story behind them. Who resided in the dungeon? How was the siege overcome? Thanks to a Goethe colleague, we met a real prince in a real castle. He told us of discovering some beautiful artwork underneath a wall covering when engaged in a cleaning project. That would definitely not happen to us.

Jolyn, then twelve, was enrolled into the Frankfurt International School and made local friends, including her first boyfriend. We drove her to and from school and to friends' homes as well. It got Jolyn and us into Frankfurt life.

The DeJonghes joined us for the first part of the trip. On the way to Frankfurt, Jan, the DeJonghes, and I visited Jennifer who was in Grenoble as part of her year abroad. Her host family had an unusual father (who occasionally walked around naked), but to us and to Jennifer they were gracious hosts. The high point was skiing at Les Deux Alpes about ninety miles away in the French Alps. I was struck by the breathtaking drive up to the ski area and

A medieval meal—with Jennifer and Jolyn

by the area's open terrain—no trees. However, the trails became dicey with no trees to guide when a heavy snowfall made the visibility nil—and we skied by some serious gorges. The girls tried monoskiing—it was tougher than snowboarding, the popularity of which was years away.

Another trip that included the DeJonghes was a leisurely boat trip down the Rhine with incredible places to stay. One lunch was on a hill overlooking the Rhine. Another featured a medieval dinner. We were dressed in costumes and served raw whole vegetables. The evening featured dancing and drinking—everyone put their glasses upside down on their head to prove they were empty. It was a trip into the distant past.

We had visitors besides the DeJonghes. Jennifer spent ten days with us and was joined by Leslie Jones, a friend with whom Jennifer would spend the fall of 1987 in Paris. An art history major, Leslie upgraded my knowledge of art and fielded some tough questions. Once in a French gallery she told me that the fashions helped you interpret the painting. Years later in New York, she explained that a MOMA painting (part of her exposition of "repulsive" art) that I could not understand was actually a vagina with teeth. We also received some of our exchange students, Hanne from Denmark and Frederick and Pelle from Sweden.

Jan, Jennifer, Jolyn,
and Leslie Jones in Frankfurt

California Casualty

In 1982 I was asked to join the board of California Casualty, a top-100 property and casualty insurance company. My friend from my Stanford PhD days, George Parker, referred me. California Casualty was run by Tom Brown, a third-generation CEO (the fourth generation is in the wings—a most unusual situation) who special-ized in serving groups such as the California Teacher's Associations. The company has always been well run and successful, even when addressing challenges such as the stock market collapse or the passage of an insurance regulation law. There has never been a stress meltdown of any kind. In 1989, the firm cel-ebrated its seventy-fifth anniversary with a black-tie party.

California Casualty 75th
anniversary party

This job, which I still hold (and will until mandatory retirement at age seventy-two), has been a joy. The people on the board are bright, interesting, and very different from my normal set of friends and colleagues. Having George on the board is a plus because he has a great sense of humor, and we can trade Stanford/Berkeley shots when the discussion slows. Participating in the strategy of the firm and in the task of being a board member with the oversight responsibilities is worthwhile and stimulating. The meetings, which occur five times a year, are always a welcome break from the routine.

The Family

The eighties saw Jennifer grow from thirteen to twenty-three, Jan from eleven to twenty-one, and Jolyn from six to sixteen. It was a time of growing, maturing, and experiencing. I was very involved in their lives at several levels—Kay sometimes suggests too much. The girls and their friends were so generous in including me in their activities, whether it was meals, movies, biking, skiing, or vacations. So I got to know their friends well. This generosity increased as they became college students. I still count many of them as my friends as well. Not many fathers get that opportunity. In part, I suppose, it was a shared family obligation to entertain me because I (like my mother) had a very limited tolerance for alone time when no activity was planned. But I also

Alice Tang

Carol Tang

feel that they really enjoyed my company (and perhaps my willing-ness to pay).

There is a long list of friends that passed through the lives of the three girls and myself. A partial list would include friends of Jolyn—Jamie Vest, Kelly Nykodym, Burke Cahill, Jenn Faeth, Amy (Poco) Little, and the members of about a dozen of Jolyn's soccer teams; Jan's friends—Michelle Meyers, Robin Forsberg, Megan Lynch, Babs and Libet Wolf, Wendy Hazzard, Debbie Bonardi, Megan Hagglund, and Amy and Todd Berryhill; and Jennifer's friends—Claudia Imkamp, Renee Chang, Leslie Jones, Susan Rolander, Aimee Drolet, Kathy Yeung, David Butler, and Michael O'Connor. Two of the many that were special during the eighties were Alice and Carol Tang. Close friends of Jennifer and Jan, they were like daughters to me, and we had many moments, including the time that we celebrated Alice's Miss Chinatown event and when we got Carol on the ski hill.

During the eighties, I first noticed that it was not so easy to give compliments out. If I told one of the girls that she really looked fit, you would think that her sisters would be happy for her. However, their first thought would rather be something like—"Am I considered fat?" or "Why is she the preferred sister?" It gets worse. The complimented sister is likely to think— "Wasn't I always fit? What is the message here?" They take flack for having such an attitude but it persists nevertheless.

We raised three wonderful girls, an accomplishment that, in my view, was about 80% (or more) due to luck (Kay tends to get more credit for our good fortune). If we did anything, it was providing love and support. I did try to encourage the qualities I look for in friends and associates whom I respect and enjoy being with, qualities like having:

- A sense of humor. Being able to laugh with others at yourself provides many opportunities to create good feelings and dissipate tensions.
- Opinions based on being informed about issues. Someone without opinions is usually boring.

- A sincere interest in others. People that are self-centered and have no interest in others wear thin after a short time.

- Empathy, being sensitive about the feelings of others and concerned about those that are in difficulty. Selfish people lose the respect of others.

- A zest for life. It is fun to be around people that are positive and enthusiastic.

- A passion for something. It makes you happy and interesting.

- Integrity—being true to yourself and to your friends, being someone people can count on.

- Appreciation for what you have. Pride and envy are both dangerous. As noted in chapter two, my retelling of the fact that my grandfather slept with four siblings in a loft in a kitchen gets boring—but it makes a point.

With respect to tactics, my philosophy, especially when they were facing social pressures, was to virtually never say no (unless safety was involved) but to put huge guilt trips on them: "You can do it, but I would be disappointed," or, "You should think through the implications of this action." The strategy was in part due to my instinct that they would dislike hearing "no" but also in part because I felt they had to learn to make choices for themselves even if it seemed a bit risky at the time. Discipline was also heavy on guilt. Jolyn still talks about how difficult it was to "discuss" some transgression, deal with her parents' disappointment, and propose a penalty.

During the summers I would discourage working just to make money, recalling my unproductive months with uninspiring jobs. However, I also could not stand seeing them waste time. So about three weeks into the summer I would start drawing up reading lists and "improvement" assignments. One year I decided that everyone, including Kay, would learn speed-reading and, to be efficient, I would teach it. I bought texts for everyone, assigned homework, and scheduled classes. I assembled chairs in the patio and prepared lectures and exercises. The first class was OK, although attention would occasionally stray, but subsequent classes disintegrated. Not only was the effort a failure, but it also became a source of ridicule. Another time I insisted that Jan learn to type at a certain standard before she could join her friends for a graduation trip. That one worked better, as she was very motivated.

Muffin, an energetic black poodle, arrived when Jolyn was around four and became an important member of our family. She is now buried on our hill with a suitable marker. Muffin was smart, knowing exactly what she was supposed to do and avoid. But when it came to food she had no willpower; she would eat whatever and then slink away looking extremely guilty, usually going under Jolyn's bed, her ultimate refuge. It was there that she had her two litters of pups. There is nothing cuter than new puppies, but nothing as messy either. I think Muffin got everyone into dogs, and Jolyn's ridgeback Oscar may be a legacy of that love.

Jennifer and Jan each had to take responsibility for one dinner each week. Jennifer did a great job. Her specialty was quiches, but she could make a variety of acceptable dishes. Jan, on the other hand, might open a can of tomato soup and make toast. Ironically, Jan is now an incredible, organized cook whether it is a casual or gourmet setting, while Jennifer does not cook but, rather, has cereal and take-out as staples. She doesn't even make quiche. Go figure. Childhood training in my view is vastly overrated.

When Jennifer and Jan were in high school, I became the president of the Parent's Club, my sole effort to be active in the community. My major contribution was to change the way the money we raised was distributed. Before I arrived, the club had committees that would agonize over how the money from our fund-raising activities would be spent. There would be proposals from teachers that would be evaluated in detail. My suggestion, which was eventually accepted, was simply to let the principal do it. I argued successfully that he was competent and willing and there was no reason to make work for everyone that would result in inferior decisions. It was a natural reflection of my tendency to be efficient and avoid unnecessary work.

Time for me is measured from the day in the fall of 1985 when we brought Jennifer to Berkeley. It was a watershed event because a family member left. But it was great that she could be at Berkeley (as opposed to Vanderbilt, the second choice) because it meant we could spend time together. You needed to be assertive at Berkeley, and Jennifer fit. At one point she was ninetieth on the waitlist to get into Phil Tetlock's intro pysch course. One month later she was his RA, and two months later she got the highest final score among 500 students. Amazing.

Jennifer and Renee Chang at Berkeley

I saw a lot of Jennifer during her tenure at Berkeley. She would study in my office and we would have yogurt together. I saw her gravitate toward a psychology major with an eye to becoming a marketing professor (influenced more by several of my friends than me). Renee Chang, her first roommate, amazed everyone by starting major term papers at three in the morning and still getting great grades. It didn't seem fair. Now an assistant district attorney in LA, Renee is one of the several special friends that Jennifer has accumulated. Jennifer and Renee joined a sorority in which most of the girls were homecoming queens (as was Jennifer—a fact that she does not spread around). I got invited to faculty days and the father-daughter dances at her sorority, so I got to know her sorority sisters.

Jennifer was there for me when I fainted in a classroom and went to the emergency room. She was expecting a lunch but instead got a note saying I was in the hospital. I was OK—it was a reaction to a hot closed room—but it was a scare. It was remarkable that this incident happened when she was so close.

This event had two good outcomes. First, I could tell concerned friends that I was among the few who know for sure that I had clear arteries. Second, I was treated by Dr. Yeung, an informed, insightful, caring physician who has since become my doctor and friend. My previous physician, equally impressive, was

Kaiser's Dr. Phil Fishbacher. Having a physician with whom you have confidence is major for me. Both would probably agree that as a patient I am somewhat high maintenance and require support and patience.

Jennifer, as already noted, spent a year abroad to experience the world and learn French. In the fall she moved from her Grenoble family to Paris where she shared a flat with Leslie Jones and studied at the Sorbonne. One reaction to the trip was her tendency to describe some men as "so French," which was not a compliment. In the summer she toured with a friend and her friend's boyfriend, an arrangement that was a bit awkward. During a low point (not too long after she was mugged in a Spanish park), I called her and said I would come over to London and spend time with her. It was such a treasure to hear her joy and relief to know that she would have some family company. We had an emotional reunion at the airport and a wonderful vacation. On the weekend, we rented a car and drove to Bath, where we saw the Roman baths, a play, and generally enjoyed the English countryside. Back in London, we saw *Les Mis* for the first time and were blown away. Jennifer really needed someone, and it was good to feel wanted.

Special days with the girls went on. Plays, skiing, basketball games, bookstores, San Francisco, and even shopping were on the menu. Jennifer and Jan could always go for a clothes outing, especially when I was buying and the measure of success was how much we could spend in the shortest time. One of the most meaningful days for me was when Jo and I went to a version of *The Fantasticks*. Even at this time, Jennifer's preference for experiences involving urban rather than wilderness settings emerged. During a sisters outing involving camping in nearby Mt. Diablo, she slept in the car.

Two of my Japan trips involved family in addition to Kay, who was a regular. In 1986 the girls joined us. It was really fun to share the Japan experience, so special to me, with the girls. Jennifer and Jan went dancing with some students of Hiro's in Rapoggi. Their blond hair and/or dancing style made them something of a curiosity. They had an audience—a picture-taking audience that mimicked their dance moves. Several escorted them home despite having no ability to communicate in English. That was the year I forgot my visa and created an enormous hassle for my hosts. When we were discussing the problem, Jan suggested that we just use MasterCard and not worry about Visa (I used the story in my talks). Jolyn ate rice. We would ask her if sushi is OK, and she affirmed that any restaurant was OK as long as they served rice. She literally lived for a week on white rice. The trip was during Thanksgiving, and we got to celebrate with a traditional dinner arranged by an American family living there. The girls all liked the hotel massage and an athletic club near our Shinjuku hotel.

On Sunday we hit Harajuku, one of the trendy Tokyo areas that has, in addition to hundreds of small shops, an outlet for the youth of the city. Guys, called teddy boys, dressed up in black outfits (think Elvis) and danced to boom boxes. Girls engaged in cosplay (costume play) with elaborate costumes. This has been going on in some form for at least twenty-five years. It makes you wonder why.

Two years later, we took Jolyn, Ida, Elin (our Norweign exchange student), and Katie and Kim Schepman, the twin daughters of Bob and Pattiann Schepman. Pattiann, an excellent teacher and a wonderful person, was the first teacher that shared a class with Kay. I tried to get them into Japanese culture. One vehicle was the sumo digest that provides a summary of the day's events. Since the action in any bout rarely lasts more than a few seconds, a half-hour show can cover a lot of ground. They had trouble appreciating the athleticism of 500-pound wrestlers. The whole group went to Korea to do some serious shopping.

Back home, we developed—nurtured in large part by Kay and Marty—a whole set of traditions that meant a lot to all of us. At Easter, there was the Easter egg hunt with the DeJonghes, Schepmans, and others, where eggs with people's names on them would contain prizes. The event was more fun with little kids, but it persisted even when the kids got older. On Mother's Day we would make a breakfast. Harry Bruno, Marty's dad, would make a special gin fizz, and Tom and I, sometimes with friends like Jorg Reinholt or Keith Turner, would make a gourmet breakfast. During the Fourth of July we would find a fireworks event. In the fall, there would be an effort on bikes to find the prettiest tree— we would bring a leaf back to recall it. Marty and Tom sponsored a wine tasting party, a decathlon (where participants would be tested by twelve events including horseshoes, nail pounding, basketball, rope skipping, ping-pong, and more—Tom and I were among the few people who took the competition seriously, an indicator that we might have been a touch too competitive), and a tree-decorating event.

In the mid-1980s, Tom and Marty bought a small resort, Shangra-La, on a rushing river called the North Fork of the Yuba near the gold-mining town of Downieville, about fifty miles north of Auburn, California. We starting going every summer with the whole family, including Ida, Mabel and Gene (her husband), Harry and Edna (Marty's folks), and Tom's father, Everett. Hiking around the mountain lakes and up to the Buttes, mountain peaks that afforded views extending hundreds of miles, provided inspiration and exercise. Bridge, fishing, rafting, shuffleboard, and just sitting by the stream were a nice change of pace. Later mountain biking became a featured activity for Tom and I as Downieville evolved into a mountain biking mecca. During the 90s, a fall couples' weekend was added, where the company of interesting people like Carole and Andy Amstutz, Carol and Don Breuner, Roy Powell and Judy Kirtpatrick, and Dick and Karen Fearon made the conversation sing.

Downieville, a two-and-a-half-mile bike ride along the north fork of the Yuba River from Shangra-La, is a sleepy town of 400, but during the gold rush it was home to 5,000 colorful characters. In the museum are 1850s pictures of the hills around the town completely stripped of trees (used then by builders), a stark comparison to the dense forests that surround the town today. Also in the museum are enormous skis with the most rudimentary bindings that reflect what transportation in nineteenth-century winters was like. I enjoy interacting with the townspeople and learning about the political issue of the day—it amazes me that a quiet town of a few hundred always has local issues people are passionate about.

Christmas was special. Each December, starting in 1975, we would rent a large room at Lake Merritt and have a party with carols after boating and singing on the lake. Somehow the Aaker lack of talent is less apparent on the water. We later changed the venue to the Oakland hills but kept the tradition alive—a tradition now nearing its thirtieth year. Regulars have included the Tom and Mary Welte family, Bonnie (our piano player) and Lee Jamison, the Schepmans, Lissa Boone (who Jan babysat for when she was a precocious child) and family, and any friends of our kids that were available. When the kids were small, a piñata would be part of the evening. On Christmas Eve there would be *Nutcracker* in the morning, special for the girls and me and Paul and Ida as well. In the evening, we would gather at the DeJonghe's, moving to our house on Christmas Day. Tom began the tradition of giving a Tiffany's present to the girls, and I got in the spirit by giving a piece of jewelry to Nicole. The tradition was harder on Tom than me because he had three girls to deal with. On Christmas Day, everyone gave a little talk about what they were thankful for. That resulted in an appreciation for how blessed we are with our extended family.

On New Year's Eve, Tom and I would plan an evening at a bed and breakfast. Because going out seemed to be a hassle, we started cooking a special dinner at home on New Year's Eve that sometimes would be augmented by the efforts of a professional (we would get some high-end take-out), but usually we opted for home-cooked dishes. On one occasion, I imposed a "healthy" home-cooked dish that was awful. Oh well.

We shared vacations each year with the DeJonghe family. In the winter we would always rent a house for skiing, usually at Squaw Valley. The best would be those powder days when the trees would be draped with new snow and the skiing experience would truly turn heavenly. Jo recalls how I would sing and Tom would grunt as we went through the trees. Tom and I would treasure these days, even though during the first years we needed optimal conditions and slope to handle powder with our narrow long skis and lack of technique. One clear morning after a snowfall, I was impatient to get to the slopes and Tom, as usual, did not forego a thorough teeth brushing after a complete breakfast. As a result, our cars got separated and we missed the first run. I always claimed that I was over it, but I did manage to keep bringing the incident up (to partially counter the seemingly endless stories about my forgetfulness). When I lost a tooth a few years ago and needed an implant, I stopped ridiculing his insistent tooth brushing.

Occasionally we would also spend a long weekend at Royal Gorge, a winter wonderland cross-country area that had sleeping facilities out in the country. It was really a chance to commune with nature, as we would ski on trails through beautiful hills and lakes covered with snow. One day Jan and I got lost skiing in a blizzard with little visibility, only to learn from a passing ski patrol person that we were twenty yards from the lodge. Our claim that we cheated death was a tough sell.

There was always a summer vacation for the Aaker/DeJonghe group as well. The J.H. Ranch in Northern California where we rode horses, played tennis, hiked, and fought off bats was the choice for two years. The Fairhills resort in Minnesota where Kay vacationed as a child (and which had activities for all ages) was another. Jo learned to dance thanks to her sisters during one trip to the resort. We all experienced and enjoyed a classic summer thunderstorm while there. Still another vacation was a week at Kona Village in Hawaii. There I took Kay sailing only to be capsized by a swell (I didn't know what a swell was—they did not exist in the Minnesota lakes), an event that Kay still recalls and recounts. In 1990 we followed Jolyn and Nicole on their trip to Sweden and Finland to play soccer. After the soccer was over we went to St. Petersberg and connected with a taxi driver (who made more money than his physician wife) who guided us for three days. We saw supermarkets that contained whole rows of Spam but little meat or vegetables and no beer. There is so much we take for granted. The Harry trips, which I'll describe a little later on, provided summer escapes during other years.

Ida was an important part of our lives during the 80s, joining us on holidays and vacations. I would get to Sun City several times a year, sometimes when a speaking engagement took me to Phoenix, where I would always play golf and hear about how short my trip was. Ida missed Oscar after he passed away in 1982, but she then had nobody to inhibit her urge to travel and she took off with trips all over the world. We had the pleasure of buying her a car, a Honda Accord. She needed a car but would never buy it herself. One day we took her outside to see a new car sitting with a big red ribbon around it. It was a thrilling moment for all. Giving something special is a real high, no question.

The car was purchased during an up period in my real estate investing period. Tom was very active in buying and managing apartment houses. I became a player around 1980 when Tom and I jointly bought a small apartment house in Oakland. We sold it at a big profit a few years later. I then begin investing with a dozen or so others in larger buildings that Tom bought, managed, and acted as a general partner. What followed was a string of successes in Oakland, Denver, and Oklahoma. Tom held several black-tie partners meetings at the Blue Fox, one of the top San Francisco restaurants of the time, to celebrate. The events were terrific; we felt like big-time successful speculators. But real estate is fickle. Some of our subsequent investments in Texas and Oklahoma caused us to lose much, but not all, of our gains when recession and a drop in oil prices hit the area. On the whole I did well and had a great time, but ultimately learned that real estate does not always go up.

My brother Paul started his career as a teacher in Iowa but was always interested in political life. He thus joined the Colorado Teacher's Association as a political lobbyist. Although his job function has changed over the years, he is a fixture at CTA. He made it a point to join Ida in Phoenix several times a year and came to California every Christmas and occasionally during the summer as well. He was popular at Christmas because he had a flare for presents and because he is family and completes the picture.

I enjoyed a great relationship with Kay's mother, Mabel, who was always supportive and easy to be with. In 1980, Mabel married her childhood sweetheart, Gene Jendro, whose court-ship was interrupted nearly fifty years before when Gene left farming in the middle of the Depression. He left the Casselton area to move to Minneapolis to enter the grocery business as a butcher. They took up where they left off—only needing a few months to get reacquainted. Gene once said, "It was like we'd never been apart." What a story! They subsequently enjoyed some twenty years of idyllic companionship in Santa Barbara—cooking, golfing, and just holding hands.

Dave, Ida, Paul

Mabel & Gene—The newlyweds

Mabel was an amazing woman. She grew up with a mother who discovered harsh fundamentalist religion (from a tent revival), took over in 1933 the management of her family's farm (bought by her father in 1893 when he was twenty-seven), learned her husband had colon cancer when she was pregnant with Kay, nursed him through a five-year illness, and raised a daughter by herself. Her story and her reunion with Gene are inspiring.

The Girls—Tennis, Skiing, and Soccer

Being involved in the sports activities of the girls has been a huge part of my life. I saw nearly every tennis match, basketball game, softball game, and soccer game in which the girls played—and many of the practices as well. And they never made me feel that I was too involved—quite the contrary. I was always so proud to see them excelling, learning, and being good representatives of themselves and their teams.

Teaching and coaching was especially rewarding. I had the opportunity to see them enjoy and compete. More importantly, it has been a chance to be part of their lives, to spend time with them, to get to know their friends, to see them relate to others, to share highs and lows, and to see them grow as a people as well as athletes. It has been a great journey for me.

My involvement in tennis and local competition continued through the 80s. And I encouraged (pushed is definitely too strong) all the girls to be involved in tennis. All became doubles players on the high school tennis team. I would watch nearly all their matches, which was nerve-racking because each point had the potential to be crucial. Jennifer made the team as a freshman with a nail-biting challenge match at Sleepy Hollow while I watched from the shadows (a bit pathetic, actually). She became an excellent doubles player (which meant that there were six singles players ranked above her on the team) with a strong two-handed backhand and a great lob. Lacking in competitive fire, she was the ultimate good sport—she used to say "good try" when an opponent double faulted. I played in a half-dozen tennis tournaments with her and did well in several as my net game and her excellent lob and two-handed backhand were not easy to play. It was one of the few times she seemed to enjoy serious tennis.

Jan was in Japan with me as her freshman tryouts were starting. To get her prepared, I created footwork and racket preparation drills that we conducted in our Hotel Okura room (a bit over the top, I know). Jan became a good doubles player with an excellent net game. Before high school, she went twice to a tennis camp in Santa Cruz with her friend Kari Shepman. I recall bringing them and watching them warm up. If Kari had to move a step to hit the ball she simply let it go by. That struck me as odd, but she never did understand my suggestion that moving to the ball might make the warm-up more useful. They had a great social time, but tennis was definitely secondary.

Without doubt, Jolyn had the best forehand and serve of the group. I taught her a two-handed forehand in a moment of inspiration and desperation because her forehand was holding her back. I had her choke up enough that she could get two fingers of her left hand on the racket (a technique used by someone I played with). From the first shot with perfect shoulder rotation, her shot became powerful, reliable, and pretty to watch. It was without question the high point of my instructional career. She also had a picture serve (achieved with a long series of lessons from a top coach). She won the club under-twelve tennis tournament, beating the pro's daughter, who went on the play for Cal. She (unenthusiastically) played in some regional tournaments and for the high school team but again did not enjoy pressure points. One of my contributions was to keep the high school coach (who liked to verbalize clichés) away from her during matches so she would not get irritated and distracted.

Jennifer was an excellent skier, and her technique became polished during winters at Grenoble when she would bus up to the slopes nearly every weekend. Jolyn skied well enough but decided early on with Nicole to learn snowboarding—a sport she mastered, at least to my eye. Jan had a real flare for skiing. She was just a natural. Her ability was refined when she spent a year being a ski instructor (to three to five-year-olds) and waitress in Aspen, hitting one hundred days of skiing. The Aaker/DeJonghe family spent a week there with her. That is where Tom and I were stunned to learn that we could not keep up with our kids. It hit us on our first run when our kids shouted up to us from the bottom of a steep run asking if we were OK. What's wrong with that picture? We were always the experts. At least, I thought, I would finally get coaching from Jan that would be a payback for all those years of teaching her. Unfortunately, Jan could ski beautifully, but it was all instinct; she could not verbalize how she skied or give me one pointer. Bummer.

Jolyn turned out to be a terrific athlete. In elementary school she was always chosen first in the coach's draw in soccer, basketball, and softball. In softball she was an exceptional pitcher. I spent hours coaching her as she refined her pitching style; it was a both fun and rewarding to observe her talent. However, she considered softball boring and disliked the pressure of clutch pitches. It did not help when an opposing coach yelled at her for not toeing the rubber correctly. In basketball, she was a talented

Jolyn as a softball pitcher

ball handler and shooter (she learned early on our backyard basket that was two feet lower than normal). As an eighth-grader, she did well against the star high school guard (the coach's daughter) in some drills at a summer camp. Her two teammates in junior high went on to start on the high school team, and it is likely that Jolyn would have as well had she gone in that direction. However, soccer was her sport.

Jolyn had exceptional soccer skills: aggressiveness, quick feet, ball control, moving without the ball, and an ability to use both feet. She was particularly good at seeing the field and making good decisions. And she had an attitude. When she got beat,

Jolyn at Davis

and it wasn't often, she went into high gear to get the ball back. Throughout her fourteen-year career, she was always a good role model, often winning the "Coaches Award" or being named captain. I frequently told her that she should appreciate her special talent. Few get to excel at the highest level.

The first four years were spent with a very inadequate but involved coach. My teams would bunch around the ball (I never did understand how another coach got those kids to spread out). Jo was one of the best ball handlers. Even in the third grade, she would juke five or six players only to have the seventh get in her way. In the seventh grade she moved up to a traveling team and I got demoted to assistant coach. My high point as an assistant coach came when I pulled the goalie, a decision that led to a goal and a victory against a heavily favored team with a vastly superior coach. I still have a ball signed by the team to commemorate the day.

Seeing young women adjust to different social contexts was fascinating. Once, we were playing in a Sacramento tournament against a rough team from a community very different from Orinda. One girl on that team was foul-mouthed and vocal, particularly to Kim Levitt, one of our best players, who eventually played for USF. Kim, after ignoring her for a considerable time, finally turned to her and calmly said, "You have thick thighs." That stopped her cold. I would never have thought of that tack. The trips were a good chance to get to know the girls. We really got to know them during that ten-day, three-country trip to Sweden in 1990 with Jolyn's under-sixteen team.

At sixteen Jolyn joined the premier league, which housed the top players in the state, and my coaching talents were no longer requested. In the premier league, Jolyn, in two memorable games, shut down a player who later started for North Carolina, a perennial Division I power. We found out later that the coach of one of Jolyn's premier teams had gotten involved with one of the players. That was a shock to say the least.

Jolyn's ability to excel at the next level always surprised me. At one point I thought she should be a goalie because of her reflexes and because I assumed she lacked the talent to play in the field at the highest level. I was always underestimating her.

I wondered if she could make the high school team, particularly since a back problem restricted her during tryouts. In fact, I didn't bother to come at the start of her first high school game because I thought she would be a substitute. Instead, she was a starting middle halfback and went on to be second team all-league as a freshman. I recall watching one game that year and hearing a spectator yell to the coach, "Put back number sixteen, you are getting killed in the middle!" That same year, Jolyn told the coach that it was unfair to use your hip to get position on a throw-in and broke up the team, who knew she used that maneuver more than anyone. During her senior year, her team got to the finals of the high school regional competition where she competed (and lost) against her future college teammate and best friend, Jenn Faeth.

I created a video to sell Jolyn to college coaches. She did have offers at Division I schools, but she decided that Division II was more comfortable and that UC Davis, where Jan had gone, was an appealing setting. So Davis it was, and I started the eighty-minute commute to see games. After playing a third of each game as a freshman forward, she became a starter thereafter. One highlight was watching her hold her own when playing Stanford, a top Division I women's college team. As a senior she was captain and got named to the all-conference team.

So many soccer memories. The games, the key plays, the wins, the losses, the coaches, the post-season parties, the friendships, the camaraderie, and the trips. It was an incredible ride for me as well as Jolyn.

Exchange Students

A set of exchange students has enriched my life and, according to Kay and others, filled my need to have playmates. They have been additions to our family and provided relationships that have extended over time. About eight exchange students stayed with us, but five were with us for extended time periods.

The first, Hanne Andresen from Denmark, arrived in 1985 just as Jennifer left for college. She was a charming, serious girl who became a marketing professional and in 2003 returned to visit with her family, which now includes two girls. Then came Elin Aksdahl in 1987, a relative from Geilo, Norway, whom we

Elin—Norway

Hanne—Denmark

Gry—Norway

Pelle—Sweden

invited while visiting her family. A gifted skier and soccer player, she was a quiet but welcome addition. I still recall her opening some eyes by handling deep powder with her telemark skis at Alpine Meadows. She joined us on a Japan trip and later became an optometrist back in Geilo. In 2004, she also returned to visit with her two children and her husband, who is a trainer of Norway's junior snowboard competitors. Pelle Zerain in 1988 was a cheerful, bubbling Swede who was always quick to laugh—especially if it involved someone else taking a pratfall. Not a serious student, we encouraged the teachers to give him the grades he needed to graduate. He was a very proud graduating senior. We got to see him and his family, who were into soccer, during our 1990 trip to Sweden with Jolyn's team. He calls every New Year's, and we have seen him several times in Sweden and once in a 2005 visit to Nice where we met his wife.

Gry Brusletto from Oslo, who arrived in 1989, was (and is) a gorgeous, personable, fun person who was also a relative of mine. I kidded all the exchange students, but Gry especially shared my sense of humor. I would playfully suggest that because of her looks and personality she should simply walk up to people and say, "Hi, I'm Gry." She did not take my suggestion but did get the humor. When she did not share some of her relationships with me I would accuse her of having imaginary friends. Once, to make a point (I'm not quite sure what the point was), Gry and Kay left a jacket of mine on the floor for several days, watching me walk around it. Gry later became close friends with the princess of Norway (who in a subsequent trip with Gry visited our home) and spent a lot of time with Norwegian security forces. Gry now has two lovely children and a terrific husband, who she married in Geilo. Gry's sister, Hannah, now in the Norwegian Foreign Service, also spent several months with us.

There was one exchange student, our last one, that provided an interesting but different experience. Tros was a relative of a friend of ours. He got into the wrong crowd and eventually we, even naive as we were, realized that he was using marijuana. I had a long talk with him and explained that either he could go back or sign up for my program, involving a written exercise and group counseling. I had him list five or so reasons why smoking pot was good or fun and five reasons why it was a bad thing. I wanted him to learn about the pros and cons so the decision to continue to use pot would become more rational. The next step was to engage in group counseling. Both Kay and I would join him in group sessions. I was proud of the effort and got a lot out of it, but we later learned that Tros was not really affected (except to be a bit more discreet). He lasted out the term but did not change friends and habits. I learned how hard it is to reach young people and influence them in the face of social needs and peer pressure.

The Harry Trips

Harry Bruno, Marty DeJonghe's father, was one of my favorite people. He was Bjarne Nielsen (introduced in chapter two) quality—the ultimate compliment. His warmth, love, and remarkable zest for life permeated his friends and family. It was just fun to hear him talk and to vicariously experience designing buildings (he was an architect), planting lowquats (he planted them all over the world, including in our back yard), studying the turtles in the Galapagos Islands, cooking beans, sailing the Atlantic, corresponding with the famous conservative writer (and sailor) William F. Buckley, or playing in the Rose Bowl. He was the back-up quarterback in Cal's last Rose Bowl team—the "Wrong-Way" Reigals team. A star running back and longtime Harry friend, Roy Reigals became famous when he ran ninety yards in the wrong direction in the Rose Bowl before a teammate tackled him. An avid bridge player, Harry never tired of describing a hand that he and I played at the duplicate boards where the opponent bid seven and went down twelve vulnerable and doubled. Harry sailed all over the world, crossing the Atlantic more than once, and competed in the Transpac race to Hawaii. He would make friends in yacht clubs in exotic and far-off places, introducing himself to the bartender as the maker of the second-best old fashioned in the world (there must be someone superior, he concluded). He was Teddy Roosevelt reincarnated.

Harry loved to organize trips and designed four of them for himself and his lovely wife Edna, Tom and Marty DeJonghe, and Kay and me. The first was to the Caribbean in 1982.

1982 Caribbean Cruse—Dressing for dinner

Kay, Tom, Edna and Harry Bruno, Marty
getting the boat ready

Harry captained (and he was the captain—Tom and I were relegated to work the anchor) a forty-nine-foot sailboat that had three staterooms. We visited the Bitter End Yacht Club, Dead Chest Island, Norman Island (termed Treasure Island in Stevenson's novel), and Big Reef Bay (where we saw a sixty-foot, five-foot-diameter log that had to have journeyed hundreds if not thousands of miles). We snorkeled in Treasure Caves (and encroached on some unfriendly black cattle and went nose-to-nose with a barracuda), cooked and slept on the ship, and dined in some exotic restaurants such as The Last Resort, owned by a colorful former RAF pilot turned actor turned resort owner. Once when dining on board we all dressed up with swimming suits and ties to add some class.

For our next adventure, in 1983, we chartered a barge and drifted down the Midi Canal, which was conceived by Leonardo de Vinci to link the Mediterranean to the Atlantic and was finished in 1681. The barge was thirty-five feet long and passed through a land of endless vineyards, quaint sleepy villages, and the double-walled 700-year-old citadel city of Carcassone. It was an active trip because we had to navigate dozens of locks and because we had bicycles along. We would bike to a village for pastry each morning and bike along or near the canal during the day. One day Marty and I were biking to a meeting place

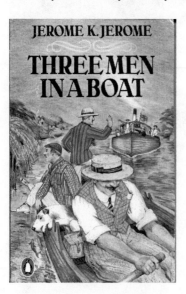

that Harry and Tom missed and motored on by. As a result we did not arrive until nine at night. Tom biked back to find us and displayed a (for him a very rare) hint of visible irritation about our inability to find the meeting place (of course we were blameless, but Harry and Tom had the worst time seeing this). We were extremely pleased with the food, people, and scenery in rural France and, most of all, to be on the water with Harry.

In 1986, the group boated down the Thames following the model of Jerome's highly entertaining book *Three Men in a Boat*, the (very) humorous exploits of three friends taking a Thames boat vacation. It is a book that has a laugh-out-loud description on every page. We got to experience colorful pubs and quaint hotels. Each had a story. Then we went to Wimbledon. It is so special because of the tradition, the museum, the center court, the players, the strawberries and cream, and on and on. I have been perhaps five times. We always go early in the first week during the early rounds when you can walk around, see the players up close, and watch doubles, often involving Cal players. On this occasion we got to see Mike Bauer, the Cal player whom I knew growing up. He won an exciting match against a German player, only to lose the next day in the second round.

In 1988 we chartered a sailboat, a Sailbird 37, in Comax, a small town north of Vancouver reachable with a small plane. The goal was Desolation Sound, and it was well worth it. It was on this trip that I pulled in very large salmon that provided dinner and a chance for me to be a hero. Going home was an adventure as the seven-hour sail became impossible with a very stiff head wind. So we chartered a floatplane. We found out later that if its single engine had faltered during a twenty-minute window we would have not have made it because landing would not have been possible. Wow! The kids then met us and we spent a week at the Lake Okanagan Resort in Central British Columbia.

Barnavan

The Aaker family, my six aunts and uncles and seventeen cousins, as noted in chapter two, were close during our growing-up years, even sharing a week each summer together. Since then, a prime vehicle to keep connected has been Aaker family reunions, often held at Child Lake (off Women Lake) in Northern Minnesota, Bjarne's place. We have these reunions about every four or five years, sometimes stimulated by my trip to Minnesota. They are a wonderful time to renew relationships, catch-up, and learn to know the nieces and nephews. I would try to provide for the next generation some feel for the special relationships my cousins and I had, but it is hard to put it into words.

Uncle Bjarne, as already noted, is one of my favorite people because of his exuberant, infectious personality. Decades ago, he bought a peninsula on Child Lake. Over time he cut down trees, put in roads, sold off lots, and built, furnished, and improved a cottage using wood from his property. He enjoyed every minute of it. He took great pleasure in taking people around a walking path—he would briskly stride along, swatting mosquitoes with a branch. There were all sorts of lake activities, but my favorite was canoeing around the point into Women Lake, an unbelievably peaceful and beautiful trip with a loon often keeping us company.

At our 1981 reunion, Jolyn, then eight, got a leech while swimming and went berserk. My cousin, Doug, with my support, finally convinced her that such an incident was so rare that he

Dave Minge, Jolyn, Bjarne, and John Aaker at Barnavan

had never gotten one in his whole life. Finally she went back in the water, but she had someone check her for leeches every few minutes. The next day, during a canoe outing over to my Uncle Ted's cabin in a nearby lake (Blackwater), damned if she did not get another. Doug's credibility went to zero—and mine as well.

She stayed out of the water until we got to the Minneapolis home of Tom Wright on Lake Minawashta, where the enticement of learning to water ski and Tom's assurance that leeches do not live in Minneapolis got her in the water again.

Cal Bears

The 80s were another frustrating decade for a Cal fan. However, there were some bright spots. The Cal basketball team broke a losing record to UCLA that went back decades. In a memorable night, Cal, led by Kevin Johnson, decisively beat UCLA. The stadium and the school went mad. It was one of my most exciting moments anywhere. Most cannot understand how humiliating it was to always lose to UCLA and by more than twenty points. Kevin Johnson, class of 1985, and David Butler, a power forward and class of 1987, became good friends of Jennifer, in part because she spent her freshman year in a dorm where many athletes stayed. She dated David, and he would come over and shoot baskets with me and would cheerfully take my advice on how to box out.

And in football there was The Play. We have gone to every big game with the DeJonghes, and every once in a while it is worthwhile, even in a bad season. In the big game in 1982, Stanford kicked a field goal with only four seconds remaining after John Elway made a spectacular drive down the field to make the score 20-19 in Stanford's favor after Cal had seemingly won the game. In the ensuing kickoff the Cal players lateraled five times to avoid being tackled until Kevin Moen raced across the goal, knocking over a Stanford trombone player in the process. It has been called the most spectacular play in college football, and I was there at this historical and emotional event. I played the tape of this play during the last session of many of my courses, using it to comment on achieving victory under adversity. Except for "The Play" and some outstanding linebackers like David Ortega (who became the recruiting coordinator for the team and a close friend), the Cal teams of the 80s struggled.

The 80s

A great decade for me. Professionally, my work started to get more impact although still with little focus. My articles with Doug Stayman and Bob Jacobson got traction. I had a book that was a big winner. Best of all, I was posed to begin the work on branding. Life as a professor at a research university was good on practically all dimensions. Personally, the Aaker/DeJonghe extended family kept on trucking, making vacations, holidays, and activities more fun and memorable. It was rewarding to be involved in the lives of all three kids, to see them excel, and to see them create meaningful career platforms.

8 The Nineties

It all comes together under the brand equity umbrella. And the kids become adults.

Research—The Brand Years

The work on branding that I started in the mid-1980s soon eclipsed all of the work of my first fifteen or so years in academia. The topic was timely and well positioned. I had caught a wave. The 1990s saw my academic work relating brand equity to stock return with Bob Jacobson and exploring brand extensions with Kevin Keller gain significant influence and impact among academics. With my series of brand books, I also influenced operating executives, a first for me. These books made me realize how invisible my prior work had been with respect to the "real world." There is no question that the second fifteen academic years were more successful by any measure than my first fifteen.

My work on branding started with research on brand extensions and the development of my first of four brand books, *Managing Brand Equity*.

Brand Extension Research

I met Kevin Keller, then a Duke PhD student and promising cognitive psychologist interested in memory issues, when he was interviewing for an academic job in 1985. Instead of

Kevin Keller

the normal screening interview, I greeted him with "How can we get you to Berkeley?" which was an impressive statement of our interest. He came to Berkeley but left a year later for Stanford, where he stayed for some nine years, long enough to be the dissertation advisor to Jennifer. She (and I) benefited from his depth of knowledge of psychology and experimentation.

Kevin and I shared an interest in branding and advertising and, even more bonding, in college athletics and tennis. He was really into basketball, and since Duke was a long distance away, he got interested in Cal and Stanford. And he liked tennis but was, to be charitable, not a strong player. I played him just the opposite of Bob. I hit to Kevin's forehand because it was a reasonable shot and his backhand was a zero. After about a set of seeing only forehands he would finally realize what was going on and insist that I play him straight up. He wanted no advantage.

Brand extension research (to what products should your brand be extended and what are the risks of doing so) seemed like a good place to start a brand-oriented research stream. Kevin was up for it. Four articles emerged from the effort, but it was the first that turned out to be a home run in the sense that it was widely referenced and precipitated a host of brand extension studies. Replication of studies is rarely done in marketing, but this one was replicated perhaps eight or more times all around the world and extended at least once. Several of these articles termed our paper as seminal, the ultimate compliment in the academic world.

The article, entitled "Consumer Evaluations of Brand Extensions," was published in *Journal of Marketing* in 1990. For each of six brands, reactions were obtained of respondents to proposed extensions that varied as to their fit with the brand. McDonald's, for example, was conceptually extended into frozen fries, a theme park, and photo processing, and Crest into mouthwash, chewing gum, and shaving cream. The results were provocative. A brand's perceived quality was found to be a predictor of extension success, but only if there was a basis of fit. The perceived ability of a brand to make the extension was another success predictor. However, a trivial extension such as Heineken popcorn was vulnerable because it cheapened the brand and because the extension was perceived to be overpriced. Abstract attributes (such as Vuarnet's fashion) or nonproduct attributes (such as McDonald's kids and family) could travel further than product attribute associations. Finally, an elaboration of an extension attribute, such as the convenience delivered by McDonald's photo processing, can reduce the possibility that a negative attribute such as greasiness will become salient.

This *JM* article, like the warmth article with Doug Stayman, had enormous academic influence because of the subject matter, the findings, and the solid methodology. We could be very confident that the provocative results were real. However, even these articles had very limited visibility among practitioners, in part because they did not read academic journals and in part because they believed that any experiments using student subjects and involving only one exposure to stimuli in a laboratory setting had limited generalizability. In real life, of course, an ad campaign is exposed to adult audiences many times often over many years. We academics did not stay up nights worrying about these issues because publishing an article in a top journal that attracted the attention of our peers was our scorecard.

In a second article published in *Journal of Marketing Research* (*JMR*) in 1992, a finalist for the O'Dell award given the top *JMR* article, Kevin, and I showed that intervening extensions, if successful, allowed the core brand to be stretched further when the core brand had moderate quality. An intervening extension is one that represents a lesser brand stretch than an ultimate extension. Another finding was that unsuccessful intervening extensions decreased the success probability of a further extension but, unexpectedly, did not affect the perceptions of the core brand. This evidence of brand equity resilience in the face of disappointing brand performance has implications to those attempting to justify brand building. In a third article in *Corporate Reputation Review*, 1998, we showed that a corporate image of innovativeness helped the success chances of a new product while the image of being community-involved had no such advantage. Our fourth article commented on the differences between the many replications of the original *JM* study.

The methodology used in the experimental research with Kevin was sound. However, the design tended to be complex because both of us had a tendency to try to answer too many questions with a single experiment. The analysis, the interpretation, and the communication of the results thus became a challenge. We looked with some envy on others, like our colleague and friend, Itamar Simonson, who would always use elegant 2x2 designs that would result in non-intuitive insights. He would conduct dozens of experiments to uncover those findings that were eye catching. We, in contrast, had to have one experiment do it all.

Kevin subsequently moved from Stanford to Dartmouth, with stopovers at North Carolina and Duke. He has been a prominent contributor to the understanding and management of brand strategy and wrote the definitive text, now in its second edition. Before leaving Stanford he married Punam, an energetic and successful marketing professor who now also teaches at Dartmouth. They have two girls and manage to avoid most of the outdoor activities associated with rural New Hampshire.

To understand extensions from another perspective, I systematically gathered as many examples as possible of extensions that had failed and succeeded and categorized them into the "good," the "bad," and the "ugly." Good" was when the brand contributed to the extension by its associations (Healthy Choice). More good occurred when the extension enhanced the brand name (Sunkist Juice Bars and Vitamin C Tablets). Bad was when the name failed to add value (Pillsbury Microware Popcorn) or added confusion (Betty Crocker Cookbook Chicken) or created negative associations (Levi Tailored Classics men's suits). Ugly was when the brand name was damaged because the extension created undesirable associations (Sears Financial Network). The article, entitled "Brand Extensions—The Good, the Bad, and the Ugly," appeared in the *Sloan Management Review (SMR)* in the fall 1990 issue and became a chapter in the first brand book. It was one of my very rare good titles.

Managing Brand Equity

Brand equity as a concept was just starting to emerge in 1988 when the Marketing Science Institute (MSI), an organization that funds, influences, and stimulates academic research,

held its first brand conference. However, there was no consensus as to what it was and was not. I decided to write a book, which became *Managing Brand Equity* (*MBE*), published in 1991, to define and illustrate the concept and to introduce some basics in its management.

Taking on a book on an emerging topic was formidable. However, writing three texts gave me the confidence that I had the ability and persistence to write books. I could develop conceptual models to structure ideas, create process models, and evolve a chapter flow. Further, I was blessed with some material from which I could draw. In particular, the content of the three texts could all be accessed in the new brand book because the concepts and tools of advertising, marketing research, and strategic management were all relevant to the conceptualization and management of brand equity. Further, my article on brand extensions in *SMR* provided a solid chapter. So I was about 30% there before I even started.

A major book task was to define brand equity. I defined it as a set of assets and liabilities linked to the brand name and symbol that add or subtract value to the offering and can be grouped into four categories: brand loyalty, brand awareness, perceived quality, and brand associations. The characterization of brand as an asset (or liability) was a powerful idea. A business asset (or liability) is the foundation of strategy and needs to be managed at the highest levels of a business. In contrast, a brand image is a tactical concept that can be delegated to the advertising manager to handle. Conceptualizing a brand as strategic rather than tactical has significant organizational and resource implications.

The book detailed how a brand will provide value to firms. For example, brand awareness (e.g., Intel Inside) not only enhances the chances that a brand will be considered, but also affects perceptions, suggests familiarity, and signals substance and commitment. Loyalty ("I always use Crest") reduces marketing costs and provides time to respond to competitor moves. Perceived quality ("Lexus makes reliable cars") provides a basis for choice. Associations such as attribute superiority ("Volvos are safe") or brand personality ("Southwest Airlines is fun and friendly") provide a point of differentiation. Brand equity is also shown to add value to customers by providing information about the offering and confidence in the purchase decision.

My definition of brand equity included the dimensions of perceived quality and brand loyalty, not found in the treatment of the topic by others. Perceived quality is unique in that it has been shown in several studies to affect financial performance. It is also often a key determinant of purchase decisions and loyalty. Further, it represents a direct link to the total quality programs that are the key to operations strategy in many firms.

Brand loyalty is included for two reasons. First, when a firm buys a brand from another, a major asset that is being bought is the loyalty of the customer base. Second, a prime task in creating or building brand equity is to build and strengthen customer loyalty and to develop programs to make the relationship between the brand and its customer stronger. When brand loyalty is considered a result of brand equity rather than a component, the focus of brand equity management can too easily turn to image instead of substance.

The book also contained four case studies of billion-dollar magnitude, each illustrating one of the four dimensions of brand equity. For example, Nissan spent hundreds of millions to change their name from Datsun, only to find that Datsun was still as strong a brand as Nissan some six years later. And Schlitz beer never recovered from the loss in perceived quality caused by an effort to reduce production costs. These studies were captured in a contribution I made to a book that Alec Biel and I edited based on the proceedings of a conference on brand equity and advertising we chaired in 1990. More on Alec shortly.

The author of a trade or bookstore book attempts to get well-known friends (or well-known strangers if there are not enough friends) to write a complimentary note to put on the back cover.

I have done this many times for others. One of the seven people who wrote such a note for me for *Managing Brand Equity* was Tom Peters, one of the foremost lecturers and business book authors in the world, who wrote, "A must for all managers' bookshelves. In an increasingly crowded marketplace, fools will compete on price. Winners will find a way to create lasting value in the customer's mind. This book is for those who would be winners—it mixes snappy case studies with sound academic research." I have used the middle two sentences in many of my talks. He has a great way with words.

The best press comes from independent writers who talk up the book. John Dvorak, an influential columnist for *PC Magazine*, in one of his columns called the book a "must-read for any marketing maven or would-be marketer who wants to know how brand names work in today's market ... even if you are not in marketing, this book is fascinating." I really like the last word. Such sentiments about my writing, unfortunately, are too rare. The book also received a full-page review in *The Economist*. That was a big day, although the only call I got was from Lou Stern. My social set, outside of Lou, apparently does not read *The Economist*.

Again, I made an effort to find humorous or insightful quotes to open each chapter. Here are four of my favorites from *MBE*:

A product is something that is made in a factory; a brand is something that is bought by a customer. A product can be copied by a competitor; a brand is unique. A product can be quickly outdated; a successful brand is timeless.
—Stephen King, WPP Group, London

A good name is better than riches
—Cervantes, *Don Quixote*

A man is known by the company he keeps
—Anonymous

Three things I never lends—my 'oss, my wife, and my name.
—Robert Smith Surtees

I published the book with the Free Press—its editor, Bob Wallace, expressed immediate enthusiasm for the book and got a contract to me in days. I knew and respected Bob because he was the editor for George Day and me on our *Consumerism* book through its four editions. So I signed and have never regretted it. The Free Press is a fine company, and Bob is simply the best. He is astute, professional, supportive, has a feel for positioning a book, and knows when to make forceful recommendations and when to encourage. Because of Bob I have used the Free Press for all four of my brand books. In each case, the contract includes no advance (I don't see any point in going into debt) but some assurances about the advertising program and a grant of free books to be used for promotional purposes. Knowing Bob and his outstanding assistants has been a side benefit of my book writing. His tenure as editor is remarkable. Most of his peers in the industry seem to be around only for a few years.

For each book, I would send a copy to marketing and advertising executives. I reasoned that even if the book sold no copies, some key people would be exposed to my ideas and me. It is surprisingly expensive to create a good list and send books out. In the case of *MBE*, I figured that it cost around $10 to send out a book, not counting the cost of the book itself (which I either got free or at reduced cost). Although the book is promoted through my talks, PR releases, and advertising, I think that putting the book into the hands of influential people played a key role in the success because it generated some buzz. I expanded the program for the other brand books. The *MBE* book sold some 65,000 copies in English during its first fourteen years and has been translated into eight languages—the Japanese translation sold around 12,000 copies. It still sells around 1,500 copies per year.

Modeling the Impact of Brand Equity

It is a challenge to demonstrate that investments in brands (or other intangible assets such as people or information technology) really pay off, in part because most of the payoff often occurs years later. Therefore, brand builders in firms have a difficult time justifying investments in brands, especially when the business is not making their sales and profit "targets." As described in the

Stock Market Reaction to BE & ROI

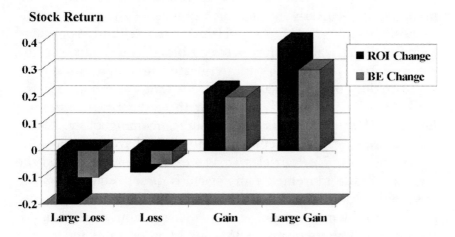

Effect of brand equity and ROI on stock return

last chapter, Bob Jacobson and I showed, using PIMS data, that brand equity as measured by perceived quality does affect financial performance as measured by ROI (return on investment—the accounting measure of profitability). We now turned to a more definitive criterion variable, stock return.

Our first effort to relate brand equity investment to stock return was published in *JMR* in 1994 and used data from Total Research, a firm that had tracked brand equity for over a hundred brands for several years. We selected thirty-four brands that were associated with publicly traded firms such as Kodak, Ford, IBM, and Campbell's. In the database, brand equity was measured by perceived quality. Remarkably, we found significant evidence that brand equity drives stock return, as the figure above shows. In fact, the brand equity impact in terms of explaining variance was comparable (actually 70% as powerful) to that delivered by ROI. This study was important because it showed that, on average, improving brand equity pays off in terms of stock return.

Interestingly, advertising expenditures were found to have no effect on stock return independent of its possible impact on brand equity.

A second study, published in *JMR* in 2001, was based on the Techtel database (courtesy of Mike Kelly, the CEO of Techtel, who became a friend and biking companion), which tracks brand equity quarterly for high-tech brands. We focused on nine brands, including IBM, Dell, HP, Microsoft, and Apple and found a similar relationship between brand equity changes and stock return. The results were replicated in a third study with eighteen dot-com brands as well, a study that was reported in the *Wall Street Journal*. Our results, over three databases representing very different contexts and measures, unambiguously showed that, on average, investments in brand equity have large payoffs.

In the 2001 *JMR* article, we also examined what caused the few significant movements in quarterly brand equity that we observed. Among the causal forces were product introductions, product problems, changes in top management, and competitor actions. The innovative IBM ThinkPad portable moved the IBM brand up, and Windows 3.1, with a huge promotional push, affected the Microsoft brand. The demise of the Apple Newton and some defects among Intel chips adversely impacted the Apple and Intel brands. The arrival of Lou Gerstner at IBM and the going and coming of Steve Jobs at Apple affected their brands. Finally, some hard-hitting Compaq advertising hurt the HP brand, and Windows 95 adversely affected the Apple brand. This type of exploration made academic reviewers uncomfortable because it was based on a small number of data points, but the results were intriguing even to them.

Building Strong Brands—
The Brand Identity System

After *Managing Brand Equity* appeared, an interest and motivation to build brand assets became apparent. However, my interactions with executives led me to believe that there was a lack of tools, processes, and conceptual models to help brand builders. The *MBE* book was primarily designed to understand brand equity and related topics. What was needed, I concluded, was a

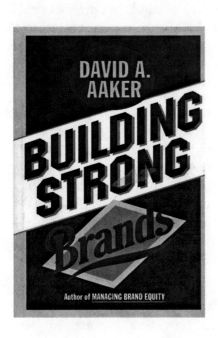

DAVID A. AAKER

BUILDING STRONG Brands

Author of MANAGING BRAND EQUITY

book that would help structure the creation and management of brands in a way that allowed managers to move beyond a three-word phrase. The result was the book *Building Strong Brands* (*BSB*), published in 1996.

The cornerstone of the *BSB* book is what I term the "brand identity system," which others sometimes call the Aaker Model. Representing a much broader perspective of a brand's role and message than is the norm, it is aspirational and multidimensional with a structure that includes a core and extended elements plus a value proposition.

- **Aspirational**

The central construct, brand identity, is aspirational (thus differing from brand image). Although aspirational, it does not represent empty dreams, but, rather, what the organization actually has the will and resources to deliver, if not immediately, then within a reasonable planning horizon.

- **Multidimensional**

The identity presents a rich, complete picture of the brand. Rather than a single thought or phrase (favored by many advertising agencies), a brand is defined in terms of eight to ten dimensions. It potentially should represent the brand-as-product (product scope, attributes, quality/value, uses, users, and country of origin), brand-as-organization (organizational attributes, local vs. global), brand-as-person (personality, relationship with customer), and brand-as-symbol (visual imagery, heritage). The Haas School of Business at UC Berkeley developed an identity that included eight dimensions. They aspired to have a brand that meant world-class, innovative, provocative, UC Berkeley (connected to a university that is rated high in many fields), accessible, collaborative, confident, and Haas (the Haas family).

- **The Core Identity**

  These identity dimensions are divided as to priority and importance. The most important three or four elements are termed the core identity, generally because of their power to differentiate and resonate with customers. The core identity elements play a driver role in developing both internal and external brand-building programs. For the Haas brand, the core identity elements were world-class, innovative, provocative, and UC Berkeley.

- **The Extended Identity**

  The balance of the identity is termed the extended identity, the "rest of the story." The extended identity helps broaden the brand perspective, often providing a home for the brand personality, and contributes the richness and texture needed in order to make decisions about what fits with the brand and what does not.

- **The Value Proposition**

  The model suggests that the brand should deliver a value proposition that, when possible, should go beyond attributes and functional benefits to include emotional and self-expressive benefits. Haas students might find emotional benefits by meeting the academic challenge and self-expressive benefits by achieving their full potential. Strategies restricted to attribute-based messaging often fail to achieve differentiation and miss opportunities to connect to customers.

Three other *BSB* chapters are worth mentioning. One was a description of how to measure brand equity based on the four brand equity dimensions of the *Managing Brand Equity* book. The resulting "brand equity ten" were published in *California Management Review* (*CMR*) in 1996. A second was a discussion of vertical brand extensions (moving a brand down to a value offering or moving a brand up into a super premium arena) that was published in *Harvard Business Review* (*HBR*) in 1997. Vertical brand extensions enable two of the most common strategic growth options facing many firms. The third was a case story of Saturn, one of the most impressive brand-creating stories of the last few decades (unfortunately, GM allowed this asset to wither by failing to augment its product line). The Saturn story also appeared as a 1995 article in *CMR* and won an award for the best *CMR* article that year. I learned from that case that there were seven ingredients to its success, each of which was critical, a finding that suggested to me that the search for the one key to a successful business strategy would often be futile.

Because of the prominence of the Saturn article, I was selected to be the model for a major Saturn advertisement that was to show that business schools were using the Saturn story as a model of brand building. The ad had four attractive khaki-clad "marketing students" sitting on the ground looking up at me on a campus setting. I was a bit temperamental during the three-hour shoot. The wardrobe people wanted to put me in a light suit with a bow tie. I told them I wasn't wearing a bow tie and that I was not excited about taking three hours to take one picture at zero pay. Nevertheless, I went through with it, and the ad appeared in thirty-five publications including *Time* and *Newsweek*. I still am puzzled why, with all that exposure, I was never contacted to do another.

Some of my favorite pre-chapter quotes from *BSB* include:

A brand that captures your mind gains behavior; a brand that captures your heart gains commitment.
                    —Scott Talgo, brand strategist

An orange ... is an orange ... is an orange. Unless, of course, that orange happens to be Sunkist, a name that 80% of consumers know and trust.
                    —Russell L. Hanlin, CEO, Sunkist Growers

Customers must recognize that you stand for something.
—Howard Schultz, Starbucks

What do you need to be the best? Concentration.
Discipline. A Dream.
—Florence Griffith Joyner, Olympic Gold Medalist

The *BSB* book benefited from my discussions with another industry guru, Scott Talgo—the author of the first quote. Scott had a small brand-strategy consulting firm, St. James Group, in Chicago and had some San Francisco clients. Scott was (and is) one of the most insightful strategists I know and one of the most open about talking about his experiences working with brands. In one of our many stimulating discussions about brands, he helped me refine the brand identity model.

Over the years Scott tried to get me to join St. James. I participated in three engagements with him—Kaiser Permanente, HP, and Rice-a-Roni—and referred other clients to him. But the facts that he is not a gifted organization builder (a lot of his organizational energy was spent getting a "divorce" first from his original partner and then from a research company he merged with) and that any office would be a satellite to the Chicago headquarters made a formal arrangement unattractive. Incidentally, Scott was one of several industry people who wanted to write articles and books with me but never seemed to find the time.

There were eight comments on the back of the book, one of which again was by Tom Peters, who called it "... a masterpiece ... sophisticated, practical, and readable." My editor, Bob Wallace, has pointed out that Tom gives glowing comments to many books, but I chose to ignore these reservations; to me Tom Peters is Tom Peters. The best was by Joseph V. Tripodi, then the CMO of MasterCard and now CMO of Allstate, who wrote, "Rarely is the sequel as good as the original. This time it's better! With compelling case studies and insightful discussion, Aaker extends the concepts put forth in *Managing Brand Equity* to create the first true owner's manual for brand managers. Aaker is the brand name in brand management." I really like the last sentence.

Too often the reviews of my brand books fail to suggest that the books are easy and fun to read. The word "fascinating," used by Dvorak to describe *Managing Brand Equity*, as noted above, is rare. Despite my extensive use of case studies and illustrative examples, comments suggesting that my writing is serious and academic are much more common. For example, a review in WorldBusiness in January 1997 of *Building Strong Brands* said, "Aaker's analysis is both solid and intelligent, sharp enough for readers to overlook his professorial prose and academic point-counterpoint style." Jennifer says that such comments mean that my books have substance and are not just fluff like so many business books. But I could stand to hear more use of words like "fascinating."

Bob Wallace always involves me in the cover design. In this case, I did not like the design, believing it to look like a Tide detergent box. However, he was forceful in arguing that the cover was both different (making it stand out on the shelf) and punchy, qualities that surely helped the book. His judgment turned out to be much better than my instinct. The only cover to which I objected turned out to be the best cover of all my books.

The *BSB* book, published in 1996, really hit at the right time. I have on numerous occasions been surprised to hear people from major companies tell me that their firm had distributed the book and used it as a basis for their brand management. I have also learned that major management consulting and advertising firms use it in their training programs. I am usually surprised, pleased, and honored to hear that news but wonder how it happened. Why my book? Why don't they develop their own model or use another's? I suspect my book wins because there is a believer in the organization that pushes it, because it has a good reputation, and because they have better things to do than reinvent what I have already done.

The *BSB* book sold over 85,000 copies in English in its first eight years and still sells at a rate of 3,000 per year. It was translated into eleven languages; the Japanese translation sold over 10,000 copies and the Spanish edition sold around 5,000. It was to be my most successful book (unless you count all of the editions of the strategy book or the marketing research book). Its sales pattern was also highly unusual in that sales did not fall off until the fifth year, which meant that word-of-mouth was generating new readers for four years. The initial promotion push—including giving away 1,500 books—helped get it off to a good start, but the acceptance by companies kept it going.

Erich
Joachimsthaler

Brand Leadership

I first met Erich Joachimsthaler in 1983 when he was completing his PhD from Kansas and was interviewing for an academic job. As a student, he had an impressive research stream that included a *JCR* acceptance. He ended up at the University of Houston were he was remarkably productive with a string of articles in top journals, showing that the top research universities made a mistake by not taking a chance on a Kansas student.

Shortly after he moved to IESE in Barcelona (the leading business school in Spain) in the early 1990s, I was invited to come to IESE and give a talk and join a panel consisting of the two of us plus V. Kumar (VK), his former colleague from the University of Houston (VK eventually took over the Aaker/Day *Marketing Research* text). Erich, who does not play tennis but does bike, took me on some awesome rides around the Barcelona hills. He recounted the difficulty of being at a school that is controlled by the religious sect Opus Dei (which played a role in the popular novel *The DaVinci Code*)—you are always an outsider, much more so than being a non-Mormon at BYU.

On a subsequent trip to Barcelona, Erich and I discussed writing a book on European case studies of brand building. We (mostly Erich) did develop some 300 case studies through articles and interviews toward that goal. However, the book, *Brand Leadership (BL)*, published in 2000, evolved to have four thrusts positioned as the four keys to creating brand leadership.

One thrust was close to our original concept for the book: brand building that goes beyond mass media advertising. We suggested that brand builders attempt to link the brand to a customer's sweet spot, activities, or values important to that customer. One example was the Adidas Streetball Challenge, a series of three on three basketball tournaments, each surrounded by a weekend of games and music. This model formed the basis for a *HBR* article entitled "Brand Building in the Post-Media World—Lessons from Europe" (January, 1997). Our position, that the Internet be viewed as a way to augment the offering and create a relationship to the customer rather than simply another advertis-

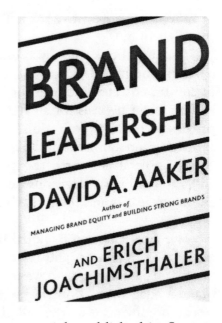

ing vehicle, formed the basis for an article published in *Strategy + Business* in August of 2002. We also opined that sponsorships, to be effective, should fit the brand and its objectives and should be managed as a long-term brand builder rather than an isolated promotion.

Another thrust was to extend the brand identity model in two ways. First, an optional brand essence—a single thought that would represent much of the brand identity—was added. When the right brand essence is found (and sometimes it never emerges), it can be helpful in communicating to and inspiring employees and customers. For the Haas School, the brand essence was "challenging convention," which does capture much of the core identity and the spirit of the school. Second, we noted the value of elaborating the brand identity in order to crystallize its meaning by finding internal and external role models. So if the Haas School wanted to be perceived as provocative, an external role model could be Victoria Secret and an internal role model could be the entrepreneurial program at the Haas School. These role models not only clarify, but also can suggest programs and initiatives to make the core identity come to life. What is it about Victoria Secret and the entrepreneurial program that make them perceived as provocative? What can be learned that might help the Haas brand?

The third book thrust was brand portfolio strategy. We developed the brand relationship spectrum that structured the roles of sub-brands and endorsed brands in the total brand portfolio and formed the basis for a *CMR* article (Fall, 2000). We further provided the first definition of brand portfolio strategy (then termed brand architecture). The starting-off point for my fourth brand book, it set forth the scope of brand portfolio strategy and specified what decisions need to be made in order to create and manage a brand team that will generate synergy, clarity, and leverage.

The final thrust was global brand management. Erich and I interviewed managers and reviewed case studies from thirty-five or so firms, inquiring as to what they felt were issues facing global brand managers and how they were dealing with these issues. Our research convinced us that all global brand managers needed to find ways to communicate insights and program across countries, to break down the "my country is different" syndrome, to develop a brand management process that everyone uses, and to find ways to allow excellence in brand building to emerge. Erich and I published this material in *HBR* in November 1999 as "The Lure of Global Branding."

Among the notes for the book's dusk jacket was one by Peter Sealey, the former CMO of Coke who is now associated with Berkeley and a good friend, who wrote, "What Frederick W. Taylor did for scientific management and Peter F. Drucker did for the concept of management, Aaker has done for our understanding of brands. Now, in collaboration with Erich Joachimsthaler, he has taken that life's work to a new level of perception, insight, and sophistication. *Brand Leadership* is a highly needed roadmap for the multi-brand marketer, which is as up-to-date as tomorrow morning with chapters on how to incorporate sponsorship and the Internet." Friends come in handy when a new book emerges, and Peter is always willing to oblige and not afraid to stretch.

The pre-chapter quotes included:

I don't know the key to success; but the key to failure is trying to please everyone.

—Bill Cosby

A brand strategy must follow the business strategy.

—Dennis Carter, Intel

You cannot win the hearts of customers unless you have a heart yourself.

—Charlotte Beers, J. Walter Thompson

The way a team plays as a whole determines its success. You may have the greatest bunch of individual stars in the world, but if they don't play together, the club won't be worth a dime.

—Babe Ruth

The book was perhaps not as well positioned as it could have been because it covered brand portfolio strategy, brand identity, brand building, and organization structure, so it was hard to identify one message. Nevertheless its sales were still good—over 38,000 during the first four years. It was translated into thirteen languages—the Japanese version sold over 8,000 books in its first three years.

A Research Appraisal

My research and writing clearly changed in the 90s. On balance, it became more managerial and more oriented toward books. Of my twenty-five articles during the nineties, eight were in journals that academics would consider "A-level." Two of them, the 1990 *JM* brand extension article with Kevin and the 1994 *JMR* brand equity article with Bob, were widely referenced and influenced the research agenda and thus would be considered home runs. Twelve were in academic journals with a managerial focus. One of these, the *CMR* Saturn story, won a best article award, and three others were in *HBR*, the managerial journal with the most impressive circulation. In addition, I wrote seventeen managerial notes in publications like *Ad Age*, *BrandWeek*, and the

Wall Street Journal. This writing pattern continued in the first half of the next decade.

However, with respect to influencing the business world, it is books that matter. I was frankly stunned by the impact that the three brand books had on managerial audiences. It made me conscious of how little visibility and influence I'd had before the books appeared. I now realize that books influence executives much more than articles, even *HBR* articles. They read books and implement ideas that catch their eye. There is no doubt that many managers at all levels have read my brand books, and that many have adopted the ideas and process models. I suspect that the books, just because of their titles and visibility, helped to change perspectives on brands from tactical image management to strategic asset creation, even for people that never got around to reading the books in any detail.

Three other comments. First, my books have high visibility outside the States. In some countries, such as Japan, I am better known than in the U.S. A significant number of books are sold abroad. For *Building Strong Brands* and *Brand Leadership*, for example, about 30% of the books were sold outside the U.S.—and that number probably exceeds 50% if translations are counted. Second, the cumulative effect helps. It is hard to get your book to break through the clutter. My prior brand books created a visibility and acceptance of my work so a new brand book authored by me will often get considered. Third, on a few occasions I have observed that firms applying my *BSB* models could have benefited from the guidance of someone with talent and experience in using the models, such as a team from Prophet, the consulting company that will be described in the next chapter. Brand identity work is difficult and benefits from having people participating that have experience, creativity, strategic flair, and a sense of how it will be used. Further, my exposition in *BSB* was not as good or developed as it could have been. The *BL* augmentation helps, but many rely solely on the *BSB* book.

Speaking and Consulting

After my first brand book came out, my life changed. I became part of the (minor) celebrity speaker circuit. The length of the talks would vary but the most common length was around sixty minutes, of which around twenty minutes would be allocated for Q&A, which I always enjoyed and found stimulating. It was rare to extend it to two hours. The venues were often glamorous. Usually I was treated like a rock star with the best rooms, a large support staff at the venue itself, often an elaborate reception after the talk (particularly in Japan and Europe), and, occasionally, a limo as well. And the turnouts were substantial. Most were in the 200 to 400 range, but some were around 800, and a few were over 1,000. It was really a trip.

Since 1992, I have given around thirty academic seminars, eighty company presentations, and more than one hundred public talks, which means I have averaged around eighteen talks a year. About thirty of these were in Japan, and another twenty-five were in Europe. Several were in other locales such as Korea, China, Taiwan, and Argentina. There are a lot of memories.

My first brand talk was at Intel where there was an audience of some 350 Intel managers. The speaker before me was Faith Popcorn (who charts trends like cocooning—hunkering down in your home), and she explained her methods (look at what women are reading in airports) and stopped thirty minutes before her time was up. I felt sorry for her and was sure that I would look good after the audience had heard a speaker with weak (to be kind) methodology giving insights not relevant to Intel while sitting down with half her time left. Wrong. She was a big hit, and my approach, using a rough outline and crude slides, was not well received. From then on, I was rehearsed, had a very detailed outline, made an extra effort to use relevant examples, and professionalized my slides. I never read talks, but I was always very prepared with transitional remarks in mind and persuasive examples to illustrate points.

I got invited back to Intel three or four times despite this rocky start because of my friendship with Dennis Carter, the Intel CMO. Dennis has visited my class many times and shared with me ideas about high-tech brand strategy. He is, in my view, the most talented strategist in that world and, with the support of the Intel CEO, Andy Grove, developed "Intel Inside" and other brand initiatives that are the envy of his industry.

I spoke at two innovative thinking conferences in Phoenix sponsored by Barry Shepard and Will Rodgers' SHR Perceptual Management, a firm linking design to brands. At one conference, I partnered with Barry to give a talk that featured a host of props—some of which would drop from the ceiling. (He wanted to write a book with me and designed a terrific cover, but he never found the time to actually write words.) We had a dinner that allowed me to get to know other speakers like Bill Russell (the Celtic center), Dick Fosbery (the high jumper who invented the Fosbery Flop and won the Olympics after all the coaches told him his approach would not work—the message was not to be afraid to chart new paths), and the creative thinker guru Edward de Bono. De Bono gave a mesmerizing talk while sitting down and writing on a rolling transparency as he talked. He broke all presentation rules but was incredibly effective. It was amazing.

In 1997 I went on a speaking tour of Europe. I spoke to crowds of some 300 in Oslo, Stockholm, and Helsinki. In Helsinki, they had a large reception in my honor and took me to a vacation chalet for a dinner. It felt like I was at the dacha of a Russian

Speaking in Finland—1997

politician. I then spoke to around 900 at the German Marketing Association in Frankfurt where I got to meet several CEOs and explore their approach to global brand management, my research interest at the time. I ran in the Frankfurt marathon that started at my hotel—at least for the first three miles. Finally, I went to Seville where I stayed in a huge, ornate hotel that was justifiably labeled as one of the best hotels of the world and spoke to 600 people at the annual meeting of a marketing association. On the plane to Seville I sat next to Jackson Browne, a major singer with some dozen albums and a distinctive style. We had a nice talk after we got over the fact that I had no idea who he was. He later sent me some cookies made by his brother's company. During my initial talk in Stockholm, I felt faint and was afraid of passing out in the middle of the talk and suffering all the associated embarrassment this would entail. For the other talks I made sure there was a chair on stage, but the fainting feeling never reappeared.

I have made around eight or nine trips to Spain, most of which involved a talk arranged by Roberto Alvarez, the translator of all of my books, a great friend, and one of the most interesting people I know. I first met Roberto when he visited Berkeley on a post-doc in the late 1970s. Since then he, his wife Maria, and their son Fedrico have spent several summers in Berkeley, sometimes staying at our home, and we have visited them in Barcelona many times. In our last visit (with Tom and Marty DeJonghe), we stayed in their summer home in the midst of charming towns and fields of sunflowers, which we saw up close on our bikes. During that trip we played golf with one of the top senior women players in Europe, Catherine O'Brian, a delightful person who also ran a store carrying an array of unique items to make a country home comfortable and interesting. I can sympathize with those pros that have been beaten by Michelle Wie.

Roberto became the head of the committee that attracted the Olympics to Barcelona in 1992 when the city fathers decided that maybe a marketing professional would have something to offer. A thoughtful, thorough program culminated in a night of celebrating when Barcelona was selected. The moment the announcement was made, according to Roberto, generated feelings of being tense, relieved, and joyous all in the space of a few seconds.

Roberto Maria and Fedrico Alvarez—around 1995

Roberto left nothing to chance, even training the taxi drivers so that when an Olympic Committee member entered a taxi, they would get the right experience.

Roberto also developed a huge fish cannery (which was about to be destroyed) into a building now housing the Barcelona museum, a dozen fine restaurants, and numerous shops. In doing so, he researched other similar developments, found a San Francisco architect that had done several, and dealt with the political and regulatory issues. After doing all that work and committing all his assets to the project, the city insisted on an open bidding process. On a Friday he learned that his bid was second and that he had lost everything. But by Monday he had convinced the city that the winning bidder was a government entity that did not pay taxes and got the decision reversed. What a weekend. Roberto is also an archeologist and art collector, and his home has ample evidence of each passion.

On one trip to Barcelona, Roberto introduced me to Louis Bassant, the CEO of the O&M agency in Spain (Louis joined O&M when they bought his agency). A gifted advertising professional, he was a true renaissance man with an impressive art collection he had accumulated over the years. At one point an art dealer lamented that people wanted to buy $10,000 pieces while his million-dollar Picasso was hard to move. So Luis told him to pick out one hundred paintings from his collection (after holding back five) and got a wonderful large Picasso that is now worth a fortune. He had an elegant dinner in his Barcelona home for Roberto, Erich, and me (with our wives) where the Picasso was hanging in his living room. His tutorial on his collection and his

Louis Bassat, advertiser and art collector

various acquisition stories were fascinating.

I was in Japan four or five times during the 90s. The Japanese talks and meetings were made more interesting because top executives would often attend. In fact, I was twice a speaker at

Hiro, Dave and students at a snowy bath

an event organized by Hiro and Jiro, the Twenty-First Century CEO lectures in Tokyo that attracted about 200 or so—all CEOs. Amazing. It would not happen in the U.S.

On a 1998 Japan trip, Hiro invited me to join him on one of his outings with his students. We went by bullet train to Nagano and a slower train to a ski area deep in the mountains. I have never seen such a blizzard—there was four feet of fresh snow. The trouble was that the only skis that they could find for me were very long and stiff, so I did not handle it well. But I was able to coach some students that were beginners and got to see the skits and bonding that took place. The highlight was the open air hot springs where you sat in hot water with snow coming down as thick as I have ever seen—and I grew up in North Dakota. What an experience.

I got to fly in a company plane twice and the Concorde once. The first company plane ride was in the early 1990s when I attended a guru summit organized by Peter Sealey, then Coke's CMO (and the architect of the multiple-commercial campaign which included a polar bear ad that got real traction) for five top Coke executives. The plane actually came to pick up Peter Drucker (who was easily the star of the meeting—an amazing man still writing books at age ninety), but I got to tag along. In 2003, a firm flew me to their home office and back. I met with the CEO to get prepared for a talk that I was to give in their annual meeting of the top 300 marketing executives. I have done such pre-meetings several times, and it always results in a more effective presentation. Private plane transportation is definitely a cut above—no hassles or waiting. When you think of the travel demands on executives and the value of their presence in the field, private aircraft, although expensive, can be justified. My Concorde supersonic experience occurred when MasterCard wanted me back from Europe to speak to their international board about a proposed change in brand strategy, a trip orchestrated by Arnene Linquito, a forceful brand strategist and friend. Years later, in August of 2001, Arnene and I shared lunch at the top of the World Trade Center in NYC only weeks before 9/11 when two planes crashed into the building. It makes you think.

Especially in Asia and Europe, I am often treated as a celebrity. For one talk in Seoul, for example, there were signs around town and banners across the main streets announcing my talk. The Seoul publicity was extreme, but other events had publicity that was visible as well. It is a weird feeling to see your name "in lights." I usually do a double take. I am interviewed at nearly every stop when abroad, usually resulting in a newspaper or business magazine article, often with a picture. I frequently get asked to autograph books. I usually think, What is wrong with this picture? I'm not exactly a major name. And if I am so great, why is this treatment so rare in the U.S.? One answer is that other more worthy people have not traveled as I have because they lack my contacts or lack interest. Nevertheless, being a celebrity, if only for a short time, has been a kick, but I would not want to be constantly playing that role as real celebrities do. Kay and my family, of course, would always bring me back to earth, as would an occasional incident like the time I was scheduled to have a big news conference after a talk in Madrid. A presidential candidate spoke before me and made a provocative announcement. Every reporter followed him out and didn't even hear my talk, to say nothing of the interview. I was completely forgotten.

At the big events there would usually be two huge screens that would contain my slides. An audio/video team of from five to twelve people would be working to make sure the event went well. The A/V people were always impressive, but things happen. Once they spent twenty minutes the night before making sure that a video clip was cued to the second. The next day it ran with no audio. So much for professional preparation. Sometimes the other speakers would use a teleprompter. I tried it once at the Saturn dealers meeting and nearly went crazy because I had never read a script before and it was a distraction. Especially in the Far East, there would often be a person just assigned to me to make sure I did not wander off and was in the right place at the right time. I'm not sure if everyone gets treated this way or if they somehow had the perception that I was unreliable or spacey.

I can see how a real celebrity could easily get jaded and become picky. Travel is demanding and tiring. Competence and extras come to be expected by speakers, and when there are imperfections it is easy to get impatient. But although I can understand the actions of prima donnas a bit, I tried to resist that tendency and attempted to be remembered as a low-maintenance speaker.

I developed a set of speaking principles that I followed, most of which have evolved over the decades starting from my early teaching days at Berkeley.

- **Never read.** For me, reading anything more than a single sentence is deadly boring and although I am usually very prepared and have transition phrases in mind, I don't read and, thus, don't use teleprompters. When I do read a sentence that defines an important concept, I read it slowly with pauses, repeating the important phrases.

- **Be prepared.** Even though I don't have a text, I do have detailed notes and have them at the podium. In most cases, I rarely refer to them, but the process of creating them is valuable.

- **Understand the audience.** Every audience is different and a misunderstanding of what the audience knows or expects usually results in some disappointments. If the group is not too large and the setting informal, I usually spend the first part asking the audience to tell me their issues. I then deal with some and refer back to others during the formal talk. When I get to spend time with the organizers of an event, my talk is more likely to be on target.

- **Have few words on a slide.** My slides average seven or eight words each and some have only pictures. I believe that slides with a lot of words detract because the audience will try to read what is there. Further, it is easy to expand or contract a talk when a slide has few words. Many of my academic and Prophet colleagues have success with slides that average dozens and sometimes well over a hundred words. But it doesn't work for me.

- **Never apologize.** I think that the speaker who starts off with an apology such as "I don't know much about this but..." or "My slides were lost..." loses credibility and creates a distraction, and no attempt at humor is worth that. Several times I lost the use of my slides because of a technical problem and I just gave the talk without them and never mentioned the fact that they were missing. I once walked into a class having prepared to teach the wrong case. I shifted gears and taught the one assigned—most students had no idea that I was less prepared than usual.

- **Illustrate.** I avoid writing or talking in the abstract. I always try to have one or more examples to illustrate concepts. For me examples both clarify and add interest.

- **Add humor.** Humor rewards the audience and extends their attention span. I am not good at remembering or telling jokes, but have the facility of creating spontaneous humorous asides. When I get one that works, I keep it in the talk.

- **Encourage Q&A.** There is an attention-span limit for most speakers. For me, talking at people for over forty minutes and certainly over sixty minutes gets long. I always try to build up the Q&A part of the talk because I enjoy Q&A and find it creates not only involvement but speaker energy.

I started to do some serious consulting for the first time. One assignment in 1995, for example, was for Providian, who were just

Dave, Katy, Jerry preparing
for a talk in Korea

introducing that name to the marketplace. One of my assignments was to help them choose an advertising agency. J. Walter Thompson was competing with a small creative shop from Texas. The small agency proposed warm ads showing couples walking on the beach—ads that were identical to what competitors with ten times (and more) the Providian budget were showing. Thompson had a clear strategic view of the problem and proposed a bridge metaphor that was sure to stand out. The Providian executive team all rejected Thompson, claiming that they "didn't understand us" and loved the warm ads. It took me about ten minutes to make them see the error of their thinking. Without my input, they would have made a disastrous decision. Rarely have I felt that my contribution was so visibly helpful.

Another job, in 1996, was to advise a major Korean firm about their brand portfolio. I worked with Katy Choi and Jerry Lee, now the owners of Brand and Company in Seoul, who are gifted brand strategists. They have since translated all my brand books into Korean and have arranged several speaking trips to Korea for me. We met in San Francisco with some client representatives from Korea who turned out to be more interested in sightseeing that in the project. Our position, that the established value brand should be retained for value offerings and the corporate name reserved for premium products, was rejected by the CEO despite a forceful memo from me (using terms like a billion-dollar mistake). He wanted to create a premium brand that would cover the whole line, and nothing would dissuade him. In the long run, his approach may succeed but, in my view, it involved brand risk and resource expenditures that were unnecessary.

Working alone was not fun and could be stressful as I was always on point. I usually felt that I lacked the time or resources to analyze the situation adequately, and I wanted the camaraderie of a colleague. In the meantime, Erich had moved from Barcelona to Virginia and we were working together on a book. So in early 1997 we started working as a consulting team and eventually joined Prophet, a brand-strategy consulting firm based in San Francisco. That story is told in the next chapter.

Berkeley

At Berkeley the marketing group thrived. We added in 1996 Priya Raghubir, an experimental psychologist from Hong Kong University (who moved closer to her husband then at Harvard—he later moved to a Bay Area school, but for a time this was a commuting marriage that set records). Two years later, we added Florian Zettelmeyer from Yale, a gifted teacher and creative quantitative researcher. Both were excellent additions to the faculty in terms of quality of research and teaching and also with respect to the faculty dynamics. It was a congenial and productive group. We would get together nearly every day for lunch and also have social events through the year.

After 2000 the group made three hires at senior levels, a difficult task because there are not many who qualify for tenure at Berkeley. Tech Ho, attracted in 2002 from Wharton, had an operations background and was an authentic research star. As a bonus, he turned out to be a gifted teacher of pricing and someone who could take over the marketing group. A year later, we hired Barbara Mellers, a prominent psychologist (once holding a full professor appointment at Berkeley), from Ohio State. Barbara studies emotion and decision making from a psychological perspective. In addition, in 2000 Ganesh Iyer, then with four years' experience, was hired. He went on to gain tenure and fit well. So Berkeley, I would say, developed a marketing group that was in the top half dozen in the country.

In 1996, I started a course on brand strategy that was supported by my first two brand books. In addition to some meaty Harvard cases, I also used the short case studies that preceded each chapter in my book. Thus, the students were exposed to brands such as Harley-Davidson (the power of brand personality), L.L. Bean (brand heritage), Schlitz (the pain of losing perceived quality), Nissan/Datson (the difficulty of a name change), Levi's Tailored Classics (the need for an extension to fit the brand), Gillette (introducing a man's brand to women), Ralph Lauren (sorting out the logic of a complex brand portfolio), Healthy Choice (the power of a strong brand platform), Intel (the justification for the Intel Inside program), Virgin (differentiating an airline), Saturn (a different shopping experience), Asahi (creating a new category), GE (moving a brand up), Marriott (endorsing a value brand like Courtyard), Adidas (using the Street Ball Challenge to invigorate the brand), and Heineken (global brand issues). As usual, I pushed the students to defend their opinions so superficial answers did not survive. The course also included a field brand project that, as predicted, was an outstanding learning experience. My branding material was introduced into executive programs where I felt more confident than ever that I had something to say.

My teaching load at Berkeley was light—I only taught one semester and often only two or three courses (the third being in the evening MBA program). One reason that I virtually never took a sabbatical was that I didn't need time off from teaching. In part to make my workload seem more respectable and in part because I thought the program worthwhile, I taught a freshman seminar on consumer behavior designed to expose freshman to senior professors. My class consisted of a discussion of the project of the week. One, for example, was to talk to others to determine the image of Gap, Nordstorm's, and Macy's, and to hypothesize why the images were different and how they could be changed. Students were challenged—just like an MBA class—which was intimidating to some but appreciated by most.

Even as the 90s began, I was beginning to tire of the academic world. Teaching was still fun but not the preparation, the grading, and the confining schedule. If you have a class at two on Tuesday they expected you to show, even if it isn't convenient (and I rarely missed a class). Thus, I had trouble doing any consulting or speaking that involved travel outside the West Coast during a teaching term. Much more troubling was the fact that academic research, although impressive on several levels, was getting increasingly abstract and theoretical. It was often linked to managerial problems and realistic market contexts in only the most remote and convoluted way. I felt obligated to attend our weekly seminars and review papers for journals, but it was becoming painful to do both because I was intellectually and professionally drawn to real-world managerial problems. Increasingly, I enjoyed associating with and communicating to (with talks, articles, or books) executives and making contributions relevant to them. Executives and academics are very different.

Although I was ready to move on, I always appreciated the academic life I had enjoyed for nearly thirty years. Academia in general, and Berkeley in particular, represented a wonderful career. You get to teach. The satisfaction from creating a good course, interacting with students, and influencing careers is very rewarding. Being on the classroom podium with a receptive audience is a feel-good experience. The ability to spend time on research is priceless. It is so stimulating. There are literally no constraints on what research you do or who you do it with—anything that interests you is fair game. Getting an article through the review process is extremely satisfying and knowing that it is a home run is a real high. Seeing your book on a shelf has its own reward. My marketing colleagues, not only at Berkeley but everywhere (people are surprised when I say that all research-oriented marketing professors in the world know each other, but it is close to the truth) are just joys to be with because they are so bright and curious and because some part of that group is so fun to hang with. Except for meeting classes, your time is your own. You can play tennis or golf or travel any time you want. When you do your research, or where for that matter, is up to you.

Dave, Dean Ben Hermalin, Russ Winer, Pete Bucklin, Laura Tyson, Carol Chapman (my assistant), and Priya Raghubir

Assuming that you are not intimidated by the research or teaching demands, being a professor at a research school is an ideal job. I always appreciated it. I recall when I got tenure in 1972, less than four years after arriving, saying "Wow! Tenure at Berkeley!" Just think of the talented tenured professors in other departments at Berkeley—some were even Nobel Laureates. I had similar thoughts when I got full in 1976 and when I received a chair in 1981. Berkeley certainly had shortcomings, but in the big picture I was thankful to be at such a fine university and proud about the company I was in.

When I left the university to become associated with Prophet, there was a reception where I was given a framed picture of the building. To give back to the school I committed to give a lecture each spring on my current thinking around brands. I also committed to sponsoring a lecture in the fall. Lou Stern, my golfing buddy and one of the leaders in channel management, gave the first one. Hiro Takeuchi gave the second. Jennifer gave the third and said some touching things about my support during her career. The fourth was Kevin Keller, my brand research partner at the outset and a brand guru in his own right.

Recreation in the Nineties

I was still an active tennis player throughout the nineties but increasingly played for the social benefits and exercise rather

Frank Stahlschmidt

than the competition. Singles with Tom DeJonghe provided a chance to exchange opinions on the topic of the day—from health care to the greatness—or not—of Clinton. Doubles at Moraga Country Club provided a way to exchange witticism with people like Jerry Mosher, Mark Bohuslov, Alan Smith, Hank Lancaster, Frank Stahlschmidt, and Larry Evans.

The humor revolved around apparent compliments. When I would call attention to one of my exceptional shots, Frank might observe that my shot was so impressive that Aggazi would envy it—Semour Aggazi. If Frank would criticize my shirt, I would note that my goal in life was to dress as tastefully as he did, even though everyone realized that his wardrobe was hardly exemplary. He would also cheerfully give permission for others to watch and even film his shots without charge. Frank doubled as a golfing partner and speaker at our anniversary party (discussed in the next chapter). During his talk at the party, he claimed that when I asked an opponent to repeat a comment after a disagreement that I did it in a threatening way that made him believe that we were going to engage in fisticuffs. I am too passive for that to be true.

Larry Evans became my art mentor. In part because of Larry, who became a full-time art dealer sometime in the early 90s, I became fascinated with contemporary art. I wondered about how paintings that were just weird sold for so much money and how the painter's name got to be valued and prominent (to me it was a brand problem). On Larry's suggestion I once went to a preview of an art auction in New York. I noted that a canvas by William Ryman was completely white (what I thought was a black spot turned out to be a bit of dust) and was expected to sell for over $200,000. Larry explained that Rymans were valued because he represented the logical end point of the minimalist school; the historical context of a painter is important. A piece by anyone (like me) that copied Ryman would not be valued even though the end result would be indistinguishable from the real thing. A wonderful, funny play, *Art*, was based on a roommate that bought and was proud of a Ryman and tried to explain its beauty to others. The absurdity (and appeal and humor) of modern art was never more exposed.

When I go into a city, I gravitate to the modern art museum just because they are so interesting—I have been to MOMA in New York and the Tate Modern in London many times. Once in the Tate I was struck by a work that involved a person hitting himself with boxing gloves and then pouring catsup over his body. Even with Larry's interpretation, it defied logic. However, I realized that I had seen hundreds of art works that day, and that was the one that stuck in my mind. I still recall one work that I saw in an Aoyama art gallery over fifteen years ago that showed real shoes on an old table that was out of balance. Again, art is a lot like branding—you need to be noticed and to be memorable.

I was still interested in tennis and developed a taste for art, but my passion turned to biking and powder skiing.

Biking

Riding through a field of flowers in a single track in Jackson Hole with Tom. Going up Mount Tam with Alec Biel and seeing a dramatic but different view every fifteen minutes and sharing ridges with hawks. Visiting a remote art gallery while biking the North Coast of Maui with Mike Kelly. Observing a dozen ridges while riding the East Ridge of Redwood Park by my home with Bob Blain. Riding with Jan into Telluride in the rain or into Zion in the heat. Pedaling down the Colorado at Moab between two rocks hundreds of feet high some with 3,000-year-old artwork on them. Seeing the bald eagles nesting in Shell Ridge while biking with Jolyn. Both mountain and road biking have added a lot to my life. It gets you off the beaten path where you can enjoy great vistas, quiet and not-so-quiet streams, wildlife, majestic forests, and peaceful meadows. Plus, it is a good workout and chance to share experiences.

One vehicle for road biking is Backroads, a Berkeley organization that organizes trips that are mostly road biking. We got started one summer in the late 80s when George and Marilyn Day had extra space in a Backroads trip to the Sonoma wine country that they had organized. So the DeJonghes, Kay, Jennifer, Jan, and I went for a five-day trip and got to see some country in our backyard. It was some tough biking in hot weather, but each night there was a great dinner and a quaint, interesting place to stay. Van support meant that you could ride whenever the hills or the heat were too much. A big plus was living for a week with interesting people, in this case some friends of the Days from Japan. My kids often compare our family to George's, all of whom seemed to be relentlessly positive, enthusiastic, bright, successful, and wonderful bikers. Marilyn, in particular, was a delightful, upbeat person who never wasted a day.

Our second trip, to Maine in 1995, involved Kay and Jan. On one of the days, we biked through an island that contained the plush summer homes to which the New Yorkers of a century ago escaped the heat of Manhattan. It was fun to imagine the lifestyles of the wealthy at the turn of the century. On another, we did some kayaking. Charming B&B's and excellent restaurants tempered the biking. The leader was Jan's friend, Megan Lynch, with whom she had lived in Aspen for a year. Megan is a bundle of enthusiasm and capable of fixing a broken chain in seconds. Her latest venture is to open a coffee shop around a bike theme near Golden Gate Park in San Francisco.

The next two trips were with Jan. In Sun Valley, Jan and I biked through some lush valleys and got to experience some charming and challenging mountain biking trails. On one I fell and missed a sharp tree fragment by inches. Off-road biking is not without risks. This was my only camping trip since Boy Scout days. Each night we would set up a tent, an activity that was hilarious. We were incompetent at both putting it up and in organizing the interior. Jan claimed I had stuff all over the tent. It was a scene from *Three Men in a Boat* by Jerome, a book that was introduced in chapter seven. We did improve during the course of the week. I am not a camper but must admit that it gets you to some neat places for which there are no hotel alternatives. I vividly recall setting off with Jan one crisp, sunny morning after we had camped by a lake. It was a precious moment—we observed that life could not get much better.

The next trip was in Western Colorado where Jan and I did a big loop which included the ski areas of Telluride and Purgatory (where we got to have a mountain bike ride). It was on this trip that I did a century (100 miles). It was a 115-mile day with 60 miles downhill and four big hills. I rode the van up three of the hills and had to ride around Durango for three miles to make the century, but I made it. There are a lot of people that do not need to hear about my century one more time.

The fifth trip was in Canada in 2002 where Jan, Jolyn, and my friend Mike Kelly joined me. We biked from Banff to Jasper and saw dramatic mountains and declining but still awesome glaciers, one of which, a huge hunk of ice, we walked on. Comparing the pictures of glaciers over the years makes the global warming trend visible. The trip was along a busy road, but the scenery compensated for the noise of the trucks. I played a picturesque, great golf course at Jasper on the last day—a bonus activity. Each hole seemed to be facing a mountain.

The sixth trip was in 2003 when Jan, Mike Kelly, and Bob Blain, another biking friend, biked the canyons in Utah (Zion, Grand, and Bryce). I saw these geologic marvels for the first time and got to do some desert biking as well. On the most spectacular 127-mile day, I did about 65 miles. Jan and I started early from the Grand Canyon and biked four hours through the rolling forest. Jan continued biking while I shifted to the van, thereby missing three humongous hills. We hooked up again for the ten or so miles into the spectacular Zion Canyon, a breathtaking sight. Both Mike and Bob like to "chat up" passersby while hiking or stopping on bikes. That sometimes challenged my patience but, upon reflection (as noted in chapter two), I always concluded that I should work on slowing down and be more like them. I took some pride in keeping up with Bob, a faster biker, for three hours one day until he charged ahead after an attractive member of our group. Bob tells the story differently.

In the late 80s, I began to get into mountain biking, where, unlike road biking, there are no noisy, dangerous cars and often no sign of civilization. The setting is some version of wilderness—albeit sometimes shared with others. In several rides, we saw postings of mountain lion sighting but my wildlife experiences are limited to a fox at Tilden Park, some wild boar in Briones Park, two eagles at Shell Ridge, moose at Jackson Hole, and hawks on the ridges of Mt. Tam. We do know that if a lion or bear are sighted we need to make ourselves as large as possible. Mountain biking has been a vehicle to see some amazing sights in the Bay Area and elsewhere. There are dozens of trails that are literally ten to fifty minutes from my home that I never saw until I started mountain biking.

My inspiration and mentor has been Alec Biel. I met Alec in the late 1980s when he became the director of an advertising research center in San Francisco set up by David Olgivy (founder of Olgivy and Mather, or O&M). We shared an interest in brands and research and, as already noted, we co-edited a book for a 1990 conference. Alec regularly accuses me of sending rough unpolished drafts of books and papers out with the goal of getting my friends to share in the writing and editing. There is some truth to that. My style is to get some kind of first draft and then improve and structure it later, drawing on whomever I can get to comment.

Alec had a lifestyle that I always envied. He had (and has) a home in picturesque Mill Valley at the foot of Mt. Tam, where he summered, and another, at which I have been a regular visitor, at the base of Aspen Mountain, where he wintered. That was when he was not on a consulting assignment somewhere around the world or on one of his exotic vacations—every year, for example, he would go mountaineering (where you ski up a mountain and then ski down) and biking in Austria. Recently, he spent a week helicopter-skiing at 16,000 feet in India. Just hearing about one of his trips was a kick. Alec and I explored over fifteen mountain biking rides, most with variants, throughout the Bay Area.

There have been memorable partners and incidents. Once I was biking in Tilden with a group that included Jan's friend Wendy Hazzard (who once was a competitive skier and now is Wendy McClain, a mom who lives close to Jan). Wendy and I decided to take a road less traveled and ended up in a ravine down a twenty-foot steep embankment. I searched for an outlet and came back to find my bike gone. Wendy had carried two bikes up a trail I could not navigate without holding onto branches. A

Jan, Dave, and Jolyn in Canada

Mike Kelly and Dave in Maui

Alec and Erich at the
Top of Mt. Tam

Tom in Moab

few minutes later, she cheerfully repaired my flat in about two minutes. She is not the only biking partner that has been out of my league. Our backroad trips were populated by some people who apparently viewed a marathon as a relaxed weekend. When on my bike, I was better off with people more my speed like Mike Kelly, Alec Biel, or Ivan Peterson (a mortgage broker and friend who can change tires effortlessly).

Mountain biking is safe in that you can always walk down steep hills and there are no cars. But I went over the handlebars on three occasions, landing on my shoulder each time. The incident happens so fast that there is no time to even instinctively protect yourself. I have been lucky not to have a neck injury like Christopher Reeve did. The worst time was on cement when I turned a corner only to see two small children on bikes. I separated my shoulder and aggravated a neck problem that meant that my tennis days were over—after forty-five minutes of tennis I now get an aching shoulder. I kept on biking, but I no longer urge others to take up the sport.

I'm sure that I have gone on over a thousand mountain bike rides in over one hundred venues. Some of these rides involved biking with Tom DeJonghe on our vacations in places such as Taos, Jackson Hole, Seattle, Downieville, and Sun River. The worst rides are picturesque and enjoyable. The best are wonderful. Here are my top dozen rides:

1. Mount Tam, Marin County, California The vistas, which go from a forest to the Bay to the city to the hills overlooking the ocean and to the ocean itself, are simply awesome. There are a lot of Mt. Tam variants, but one of the best rides is to go from the base to the West Point Inn (about two-thirds up) and then out to the ocean. When you break from the forest to the meadow above the ocean you want to sing (unfortunately, I can't sing at all) "The Sound of Music," "Oklahoma," or the "Alleluia Chorus."

2. Jackson Hole, Wyoming There is a trail along a stream that leads to a path through wetlands where you ride through shoulder-high flowers and often see moose hanging out.

3. Harrah Pass, Moab, Utah A ride through a cathedral of rock hundreds of feet high. One of the most dramatic sights I have ever seen.

4. Sun River, Oregon A spectacular but mellow trail along a scenic river that is mostly peaceful except for three or four impassable rapids.

5. Downieville, California The new mountain biking mecca in the Gold Country north of Truckee has the Downieville downhill, a ride through rugged forest terrain and along rushing mountain streams. Racers do the downhill in forty-five minutes but for me it is well over two hours.

6. Tahoe, California The Flum Trail runs above Lake Tahoe and provides a dramatic view of the lake. The five-mile ride up to the trailhead is a good warm up.

7. Moab, Utah Klondike Bluffs is a trail up solid rocks to a mesa with a view of the Arches National Part and the Monitor and Merrimac Buttes. Along the way there are a half-dozen dinosaur tracks in the rocks. Really.

8. Redwood Park, Oakland, California Only minutes from my house, there are two ridges from which to choose. Each provides a view of an extensive set of forested hills and ridges. The park is preceded by four miles of road biking through an incredible forest.

9. Downieville The Chimney Rock trail, which takes me over five hours, extends far into remote mountain country. At one point around a sharp turn in the trail some giant rocks, some four stories high, appear. One of them, termed Chimney Rock, seems suspended out in space. On my first ride on this trail, I was two hours out with Jan, Rich (Jan's husband), and Nicole DeJonghe when we ran out of water (we were told it was a short ride) and seemed lost as the trail was going down into an isolated canyon. We almost turned around four yards from a switchback leading in the right direction.

10. China Camp, Marin County, California A rugged trial through the trees ending up at a peninsula that houses

a museum commemorating the life and times of the Chinese population in the Bay Area who had found a refuge in this remote area in the late 1800s. They prospered by fishing until that avenue was closed to them by the politicians of the day. A sad chapter of U.S. history.

11. Bolinas Ridge, Marin County, California A twelve-mile ridge that goes through a rain forest and emerges onto a rolling pasture.

12. Lake Chabot, Oakland, California A rolling ride through a forest and around a large lake.

Powder Skiing

Powder skiing is incredible on several levels. First, the surroundings are pristine: new untracked snow; mountain terrain; rock cliffs 3,000 feet high; ridges with awe-inspiring, 360-degree views; skiing through aspens or through forests—and new snow makes the scenery even more unreal. Second, the skiing itself, when you get into the groove through virgin snow (and that is actually easy with wide skis), is like hitting twenty consecutive 300-yard drives. The snow pushes you up so you are weightless half the time. Third, the camaraderie with others sharing the experience is special. Talking about it afterward extends the pleasure.

Tom and I skied regularly through the 70s and 80s. We had ski weeks in Squaw for many years. In addition, we made a host of day trips to Sugar Bowl, around four trips to Utah, a trip to Aspen (when Jan spent a year being a ski bum after college), and another to Breckenridge (where Nicole DeJonghe was spending a year after college). We enjoyed skiing but really looked forward to powder days.

Learning to ski powder was a challenge. For a long time we required powder on modest slopes so that we did not lose control. It was several years before we developed the confidence to point the skis down on steeper terrain. It turns out that powder skiing is easy when you can go down a fall line with a reasonable pitch. It became easier yet when they invented "Fat Boys," which are extra-wide skis that allow you to float on the top and bounce

Helliskiing—Dave, Tom, Bob Blain,
Bob Bisno, Jan Bisno—1993

Jolyn in powder   Fat boys, Jan, Tom

through turns (rather than power through them). We spent (and still do spend) a lot of time searching out the edges of a ski area looking for a place where a few turns in powder might be possible.

In 1993 we started helicopter skiing out of Elko, Nevada. It turns out that Nevada is not just desert—it has mountain ranges including the Rubies near Elko. Our friend, Bob Bisno, organized the chartering of a small plane that made the trip extremely efficient. We would go up late Thursday, ski two and a half days, and return Sunday often in time to play some tennis on Bob's court. And we would stay at Red's Ranch, which featured a central lodge with an enormous fireplace, where we would enjoy great breakfasts and dinners and all the popcorn you could eat.

Bob was and is an unforgettable person with an unbelievable repertoire of mostly off-color jokes that he would tell with enthusiasm and lead in the laughter. Starting with a rental home in Oakland in the '70s, he became a major California developer and operator of properties with the latest being a large and very upscale hotel and condo complex in Sun Valley. His tales of his latest venture are always interesting. He lives in a home in L.A. about six times the size of mine but never makes me feel anything but a friend who would always be included in his very different lifestyle.

The skiing is relatively safe. We are all checked out with beepers. There is a guide for four skiers and four sets of skiers per helicopter. When there is any chance of an avalanche, only one skier is on a hill at a time. Very different from the systems in Canada where there are two guides for fifteen skiers and there is much less discipline about who is where. However, I did learn that avalanches move fast and result in a run-off that is somewhat like concrete—if you are in one, you don't have much time. Also helicopters are not foolproof. Two weeks after my second trip, the helicopter I was skiing in crashed, killing five people including the president of Disney. It makes you think.

Memories ... driving to the airport and just walking on the private plane; hitting twenty turns on a wide-open virgin field of snow; catching a ski in a hidden treetop in an open snowfield and spraining a wrist (the next day I did not ski and was perversely glad to learn that I'd missed breakable crust—the worst snow possible); lunch beside the copter in a valley; kicking the snow off the bindings after leaving the helicopter; fresh popcorn by the fire; seeing the girls (each of whom joined me on one trip) be so exhilarated by the snow and handle it so well—Jolyn on a snowboard; interacting with the guides. (What is the difference between a guide and a savings bond? The bond eventually matures.)

My Ruby's adventures lasted for seven years. Then I got touches of altitude sickness—the first time I was moving at slow motion at great effort and had to be lifted to lower elevation. So the next year, 2000, I went Cat skiing in Canada with Alec outside of Fernie, about one hundred miles from Calgary. We skied out of a lodge in the wilderness and resulted in some great powder in mountains much lower than those in Nevada, so there was no danger of altitude sickness. Seats on the Cats, however, are hard to come by during the prime weeks. Over the years I have also visited Alec in Aspen and have done Cat skiing there as well when my visit corresponded with a storm. Powder skiing never gets old. It is, for me, the pinnacle of outdoor activities.

Politics

A Goldwater Republican during the early 60s, the Vietnam War caused me to become an anti-war Democrat—but a moderate, fiscally conservative Democrat (my father's Republican influence lingered). At the end of the 60s and the early 70s, anyone that opposed LBJ's war had my support. I was particularly irritated by Nixon's position that opposition to the war was unpatriotic and was hurting his efforts to end the war (which included massive bombing of Cambodia and numerous initiatives to increase the body count). I listened to the Watergate hearings with fascination (the movie *All the President's Men* with Robert Redford and Dustin Hoffman captures the drama well) and was glad to see him removed.

In the 80s, I was disturbed about Reagan's fiscal irresponsibility and made multiple bets with Tom that they would result in inflation as my undergrad econ course had taught me. I lost all those bets and still don't understand why. I was so pleased to see Clinton arrive, finally a moderate. I thought that he was a brilliant president both domestically and internationally. Hearing him speak after his term (in a speakers series to which we subscribe) did nothing to change my view. His impeachment and the actions that precipitated it were, in my view, a tragedy because they inhibited his effectiveness and accelerated the partisanship that has poisoned Washington.

During the 90s, I got an up-close look at Washington politics through my friend David Minge, the husband of my cousin Karen (a picture of David appears in chapter seven). When David turned fifty in 1991, he was practicing law in Montevideo, Minnesota. He decided then and there to run for Congress, to do something besides complain. An unknown, he became the compromise winner of the Democratic primary and subsequently upset a strong Republican (by 500 votes). As part of his campaign, he and supporters biked across his district—an activity that represented his values, lifestyle, and energy. He ultimately served four terms before he was defeated by special interests (primarily the NRA) in 2000. Governor Jessie Ventura then appointed him to the Minnesota Court of Appeals, where he now sits.

Having a friend in Congress and being involved in his campaign was fascinating. I was in charge of raising family money. Our money was not big, but it was early and it turns out early money is huge in a campaign because it gives the candidate timely credibility and momentum. I got to discuss politics and issues with David on a regular basis. And Kay and I were invited to the 1996 inauguration ball for Bill Clinton. The ball was a black-tie affair, and the women's gowns were a sight to behold. Actually there were many balls, and we went to the California one. It was a memorable night, the highlight being the appearance of the Clintons and the Gores. When I visited David, I would make it a point to attend congressional committee deliberations. I recall one in which Diane Feinstein was particularly impressive (and some others were not).

Dave was a moderate, fiscally conservative Democrat—one of some two dozen like-minded "blue-dog" Democrats in Congress. He was thoughtful about issues (he would call me to get names of economists at Berkeley from which he could get outside opinions of issues before his committee) and principled (he voted against

From Fargo to the World of Brands

pork barrel projects in his own district). We need more people like David in Congress, people who are moderate and thoughtful. Decades ago there used to be "Rockefeller Republicans" and conservative Democrats that actively competed for their party's nomination. No more. Moderates can no longer be nominated from either party despite the fact that the majority of voters prefer moderates. There are therefore few that look at issues objectively and have the ability to work across parties. It is a shame, and it only seems to get worse.

In fact, I worry about the future of our republic, as extremism seems to be winning. It is becoming impossible for anyone in public life to compromise because the special interests are so committed that they regard those that do not toe the line to the letter as opponents. And the special interests are powerful because they provide money, a voter base, and people who are willing to be involved. Further, the election process has been distorted because the congressional boundaries have been drawn so that less than 5% of the 535 or so congressional seats are even competitive. Thus, the special interests can target these few districts that are not safe. In my view, one small step toward recapturing our democracy is to get impartial bodies to draw up the congressional boundaries. Arnold Schwarzenegger, a moderate who got on the ballot because of a recall and thus bypassed the nomination process, attempted to do that in California, but opposition of entrenched interests has been vigorous.

Although I am a Democrat, I would support a moderate of either party. I would have been happy to see John McCain as president (and donated money to his campaign), but instead we got George W. Bush, who, to my eyes, was a disaster with respect to fiscal responsibility, foreign relations, and the handling of the Iraq war. Of course, in the polarized climate of today, I too, am hardly objective and know that I filter information and judgments through my biases.

Cal Bears

Being a Cal fan was marginally better in the nineties. The football team was better with four bowl (albeit minor ones) appearances. Two (1990 and 1991) of the three bowl wins were due in large part to quarterback Mike Palawski, runner Russell White, and coach Bruce Snyder (who left in 1992 to go to Arizona State). Another, a losing effort in 1996, was led by quarterback Pat Barnes, linebacker Matt Beck, and coach Steve Mariucci (who only coached in 1996 before going to the pros—the Berkeley curse). For a Cal fan, that was a good decade.

Basketball got to the post season six of the ten years. By far the high point was the first Jason Kidd year (1993-94) where we beat heavily favored Duke in the second round of the NCAA tourney—a thrill comparable with the first UCLA victory of 1986. It was to be our only second-round win in the NCAA tournament, but for a Cal fan that made a good decade. In 1999 the new Haas pavilion opened with 11,500 seats; I grabbed four of the most comfortable. So we were poised for the next good team.

I became involved in football recruiting, often going to Saturday morning breakfast meetings with recruits. I was always the lone voice talking about how fun it is to take courses at a school like Berkeley with all its great teachers. Others would talk about Berkeley prestige and how the recruit could help build a winner. I thus got to be on the field for a game (and hear the awesome collisions) and go into the locker room before the game and at half time. The coach would have to get the team up or to keep them going if they were behind. A lot of yelling and praying occurred. I wondered if it did much good, as we often lost, and I also wondered what those players who were not Christians thought about praying in the name of Jesus.

I contributed to Cal athletes in other ways as well. I taught a seminar one year on marketing Cal athletics, focusing on women's basketball (players sponsoring a free throw shooting contest in the central plaza was one idea) and football (we studied suggestions to change ticket pricing to attract students). I also worked with a group that was redesigning the logos. It turns out that there are two brands. One, Berkeley, is the brand that the academics use (I teach at Berkeley) and another, Cal, is used in an athletic context (Cal played today). The visual presentation of the brand needed to reflect that reality.

At the suggestion of Mohammed Muqtar, a good friend and one-man moral support staff to Cal athletes, I also helped the football coaching staff develop a brand identity for the football team and the university so that coaches and players could be more capable of being "on-brand" when recruiting. There were actually two identities. Cal football had a core identity around team excellence (to be top of conference), individual excellence (coaching, goals), responsible players (character, empowered, discipline), and student first/athlete second (graduation, academics a priority). The University of California brand had a core identity of top school (rankings, students, career preparation), cultural experience (diversity, students, and speakers), and fun/exciting place (variety of majors and courses, professors, social life). The result provided a tool for the coaching staff to sharpen their ability to describe the experience of being on the team and to create the right culture. However, it did not seem to help them on the field.

The Family

An important part of my life continued to be Kay and the kids. It is remarkable how important. We have been blessed to have them close so I can interact with them frequently. More significant is the fact that I can follow and take pride in their lives, friends, careers, and families. It is much of my life's purpose and joy.

The nineties saw Jolyn grow from seventeen to twenty-six. She entered Davis, majored in history, and spent four years playing college soccer. When it was over and I had no team to follow around the country, I had serious withdrawal pains. We got to visit Jolyn during her semester in London and saw what student living is like when we stayed in one of the smallest hotel rooms ever constructed—selected because it was close to her housing.

Jolyn in college got interested in social service. Upon graduation she worked for a county group that provides caregivers to some 7,000 low-income elderly and physically disabled people in the county so they can continue to live in their existing homes. It is a program that does so much for those affected and is incredibly cost-effective, as many of these would be institutionalized at enormous cost. By providing minimum wage caregiver jobs, it helps the community as well—a win-win program. I use it as an example to my friends, many of which believe that all government programs are wasteful. She then got her master's in social welfare at Berkeley (where my parking pass made me a valued friend). Upon graduation she joined the regional center where her caseload involves forty or so developmentally handicapped adults that live in supervised care facilities. She has always got accolades about her caring attitude and her skill. Her clients and their caregivers really appreciate having her involved. I am so proud of her, her talent, and her choice of a career.

Jan graduated from Davis in 1991 after spending a semester in Australia. With the DeJonghes, we visited her in Sydney and went snorkeling on the Great Barrier Reef. It was there that I almost took a swim one morning not realizing that the waters contained poisonous jellyfish—very dangerous. Luckily I don't like to swim. Jan spent a year at Aspen teaching three and four-year-olds to ski, and our group again followed her. She lived there with Wendy Hazzard (McLain), Megan Lynch, and Babs Wolf. Babs was and is incredible. She has scuba dived below the North Pole (the third women to do so), taught scuba diving in the South Pacific, served as a ranger in the mountains of Alaska, hiked through forbidden jungles in Southeast Asia, and led extended trips through Africa driving a huge truck. And that is only part of the story. We all share her adventures vicariously. It is exhausting just thinking about it. Her sister, Libbit, became Jan's roommate, close friend, and bearer of news about the latest exploits of Babs.

After the Aspen break, Jan was ready to get a teaching credential and begin her career in the classroom. One reviewer of her teaching style said that her "... planning, caring, and calm demeanor all help to make a wonderful and stimulating learning environment," and that her innovations like a "book club" approach to literature make learning come alive. In the classroom she is relaxed, calm, humorous, and positive. The kids clearly enjoy themselves. One fifth-grader said that Jan was "... easy to talk to and would laugh when I said something instead of telling me that I was in trouble." She, like her mother, was born to teach.

In her first class, I was called on to give the students a soccer lesson on a wet day. At the end, I jokingly asked those kids that were not dirty enough to slide in the mud. Seven kids started running, and I still recall the horrified look on Jan's face. I was not invited back.

Aspen ski bums—Megan Lynch, Wendy Hazzard,
Jan, and Babs Wolf

Jan lived in a funky apartment in San Francisco with Megan and Libbit. I got out there frequently for dinners in or out. Rich Broad, who Jennifer knew at Berkeley, became a roommate until he and Jan connected when he moved out in order to have a more conventional dating relationship. He proposed to her while hiking in the Dolomites just after our family trip to Florence with the DeJonghes and the Garmans (Mark Garman, also a professor at Berkeley, and his wife Barbara are members of our bridge club) in 1997. Rich and Jan were married in 1998 in a retreat in the wine country. I gave a great talk during the groom's dinner, full of warmth and humor. With all my good material used up, I then discovered I needed to give another after the wedding. I never made that mistake again.

At the wedding, I got to spend some time with Jan before walking her over a bridge to the ceremony. Some in the group did not recognize it as a wedding highlight, but for me it was a thrill of a lifetime. It seemed like the culmination of so many special

Crossing the
bridge—1998

Dave and Sue Broad, Rich Broad, Jan, Kay, and Dave

times I had shared with Jan. I basked in the glow of the feeling for hours. After the vows there was a party at which Rich sang a song to Jan that he'd composed, thereby setting a high standard for my future son-in-laws. There were talks as well. Tom recounted ten reasons why they made such a great couple, several of which were a bit racy. The professional speakers in the family (Jennifer and I) were concerned about the amateur, Jolyn, so we let her go first. Big mistake. It turns out that she is not only articulate but also sincere and emotional; she had everyone crying. Jennifer and I agreed such tactics were a bit unfair to other speakers. The word now in the family is to avoid going after Jolyn at all costs.

Rich's parents are wonderful, laid-back people. Sue is the perfect mother and grandmother and Dave is a painter of landscapes. Rich's brother, Steve, and his wife, Annie Chun, have a small but growing firm that makes packaged Asian food, Annie Chun's, which I have been involved in as an advisor and investor. Well positioned as a good tasting, natural, convenient, Asian, and interesting cuisine, the brand captures several of the positive trends in food retailing.

Rich and Jan bought a charming house with character in Lafayette, less than ten minutes by car and thirty minutes by bike from our house. It has location, location, location, as it is within walking distance from the downtown area, playgrounds, and great schools right up through high school.

Jennifer became a marketing professor. It sounds like a remarkable coincidence, except she is not the first person to follow a parent's career path. After a year of working for an advertising agency in New York, she studied at Stanford (note the similarity) and took her dissertation on brand personality under my friend and coauthor Kevin Keller, an excellent but tough mentor. In 1995 she graduated and started teaching at UCLA where most of her students were older than she and several were fellow students from high school or Berkeley. So she tried to look older by wearing suits and (unnecessary) glasses, but it was tough with her California blond looks. At least one former high school classmate wanted to know when she was taking marketing only to learn that Jennifer was his professor rather than fellow student. I would go down every five or six weeks and roller blade or play tennis and then have dinner with Jennifer and friends like Renee Chang (introduced in chapter eight), Kathy Yeung (a UCLA MBA who designs jewelry and develops business plans for an assortment of entrepreneurs), and Aimee Drolet (who graduated from Stanford with Jennifer and became her UCLA colleague), and then catch the 9:00 p.m. flight back. It was a good rhythm.

A word about Aimee, who has been a good friend since her Stanford student days with Jennifer. Quirky, humorous, irreverent, and interesting, she is fun to be with on many levels. Unlike most business school professors she openly admits she has no interest in management; she is a psychologist and has worked as an archeologist. She once seriously considered whether being an author of romance novels would be a more appropriate career than being a professor. Curiously, she is a popular teacher despite discouraging student interaction, using academic content in her course, and even having her students be subjects in her experiments. I suspect that they appreciate her attitude, humor, and razor-sharp intellect. When I guest speak for her (in contrast to Jennifer), the schedule and content is very flexible. A movie buff, she is a wonderful source of commentary on movies, especially classics of the thirties and forties. Aimee is one of a kind—in the best way.

In 1999 Jennifer married Andy Smith, a wonderful, talented person although some might say a bit geeky because of his interest in computers and sound systems. Now at Dolby Laboratories as a global brand manager, he previously was at Intel and two dot-com companies where, like everyone else, he tried to ride the wave. In 1999 Jennifer moved to Stanford, and she and Andy bought a home in Burlingame, about forty-five minutes from our place.

Jennifer's wedding was at the First Presbyterian Church in Lafayette where she was active in youth programs as a high school student (with me as an advisor). The wedding reception, held at the Claremont Hotel, featured a poem written by Jan and Jolyn that provides some insight into personalities and relationships. It reads in part:

- *Jen is the oldest child, the favorite we say,*

Paul, Dave, Kay, Andy, Jennifer, Ida, Jolyn, Jan, Rich—1999

Aimee Drolet, Jennifer Ruger, Kathy Yeung, Jan, Jolyn,
Carrie Resh, Renee Chang, Leslie Jones

Tom, Dave,
and Alec at
Jennifer's
wedding

- *We can hear our dad reminding, "She is just more special, what can I say?"*
- *Being the favorite, more perfect she grew,*
- *Don't worry, our issues are only a few.*
- *With unending love, Jen grew a beautiful soul,*
- *And to have Mom and Dad's strengths became one of her many goals.*
- *Jen always had every shoe in perfect row,*
- *If one was out of place, watch out! She would know*
- *She gives and she gives, with others in sight,*
- *Bone marrow drives, tutoring, she does it all, and she does it all right.*
- *Absent-minded professor, and a good sense of humor, she mastered from our dad.*
- *In the classroom, she is a natural, she is really, really RAD.*
- *We pick up the phone with any feeling,*
- *Cause Jen is always our source of healing.*
- *We unload our thoughts, and all our troubles,*
- *And count on Jen to analyze, comfort, and dig through the rubble.*
- *Don't worry she has found a perfect match,*
- *Andy is a fellow computer nerd—what a catch!*

It has been rewarding to be able to be involved in Jennifer's career and to be an observer as an insider. She claims that I have been a big help to her, supporting her during tough times in graduate school, being a sounding board for ideas, reading early drafts of papers, helping her make career decisions, and just being a friend. I have enjoyed all that, plus having the chance to see her excel. She has become a star, one of the top people of her field with a worldwide reputation. She has had four or five home-run papers and actually started one research area, cross-cultural research based on experimental psychology, and restarted another, brand personality.

Jennifer moved from UCLA to Stanford in 1999. In her first year at Stanford, she taught the core marketing class (a difficult assignment because it is a required course) and proceeded to win the award at Stanford as the best teacher. This was not entirely unexpected because she won similar awards at UCLA. Her classes are interesting, relevant, and humorous, and she has a way of relating to students. They seem to sense that she cares about and understands them. Her practice of memorizing all their names before the first class contributes to that impression. Her first ten years were many times more impressive than mine.

Jennifer's career indeed has been fun to watch, but it is a bit humbling when I am called to speak or consult because she is not available. Jennifer was careful to distance herself from me from the outset because she wanted to develop her own reputation and because my managerial image conflicted with her desire to be perceived as more interested in basic (less managerial) work. She was also sensitive to connecting to me in the classroom. The first year she taught, I was hidden in the back when visiting—I even left before the break so students would not see me. The next year I was introduced and given ten minutes of airtime. That gradually increased until I now have a whole guest-lecture slot. But a student does not get points by asking if she is "the daughter of David Aaker."

Kay and I were admitted in the mid-80s into a four-couple, duplicate bridge/dinner club that has been an ongoing source of laughs, good food, and excellent companionship. By the nineties the group included Jorg and Lisa Reinholt (the original members), Barbara and Mark Garman, and Jane and Steve Roath. (When Jorg and Lisa moved to Orcas Island, Bob and Laura Wilson joined.) Steve became the president of Long's Drugs, and I enjoyed talking business strategy with him. Steve was also a golfing companion and just a bit better than I. The picture shows us on a rare outing to the mountains.

Our vacations and holiday traditions with the DeJonghe family continued unabated. Among the destinations were Whistler, Park City, Scotland, St. Petersburg, Sweden (for the Stockholm cup that Nicole and Jolyn competed in), Puerto Vallarta, Downieville, Charminade (in Santa Cruz), Aspen, Maui, London,

The bridge group
Standing: Barbara Garman, Jane and Steve Roath
Kneeling: Mark Garman, Lisa and Jorg Reinholt

Celebrating New Year's Eve with Marty and Tom

Barcelona, Orcus Island, Sun River, Jackson Hole, Florence, and Breckenridge. The trips were all active with biking, skiing, golf, tennis, and swimming part of the action. The trips were often inspired by the fact that one of our kids was on an extended visit somewhere. But the best part was the double family togetherness, especially at holiday time.

The 90s

Professionally, I had finally arrived. I stood for something: brand equity and brand building. The work with Doug, Kevin, and Bob gave me academic credibility, and the books gave me impact beyond academia. Words like guru, founder, father, pioneer, and influencer were tossed around. This is mostly during speech introductions, but still. My speaking took off, in large part because I had something to say. It was fun to suddenly be visible and well positioned.

My private life continued to be rich. Biking, tennis, skiing, and family vacations with the DeJonghes provided active, enjoyable times. Watching my girls grow in their careers and develop families of their own was a treasure. I was ready for the new millennium.

9 2000 and Beyond

A new century signals a change in professional direction and the arrival of a new generation into the family.

The Prophet Years

I joined Prophet, a brand-strategy consulting company, in late 1998; the official date was January 1, 1999. It was to be a new chapter. I always envied those who had changed jobs. They got to interact with different people and issues in different settings and therefore broadened themselves. Except for the TI years, I'd made no changes. I did not even change schools because I felt that Berkeley had too many pluses. Now I was finally going to go to a new organization in a very different role. I was ready.

The story really starts with Aaker-Joachimsthaler & Partners, which begin in mid-1996. Erich and I, already collaborating on the book, decided to try joint consulting because we both were tired of being the Lone Ranger. Erich was on the same wavelength with me and was terrific with clients, especially top executives. He would look them in the eye and say with his German accent that they had it all wrong. They ate it up, finding it refreshing that anyone (especially a consultant) would stand up to them and be honest. Further, he was excellent speaker and workshop leader, traits that were useful at our stage.

An intriguing aspect of consulting is that organizations, with all their politics and dynamics, can be seen up close. For

one of our earlier clients, we observed (and aided) the process
of making the global brand team work toward developing a
management system to deliver synergy and effectiveness in
their brand building and marketing efforts. It was fascinating to watch the team members representing sharply different
perspectives, backgrounds, problems, objectives, styles, and
contexts face the challenges of working together. Just before
we arrived, a new advertising manager was hired and was trying
to shake things up. Everyone was wondering whether he was
a needed agent of change or just wacko. It was an interesting
dynamic. We also developed a brand valuation model and were
in the middle of implementing it when a lawyer stopped it cold,
saying that determining what the brand is worth in China and
elsewhere could trigger tax problems. The realities of global
business and how it interacts with the tax laws were never more
visible.

Of our engagements, which included work for a dozen firms
such as Adidas, Compaq, and Levi Strauss, the most interesting
and successful was our work for a global firm headquartered
in Paris. The CEO in 1997 had put together a task force to
develop a brand strategy by the end of the year. In March, the
task force and its leader realized they were over their head
and called on me to help. As a stopgap, Roberto Alvarez (my
Barcelona friend) put on a workshop for them the next week in
Paris, after which Erich spent two days with them in Colorado.
Then Erich and I helped them apply the brand identity model.
I recall nailing it in a meeting in Paris—a rewarding and fulfilling experience.

The next step in the engagement was to select a design
company to help implement the strategy. The winning design
company swore they would work with Erich and me like
buddies (at one point they offered our "firm" office space in
Rockefeller Center), but as soon as they were hired they did
everything possible to get us out of the loop. We learned from
that experience. At the end of the day, their work was judged
unsatisfactory—at a key meeting the CEO dismissed their
solution during the first ten minutes, and they had no backup.
It was one of those moments. As a result, their treatment of

Erich and me backfired and our credibility (especially that of Erich, who was involved in more meetings) soared.

Our business grew about 50% or so from 1997 to 1998 with a one-person staff, but was still modest. Nevertheless, our client relationships were worth something and our reputations and intellectual capital were worth much more. Further, we felt we needed more leverage and access to teams that would support our work. So we shopped the firm. And several seemed interested. It was fun and flattering to sit with the head of acquisitions for Y&R. But we eventually decided to join Prophet.

Scott Galloway

Scott Galloway (one of my students) and Ian Chaplin (a computer wizard) started Prophet in 1991 as a market research company as they were finishing their Haas MBA program. They would access MBA students (who were capable of interviewing executives) around the country to be interviewers, provide them with computers, and download and analyze the data in real time. They quickly found that such research was basically a commodity and what companies really wanted (and would pay for) was the insight and recommendations that Scott would deliver. So Scott took over Prophet and Ian became responsible for 911 Gifts, a dot-com venture that became Red Envelope, one of the dot-com survivors—thanks in part to Prophet's repositioning guidance. In the early years, Prophet lived off Levi Strauss, doing some seventeen engagements for them, all involving marketing or strategy. Scott was good at selling, hiring, and offering authoritative strategic insights. An early hire, Connie Halquest (who in 2000 started Blue Violin, an Internet-based firm that provides products designed for the elderly), would take the leadership to deliver what Scott sold. In 1998 Scott made his best hire when Michael Dunn came on board to grow the company. Michael turned out to be an outstanding CEO, a top one percenter.

Another notable hire, also in 1998, was Kevin O'Donnell (shown on p. 345), an insightful brand strategist with a background at Disney and good people skills, who became a firm partner. Kevin and I have worked closely over the years in a wide variety of contexts. He had to adjust his expectations of my knowledge, however. During my first meeting with the Prophet team, I gave a half-hour summary of the portfolio strategy part of the *Brand Leadership* book. Kevin promptly sold a significant engagement to a software company that had evolved a very confusing portfolio. After the sale, Kevin came and asked me for the rest of the story. He was stunned when I said that was it—there is no more. But he coped and filled in some gaps on his own. I was once stumped on the complexities of brand portfolio strategy and asked Kevin what he thought it was. His definition and conceptualization helped me get over the hump. He is a clear thinker when it comes to brands and my material. He is particularly good at evaluating the work of our teams, encouraging their good ideas, and letting them know where they could do better.

The 1998 Prophet team included a precocious Jason Stavers, who was in his mid-twenties but looked like a teenager. He could and did go in front of CEOs of large firms and mesmerize them with thoughtful analyses of the Internet and its implications to a firm and industry. And he was a gifted writer, reflecting his time as an Ivy League English major. One of our major financial service companies that I had attracted signed up for a follow-up project and was more concerned that Jason be involved than I. Jason was a big selling and recruiting tool for Scott. He was such a talent that his youthful appearance, which should have been a liability, simply made him appear more amazing (just as a professor's sloppy attire is sometimes associated with genius). Jason finally left the business for the law school at Virginia where he is studying to be an appellant attorney.

I had a relationship with Scott Galloway that started early in Prophet's life. Once, he and Ian were invited to pitch a brand strategy engagement and, realizing they were out of their element, got me to sit in and provide content. I did a lot of talking but did not help to close a sale. Several years later, when Scott was selling and delivering brand strategy engagements, I was referring clients

Randall Caudell and Connie Halquest at the
"Join Prophet" dinner

to two firms, Prophet and St. James (a Chicago firm headed by
Scott Talgo, a brand strategist introduced in the last chapter).
Both tried to get me to join their firm or have a formal relationship. But all the offers were easy to turn down. In 1998, however,
Scott turned to Randal Caudell, a brilliant retired investment
banker, and told him to create a deal that I would accept. The
result was an agreement that Erich and I would join Prophet, each
of us receiving a substantial percentage of the company.

Prophet's prime offerings when we joined were around brand
strategy, largely drawing on my books. What do you want your
brand to stand for? What brand portfolio strategy will deliver
relevance, synergy, clarity, and leverage? How should the corporate brand be used? How should you organize in order to manage
effectively across products and countries? Prophet's services have
been expanded since I joined to include other related areas. For
example, we now help clients prioritize and manage all their
customer touchpoints and conduct segmentation research to
help clients understand the market and create effective strategies. Whatever direction our work takes us, we always have a
strategic perspective and look at issues through a brand lens. We
have never been in the business of creating logos or ads. In fact,
a firm that doesn't regard brand strategy as an interim step to the

real business of designing logos or making commercials is often appealing.

A key role for me at Prophet is to attract clients and employees. In many cases, this involves simply answering the phone and introducing Prophet teams. A dozen of our clients, including some of our largest, started just that way. Especially for those clients that have contacted me, I am available as a resource and sounding board for the engagement team. For UBS, for example, the CEO had insisted on my involvement in an initial brand engagement, and I went to Basel, Switzerland, twice (the last time to meet with him for two hours). On this engagement the recommendation was basically the work of Sterling Lanier, another "baby" talent who was and is brilliant and creative but opinionated (unlike me of course), and myself. The two of us hammered out a brand strategy—and hammered is the right term. It was a stimulating and rewarding time highlighted by victory dinners in Basel and a bike trip with Steve Sallie, another team member, along the canal toward Strasburg. Our adventure included discovering a charming restaurant and hotel along the way. The bike trip was to conclude with an easy morning ride to a train depot, but it turned out that there was a mountain in the way and it was not so easy. We have since opened an office in Zurich staffed by some outstanding talent including Jeff Smith, an expatriate from Chicago who loves the Zurich lifestyle and is now a firm partner.

I have also played a role in attracting employees, the heart of a consulting company—other firms lack a visible front man and credible knowledge base. My big winner in this regard was the role I played in attracting Scott Davis and his colleagues (including Jeff Smith and Mike Petromilli, now a Prophet associate partner) to come to Prophet and create a Chicago office. Scott, who joined Prophet in 2001, is a stimulating and strategic brand thinker, a gifted and active speaker and

Scott Davis

author, a masterful client relationship person, and a very successful office builder.

I also provide visibility to the firm and support knowledge development and culture building. Visibility is provided through my articles and books and my talks to client groups and to general audiences. We sponsor dinner meetings for selected clients and prospective clients each year, for example. I also give talks at commercial brand seminars in which Prophet receives complimentary sponsorship status. When I have a book out, my tolerance for traveling to speak goes way up. In 2004, for example, I gave "book" talks in LA, Chicago, San Francisco, and New York, all sponsored by Prophet. In addition, I did my second marathon tour of Europe (which, like the first one, was a bit much)—more on that later.

Prophet is always expanding its knowledge and expertise base, and I contribute in part through my books and articles, but also by offering input to knowledge initiatives. I also support the "brand culture" at Prophet by encouraging people to enjoy talking and writing about brands. I organize general hangout sessions with groups of people from time to time in order help create a stimulating place.

When I accepted a formal position at Prophet, I decided to leave the university because I felt conflicted. I did not think it appropriate to spend time at Prophet and represent Prophet when speaking while still being a professor (although others in business and engineering were doing just that). The decision to leave the university was made a bit more difficult because a major pay raise was in the offing for me that would have affected my retirement pay if I'd stayed. But in the end that did not seem like a good reason to prolong my Berkeley days.

When Michael, Erich, and I joined the firm, it consisted of eighteen people in San Francisco with local clients (mainly Levi Strauss and later Williams-Sonoma) and was doing well under $4 million per year. By 2005, it grew to over one hundred people with offices added in Chicago, New York, London, Zurich, Houston, and Tokyo, and billings approaching $30 million. There was also a solid leadership team that included, in addition to Scott Davis (who became a senior partner and Prophet board member), Kevin O'Donnell, Jeff Smith, Michael Petromilli, and eighteen other partners and associate partners. That group included several with which I have worked closely, such as Tom Agan (who was a driver behind our presence in Europe), July Hopelain (who as the head of the SF office has an office next to mine and is a bundle of talent and energy), Mike Leiser (a senior partner who brought brand insight and a sense of humor from Scott

Michael Dunn

Talgo's St. James), John Copeland (a research and analytics specialist, we share the special vocabulary of statisticians), Tim Munoz (who now handles the London office and has given me some tips on collecting ancient maps of Europe), Cindy Levine (in charge of corporate strategy and marketing, she is quick and responsive when I need help on a writing project), Andy Flynn (a talented strategist who was on board when I arrived), Steve Cirulus (known for his energy and positive outlook), and two Japanese associate partners, Haruo Koyama and Atsushi Kogoma. The offices were upgraded as well—going from being in areas that were somewhere between trendy and sketchy to downtown high rises. In San Francisco for example, we moved from the fourth floor of a funky brick building with a single slow elevator near the ballpark to the fifteenth floor of a modern high rise with a view of the Bay Bridge and a bank of six elevators.

So for better or worse we have become grown-up in image and outlook. Our clients now come from all over the States and the world—including Korea, India, and the Near East, and we have a professional IT, marketing, accounting, and knowledge management staff. It has been a remarkable ride and one of the best parts has been to watch Michael at work. He is amazing. There were, however, three major hiccups along the way.

The first occurred within a year after we joined. Prophet and Erich decided to part ways. I decided to stay with Prophet because I did not want to go back to the Dave/Erich firm and get involved in building a company from zero that would probably have to be based in New York, and because I also had confidence in the top Prophet managers, particularly Michael.

Erich started two companies. The first was a strategic marketing consulting and innovation company, Brand Leadership, now called Vivaldi Partners, located in New York, with me as an advisor. The second was the E-Edge Company, an executive education firm. To my delight, the firms have done well. They served large, well-known clients from four offices in Europe and the U.S. Their advisor group now includes, in addition to me, Kevin Keller and several visible strategy and organization theory academics from the Harvard Business School. Erich has been able to grow the firms to over fifty people without giving up significant equity, a rare accomplishment. My role initially was to advise him on organizational matters (such as how to compensate new senior hires) and associate myself to his firm as an endorser. I now also refer expert witness assignments to him since Prophet is not in that business and Erich and some of his colleagues are extremely good at it. Of course, I cannot get involved in any of his client work. When I get to New York, we usually get together for a dinner and play.

The second hiccup occurred with the dot-com crash that can be dated from April 14, 2000, when the stock market lost two trillion dollars. We had a high percentage of our clients in the dot-com world and many of them paid us in stock. All of a sudden our client base shrunk and we were overstaffed. A decision to downsize by nearly one-third was painful. Michael asked all those that were retained not to come in on one day. For the others he emphasized that business was inadequate to keep everyone and explained that three criteria had been used to evaluate people, one being how they fit the strategy going forward. Although I stayed home as well, I learned from others that the process was emotional but handled in such a way that most of those let go seemed to feel good about Michael and Prophet. Many of the people who were let go were very good, but those that remained were simply outstanding. This move, plus a renewed emphasis on bringing in new business in Europe as well as the U.S., not only saved the day but also provided the basis for future growth. In addition, some needed cash came in the form of an investment from a European firm called Catenas that had the idea of investing in many small service firms and attempting to generate synergy across them. The idea was good but the timing was bad and today we are the only success story in their portfolio—and one of the few firms that are even left standing. The Catenas connection brought to us Niels Nielsen, a seasoned entrepreneur who became a valued Prophet board member distributing wisdom and helping support Prophet efforts in both Europe and Japan.

Those were difficult times for many firms who, like us, were enticed by the Internet revolution. It turned out that those unlimited growth vectors were illusionary. The article on the perils of high-growth markets that George Day and I wrote in 1986 was never more relevant. Why didn't others and I take it to heart? The answer is that the euphoria and activity is hard to resist. So many firms had money and seemed to lack only brand strategy help. People and firms were getting rich all over the place. Why not us? We had the needed brand expertise. All we had to do was to reposition ourselves a bit to be relevant to the Internet era. We had Jason who could talk the game, Michael who had some real knowledge of the underlying computer systems, and myself who had written on using the Internet in brand building. So we were tempted ... and it was costly. We hired some people that did not fit our core mission and took our eye off the ball, so to speak.

During the height of the craze, a second tier systems integrator (a firm that designs and installs Internet enabled computer systems) made an offer to buy our firm for a price about ten times (maybe fifteen times) what it was worth. The firm was a roll-up (a combination of ten or so small local firms each with a small group of software engineers) that basically wanted our firm to provide customers to them. Since we were doing brand strategy we would be in a position to recommend a firm to implement the Internet portion of that strategy, a dubious proposition from the beginning. So Connie, Scott, Michael, and I went to Philadelphia to meet with their executives. We were ushered in for a one-hour meeting—no time for socializing. We explained what we did and the potential to provide a larger solution offering if we could integrate the two companies. It was clear they did not understand our business or the potential of expanding their offering. They simply had no concept of brands or brand strategy. They were computer and finance people. But their offer to buy our firm was incredible, even though it was in stock and not dollars. Despite Michael's strong reservation, we went ahead. However, a few weeks later, their stock (which was priced at least twenty times what it was worth) nearly doubled, which meant we would have received fewer shares of a stock that was clearly grossly inflated. So greedy though we were, we decided that the money was not real and walked. Soon after, their firm collapsed and its stock was worth almost nothing. I'm reminded of Winston Churchill's comment about the exhilaration of being shot at without result.

A third hiccup occurred in the fall of 2001 when it was apparent that we needed money for working capital and to buy out Scott and Ian, the founding partners, who, although no longer active, were an awkward presence on the board. The solution to both problems was Dentsu, the largest agency not only in Japan but also in the world. They invested in Prophet in February 2002 and made me an advisor to their firm in October 2001. But I need to backtrack.

Since joining Prophet, I encouraged the firm to look to Japan, where I was well known and well connected, but there was a lack of both interest and resources. So I considered setting up a consulting company in Japan with University of Tokyo professor Hotaka Katahira, my friend and Japanese brand guru. I first met Hotaka when he was a visiting professor at Berkeley. Since then we have enjoyed many sushi outings in San Francisco and Tokyo. Hotaka paces himself and can sit at a sushi bar for hours. One of his many activities is a monthly executive brand seminar group of around one hundred people, an event at which I have spoken at least four times. The picture shows Hotaka with Toshi Akustu, my PhD student who was introduced in chapter seven.

Hotaka and I contacted both Denstu and Hakuhodo, Japan's number-two agency, about funding our venture. As a result, some Hakuhodo executives came to San Francisco and discussed the

Japan's current and future brand guru,
Hotaka Katahira and Toshi Akutsu

idea of a company formed by some combination of Hotaka, Prophet, and me. After expressing significant interest, they went dark. We found out later that one of their major clients had insisted on using Larry Light, a freelance brand consultant and speaker. In their eyes an alliance with me would interfere with their client relationship.

As an aside, Larry, a long-term friend, is now the CMO (chief marketing officer) at McDonald's and, justifiably, is given much of the credit for their turn-around. Larry and I have shared a venue several times (once in Stockholm and another time at Ford) where we chatted about brands and consulting. He is an innovative, sound, and decisive brand thinker. In guiding McDonald's he has concluded that you need to tell different brand stories to different segments and even to address different needs for the same segment. To a world used to looking for the magical, universal three-word phrase, this represents a radical direction—a direction very compatible with my own thinking.

Dentsu, perhaps the most respected communications company in the Far East in addition to being the largest agency in the world, was also interested. They were starting an internal brand consulting operation and needed help. Further, they wanted a relationship with me to not only help the consulting group but also to give advice as to their strategy and image. When I said that I could not be much help in training their new

The Prophet/Dentsu Training Team
Top: Cautie Okada, Andy Flynn, Itsurou Hamada,
Kevin O'Donnell, Gosuke Sato
Bottom: Michael Dunn, Dave, Kazuo Miyakawa,
Katsuhiko Adachi

group without the support of Prophet's talent, they proposed a contract with Prophet to train and support their people (which was ultimately done under the direction of Kevin O'Donnell and Andy Flynn). They also proposed a separate three-year contract with me to be an advisor (plus a one year project contract). It was a done deal after several meetings in California. Then, just as we were declaring victory and had begun to celebrate, Michael said (as almost an afterthought) that we were going to raise money to buy out the Prophet founders. There was complete silence until finally the Dentsu people said that if one of their competitors (and the most likely investors would fall into that category) became a Prophet shareholder, Dentsu, by policy, could no longer have any relationship with Prophet.

The obvious solution, to have Dentsu be that investor, would take time because they would have to get approval from the top management and craft the legal documents. Thanks to Michael's relationship skills (which included singing Japanese songs in a karaoke bar), his ability to impress the Dentsu top management with Prophet's prospects, and a commitment to open a Japanese Prophet office (which meant a Aaker-Katahira firm was unneeded), Dentsu came aboard. The money actually did not arrive until the following February, but it did arrive; Scott and the others were bought out, and some needed capital was obtained.

As part of my advisor role at Dentsu I agreed to visit Japan around three times per year to engage in a variety of activities. In particular, I was to meet with clients about brand issues, advise and support an effort to develop brand strategy models and methods, and help with the Prophet-Dentsu relationship. I was also to advise the senior management at Dentsu.

Another of my functions was to give talks at Dentsu and to Dentsu clients (so I gave up my ad hoc speaking in Japan), usually in Tokyo but occasionally outside the city. On one occasion in 2002, Michael and I did a talk in Osaka at Dentsu's annual client meeting. While in Osaka we, like the Osaka mafia, were using black limousines. When Michael had me leave the car first, I suggested in jest that he might have thought there was some risk in being the first out the door.

I also traveled for Dentsu. In 2002, I gave talks in Beijing (which I dislike because of the air, the traffic, the food, and the attitude of the people) and Shanghai (which I loved—it is like Tokyo except with pockets of old China) as part of an ongoing Dentsu initiative in China. In Shanghai, I visited the first head-

At the Global Brand Forum, Taiwan, June 2004

Global Brand Forum, 2004

quarters of Mao, a rather simple austere building. One room had a picture and story of each of the other founders, many of which had suffered violent ends, often at the hand of their "compatriots." During the trip I was exposed to the some major Chinese companies who had engineering and manufacturing talent and breathtakingly low costs. I felt that they would become world powers—they just lacked brands and marketing. In 2004 I gave a Dentsu-sponsored talk in Taiwan where 1,100 people showed up. I am embarrassed to admit that I too frequently manage to bring up the fact that Michael Porter, the prominent Harvard strategy guru, only drew 700 at the same venue. My draw was in part because brand strategy was salient in Taiwan. Many of the top Taiwanese firms see their low-cost strategy undermined by Mainland China and realize that they need brand power.

Still another function was to support Dentsu with articles, books, and videos. I wrote in 2004 a series of ten pieces for the Dentsu Newspaper. Each was a short case study outside Japan of brand successes such as Dove Soap, who leveraged their moisturizer association to other categories including body wash, deodorant, and shampoo. I worked on a book on global brand management with Dentsu people as collaborators, a project intended to give them visibility in this key area. In addition, I contributed a series of video lecturettes for the "Aaker Academy," which is an effort to communicate brand strategy principles to a broad cross-section of Dentsu. So I have some accomplishments

Wet Yokahama golf with Ted Hirose,
Nakumura-san, and Shono-san

Matsuda-san, a senior Dentsu executive and a good
golfer, with Kabayashi-san, the fourth person to hold
Dentsu's Prophet board seat, in Orinda 2005.

to show for the first three years, with a modest time and travel commitment.

The Dentsu relationship has been enormously stimulating and enjoyable. With a Dentsu badge (that allows me access to even the executive floor), business cards, and my own office, I have become part of the organization. I am pleased and proud to be associated with and contributing to such a successful and admired communication company. Seeing a Japanese firm up close and having access to executives at both Dentsu and its clients is an added benefit. I get to go to Japan, my second home, more frequently, see my friends there, and support the Prophet Tokyo office through training, business development, and helping client teams. I even find the travel relaxing. Eight to ten hours to read (I bring five or six books to be sure the right one is on tap), work, nap, and dine with no phones, computers, or distractions. And the train trip between the airport and city is a pleasant addendum. In 2004, the advisor contract was renewed, so I was perceived by Dentsu to have been helpful.

The new Dentsu building is a spectacular high-rise at the edge of the Ginza. I have meetings in my own office, which doubles as a small conference room when I am not there. Further, my hotel is next door so my commute is a one-block walk. The new building has an outside elevator that takes under twenty seconds to go up forty-six floors, providing an exhilarating experience as well as an outstanding view. The interior elevators have videos of tropical fish roaming through colorful coral. Experiencing scuba diving while being in an elevator ... only in Japan. The building has a complete medical staff, which means a doctor is available within minutes if needed. It is nice to have the support of a large well-run company.

The big payoff has been the Dentsu people with whom I have worked. They are talented, supportive, and professional. It is no wonder that Dentsu has been successful. Chairman Yutaka Narita and President Tateo Mataki have both shown vision and developed an impressive business model and organization. Several top managers such as Tetsu Nakamura, Takehiko Kimura, and Kimiharu Matsuda have supported the Prophet-Dentsu partnership and my role as Denstu advisor. The people in leadership roles at the brand consulting center (BCC) and its parent, the integrated communications group, were particularly helpful to Prophet and me. Katsuhiko Adachi was a key architect for the partnership and was the first Prophet board member from Dentsu. Gosuke Sato was the second Prophet board member and had responsibility for building the consulting group. Cauitie Ocada, with a U.S. MBA, was indispensable along the way in making sure that issues were always communicated and in managing my contribution to Dentsu. Itsurou Hamada (shown in the photo of the Prophet training group along with Sato, Adachi, and Ocada) adds color and energy to the BCG group.

I interact with the Dentsu people not only professionally but also socially. We often go to sumo if a Basho is going on when I arrive. Dinners featuring incredible food and convivial company are a regular occurrence. On a recent trip, six of us—led by Hisashi Shono (who became the third Prophet board member replacing Sato-san after he changed positions within Dentsu, only to himself be replaced by Kobayashi-san when Shono-san also changed positions—large firms like Dentsu seem to reorganize often)—went to a second-floor sushi bar in a modest area of Tokyo that featured eight seats and a single person doing everything including the dishes. I was wondering how he made a living given he only served dinners five nights a week. It turns out he charges about $250 a plate and turns down people that he doesn't feel fit in. It sounds like the Nazi soup kitchen from Seinfeld, whose chef would turn away people who did not follow the right procedure. During our meal I jokingly claimed that it should take ten minutes not ten years to become a sushi chef and that I'd made sushi during a Prophet outing. Unfortunately, my comment was translated and our welcome at the bar could have been jeopardized, but, fortunately, the chef did recognize the humor and factored in my California origins.

I have been able to play golf with Dentsu people on a half-dozen occasions at several courses in Japan, including the Hakone Country Club (in the mountains outside of Tokyo), at Totsuka Country Club in nearby Yokohama, and the Narita Country Club near the airport (where membership, at $1 million when it was founded during the real estate bubble in 1991, now stands at

$50,000) plus others in California. Ted Hirose, who is a talented brand strategist with a Northwestern MBA and has a leadership position at Dentsu's brand consulting group, is a regular in our golf outings and is one of the most enthusiastic golfers I have ever seen. Several of the golfers, particularly Nakamura-san, take great delight in seeing others make bad shots. They enjoy a laugh when that occurs and they help make the outing enjoyable even if the golf is not always up to par, so to speak. Shono-san is another regular member of the group and has beat me on at least one occasion.

The Prophet Tokyo office in Ginza is not far from the Dentsu high rise. The office has done well in terms of finding clients that need our talents. The problem has been to find and train suitable people in Japan, people that have an aptitude for brands and strategy *and* speak English. A big help has been Toshi Akutsu, who has introduced us to clients, helped with client relationships, and supported our consulting teams.

Toshi was Hiro's student as an undergrad at Hitotsubashi and my student in the PhD program at Berkeley. He subsequently joined the faculty of Hiro's new Hitotsubashi MBA program in downtown Tokyo. The coauthor of a successful brand book and numerous articles, I call him the future brand guru in Japan (in deference to Hotaka Katahira). He has generated an excellent translation of *Brand Leadership* and my fourth book, *Brand Portfolio Strategy* (my first two brand books had inferior translations often based on a literal word-for-word reading, missing the underlying meaning). Toshi has joined Hotaka and Hiro as the set of people I regularly see on each Tokyo trip besides the Dentsu and Prophet teams.

Toshi was not blessed with a great dissertation advisor as my record shows. At one point, when he and I were stuck on a research direction, Jennifer came to our rescue. At a social event at our house she took Toshi aside and told him to forget my advice and set forth a new direction based on a laboratory experiment. Thanks to Jennifer's help, Toshi got on the right track and finished an excellent piece of work.

Prophet has been good for me. I get to interact with some talented, bright, fun, young people (few in the firm are older than forty) that consistently deliver outstanding advice despite often dealing with complex issues. We know the performance is outstanding because of the post-engagement client interviews that are regularly conducted. The firm survived some difficult times in order to grow to its current size and scope. It is fun to be with a winner and a pleasure to watch a truly gifted, charismatic CEO, Michael Dunn, up close. I have seen him in client pitches, in team meetings, in board meetings, in negotiations, in giving talks, in socializing with clients, in relating to employees of all levels, and in creating professionalism in what was an ad hoc organization. Impressive! And I enjoy brands and brand strategy. There is nothing more fun to me than to be engaged in brand problems, opportunities, and cases with interesting, involved people. Prophet has provided a host of opportunities to do just that. Further, communicating, giving talks, and writing books and articles is stimulating, fun, and rewarding. Writing and creating is more fun and easier than before because I have the support of the Prophet people. It was the right decision.

Writing, Research, Speaking and Consulting

My fourth brand book, published in 2004, was *Brand Portfolio Strategy* (*BPS*). A brand portfolio contains the brands affecting a firm's business, including sub-brands, endorser brands, co-brands, corporate brands, branded services, and branded features. The book set out to explicitly define the scope and structure of brand portfolio strategy and how it can be used to address issues facing business strategists such as:

- How to grow by expanding the product-market scope through brand extensions.

Creating ◎ Relevance
⋈ Differentiation
◊ Energy
⟋ Leverage
⟨ Clarity

David A. Aaker
Co-Author of *BRAND LEADERSHIP*

- How to participate in value and premium niches with vertical brand extensions.

- How to make brand alliances work.

- How to leverage the corporate brand.

- How to manage the brand issues surrounding mergers and acquisitions.

- How to improve the clarity of the offerings and provide focus to the brand-building activities. Some firms have literally become paralyzed because of the confusion and lack of priorities in the portfolio.

- How to keep your brand relevant while facing a dynamic market where "what is being purchased" is changing.

- How to energize and differentiate your brand using brand portfolio tools.

Developing brand portfolio strategy is complex and situation specific. There are no cookbook rules. There are, however, concepts, tools, and processes that help create coherent, effective strategies. I had written on brand portfolio issues in the other books but felt that there was a chance to pull it all together and introduce the concepts of relevance, branded differentiators, and branded energizers.

I became fascinated with the concept of relevance around 2001 in part through my discussions with Mike Kelly about findings in his Techtel brand database. The idea is that a brand can remain strong and still lose market share if there are emerging submarkets for which it is not relevant. It simply does not matter if your brand is perceived to be the best minivan to those that have decided to buy a hybrid or SUV. You are no longer relevant. Staying relevant means that you have to detect and evaluate trends and make sure that you have brands and offerings that are responsive. Not easy, but the use of sub-brands and endorsed brands can help. PowerBar, the developer of the energy bar category, responded to new submarkets by introducing the Pria Bar for women and the Harvest Bar for those attracted by taste and texture (both endorsed by PowerBar). In my view, understanding relevance is a key to competing in dynamic environments.

The book also introduced branded differentiators and branded energizers as a way to use one brand to help another address two significant branding issues. A branded differentiator is a branded feature, ingredient, or service that serves to differentiate the brand. Thus, Weston Hotels has the Heavenly Bed and the Heavenly Shower, both noticeably superior, which serve to differentiate their hotels. A branded energizer is a branded product, promotion, sponsorship, program, or other entity that, by association, significantly enhances and energizes a target brand and is actively managed over time. The iPod energizes Apple, the Oscar Mayer Weinermobile energizes the hot dog brand, Ronald McDonald House provides energy and image enhancement to McDonald's, and Tiger Woods adds much needed energy to Buick. A problem was that the *BPS* book was positioned around brand portfolio strategy, and reviews often did not notice the innovative thinking around relevance, branded differentiators, and branded energizers. A future book focused around relevance is possible.

Four articles were drawn from the *BPS* book. *Strategy + Business* published the "Relevance of Relevance" in the spring of 2004. A branded differentiation article was in *Sloan Management Review* in the fall of 2003. The "Corporate Brand Role" in the portfolio was published in *California Management Review* in 2004. A piece on branded energizers appeared in *Marketing Management* in 2004. In addition to the articles, a section on how you trim portfolios to gain focus appeared in *BrandWeek* in March of 2004.

During the first year the book sold around 13,000 copies, and translations were under way or completed in seven languages. The Japanese and Spanish translations by my friends Toshi Akustu and Roberto Alvarez were introduced by significant events. I spoke at both, using a video feed for the Spanish event. As usual, the first translation out of the gate was the Korean one by Jerry Lee and Katy Choi.

Among the six comments for the back of the book was one from Sam Hill, a successful author and former vice-chairman of

DMB&B, a major agency. "Brand portfolio optimization will be the value-creating management approach of the next decade, and will change the way we do business as fundamentally as has business process reengineering or six sigma. Dr. Aaker has written a simple and pragmatic guidebook that will be tremendously useful to strategists. He has almost single-handedly transformed branding from an art into a science, and no one is better qualified to lead the discussion on brand portfolio strategy."

Among the pre-chapter quotes were

It's easy, I simply get a chisel and chip away anything that doesn't look like a lion

—Pablo Picasso,
on how a block of stone
could become a lion

Nobody has bet enough on a winning horse.

—Richard Sasuly

Even if you are on the right track, you will get run over if you just sit there.

—Will Rogers

Always design a thing by considering it in its next larger context—a chair in a room, a room in a house, a house in an environment, an environment in a city plan.

—Frank Lloyd Wright

Like my other books, the publication of *BPS* resulted in extra speaking engagements and interviews in order to promote the book. My top interview ever occurred in the spring of 2004 when an editor of the *Financial Times of London*, Simon London, discussed the book and my ideas for about an hour. In a half-page article complete with a large picture he described me as having a laid-back style and an "aw-shucks" delivery and indicated that my books have been instrumental in establishing notions such as brand equity as part of mainstream business. And to top it off, he ended by saying that if there were a Nobel Prize in marketing, I surely would have won it. That was such a stretch that I am torn between feeling embarrassed and complimented.

My 2004 European speaking tour packaged a dozen or so talks all designed to help Prophet and promote the *BPS* book. It started with a talk to business executives sponsored by the business school at St. Petersburg University, which has been mentored since its inception by the Haas School. While there, we were eating at a nice country restaurant (by one of the czar's palaces) when two cars drove up and out stepped a three-man security team and a young couple with their daughter. I was told that he was the head of a rice company and that such security for an executive is prudent. My speaking tour then moved to Denmark (where 500 attended the talk), Amsterdam, Zurich (for a talk at UBS), and finally London.

I gave some seven talks in London in four days. One of the London talks was to a group of financial executives who were worried about restoring credibility after a series of embarrassing meltdowns. I suggested they develop a "branded trust creator" (like a branded advisory panel looking over their investment policy) that would be analogous to a branded energizer. Although I was rather proud of my ability to create a new construct to address an immediate problem, I'm sure it did not live beyond my speech.

Another talk, at London Business School (LBS), was on how you can get the CEO's attention and support for brand building, and I offered two suggestions. First, talk the CEO's language, positioning branding as a way to achieve growth or to gain efficiency in marketing or whatever is on top of the CEO's issue list. Second, document the payback of brand building using financial data where possible and other measures otherwise.

The biggest talk was to 300 or so senior marketing and government officials, members of the Marketing Society, the leading association for marketing executives in UK. The talk was published in their journal, *The Leader*, under the title "Hybrids, Heavenly Beds, and Purple Ketchup," a rare catchy Aaker title not developed by me but by Alex Baldock of Prophet, my guide throughout the tour, whose job it was to mine the audience for clients and to keep me on schedule. Alex taught me that shirts should not have a pocket, using the argument that if a pocket were there, you might use it for a pen—and that would be tacky. When Alex bought shirts, any with pockets were excluded. In addition, shirts, according to Alex, must have cuff links and I could not convince him that cuff links were

uncomfortable in hot weather and inefficient to wear. In the UK, traditions die hard.

The 2004 Europe trip also resulted in several interviews and articles in trade magazines in all the countries I visited. When I was in Zurich, the editor of a leading German marketing journal called *Absatzwirtschaft* came to interview me. The result was a four-page interview in their July issue complete with an artist rendition of me that was the whole cover as well. Beside my picture was the "Portfolio Power" phrase with the label "Marketing Guru." I felt like I was Phil Kotler, the Northwestern marketing professor who is the real marketing guru, for a day. Actually, the same journal ran a photo of Erich and me on the cover when *Brand Leadership* came out.

Kay joined me in London where we stayed at the Covent Garden Hotel near the Prophet office and the theater district (and a favorite of actors and producers—we, of course, were not knowledgeable enough to recognize anyone). A highlight was a dinner at a French restaurant, La Garouche (discovered by Tom DeJonghe when he dined there with Jolyn and a colleague after a legal victory some years ago), with Michael Dunn and a fun, creative, energetic, and talented women, Anna Catalona. Anna (who was once named one of the fifty most powerful women in global business by *Fortune*) left BP because she was only the "global marketing manager" of, by some measures, the largest firm in Europe and was not satisfied about her career path. Talk about high goals.

I continued to give around fifteen or twenty talks per year. One notable talk was in September of 2004 when I went to Las Vegas to speak to 1,800 agents for Progressive Insurance, my largest audience yet. They were introducing a sub-brand to serve their agents, called Drive by Progressive. This sub-brand was to be the vehicle to tell the story that an independent agent that can access several insurance companies for their clients can provide superior prices and service for you. I told the relevance story—if the independent agent story could be made visible through the upcoming Progressive advertising program and new subbrand, than agents tied to a single firm (like Allstate and State Farm agents) would become less appealing and relevant to buyers of insurance.

Print reporters from the *Wall Street Journal* and *Business Week* to specialized marketing journals frequently asked me to comment on the brand issue of the day. The norm was to have a ten-minute interview resulting in the appearance of a few sentences taken out of context. I also appeared on television several times a year to comment on some brand issue. About once or twice a year, a camera crew would be sent out to my home for an interview that would be similarly edited. In one CNN interview lasting around five minutes, I ended up with fifteen seconds on air.

The CNN interviewer asked me to comment on a story focusing on why brands like Tommy Hilfiger and Ralph Lauren wrapped themselves around the American flag. In most interviews, I know little about the subject matter but still manage to provide a brand perspective by relating the problem to other brand contexts with which I was familiar. After all, it does not take much to provide a sound bite. However, in this case I got some help and was able to come across as more authoritative about the context of interest. Heather Welte Archibald, a high school friend of Jan's and now a rising star at Old Navy, briefed me on the relevant fashion brands and updated me on the current

An at-home TV interview

vocabulary. Five minutes with her allowed me to appear as an insider rather than the clueless person I really was. I suggested that the flag helped them create associations based on a particular perspective on America, whether it be urban hip-hop, preppy, or Western, and that it activated some self-expressive benefits. Without Heather I would have had no idea that the different brands had different takes on the flag.

I continue to enjoy consulting. A brand issue is to me fascinating. I love to sit with an executive and discuss a tough brand problem. Maybe I have an exaggerated view of my talents, but I do seem to have a real flair for addressing brand problems of all sorts. I can, after a short briefing on a complex brand problem, provide structure, identify the key issue, suggest an approach to generate and test alternatives, and even provide judgments as to what is likely to be a good option and what is not—and why. I continually surprise myself. I draw upon a host of models and processes developed in the writings of others and myself; in addition, I always seem to be able to recall several case studies that frame the problem. Case studies are so much easier for executives to understand and relate to than abstract discussions. The identity of Prophet's clients is sometimes confidential. In one case, with a visible client in India with a charismatic CEO, I was personally outed as an advisor by a leading Indian newspaper. I felt like a tabloid subject.

Two books are in the "potential" stage. One would focus on how CMOs (Chief Marketing Officers) can create and manage their brand across "silos"—product or geographic organizations that have a high degree of autonomy. It would draw on the research that I have done with Erich on global brand management and on a project with Tom Agan, formerly a top Prophet partner, on CMOs facing silo issues. A second potential book would address the relevance issue. In my view, relevance is a key issue facing all firms that exist in a dynamic market. The *BPS* book did not provide the focus or depth that the topic deserved.

The Awards

I received four career awards between 1996 and 2005 reflecting my age as much as accomplishments. In 2005, I received an award given annually for innovations in marketing by the Marketing Management Association. In 2005, I was also named as one of eleven people to be included in a book on Marketing Masters described as "the collective wisdom of the most influential marketing gurus." A bit much but the company is nice.

In 2004 I received the Buck Weaver award named after a GM marketing executive who researched customer attitudes, styling preferences, and feature priorities in the late 20s and early 30s. He had such an impact on automobile design that he was on the cover of *Time*. Originated at MIT, the award was for the advancement of theory and practice and presented during an MIT seminar featuring four top young academics. Jennifer talked at the event the prior year when the winner and first recipient was Paul Green of Wharton. It was special because I am an MIT graduate and have always been impressed with the management problem-motivated research of the MIT faculty.

In my Buck Weaver talk, I noted that practitioners tend to be influenced by concepts from books and that it is ironic that books play little or no role in an academic reputation or promotion evaluation (in part because there is no peer review and in part because they lack an academic style). I presented two concepts

Glen Urban, Dean, MIT, with the Buck Weaver Award

from my latest book (branded differentiator and relevance) and identified what was new and what associated academic research would be useful. Having the last speaking slot of the day, I observed that if the morning speakers, Gavan Fitzsimmons and Bart Bronnenberg (who were actually among the best presenters in academia), worked on their presentation skills, they too would someday be asked to take the last slot in the afternoon.

In 2000 I received the first Mahajan award for contributions to marketing strategy, sponsored by the strategy section of the American Marketing Association (AMA). This award was given at the annual AMA meetings in Chicago and featured two sessions of one and a half hours each in which friends like Russ Winer (the organizer), Al Shocker, Bob Jacobson, George Day (who was to win it the next year), Kevin Keller, Erich Joachimsthaler, Lou Stern, Patrick Barwise (the UK authority on branding who came from London), Aimee Drolet, Tülin Erdem, Raj Srivastava (a Texas professor with impressive research credentials around brands), and V. Kumar (who has expertly taken over our

Converse award winners—1995
Top—Gil Churchill, John Hauser, Dave, George Day
Bottom—Glen Urban, Jerry Wind

Shelby Hunt, Kevin Keller, and Dave at Converse Awards

Marketing Research book) described me and my work. Although many enjoyed noting some of my foibles, there was a lot of sincerity as well. It was a bit embarrassing but also touching that so many would take the trouble to be there and had so many things to say—although their comments were not exclusively serious or positive. It was an incredible experience. It was made more special because Kay was there, as were Jolyn and her husband, Brian. Jennifer not only came, but spoke.

The oldest, and perhaps therefore the most prestigious, award I have received was the Converse Award, sponsored by the AMA and awarded at the University of Illinois in 1996. This award, inaugurated in 1946, is given about every four years to a group of professors, six in my group, who are nominated on the basis of a work that has been out for at least five years (*Managing Brand Equity* was the basis for my nomination). Prior winners included the mathematician John von Neumann (1967) and the management guru Peter Drucker (1975). Each professor presents an overview of their research and invites two people to comment on their work. These eighteen or so talks are published in a book. Prior award winners often attend. The photo shows Shelby Hunt,

Jennifer at the Converse awards

my friend from the PhD consortium days and a previous award winner, at the event.

The other recipients were extremely worthy, and I felt fortunate to be included in the group. Gil Churchill of Wisconsin did pioneering work on sales force management and measurement and had the dominant marketing research text. My writing partner, George Day from Wharton, was in my view the foremost researcher on strategy in marketing. John Hauser and Glen Urban, both from MIT, were nominated for their new product modeling efforts, and both have seen their models become widely applied in industry. Jerry Wind, from Wharton, who was nominated for his work on segmentation, had inexhaustible energy over the years. By 1996 he had already written fourteen books and 200 articles and was involved in a host of initiatives to advance the field. He has not slowed down since.

My discussants were Bill Wells, Kevin Keller, and Jennifer (she was an extra). Bill described my work as being collaborative (he noted that over half my works involved coauthors that span disciplines and countries), having clarity (although the first drafts may be embarrassing, the final draft communicates), and exhibiting range (using a broad set of methods and attacking a wide range of problems). Kevin called *Managing Brand Equity* a home run in the upper decks because it defined the topic and set forth its antecedents and consequences for both academics and industry people. Jennifer noted that my work was both theoretical (in that I have defined constructs and postulated relationship with some rigor) and practical (in that the work is relevant to practitioners), but the best part was when she said I was kind and supportive to everyone, especially her and the family.

Davos

The World Economic Forum, or Davos for short, is a gathering of some 2,000 people each year in the Swiss ski town of Davos. In part because of endorsements by Hiro Takeuchi and Roberto Alvarez, I was invited to Davos in 1999 and again in 2000. To be invited, you needed to be a CEO of a large firm or one its significant components, a prominent political leader, or an "entertainer." Around 200 of the invitees are (like me) the "entertainment" in that instead of paying a handsome fee they give talks, moderate sessions, and host lunches and dinners.

One objective of the conference, where spouses are welcome, is to give business and government leaders a chance to broaden their minds. In addition to topics like the economic future of Germany or South America or managerial topics such as leadership or global business, there are a host of topics of general interest such as heart care (Dean Ornish), literature (Umbreto Eco), music (Zandor of the Boston Philharmonic), knowledge, memory, climate change, stress management, the brain, philanthropy, work, physics, fighting cancer, geopolitics, refugees, privatization, space frontiers, cosmology, time, human rights, imagination, organic foods, and on and on. It is so fun to have the time to attend sessions or meals with interesting topics and fascinating authorities.

One of the thrills of Davos, especially during the first time there, is just walking or sitting next to celebrities. Bill Clinton, Al Gore, Tony Blair, and John Kerry (who would run for president in 2004) were among the speakers. People like them view Davos as the best chance to speak to the global business community. CEOs were everywhere. Theoretically you could ask for a meeting with anyone there, but I was a bit intimidated. The lunches and dinners were more informal and a good way to get to know people. I recall sitting at meals next to the CEOs of Intel Europe (who is now Intel's CEO), Nissan, Toshiba, P&G Europe, and the largest law firm in the world, but everyone was interesting. I just soaked up information. I'm sure many were glad to get away from the source of so many questions, but most people liked to talk about their firms. I also volunteered brand advice freely, but I doubt that it registered. Kay and I went to one lunch on origin of the universe issues hosted by Nathan Myrvold, the Microsoft guru and, as noted in chapter seven, the founder of the startup, Mondrian, for which I was an advisor. In attendance was the Prince of Monaco with two security people. Waiting for a bus, I once shared a cab with the HP CEO and another time was given a lift by the CEO of Starwood. In each case we talked brands—or at least I did.

I was obliged to work for my stay. I hosted two meals each trip. In one case, for example, I hosted a dinner with John Quelch, then the dean of the London School of Business, which addressed

The World Economic Forum at Davos

the problem of branding your country or city. About ten representatives of governments struggling with image problems came.
I also attended sessions as a speaker and moderator. One session
included Shelly Lazarus, the CEO of O&M, a brilliant woman who
was the architect of the IBM positioning strategy, Mark Thomson,
an EVP of Charles Schwab, and Philip Knight of Nike. I told
Knight that Nike was making a branding blunder by not having
more brand platforms. He said maybe I was right, but he did not
seem perturbed about my insight and did not suggest that we get

together and pursue the idea. Nike has since added brands but I'm sure it was not because of my suggestion.

There were many memorable sessions. I recall being impressed with Christine Todd Whitman and thought I could be a Republican if they would run someone like her, but, of course, as I noted in the last chapter, no party would nominate a moderate for anything these days. Patrick Walsh, the celebrity prostate researcher and surgeon, talked about the state of prostate treatment and his innovative nerve sparing surgery. It was very informative—little did I know that I would have such surgery in 2002. One executive I met at Davos told me that he waited for over four months to get on Walsh's calendar so that he could have the best. Kenneth L. Lay, the CEO of Enron, spoke on building a culture of leadership and also on environmental statesmanship at a time when his company was engaging in dishonest acts that would cost their investors and employees dearly. Davos was made for Ken Lay. Tim Koogle talked about the Yahoo phenomena and how it occurred. The Japanese dinner hosted by Idei from Sony had an impressive setting, dinner, and speakers. It was at this dinner that I ran into my classmate from Stanford, Hank McKinnell, who was shortly to become the CEO of Pfizer, the huge pharmaceutical company.

Davos was not all work. There was a back-tie gala party with five theme areas and outlandish buffets. One, for example, was in South Sea island decor complete with a lake, and another had a New Orleans motif. It cost around $2 million and was an experience. And there was skiing. Sunday was ski day, and I would go downhill with Hiro. But, for me, the best thing about Davos, especially the second time around, was the cross-county skiing. I would walk down a half block from the hotel (we stayed in an adjacent town, Klosters, a twenty-minute shuttle away) and skied down a gentle hill to the most incredible cross-country trail I have seen. It followed a valley along a stream that had dramatic snow formations. Every morning that I was at Davos, a ski run started the day.

Golf

My bike accident in 2001 caused me to shift my recreation from tennis to golf, a sport I had played since my boyhood but one that had always been behind tennis in priority. Tennis had created friendships, led to quality time with great people, provided regular workouts, and afforded the opportunity to excel locally (all things are relative). However, I was burnt out on tennis

The Golf Group—Lou and Rhona Stern, Kay, Dave

and now was basically playing for social reasons, so it was not so bad to move on.

In 2004 I hit a hot streak in golf, getting down to the 70s on a regular basis and driving my handicap into the single digits. I have a signed card, now framed, that shows I once shot a seventy-three (two over par) playing with Lou Stern at my home course, the Moraga Country Club, a mile from my home. Just when I was getting comfortable with this level of golf, I got a chance to play at Sunnydale, just out of London. They have two courses; the new course was built in 1921 and was the site of the 2004 women's British Open while the old course was constructed in the 1880s. Bobby Jones in the 20s once shot a sixty-eight on the old course, hitting all the par four and five holes with a fairway wood. What a golfer he must have been. But instead of a Bobby Jones day, I shot an embarrassing one hundred. Their wiry rough was part of the reason. On one hole I hit as hard as possible a ball that was a few inches into the rough and a few yards from the green. The ball went forward two inches and back five yards. A few weeks earlier I'd been playing at a very nice country club outside of Tokyo with some Dentsu executives I was trying to impress—and shot a ninety-seven. Golf is a humbling sport.

Starting around 2000 we took around three or four weekend golf vacations a year with Lou and Rhona Stern. Lou, introduced in chapter six, has long been an enjoyable companion, in part because of his ready wit and the fact that he doesn't take himself too seriously. The format would be nine holes the first day, eighteen holes the second, and another eighteen holes on the day when we would return. The venues were usually Palm Springs, Scottsdale, San Diego, or Tahoe. The rules were a bit relaxed. In particular, we allowed a floating mulligan each nine (to generate a better representation of our game), played no bad lie (life is too short), charged only one stroke for out-of-bounds (two is excessive by our standards), gave short putts (to speed up play), and occasionally took a shot over when a noise interfered with our concentration (no excuse for that one). We laughed a lot and had some terrific meals along the way. I would say that the best course that we played was Coyote Moon in Tahoe because it was away from homes and had a host of dramatic holes. I have learned from Lou how to recognize and appreciate deals and determine an appropriate tip range.

Golf is rewarding on several levels. It is a great excuse to walk in the most beautiful summer settings. Each course has its own charm and some, like Pebble Beach, are just special. Without clubs you would never get to enjoy such scenery. Further, hitting a shot just right whether it is a drive, a long iron, a sand shot, or a putt is such an exhilarating feeling. It takes a poet to express that feeling. John Betjeman, the English poet famous for his ability to capture nostalgia, beauty, and humor, described a successful golf outing in a poem entitled "Seaside Golf," which starts with a description of a drive that captures for me the magic of golf:

> *How straight it flew, how long it flew,*
> *It clear'd the rutty track*
> *And soaring, disappeared from view*
> *Beyond the bunker's back—*
> *A glorious, sailing, bounding drive*
> *Than made me glad I was alive.*

Books, Movies, and the Theater

Books have always been a passion for me. Biographies are my favorite genre. I have read my share of fiction from junk novels to John Updike (who uses metaphors like John McEnroe hit volleys). However, I am drawn to biographies. It is fascinating to me to learn how someone else lived his or her life, and I enjoy examining their experiences, choices, feelings, and relationships. My favorite author is William Manchester. Among his works are *The American Caesar* on Douglas McArther, *The Last Lion* on Churchill, and some marvelous history narratives: *A World Lit Only by Fire* about the Middle Ages and *The Glory and The Dream* about the time period between 1932 to 1972. In a similar genre are books by executives from Alfred Sloan (the architect of the GM miracle in the 20s and 30s) to Lou Gerstner (who turned around IBM in the 90s) that appeal when they offer insight into organizational change and the development of strategy.

Movies are an important part of my life. Many of my favorite films date from the 60s—films like *Breakfast at Tiffany's*, *Lawrence of Arabia*, *To Kill a Mockingbird*, *The Longest Day*, *Guess Who's Coming to Dinner*, *The Pink Panther*, *The Graduate*, *Butch Cassidy and the Sundance Kid*, and musicals such as *The Music Man*, *The Sound of Music*, and *My Fair Lady*. Before that it was the Hope and Crosby road pictures, *High Noon*, *Rebel Without a Cause*, *Blackboard Jungle*, *Bridge on the River Kwai*, and a wonderful musical called *Calamity Jane*. My favorite comedy of all time is the first *The In-Laws* with Peter Falk and Alan Arkin, followed by *Airplane*. I have seen *In-Laws* over twenty times and have imposed it on countless friends. Falk plays Vince Ricardo (who may or may not be a CIA operative) who draws the dentist Sheldon Kornpett, his future in-law, into a set of adventures. Look for the serpentine scene, the tsetse fly story, the diner scene when Sheldon learns the real story, and the Chinese pilots.

I love the theater and gorge on plays when in London or New York. We are season ticket holders for the Berkeley Rep and the Shakespeare Festival. My favorite Shakespeare play is *Julius Caesar*—as noted in chapter seven, it is the source of the frontispiece of my strategy book. A playwright I admire is Michael Frayn, who wrote *Copenhagen*, which is about a meeting between Heisenberg, the German physicist who developed the "uncertainty principle," and

Nils Bohr in 1941, and *Democracy*, which is about Willy Brandt. Both are fascinating attempts to look into the fundamental motivations of people at critical points of history. Although I also have been a long-term devotee of *The Fantasticks*, mentioned in chapter four, my favorite musical by a big margin is *Les Mis*, which I have seen six times, starting with a special trip with Jennifer during her year in Europe. All others are a cut below in my view. In addition to great music, *Les Mis* has a story that is thought provoking on several levels.

Charity

We have long tried to be sensitive to the struggles of those less fortunate, looking for ways to be involved. Kay has for decades made a direct contribution by being on the firing line. She has worked for the American Cancer Association as the coordinator of drivers for cancer patients undergoing treatment. She has also been a driver for Meals-on-Wheels and a hospice volunteer. Jolyn, as described in the last chapter, has developed programs to provide in-home assistance to low-income elderly and now assists the developmentally handi-capped. I occasionally claim that by supporting the work of Kay and Jolyn I should get some credit, but that is a stretch.

My role for the past several decades, aside for some brand strategy consulting for UC Berkeley, the Haas School, and two nonprofits, is to create a family charity budget, to research giving options, and to guide the allocation decisions. Although we have included the arts, medical research, and education in our portfolio, our priorities have been the homeless and the disadvantaged elderly. With respect to the homeless, we are attracted to programs that have high leverage. One charity that we have long supported has been the Contra Costa Food Bank because it leverages a limited budget to provide food for many. In early 2006 I joined the board of the food bank to add a marketing and brand perspective. Another is the St. Anthony Dining Hall that feeds over 2,000 people each day of the year for around twenty-five cents a plate. Our second priority has been programs directed at seniors. I saw what difficulties my mother had during her last few years, and this was a person that had unconstrained financial resources and family support. What about those that lack both? So we support several senior programs. The research and allocation process is always a chance to recognize our good fortune and to understand more about the problems and programs out there. Jolyn always helps in the process, bringing to bear information, judgment, and sensitivity. She and I have visited several charities to see their operations first hand—it is always eye opening to see the problems that are being addressed up close.

The Bears

Cal Football reached the bottom in 2000 and 2001. But then a new coach, Jeff Tedford, arrived and the fortunes changed. He developed Kyle Boller into a top quarterback and changed a one and ten team to a seven and four team. In 2003 he developed a junior college quarterback, Aaron Rodgers, into an overnight sensation and took the team to a victory in a bowl. In 2004, with Aaron Rodgers, J. J. Arrington (an All-American running back), and a host of others, we were ten and one and ranked fourth in the nation. Although we lost to Texas Tech in the Holiday Bowl and fell to number nine, by Cal standards it was an incredible season. The future looks bright.

Basketball was made more fun by a new arena with comfortable seats (Haas Pavilion), and by the fact that my son-in-law, Rich Broad, is a fan with whom I can commiserate. The teams did well by Berkeley standards, making the post-season tournaments with players like Sean Lamply and Joe Shipp but losing in the early rounds. The year 2004 was disappointing, and there appears to be a time of rebuilding ahead. The perennial question returns: Why can't we be more like Stanford or Duke in basketball?

The Family

The millennium was a big deal. With everyone having parties on the 31st, Tom and I decided to have a big party on the 28th when venues, entertainers, and guests were available. We got a charming room in Berkeley and had around one hundred people attend. The party had an intellectual side as we asked people to nominate the outstanding people and event of the millennium. A lot of discussion ensued.

On December 28, 2003, Kay and I celebrated our fortieth anniversary, a time for me to reflect on how lucky I have been to have Kay at my side and how instrumental she has been in all the good things that have happened to me. It was also the occasion

Dave, Kay, Marty, and Tom at the Millennium party

Surprise! The 40th—Devon, Cooper, Kay, and Jennifer

of two parties. One, a surprise party at Jolyn's home, had around a hundred people that managed to get there before we arrived. There were talks by Tom DeJonghe, Lou Stern, and Frank Stawschmidt, with the general theme being that any success I might have had is due to Kay; they gave specific anecdotes to support their position. Rich, Andy, and Brian my sons-in-law, wore shirts labeled "the favorite son" and explained why they should be so nominated. (Rich goes to Cal games, Andy fixes our IT/entertainment programs, and Brian bikes.)

"The Dance"

Dave, Kay, Jo, Andy Amstutz, and Brian Krug

Nicole DeJonghe, Amy Little, Jan, Jo, Jen,
Jenn Faeth, Kelly Nykodym

We also had a more intimate anniversary party with the Aaker/DeJonghe family plus Dave and Sue Broad, Rich's parents, which was arranged by Marty DeJonghe at a banquet hall at the Ironstone Winery in Murphys, a charming gold country town in the foothills, during our visit at our new vacation house between Christmas and New Year's. The talks got emotional, as there were a lot of memories this group shared. Nicole, for example, talked about us as her second parents, how Kay encouraged her to be observant and a good listener, and how I have always been so interested and supportive of her activities. Jo talked about her view that Kay and I have given so much to the extended family and how incredible that family is, in part because of the support, generosity, and love that surrounds it.

The girls now had families and homes. Jo married Brian Krug at a rustic resort above the ocean at Santa Cruz in September of 2001; our friend Andy Amstutz officiated. Andy is a delightful person with a lot of wisdom, some of which he passed on to Jo and Brian. I had spent several months learning a dance under the guidance of an instructor who drove a 50s pink Cadillac convertible. It was our special time, and we really went for it. There was a lot of emotion from Brian's brothers and Jo's sisters. The wedding was three days before the September 11th attack on the World Trade Center. Wow!

Mark and Sherry

With Brian came the remarkable Krug family. Brain has three brothers, Thomas (once a star quarterback at Notre Dame and the son-in-law of the loquacious basketball announcer Dick Vitale), Derrick, and Kevin. They gave moving talks reflecting their close relationship. The Krugs, especially Paul, Brian's father, are campers, and got me to join them on their favorite weekend camp-grounds at Lake of the Woods near Tahoe. We hiked in several miles for our two-night adventure. I got sick the first night (in part because Brian got our food mixed with lake water) and as a result we all left a day early. The hiking and scenery was awesome but I was reminded why I do not camp.

Jo and Brian found the perfect home in Walnut Creek next to Shell Ridge, a huge open space where eagles roam and mountain bike trails are endless. Jo completed her social welfare degree at Berkeley and directs her professional life towards helping people in need. Brian, a gifted software manager with exceptional people skills, went from being a project manager for a software company to being in charge of team-building websites at Chevron. They both bike and run—Jo did an Ironman in 2000 (swim 2.4 miles, bike 112 miles, and then run a marathon) with a lot of help from the Aaker/DeJonghe team. We were able to bike on the course, so we participated, at least in our eyes. I was surprised by the energy surrounding the event. It was very involving and very long (the spectators tended to give out). She has committed to do another with Brian.

Another wedding of note was when Mark DeJonghe married Sherry on October 26, 2002. I was asked to prepare a set of remarks on marriage for the occasion. I contacted several couples that I respect, like Andy and Carole Amstutz, and asked them what makes a good marriage. With that as background I wrote the following, which reflects to a large extent my marriage with Kay.

⟋⟍

A Good Marriage
By David Aaker

On the occasion of the marriage of Mark and Sherry DeJonghe

What makes a good marriage? To answer that question, I sought the insights of two dozen couples that I respect. My interpretation of their experiences is that a good marriage involves friendship and love.

What is a best friend? According to my panel, a best friend can be described in four very different ways. A best friend will:

- **Be a companion who will share interests.** There will be activities for which there is shared enthusiasm. There will be other activities that have that potential but require some cultivation—a best friend will invest the effort. There will be adventures involving new activities. It is all about saying yes to walking on the beach or seeing a movie or taking up hiking in Austria. It is all about being positive and enjoying life.

- **Be fun to be around.** There will be chuckles and laughter, a willingness to see humor in everyday life. There will be completely unexpected surprises that please and some that delight and some that remind you of being a child at Christmas.

- **Be stimulating.** There will be opinions and ideas that stretch the mind, that make you think. A best friend will be a good listener that looks to hear opinions and ideas as well as express them. Life with a best friend will never be boring.

- **Provide space to grow, to realize your potential.** Rather than trying to change you to Mr. or Mrs. Perfect, a best friend will not only accept you, faults and all, but will respect you as a unique person. More important, a friend will not be confining, clinging, and inhibiting but, rather, will give you the freedom—indeed, the encouragement—to create dreams and fulfill those dreams whether they be spiritual, professional, to climb that mountain, or to run that race.

What is deep love? According to my panel there are three dimensions. Deep love will:

- **Have passion.** It should have moments of real sizzle where there is love expressed with urgency, intensity, and intimacy. The sizzle is important—so says the panel.

- **Be expressive in day-to-day life.** It is about under-standing, listening, accepting, tenderness, and making your partner priority one. And more tangibly in notes, gifts, helping out, thoughtful acts, touching, showing affection, expressing love, and, perhaps most importantly, saying I'm sorry. The 1971 *Love Story* movie defined love as not having to say I'm sorry. It was a wonderful, inspiring movie, but I think they got that part wrong.

- **Include a deep, long-term commitment.** Things will not always go well. There will be irritations, problems, illnesses, temptations, challenges, and very likely worse. Commitment helps you cope and overcome. There will be disagreements—some large and some small. Commitment means that a way to reconcile those differences will be found and that it is OK to lose a few. It is about being there for the long haul—to support, to encourage, to help, and to love.

So try to be a friend, help your partner enjoy life, laugh, think, and grow. In the words of Ralph Waldo Emerson, "Happy is the house that shelters a friend."

And work at being a lover who offers passion, day-to-day expressions of love, and commitment. In the words of Virgil over 2,000 years ago, "Love conquers all things. Let us too give in to love."

❧

Mark and Sherry live in Monterey where Mark is an engineer making underwater camera equipment with an interest in real estate development and surfing, in not necessarily that order. Sherrie teaches and, in July of 2005, became the mother of Merrick to the joy of four grandparents.

Jan and Rich have Samantha, born in June of 2000, Maile, who arrived in March of 2002, and Kailyn, who appeared in June of 2005. Sami is the sweetest, most charming girl imaginable and is so nice to her sister—who probably thinks all big sisters are like that. She includes her sister in all activities, including sleeping. Sami, at eighteen months, was one of the youngest to go to the *Nutcracker*. She joined a tradition that now extends back some thirty years. I vividly recall Jennifer and Jan, not too much older than that, being all dressed up and participating in the contest to find the prettiest dress. Maile is personality plus, very opinionated and not easily distracted. Everything works best when she

Maile and Sami

Andy, Jennifer, Devon, and Cooper

gets her way. Blessed with incredible energy, she does everything full blast, whether it is running down the hall, riding her trike, swimming, or expressing displeasure (in one of her remarkable meltdowns)—she just puts her head down and steams. Kailyn is a model baby in all respects. Jan, who teaches half time, and Rich, in the Internet gift business, live in a charming home about ten minutes away, so I see the kids about five times per week, and Kay cares for them one day a week.

Jennifer and Andy had twin boys in April of 2002. Devon, like his dad, is fascinated by remotes, cell phones, and wires and lacks the attention span for colorful plastic things. Once when he had trouble going pee pee for his nursery school teacher, he opined that maybe his instrument needed a recharge. He is a doer. Cooper (actually Cooper David Aaker Smith), a thinker, has more patience and usually has a big smile on his face. The boys disagree but also look after each other. When one is in a "time-out," even if it is for hitting his brother, his twin will show empathy and support. Remarkable. Tea Sloane, another perfect baby, joined the family in October 2005. Jennifer became a full professor at Stanford and continues to excel. Outside reviewers call her research elegant, clever, and important ... with incredible breadth and quality ... and the product of an extraordinarily smart, creative, and productive researcher. Wow! She and Andy, the global brand manager at Dolby, have a great home in the hills of Burlingame that, thanks to Andy, is a home entertainment marvel (if only Jennifer or anyone else could operate it—a television repair man once could not figure out how to turn the TV on). The number of remotes was once up to sixty.

Kay was named Orinda Citizen of the Year in 2003. Her forty years teaching, twenty years at Hospice, and almost that many as a cancer driver coordinator were rewarded. It was a big deal with a dinner and seven speakers, including Jolyn and Marty DeJonghe, who told the Kay story from different perspectives. It is amazing how many people she has touched.

The Aaker-DeJonghe vacations continued to Taos, Sun River, Squaw Valley, Downieville, Monterey, Murphy's, and Spain, plus the big weddings of Jolyn in 2001 and Mark the next year. In June of 2004, the whole group, seventeen people in all, spent a week on

Maui at a set of condos on the beach with golfing, biking, surfing, fishing, and hanging out on the agenda. We definitely have something special.

I started having warnings of a possible prostate cancer in the late 90s. During one of those times, the girls took me on a special day of skating in Union Square to take our minds off a forthcoming test result. When in mid-May of 2002 I finally received the diagnosis of prostate cancer, the family came together. Everyone pitched in to do research on options and to help make appointments. I ended up talking to some twelve professionals and dozens of prostate cancer survivors in the course of two weeks. The bottom line is that the three major options net out with very similar results (which is why they are all being used). However, the recommendations of my current physician, Dr. Yeung, and my previous physician, Dr. Fishbacher (now an oncologist), both of whom are unbiased as to treatment and know me, steered me toward an operation. Dr. Peter Carroll of the San Francisco Medical School performed it successfully in early July, less than six weeks after the diagnosis. The whole experience does change your outlook. Each day takes on new meaning.

On Father's Day in 2002 I was preparing for my cancer surgery when my three girls all wrote letters to me. Of course, this was a time where they were looking for good things to say, but still the thoughts that came through were special to me. Some excerpts:

Jolyn—No one picks their father, so I really feel like I won the lottery with you! ...Your sense of humor makes you a joy to be with for everyone. You laugh at yourself, make light of every funny situation, and laugh with others. You are a pleasure to be with ... as a mentor and father, you have personally shown me how to be compassionate, empathetic, open-minded, and giving. You have played a large role in my path to social work. Since I can remember, you have one request for a Christmas gift— advice on good charities. Whenever I meet my clients I try to approach them in a way that you would. You care about others and are genuinely interested in people's lives and well-being. ... Your unconditional love and support ... Growing up with a dad I remember being there all of the time is priceless! You have always encouraged me to be the best I can be without putting pressure on me ... how did you do that? ... You are such a special person.

Jan—You have been the best dad a daughter can ask for. Even though I was never a star athlete, you would make me feel like I was one. You would spend hours working with me to make me better ... I have always felt completely comfortable going to you with any thought, problem, or idea. I love having such an honest and open relationship with my father. Watching you be a grandfather is an incredible sight to see. Our two girls are so lucky to have such a loving, involved, caring, attentive, thoughtful, and fun grandpa.

Jennifer—You are absolutely, hands-down, the most incredible father in the world ... the unbelievable power of support, strength, and unadulterated pure unconditional love that you give us ... every single time some challenging thing happens to us or there is joy in our life, you are next to us sharing what we feel ... the creative, open and full way you live ... the amazing special days ... even the mundane ones like flying a kite influenced how much fun I had with you, how great it was to be a kid, and, indeed, how wonderful life could be. ... Your sense of humor is reflected in all of us. We laugh and laugh and laugh, as a family, at you, at me, all together. ... Everything you are is in us; and the strength, passion, and creativity and sense of humor that defines you, defines us. Even better, it is already defining our children. We are blessed.

Reflections

My professional life to date has been, on balance, excellent. Being an academic at a school like Berkeley was simply incredible. Research and writing was challenging and fulfilling. Working with bright, creative research colleagues has been a treasure. And the freedom to research any topic and manage your own time was so precious and unique. I have never felt confined or controlled. My Berkeley colleagues and the larger marketing academic community have been a source of close friendships. Teaching has been rewarding on a lot of levels.

My second professional life, involving speaking, writing, consulting, and my association with Prophet and Dentsu, has been stimulating and rewarding. Just chatting with cool people, talking about brands or business strategy, is as good as it gets for me, and I get to do a lot of it. The bottom line is that I do not want to retire—my professional life is too much fun.

One constant through my professional life is working hard, preparing more, and going the extra mile to make sure the result represents my best work. Whether trying to excel at high school debate, survive at MIT, make a mark at TI, make a small business thrive, pass an Stanford PhD exam, stretch a research project, refine a journal article, teach up to my capabilities, make the book as good as it can be, or please an audience, I always give it my best shot. My desire to deliver frequently bordered on the absurd, but I had few second thoughts. When I failed, I rarely had to regret not putting in more effort. For better or worse, I have been an overachiever.

I have developed an ambitious set of objectives during the last fifteen to twenty years. I decided I wanted to influence the way brands (and, by extension, firms) are managed. One goal is to encourage firms to look at brands as assets and manage them strategically. Another is to provide a set of tools and concepts to enable them to do that well. I want to leave a mark on the management world, noticeable if modest. That is one reason for the books, talks, and consulting. History will decide if these efforts to make a difference will bear fruit or will fade.

My work has also provided the chance to travel, not as a tourist, but as a part of a culture. Japan became my second home and provided a host of cultural experiences, many shared with Kay, and several close friendships. In Europe there were memorable speaking events, Davos, our Germany adventure, our exchange students, and my Barcelona connection.

I have been blessed also with a set of activities that have enriched my life: the opportunity to excel (all things are relative) in tennis, skiing, and golf, the experience of seeing the wonderful outdoors up close through boating, mountain biking, and cross-country and powder skiing, and the chance to be active and fit.

My family and the extended Aaker/DeJonghe family have been a treasure and source of enjoyment and strength. My wife, Kay, a great friend and the love of my life, has made so much of what I value and enjoy possible, from the holiday times to the day-to-day pleasures. The DeJonghe family has added so much as well. My interactions and activities with Tom have enriched my life immeasurably. And my three girls—and now their families—are what it is all about. I cannot envision life without them.

Writing this book has been a joy because I got to remember so many good times and reconnect with so many people—if not in person, then in spirit. When packaged, it does seem that a lot has transpired. I hope the story is not all told, and that it will go on. Jennifer says that she is already looking forward to a sequel. A nice thought.

10 Epilogue

Seven years have passed. It is well past mid-2011 and time for an update. The story continues. A lot has changed in the world and in my life.

Prophet Blossomed

Indeed Prophet has blossomed under the leadership of Michael Dunn, Andy Pierce (president of Prophet USA), and Scott Davis (CGO—chief growth officer). In 1999 when Michael and I joined Prophet, it had eighteen people and local clients. In 2011, it employed well over 200 people, made its second acquisition in the form of a strategy consulting firm in Berlin, had seven offices in the U.S. and Europe, and dealt with global clients and projects. Getting to $100 million in sales was no longer a dream but a realistic forecast. It has been on a tear.

The quality of the people and their ability to adapt and contribute is remarkable. To a person, they are both impressive and likeable. The strong Prophet culture and leadership are in large part responsible. New hires are expected to be competent, knowledgeable, and bright, but also approachable, likable, team players, and client-centered. There is a history of making sure that a new hire represents a culture fit. Hiring is never a sure thing but the batting average is higher than most. Evidence comes from the post-engagement interviews with clients in which phrases like "fun to work with," "understand our business," and "made a real contribution" abound.

A growth has been stimulated in part by the expansion of the scope and IP (intellectual property) of the firm. Even a

389

half-decade ago, we were known as a brand strategy firm doing brand identity and positioning engagements and applying the brand portfolio concept and frameworks developed in my *Brand Portfolio Strategy*. In 2011, less than one-third of our revenues is expected to come from branding projects and there are five other growth platforms.

The first of these is marketing. Typically, as we help clients with brand or brand portfolio issues, they gain confidence in us and our knowledge of them and their markets. It becomes logical for them to ask us to address broader marketing and customer relationship issues. One key perspective has been the concept of customer experience and touch points that was codified in the book *Building the Brand-Driven Business* by Scott and Michael.

The second area is analytics, the ability to develop and harness databases and experiments to generate marketing options and measure their performance and potential. We now have the capability, for example, to provide data-based segmentation strategies and to design a "test and learn" process of evaluating marketing programs. These are reported in Michael's book *The Marketing Accountability Imperatives*. One aspect of our analytical effort that differs from others is that it is always forward looking and linked to the "big picture" strategy rather than being described as data mining and backward looking.

A third area is design. We had long pointed out with some pride that we were focused on strategy and did not do logos. However, over the years, this posture cost us many large projects because clients resisted having to hire a team of firms and recognized that handing off visual branding to another firm risks losing control of strategy. Perhaps as important, our pitches and our final presentations were excessively left-brained and verbal. We struggled without any visual expertise to provide energy and amplification. So we decided that design should become part of our offerings, but it should be design linked to and driven by strategy. And to develop it organically. Peter Dixon, a gifted and seasoned design executive joined and established from zero a first-class design practice with a cadre of talented people. He has had a significant impact, from designing the visuals for major retailers to designing the logos for complex brand architecture.

He has also touched many of the Prophet engagements by adding a design dimension or visual flare element to the pitches and recommendations.

The fourth area is innovation. Our innovative process ranged from dysfunctional to haphazard. There was no "Prophet" take on the creative process. When I arrived at Prophet, I actually bought everybody two books on creatively and with Karen Woon developed a process tailored to us, but it was not used, not even once. But in 2008, we bought the firm Play, developed by Andy Stefanovich, a charismatic speaker with boundless energy. Play had developed at least twelve tools to get people out of their comfort zone to gain new perspectives. The two firms clicked. Play provided Prophet with a huge upgrade in its ability to lead creative thinking. Further, this upgrade was visible both to clients and prospective clients. We suddenly had a broader and more persuasive value proposition. And Play's efforts, which had largely occurred in isolated workshops, were placed in a larger context in which they could be leveraged. This win-win result, rare for two firms attempting to merge, was accomplished in the face of organizational difficultly.

The fifth area is business strategy. We get asked to weigh in with analysis and judgment about basic marketplace dynamics and big strategic decisions sometimes involving billions of investment dollars. This is a stretch for Prophet, but credibility comes from our people and prior engagements. The fact that we can employ innovation skills and brand strategy expertise helps. It is a heady and stimulating experience to go up against the top strategy firms and win.

My role continues to be the guru in the corner writing books, giving talks, and being a resource to the Prophet teams. Very modest but also very low stress. I get a great office and interaction with incredible people about fascinating issues. And the group seems to value my presence. From around 2007, Prophet has recognized high performers along a dozen dimensions by awarding "Aakers." Nice but hard to know how to react except to feel embarrassed and ancient. Around 70 contributed a single word descriptor for me (a very Play project). Got words like inspiring, insightful, witty, provocative, inquisitive, and thought leader but nothing like life-of-the-party, good looking, or fashion leader.

My eleven years as the executive advisor to Dentsu finally wound down. My three visits a year dropped to two in 2010 and one in 2011. The last one coincided with the translation of *Brand Relevance* and involved a farewell talk to Dentsu. I commented on my ongoing objective to encourage Dentsu to be a brand strategy advisor and my efforts to help the firm elevate brands, brand building, and business strategy into their practice and thus help their clients realize their potential and help Dentsu become relevant at the CEO level. The Dentsu part of my life was special professionally and personally. I got to experience Japanese culture through working with Dentsu and its clients and through skiing, Sumo, Takarazuku, Kabuki, the fish market, and golf. Special memories of a great company, wonderful and talented people, and a fascinating organization and culture. I'm sure I will be back from time to time.

My Brand Efforts Go On

I continue to try to advance the cause of brands and brand-building, the thrust of my professional efforts during the last twenty-five years, sometimes feeling a bit like Don Quixote. This effort, as I noted earlier, was stimulated by the short-term perspective in the executive suite caused by pervasive use of current earnings to measure the performance of individuals and firms. The alternative, in my view, is to build assets that will support a forward-looking strategy. And one of the key assets is the brand.

Two books emerged, *Spanning Silos: The New CMO Imperative* and *Brand Relevance: Making Competitors Irrelevant*.

Spanning Silos

I watched Prophet deal with a client that needed to change its branding strategy in order to support a business strategy that required synergy across product silos and cooperation across country silos. The process exposed me to the difficulties of dealing organizationally with silos and some solutions that worked. I also through my work at Dentsu realized that managing a brand across country silos was a major issue for most global firms. Clearly a set of silo issues was receiving attention at the highest strategy levels. I resolved to study the problem more systematically.

I came to realize that nearly all organizations dealt with country and product silos, often acting very autonomously, and this structure inhibited the development of strong brands and marketing. Further, the problem was not easily solved because the decentralized organizational structure was institutionalized, had a lot of positive qualities (put the decision making close to the customer, market trends, and relevant technology), and was aggressively defended by those enjoying their power. I inter-

viewed over forty CMOs (chief marketing officers) to determine the nature of the problem and what could be done about it.

They agreed that the silo autonomy, despite its advantages, was just not working in the modern marketplace. In particular, silos were standing in the way of short-term and long-term success because of the following four realities and others. First, customers were demanding offerings that spanned silos. Second, marketing programs such as sponsorships required cross-silo cooperation in order to achieve critical economies of scale. Third, brands that spanned silos risked becoming confused and inconsistent. Fourth, really great marketing programs were rare and needed to be leveraged across silos. Many firms recognized that silos were preventing the development of winning products and programs or preventing them from reaching their full potential. Their response was to create or revitalize the office of the CMO and charge it with providing a fix. It turns out that the fix was not so apparent or easy.

My approach was to find out from the CMOs what does work and what does not. The research yielded some surprising results. The headline-- the best course in most firms was not to centralize and standardize but, rather, to find unthreatening ways to encourage cooperation and communication. Movements in this direction come if the CMO office acts as a facilitator (e.g., organizing meetings and creating teams), service supplier (e.g., conducting segmentation studies), and consultant (e.g., helping to interpret tracking data). In these nonthreatening capacities the CMO team can get the silos to talk and work together. In doing so the use of teams, information systems, and even meetings can be very helpful. It is amazing what can be accomplished with such a low-risk approach. There are times of crises in which a more aggressive approach is needed. But in general, imposing centralization and standardization will lead to a flameout and is part of the reason that the average tenure of a new CMO is twenty-three months.

The pre-chapter quotes include one from cartoonist Walt Kelly, who has his central character, Pogo, say, "We have met the enemy and he is us." That summarizes the nature of silo barriers.

Spanning Silos represented a departure from my normal writing style, which is to develop some conceptual models supported by case studies. This book was instead based on interviews. I did not feel the result was as interesting or involving a read. The interviews resulted in good insights and anecdotes but not many stories. I resolved to go back to the style that had worked in the past for my next book.

Brand Relevance

I introduced the brand relevance concept in *Brand Portfolio Strategy* and made the point that it does not matter how good your SUV brand is or how loyal your customers are if they are now buying a hybrid sedan. It just does not matter; your brand is not relevant. Since then I have been amazed by how often the brand relevance concept explains market dynamics. Whenever there is a disruption of the marketplace there is a brand relevance explanation. So I decided that I wanted to elevate the concept to a book.

The basic idea is that there are two ways to compete in existing markets, which I have labeled brand preference competition and brand relevance competition.

Brand preference competition, the most commonly used route to winning customers and sales, focuses on generating brand preference by beating the competition in established and stable categories. The winning strategy is to engage in incremental innovation to make the brand ever more attractive or reliable, the offering less costly, or the marketing program more effective or efficient. It is all about continuous improvement—faster, cheaper, better—which has its roots in Fredrick Taylor's scientific man-

agement with its time and motion studies a century ago.

This "my brand is better than your brand" approach is an increasingly difficult path to success in today's dynamic market because customers are not inclined or motivated to change brand loyalties. Brands are perceived to be similar at least with respect to the delivery of functional benefits, and often these perceptions are accurate. Why rethink a product and brand decision that has worked when alternatives are similar? Further, competitors copy or give the appearance of copying most incremental advances.

The alternative is brand relevance competition, which involves developing an offering so innovative that it creates a new category or subcategory that affects the purchase decision and use experience. The goal is no longer to beat competitors, but rather, to make them irrelevant by enticing customers to buy a category or subcategory for which most or all alternative brands are not considered because they lack context visibility or credibility. The result can be a market in which there is no competition at all for an extended period of time, or one in which the competition is reduced or weakened—the ticket to ongoing financial success. The Chrysler minivan, Enterprise Rent-A-Car, Zipcar, iShares, Whole Foods Market, Westin's Heavenly Bed, Gatorade, CNN, the Discovery Channel, ESPN, Tide Coldwater, IKEA, iPod, Go-Gurt, and hundreds of other brands have created categories or subcategories and enjoyed the absence of viable competition for a long period of time.

The brand relevance strategy is to engage in substantial or transformational innovation that will develop offerings containing some "must have" attributes that will define a new category or subcategory. Competition is now between categories and subcategories. The challenge for the brand is to own and actively manage the perceptions, the acceptance, and the loyalty toward the new category or subcategory. It involves becoming an exemplar, the brand that represents the new category or subcategory, and being persistent in communicating why the customer should choose the right category or subcategory. This task will be unfamiliar to those used to focusing on brand building.

There are a few pitfalls making the brand relevance competition difficult. First, it is hard to distinguish between incremental and substantial innovation. There is the tendency to inflate incremental innovation and come to believe that the brand has created a new category or subcategory when the market is not that impressed. There is also the companion tendency to overestimate the apparent barriers to making the concept based on substantial innovation operational. The result is a missed opportunity to create a new category or subcategory, a blunder that is hidden in that it does not appear in the financials.

Second, there is often a failure to adequately fund and support a concept with new category or subcategory potential, not only throughout its introduction into the marketplace, but also as it attempts to build ongoing barriers to competitors. There are always many times in which a "kill" decision will be justifiable.

Third, even if the vision is there, the timing might be off or the offering could be missing a key ingredient. Few realize that Sony introduced a iPod-like device two years before Apple, and Microsoft introduced an iPad-like device ten years before the iPad emerged. It was not the vision that led to the Apple success, it was timing and the ability to get the offering right.

Among the pre-chapter quotes is a great one from Mahatma Gandhi, who said "First, they ignore you. Then they ridicule you. Then they fight you. Then you win." That idea captures the efforts of a firm with a truly innovative offering that forms a new category or subcategory. Another, from Peter Drucker, is one of the wisest business management commentaries: "Results are gained by exploiting opportunities, not by solving problems." That is what wining the brand relevance war is all about.

A side note. The cover developed by the publisher was pleasing but not suitable for a book on innovation. So the Prophet design team set to work and designed a cover around the charge to be bold. The middle, the longest arrow in white, represents a brand breaking out of the clutter with an innovative offering that defines a new category or subcategory. The other arrows in gold represent the also-rans. It was nice to have a Prophet backup.

Another side note. Joe Tripodi, who has been a visible, transforming CMO of MasterCard, Bank of NY, Allstate, and now Coke, has written an endorsement for my last five books. Of *Spanning Silos* he wrote: "David Aaker has brilliantly dissected the CMO role with complex global organizations and laid out a compelling 'how-to' manual for success. Aaker offers up pragmatic solutions that will enhance the collaboration and connective tissue between siloed business units. This book will unquestionably turbocharge the impact of the CMO and central marketing organizations worldwide." Of *Brand Relevance* he said, "Aaker has nailed it (again)! The long-term viability of a business is inextricably linked to gaining a brand relevance advantage through new category and subcategory development and unique positioning." He is a good friend which helps explain his willness to be so positive. Nevertheless, his eloquent endorsements are real uppers.

Spanning Silos had modest sales. *Brand Relevance*, named as one of the top three marketing books of 2011 by S&B which is a leading management journal, should do better but will not be a best seller. Bob Wallace, the editor of my first four brand books, noted that because these books all did so well, I had little perspective about how hard it is for a book to have breakout sales. I do now. However, I do feel the books have made a contribution by introducing new perspectives on important issues in a readable form. Further, the books have sold well outside the U.S. in the form of translations in Korean, Chinese, Japanese, Russian (*Spanning Silos*), Portuguese (*Brand Relevance*) and Spanish (*Brand Relevance*). But book writing is fun for me and I will continue whatever the sales. My role model is Peter Drucker, who was writing in his nineties.

The next book is likely to be shorter. One option is *Aaker on Brands* which would present the 25 top brand concepts from my past writings and elsewhere. Another is *Energizing Your Brands* which would discuss the importance of brand energy and how to get it. Still another would be a book around the concept of shared interest, one of my research streams.

Find a Shared Interest with Customers

Most marketing is geared to support the offering. The focused goal is to build the brand, deepen the relationship, grow sales, and increase loyalty. The problem is that while firms are interested and involved in such objectives, customers are not. Another route is to find a shared interest with customers for whom the brand is relevant and use that as a vehicle to involve and interest. The result can be a way to add energy, improve an image, create a deeper relationship, and stimulate a social network.

Shared interest programs need to have a link to the brand or firm. As a minimum, there needs to be a fit or natural connection with the brand. Would you expect the brand to be involved in the shared interest? Or is it incongruous? Pampers, for example, has a connection with a shared interest in baby care and Avon's Walk for Breast Cancer connects to Avon because of the interest that its customer base has with breast cancer. Sometimes the assets or skills for the firm can be employed. General Mills has a recipe bank and kitchen that can provide credibility to a shared interest in gluten free eating. The strongest link is when the offering is integrated to the shared interest and how it is implemented. Kaiser Permanente, for example, an integrated medical insurance and delivery system, focuses on the shared interest in health enhancement and involves members controlling their own health with "My Health Manager," (a secure on-line way to access health records, contact physicians, monitor program participation, etc.), and accessing a wide array of preventive health programs online and through classes which include areas such as weight control, exercising, stress management, insomnia, smoking issues, and healthy eating.

Firms are struggling to create effective social media strategies. Shared interest programs provide motivation for people to talk and listen, the keys to an active social media audience. In contrast, it is a rare product that is intrinsically interesting and involving. A shared interest program starts with the customer, his or her activities, interests, opinions, issues, and possessions rather than promoting the product or service. It involves a new way to look at building brands and customer relationships.

Speaking

I continue to give a dozen talks or so each year including an annual public lecture at the Haas School. I have been pleased when 150 or so show up but then Haas started to put then on YouTube and one lecture on my Spanning Silos book got 15,000 uploads. It would take me 50 talks to reach that many people live. Welcome to the new world of digital media.

The international ones are special because of the venues, the large audiences, and the fact I am treated as a media celebrity. Five stand out: three in Korea in which my presence was promoted by Katy Choi (whose picture is on page 302 with her partner Jerry Lee), one in Singapore, and one in Portugal.

The first Korean talk involved an audience of over 900 people at the W Hotel in 2007, each of whom was given a leather-bound translation of *Spanning Silos* with my signature embossed on the cover. The translation and the event were all planned and executed in under three months by Katy. Incredible! I was treated as a celebrity with autographs and requests for pictures. Kind of fun but a half day of that is enough. I feel for real celebrities.

The W hotel was located on a hill overlooking Seoul. Our three-room suite was dramatic but not so usable. It had a tub in the middle of the living room that took two hours to fill, and we had to get help to turn on the lights, close the windows, or use the alarm. The whole hotel was like a living contemporary museum in many respects, designed to be seen and not used. The bar area had tiered small conversation areas with unusual but comfortable chairs, and around the corner there were restrooms resembling cabanas. The hotel was so different and pleasing to the eye, it was just fun to soak it up.

The second Korean event was the 2010 World Knowledge Forum in Seoul, an annual event to showcase Korea to thought leaders around the world. (Katy sold me to the organizers even thought I was marginally qualified). My talk, again to around 900 people or more, introduced the *Brand Relevance* book translation, a book that thanks to Katy appeared three months before the English edition. For three days each breakfast, lunch, and dinner was an intimate affair with the speakers, and they contained a bunch of luminaries. So I got to dine, hang, and chat up some really interesting people. I took advantage. For example, I had breakfast with Donald Trump Jr., to whom I said, "I am wearing a Trump shirt" (I did not say I bought it at the van Heusen outlet store), and he replied that he wore one as well. He was in charge of the golf course purchase programs. Basically they buy really upscale courses that are in financial trouble. Sounded like he had a terrific job. And I exchanged opinions with Christopher Hill, who just stepped down as ambassador to Iraq and had been the chief U.S. negotiator with North Korea before that. Amazing inside stories. Among the others were Ferguson and Zakaria.

I had several meals with and got to know Niall Ferguson, the Harvard economic historian who has written extensively on the decline in the dollar, a subject that I have followed intensely along with my friend Mark Garman. Both Niall and Mark have a pessimistic view. One of his dramatic conclusions is that within a few years the interest on the U. S. debt will exceed our total U.S. government revenue. (As a result of this logic, I decided to overweight gold, silver, energy stocks, and bonds from Norway, Canada, and Australia in our portfolio). Because of my interest and the knowledge I had gleaned from Mark, I could ask some reasonably probing questions.

On the night before my talk, Kay talked me out of chatting up one of my heroes, Fared Zakaria, the *Time* columnist and TV personality who specializes in international issues; he was on a cell phone. However, the next night I was seated across from him at dinner, and my wife decided to shop, so it was just Fared and me. I learned about his life in New York, his kids' soccer activities, how he gets guests, and so on. He did not inquire about my kids or ask my opinion about world issues even though I had a lot to say in readiness. He apparently has other sources.

The third Korean event was part of the Korean President's initiative to build a Korean band and was sponsored by the national brand council that he set up. I was to meet him but he apparently believed a trip to Mongolia was more important. His absence meant also that the ministers that appeared for the opening ceremony with its intense press coverage did not feel obligated to stay for the talks. About fifteen dignitaries and I cut a ribbon each using gold scissors and white gloves. Felt like I was in a period movie. I chatted up the Russian ambassador who did not seem comfortable shared thoughts about North Korean issues. I became skeptical about the ability of a council to deliver effective building strategies for Korea with brand naive people playing prominent roles. One council member, who managed to drop the fact that he was a former UN ambassador, confided to me that the key to branding success is to get the slogan right. I tried to tell him how wrong that was but we clearly did not communicate.

I can't express enough how very weird I find press conferences and interviews at these events. In this trip I even had a thirty-minute special on a TV station. What is wrong with this picture? If our local paper in Orinda even knows about me it is as the husband of Kay Aaker.

A highlight of the trip was meeting two young executives, both sons of founders of major firms. Mr. Yong-Jin Chung of E-Mart, a large retailer and a Prophet client, invited the Prophet team to an evening BBQ at the pool of his sunny 25,000 square foot home which had four levels, marble floors, an exercise area with around 44 pieces of equipment, a half dozen grand pianos, suites for his two children, a theater, and an impressive car collection. The home was tastefully and elegantly furnished and Mr. Chung and his wife were gracious hosts. Mr. Dong Kwan Kim of Hanwha, another Prophet client, was a graduate of Harvard's undergraduate program who is helping to run a 25 billion company. He is extremely young but thoughtful, informed, and with a real grasp of strategy. I suspect he has the talent to eventually become a

CEO. In Asia, many of the largest firms are family affairs, very different from the West.

I spoke at an annual brand conference in Singapore and later at a Dentsu event in Thailand in 2006. I went there with a back spasm and almost canceled. However, I got to fly first class on Singapore airlines and thought I could handle that even with a bad back. I had the chance to chat with Martin Lindstrom, who does innovative research on consumer behavior despite giving 150 or so talks around the world each year. In his talk he presented data about the relative time kids spend on TV, on the computer, and with games. He correctly forecast then that TV was not the way to reach them. I also spent time with Jack Trout, who with Al Ries wrote the first popular brand book, *Positioning: The Battle for your Mind*. Their book was well done and helpful to those who needed some provocative ideas. The trouble is that many take their word as gospel, and that sometimes leads to unfortunate outcomes. One of their brand rules, for example, is that you should never extend your brand. If Disney had followed that rule they would still be relegated to making cartoons. Jack is colorful if a bit grumpy. One of his typical over-the-top statements: "More money is wasted in marketing than in any other human activity." Provocative even if unsupported and undoudtedly wrong. Even so, I enjoyed getting to know him, we have a lot in common.

Finally, I spoke at the annual QSP Summit marketing event in Porto, Portugal, in 2010. Porto is a charming town in the North of Portugal with old world streets and shops. After the event several of the speakers who stayed over enjoyed a boat ride down the river, as well as a wine tasting and dinner with the manager at a winery that is the world's pioneer and market leader of port. They served some white port on the rocks as a before-dinner drink that was not so sweet and a nice change of pace. The winery overlooked the city and a bridge and the vista at night ws memorable. I was sad to learn that Portugal's economy is so bad that a whole generation of students have no chance to get a professional job unless they leave the country. It is hard to see how Portugal can climb out of their tailspin. Education is said to be the route to economic health, but it is not working there.

I like to see countries in the context of an event like those I've described. You get to be with the fellow speakers, who are often

In Porto, Portugal, 2010

informative and interesting, and you get firsthand insights into the culture and politics of the country from natives. Plus, there are always a few afternoons to see museums, which is about right for me.

I should mention a rare opportunity to work with Jennifer. We put on a "Dueling Professors" act first for the Haas Alumni in 2008 and then for some Stanford donors in 2009 (this version appeared on YouTube and got 3,500 hits). We each described our research and analyzed the other's. I noted that Jennifer was so productive because she multitasks. Her family knows that if she is on the computer she is at 60 percent attention during a conversation, but if she is writing that falls to 30 percent, and everyone can tell especially if they hear the typing. She put forth a set of "DavidAakerisms" like, "that is the worst sentence I have ever read," "average under ten words a slide," "good question, I wrote a book on that," "in raising kids if you buy them things they will like you more" (a model Jennifer claims to follow), "talk about the weather to a colleague you dislike," and "stake out areas of incompetence" (Jennifer has done that well with cooking as I did with administration). It was a treasure to be on a stage with Jennifer. I noted at the close of my talk that she is special in so many ways and is my best friend. Jan and Jolyn know that in the right context, one of them would have been named as a best friend.

One more thing. A survey was conducted of a group of 1,700 senior marketing people in 2007; 600 responded. One question asked respondents to identify the most important marketing/business gurus. It is not false modesty for me to say that the result has not a lot of meaning. I suspect that no one got many votes, so the rank order difference means little and the methodology was suspect if not flaky. However, I placed fifth behind Seth Godin (a best seller of short pithy business books and the top marketing blogger), Steve Jobs, Peter Drucker (author of classic management books), and Warren Buffet, and ahead of Tom Peters. Jim Collins (who shares with Peters the honor of being a megabookseller), Jack Welch (the legendary GE CEO), and Phil Kotler (the real marketing guru). I have the *Ad Age* article with pictures describing the results in my room and look at it whenever I get depressed, not really knowing whether to laugh (because seeing my face with that group is so incongruous) or cheer.

More substantial and credible was an invitation to give the 26th annual Wroe Alderson Distinguished Lecture at the Wharton School. It was a stretch to call me a present day researcher, but I was honored to have my name beside some notables of marketing academics.

Joining the Social Media Craze

In the spring of 2010 I entered the digital world by becoming a tweeter. I commented on articles that had relevance to branding. I learned how to befriend influential others and grew my followers from 500 to nearly 4,000 a year later (during which time my daughter grew hers from around 3,000 to 13,000 but who is counting). I also became active at LinkedIn. I have concluded that that the Twitter population has, on average, bad demographics (about 15 percent of my followers are relevant and 1 percent are active in the sense of commenting on my stuff) while LinkedIn, where I have well over 2,000 connections, has great demographics, but the members do not check their messages regularly. I sent a note to thirteen top Indian executives; only one replied and that was over a month later. I suspect that most LinkedIn members in my audience check their messages once or twice a year. Facebook was a mystery to me, but I finally got some help and a program emerged with videos that has promise.

At the end of 2010, I started a blog on branding, davidaaker. com, posting a comment once or twice a week. I enjoyed being able to comment on whatever without polishing it into an article or book chapter and fighting with editors. During the first few months my blog grew to 3,000 visitors and 5,000 page views a month but then seemed to plateau. One reason is that many of my core target audience, senior marketing people, do not spend time on social media, and if they do, they do not know of my effort. Social media is all a numbers game. If you have enough of them and they can be stimulated to pass on your stuff, it can all be worthwhile. But it is a battle and whether my blog davidaaker. com will be successful is at best an open question.

To reach a more robust blog audience, I decided to blog on major established outlets with large audiences and the right demographics like HBR. My fourth HBR blog, titled "Secrets of social media revealed 50 years ago," caught people's eye possibly because so many in the audience were social media people and this was a different take. During the first two days, 240 people with over 750,000 followers twittered about it, and it attracted over 50 comments. In contrast my postings on my own blog might get ten or fifteen Twitter mentions and a dozen comments if it connects.

The blog posting described a large study that Ernest Dichter, the father of motivation research, did of word-of-mouth persuasion. Reported in a 1966 HBR article, a major finding was the identification of four motivations for a person to communicate about brands. The first (about 33 percent of the cases) is because of product-involvement. The experience is so novel and pleasurable that it must be shared. The second (about 24 percent) is self-involvement. Sharing knowledge or opinions is a way to gain attention, show connoisseurship, feel like a pioneer, have inside information, seek confirmation of a person's own judgment, or assert superiority. The third (around 20 percent) is other-involvement. The speaker wants to reach out and help to express neigh-borliness, caring, and friendship. The fourth (around 20 percent) is message-involvement. The message is so humorous or informa-tive that it deserves sharing. Those who aspire to use social media to build brands today need to respond to one or more of these motivations. The fact that a study done nearly a half century ago could be of practical value to those using social media to build brands is truly astonishing.

My sixth HBR blog post, which got 145 comments, was stimulated by a book by Bob Lutz, the outspoken auto execu-tive, who opined that an auto CEO should be a car man, not be a bean counter, and be something of an autocratic. My blog was entiled "Great CEOs are born, not made" and argued that only those with innate talent will become a Steve Jobs and many of the successful CEOs like IBM's Lou Gerstner had no prior industry experience. But you had to have executive talent (with respect to being able to handle the deminsions of an executives job) and a strategic flare (having a feel for strategy). You did not have to be a car man and could be a bean counter. The title and content clearly hit a nerve. Many argued that training could create talent. The basic idea followed a long-held belief that talent is underap-preciated. Many feel if only they had a chance to play more golf they would be better. Wrong. A golfer that lacks the talent to be a ten handicapper can play every day with a pro and never achieve that level. You cannot teach talent.

The blogging and to a lesser extent tweeting is fun and a good way to interpret the news of the day and to keep up to date on ideas and trends. It provides an excuse to write and an outlet for the resulting writings. I really like it, which is enough motivation to keep it up.

Politics

I am fascinated but discouraged by politics. It seems like special interests have taken over the process because of campaign contributions and the nomination process. There used to be liberal Republicans and conservative Democrats. Politicians used to hang out in Washington during breaks, drink Bourbon, and make deals, and the country functioned. No more. If any politician strays from the dogma of the party and entertains compromise, he or she will not be nominated. So the politicians are polarized and the government is paralyzed. I worry about the future especially of our grandkids.

The solution seems so common sense.

- Reduce the cost of medical care and improve its coverage (remove incentives to overtreat and copy any one of fifteen Western countries)

- Reduce entitlements (the current system is not sustainable—reduce the safety net for those who do not need it)

- Increase revenues while rationalizing the tax structure (you cannot run a major country with the current revenue base; undo the Bush tax cuts, get rid of the tax loopholes that create complexity and usually the wrong incentives, have a reasonable inheritance tax, and reduce the corporate tax rate)

- Reduce the defense budget (get into fewer wars and get out of the ones we are in)

- Improve education (improve the quality of teachers and support trade schools—just copy Finland or Denmark)

- Invest in infrastructure (we are third-world next to China—compare our airports, rail system, roads, and power grid)

- Pursue energy independence by providing the right incentives to move beyond oil starting with a tax on gasoline (deliver what seven presidents have promised)

- Through regulation or breakup insure that the "too big to fail" banks do not precipitate another meltdown

- Reduce the regulatory barriers to building infrastructure and starting and running a small business (almost no cost involved)

A balanced, reasonable approach to fiscal discipline and strategic priorities. But my opinion has never been asked.

All of these ideas have a home in one of the two parties and generally have strong support from the majority of the voters, but interest groups and the polarized parties stop any reasonable compromise. I think both parties share blame but the Republicans, to my mind, are the most inflexible and ideological. As the conservative columnist David Brooks noted in July 2011, the Republicans by their intransigence may have ceased to become a "practical, governing alternative." A third party that is moderate and proposes pragmatic, common-sense compromise programs may be a solution, but third parties have steep barriers. A more feasible option could be the emergence of a third force that would support moderates in the nomination process. In any case, something needs to be done or paralysis will win.

I love what our country stands for and what it has done for me. There are bright spots. There are a host of informed and dedicated people that are trying. California has taken the congressional boundary setting away from the politicians. The U.S. has still enormous assets and incredible vitality. So I remain cautiously optimistic that it will survive this time of difficulty as it has similar ones in the past.

Giving Back

I have a theory that charity budgets should be managed like an investment portfolio where you objectively allocate over investment options—stocks/bonds/gold/real estate, foreign/domestic, sectors, etc. Too often in my view charity giving is governed too much by the excitement of a fund raiser, supporting a friend's charity, and not getting around to planning a giving strategy. Rather, an objective judgment should be made about the budget size and how it should be allocated over options such as the disadvantaged, education, medical research, the arts, education etc. before picking individual charities. Following that logic, we decided to change our allocation to include a foreign charities component. We picked out Doctors across Borders (sending doctors to the front lines of disease), Nothing but Nets (distributes insecticide-treated bed nets that cost $10 each and provide protection from Malaria—over 1 million lives saved many of which are children), and GAVI Alliance (an inoculation program for the third world already estimated to have saved

5 million lives during the last 10 years). I am attracted to big numbers.

In addition to financial help, the donation of time and talent is important as well. Kay does way more than her share and my efforts in comparison is modest. I am on the board of the Food Bank of Contra Costa and Solano Counties, an activity that is such a pleasure because the director and staff are so competent, the board functions so smoothly, and the output is just incredible. The organization distributes food to over 130,000 people in need each month (nearly a third of which are children) and has initiated a host of programs such as the Farm 2 Kids which delivers fresh fruits and vegetables to 6,500 low income kids each week at their schools. I have seen the excitement in their faces as they pick up their bags. Did I already say I like large numbers?

I have helped several non-profits with branding. One notable "client" was Dean Richard Lyons of the Haas School. The process and the output has been extremely influential. Our first brand essence, "Leadership through Innovation" resulted in elevating an innovation thrust in the school through changes in existing courses, new courses, hiring professors, research programs, and the ways that alumni and prospective students are linked to the school. The brand vision evolved into "developing leaders who redefine how we do business" that is broader and bolder. A redefinition, for example, can involve social programs and strategic changes that may not be innovation led. Among the core identity elements was one that was highly distinctive—"confidence without arrogance" (Stanford, Harvard and other tend to have students and even faculty with more of an attitude). It is a substantive quality of Haas that is admired and appreciated.

Cal Sports

College sports, particularly football and basketball but also volleyball and softball, are exciting and involving. So we are still into the Cal Bears. The football team continued its ways of finishing in the middle of the conference or a bit higher but never near the top. There were some exceptional players like Marshawn Lynch, Jahvid Best, and Desean Jackson, but something always seemed to be missing. Still, there is always next year. The basketball team did win the conference title, the first in fifty years, in 2010 with a newly hired coach, Mike Montgomery, and players like Jerome Randall, Patrick Christopher, and Jorge Gutierrez. It was a thrill even though the team lost in the second round of the NCAA tournament. The taste of being on top was great, but it might be another fifty years to see it again.

The Family

We are blessed to have our three girls and their families including the seven grandchildren live within biking distance from us. We see them nearly every day. What a treasure. A quick update.

Jolyn and Brian (Krug) are still living in their perfect house right on Shell Ridge with its mountain biking and running trails plus eagles, deer, coyotes, snakes, and other wildlife. No one likes it more than Oscar, their ridge back dog, who bounds after anything that moves, even coyotes, which is not smart. He particularly enjoys visiting Jan's house, because there is a lot of food on the floor, and seeing Dave as he brings treats—the way to a dog's heart in through treats. Brian continues to excel in making clients happy with his firm's software. In 2011, he enjoyed adjusting to Cisco, which bought his firm.

Jolyn is a compassionate, active social worker now qualifying people for the state's assistance program. She has seen up close some difficult family challenges and that helps all of us be thankful for what we have. The stories she brings back are amazing and heartrending. It is difficult to see how families can cope with the physical, mental, emotional, and social problems of their kids, some of whom are well into adulthood. Of course, they often simply can't and that is why Jolyn and her agency are there.

There is no typical case that Jolyn evaluates. However, the following is illustrative although not a real case. One family is coping with a "high-functioning" autistic boy in his late teens who has limited social skills, becomes extremely apprehensive when away from the family even for a matter of seconds, speaks in a monotone, rambles with odd directions of thought, occasionally makes loud and inappropriate sounds, has major meltdowns lasting hours periodically, requires a one-on-one school context in order to both focus and avoid behavioral disruption, and has an uncertain prognosis as far as independent living. However, the boy has up-times when an artistic or other talent emerges, or when he experiences periods of near normalcy. In general, seeing this case and others up close makes it clear that having such a child in a family is stressful and draining for siblings and parents. Can you imagine what the family goes through on a daily basis? And the family will often be coping with other health and financial issues as well. Fortunately, Jolyn's agency can provide assistance but the situation is still debilitating.

The big news is the addition of Landon in 2007. Landon has always been active, outgoing, and positive. At ten months he was staggering, careening, falling but always with an exuberant smile. Instead of fussing when things go wrong, he just moves on. Large for his age, he is very assertive and doesn't walk, he lunges. Even at three, he shows signs of being a division one athlete when skiing, golfing, biking, or playing ball. Affectionate and demonstrative, he hugs other kids sometimes too forcefully. Cousins Kailyn and Tea love to mother him.

Landon at age 3

And he is clever. When told this is the last hide and seek game, he walks by the hiding place five times looking but not "finding." And directive—he'll say that he should not be found right away. Additionally, he has no trouble getting his response right, and facts or truth do not stand in his way. When told you have to be five to do something, he promptly becomes five. When caught with gum he puts one hand behind his back and holds out the other to support his assertion that he has no gum. To prove the point, he reverses hands to demonstrate that there is still no gum in the exposed hand. One night Jo, when getting him to bathe became a problem, pointed out that Batman and Spiderman take baths. The next day Landon told me about Sadie, a hero with a purple outfit who did not bathe. He created a counterexample.

Jan and Rich (Broad) have made a leap by moving one mile into a wonderful home. After looking for five years, the perfect house appeared only a few weeks before they were going to tear down the prior home, the one with foundation problems, and build a replacement. What a nightmare that would have been. The house was priced aggressively, and Jan and Rich snapped it up before the first open house. What a great feeling after so long looking for something that would work and be special. The new home has a dramatic dining room overlooking a living room sunk a half floor, extensive decking around a swimming pool, and lots of forest. The running/hiking ridge around the reservoir is a few blocks out the door. The three girls can walk to school, and they have their own rooms plus a playroom. Super cool. Rich is an executive for wine.com, the leading wine-oriented e-commerce firm. Jan is a great teacher, calm, humorous, motivating, supportive. One of her students in 2011 was Devon Smith, her nephew. She converted him into an avid book reader, one of her many successes.

Sami Broad at age eleven

Samantha, 11 in 2011, has always been the mother of the team and leader in activities. For the last five years she has orchestrated a host of role-playing games involving "family" or "school" (grandfather is not invited). She and her sister Maile can discuss how to parcel out dolls and "roles" for hours. It comes naturally to her as she has always been a performer and loves being in plays at home or on a real stage. She is always thoughtful and helpful, she was awarded the citizenship award upon graduating from elementary school, and is an exceptional babysitter. My special days with the kids continue. One of the most special was when I introduced Sami to *The Fantastics*, my second favorite musical. She has tried all the activities from Ty Con Do where she learned politeness (didn't completely take) to swimming (where she has a social network) to soccer to tether ball to volleyball, each of which had its turn as the "best."

Sami joined us on one of our Japan trips. She got to see Disneyland not too long before the earthquake hit the park. But most of all she got to hang out with her Japanese "sister" Marina Akutsu (the story of the Akutsu family appears below). She ate Japanese food, rode the subway, did monster shopping adventures, and attended a Japanese school where she was treated warmly.

Maile Broad at age nine

Maile, 9 in 2011, has turned into the nicest person, always ready to be friends to her peers and to help her folks. Who would have thought, given her awesome pouts as a two-year-old. Simply exuberant, her high energy and dazzling smile are infectious. She plays soccer like she plays life—she gets the ball wherever it is and then charges up the field, changing direction to avoid opponents and often scores. One of the top athletes in her class, she is already a gifted skier in part thanks to her mom, the former Aspen ski school instructor.

Maile is a collector whether it is rocks or random whatever. Her bed contains twenty-nine stuffed animals, numerous books, and much more—the ultimate survival shelter. Periodically she has a garage sale of the less prized items and is a tough bargainer.

Kailyn, 6 in 2011, is unusually beautiful, charming, and happy. As a one-year-old, she would pull "doggy" (Oscar) to his water using all her strength. When her sisters were discussing trophies Kailyn announced that she had two and they were in the bedroom—she wanted to be part of the group. When invited to read one book, she counters with four but she means eight. Kailyn has a dazzling smile that comes out when things go well like when she makes

Kailyn Broad at age six

the "best eggs in the world." However, she can fold her arms across her chest and push out her lower lip in a pout just like her mother (and Maile) used to do. She is often on her play cell phone talking to her pal, Tea Sloane.

Jennifer and Andy (Smith) made the decision to move to Lafayette to be closer to the family in 2007. The home is a gem with interesting design and workmanship. Thanks to Andy the garage has become a real movie theater and workout room and the driveway a basketball court and trampoline area. There is a living unit by the pool that is being used productively by a stream of terrific au pairs from Sweden. In 2010, Andy left Dolby Labs where he was VP of global brands to be an adviser for and investor in startup high-tech firms, usually with a social media dimension; public speaker; and coauthor (with Jennifer) and chief marketer of the "social media to drive social good" book, *The Dragonfly Effect*. The book was named after the dragonfly, whose four wings represent the book's process model: Focus, Gain Attention, Engage, and Take Action.

The book was inspired by Andy's interest in harnessing social media to grow brands, and Jennifer's (very slight) interest in social media and (significant) interest in giving back and making a dent in cancer. The core motivating story involved Sameer Bhatia, a Stanford grad and successful entrepreneur in the mobile gaming arena, an exceptional person—respected, positive, charismatic, and extremely well liked. In 2007, at the age of thirty-one, he was diagnosed with AML, an aggressive form of leukemia. The only hope was a bone marrow transplant but no matches emerged in part due to the low incidence of South Asians in the US registry (only 1.4 percent) and the ill-developed Indian register. The solution was to get 20,000 new South Asian registrants and to do it fast as there was a clock ticking. His network of friends considered that a challenge and, using social media and a refined system of parties, actually got over 24,000 in eleven weeks. A perfect match was found. The procedure ultimately did not save Sameer but the process left a legacy that saved hundreds of others, changed how the register is managed, and inspired a new direction for Jennifer.

Andy and Jennifer put the model and the book ideas to work with an effort to motivate and publicize the registrar among South Asians. In October 2010, they initiated the 100,000 Cheeks campaign, with the single focused goal to use social media to inspire 100,000 people in just one year to give a cheek swab. A host of talks, one of which involved Jennifer going to a site six hours' drive from Mumbai, India, generated swabs but also some important buzz and real impact. Twelve Stanford students adopted the project and should put it over the top. It is happening. Andy, Jennifer, and the others are making a difference!

Jennifer has a stimulating professional life. She hangs with a remarkable set of people. At one event she spent thirty minutes chatting with the mayor of New York. Some of her class visitors are celebrity movie stars or executives. As an experimental social psychologist, Jennifer has impacted her field by pioneering several research streams. Her subjects have included brand personality, cultural psychology, emotions and health, psychology of giving, and finally (yes, there is more) time, money, and happiness.

In a study with Susan Fournier, two personalities were created for an online photographic service brand called "Captura"—one sincere, the other exciting, each with its own website. After six weeks of interacting with Captura, half of the participants in each group were told that an employee had accidentally erased their online photos. Two weeks later the photos were "found." While the sincere brand enjoyed stronger consumer-brand relationships than the exciting brand before the photos were lost, its ensuing sharp image decline was not relieved by recovering the photos despite the brand's apology and attempts to make amends. Surprisingly, the exciting brand who let consumers down (and then apologized) actually did better even than the exciting brand which didn't let consumers down. There is a dark side to promising trust, and a significant upside to promising excitement.

More recently, Jennifer's work focuses on time, money, and happiness. She addresses on questions such as: What actually makes people happy, as opposed to what they think makes them happy? How can small acts create infectious action, and how can such effects be fueled by social media? In one study she found that on average, older people find happiness associated with calmness rather than excitement; her father is the exception that proves the rule. In another study she showed that nonprofits will get larger donations if they first ask people to donate time, even when the people actually declined to give time.

Devon Smith at age nine

Devon (age nine in 2011), like his Dad, is fascinated by remotes and all things electronic. He is the only one who can run the family entertainment system and once outsmarted his dad, who disabled his computer, by simply plugging everything back in. He was the only kid in the history of his school that, when asked to bring a book to school, brought a Kindle. The acorn does not fall far from the tree. His parents are into politeness so he learned to say "Excuse me" before interrupting. He coined the phrase "Excuse me first" to handle situations when there are multiple "excuse me" requests.

Devon also likes things that fly. During a golf lesson he paused thirty seconds on a backswing to discuss an airplane he noticed in the sky. A real trooper, at six he went through three operations to align his right eye. In telling the story, he begins by saying that sometimes they can figure out a diagnosis—too true. We took him and his twin brother Cooper, then seven years old, to Legoland, and they learned to drive by ignoring the signs; there is speculation that they have inherited driving skills or lack thereof from their mom.

Devon is known for his empathy. He cares about others, of all ages. And he has a sensitive side. At age seven he wrote a poem entitled "My Heart Soars" as part of lesson taught by his grand-mother, Kay:

> *My smart computer, my big theater, and my small phone, speak to me.*
> *My strong heart-beat, my smart brain, and my strong bones, speak to me.*
> *My caring mom, my smart dad, and my funny sister and my touchy brother,*
> *All speak to me.*
> *And my heart soars.*

Cooper, Devon's twin, usually has a big smile because he is enjoying one of his many interests and because of his sense of humor. Known for his speed, Cooper is a gifted athlete. Like Maile, he excels in soccer, basketball, and skiing. I recall that as a five-year-old he invited himself into a basketball game with eight–year-olds and was the best ball handler and passer on the court. He is good at academics, especially math. He knows the age and birthday of everyone and loves to do number tests in his head. And quick—when asked how to tell the difference between beer and wine he knew instantly that it was the size of the bottle. He also has an artistic side with real talent in drawing, cartooning, singing, and piano. He has actually composed songs. In fact, he aspires to be a renaissance man, with a wide range of interests.

With his brother, he has participated in a host of entrepreneurial activities such as the lemonade stand that was written up in the newspaper where some or all of the proceeds go to charity.

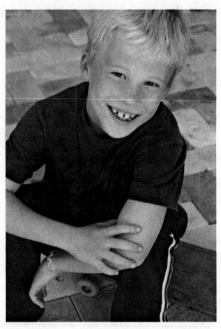

Cooper David Aaker Smith
at nine

Encouraged by his parents to think of others, Cooper on his own turned in the toy guns he got at a birthday party and gave the proceeds to the church to help the less advantaged. He knows he is lucky to have Devon as a best friend. Amazing relationship.

Tea Sloane, six in 2011, is very strong willed, and things go a lot better when she gets her way—but she can melt anyone with her smile. She has been described as "irresistibly adorable," "large and in charge," "infectious enthusiasm," "the shy smile," and "spunky/cute-tough." She is excellent at rules that apply to others such as, "Say sorry, Cooper." Cooper, a bit of a creative diplomat, suggested that the impasse created by Tea's decision of "clothes (pants)—NO DRESS" could be resolved by relabeling dresses as clothes.

Tea Sloane has their house activities structured and typically gallops through the house because she is "very busy." She set up a desk near her mom and turned out a ton of work. She knows what she wants: "I wish for a fairy for the family. I like fairies because they are beautiful and pretty!" And has opinions—"Angels have wings and them can fly and they are soooo beautiful! They are like fairies so they are magic. To have magic is good cause then you can do good stuff to people. I think of mom when I think of angels!"

Tea Sloane and I played catch with a football one day. After five misses she caught everything, even when we were about fifteen feet apart, but after twenty tosses (when many would be just getting into it) she asked, "Can we quit now?"

Tea Sloane at six

Shades of Jennifer—don't let any activity overstay its welcome. Another Jennifer hint: I took Tea Sloane golfing. We were doing fine hitting, but then it occurred to her that we should organize the next activity. So we talked about what we would do when we got to Nana's house—one issue was that Nana was not there to do a puzzle. Where does Tea get a compulsion to plan?

Kay Retires

Kay retired from teaching in 2010 after some forty-six years—a big decision. She was honored with five events. The best was when the kids at her school gathered and gave their appreciation of her talent and effort in their own words. A song was written for her and sung by the whole school that went in part, "You've taught a lot of children and gone the extra mile. Your patience is enduring as you teach us with a smile. Our community is better because of what you do. You're the Yellow Rose of our school. We give out thanks to you."

Ten students spoke. One compared Kay to the sun because her rays reached so many people. Another commented on her well-known home visits, talking about how she always took "the time to get to know each of us inside and outside the classroom. When she came to my home to see my room and my life she taught me dominoes. I now often play dominoes with my family and give credit to Mrs. Aaker each time I win." They remember Flat Stanley, a character who is sent by class members to distant friends who are asked to pass it on. A very unique way to learn geography. President Obama was in the loop one year. They talked about the field trips, including one to a working farm. Most of all they talked about the fun in her class and the impact on their lives. Very moving.

A bit apprehensive at first, Kay now seems to be in a good groove, enjoying her grandchildren and being a mentor to several teachers. Her volunteering contin- ues—coordinating cancer

Marina

drives, being a caring hands caregiver, and leveraging her long career as a hospice volunteer by helping them staff clients. She is very good at all these activities and regularly received recogni- tion of her long, dedicated service. She also manages our vacation home near the gold town of Murphys located in the foothills.

One of Kay's special projects has been our friends from Japan, Toshi and Muiko Akustu and their daughters, Marina and Leana Kay. They came for a two-year visit while Muiko was only months from giving birth. Kay helped her find a home to rent, friends, schools, doctors, and hospitals, and supported her during the whole process. Leana Kay is named after Kay. After the earthquake they came back to stay with us to escape the uncertain times in Japan. They are part of our family. Marina stayed on to complete her third year in U.S. schools. Leana Kay at three became fluent in English after only two months here. Amazing.

Extended Family Vacations

We have had many memorable vacations and events during the past seven years. Some of the most special:

In 2011 we went on a one-week biking adventure to Morocco. What a cultural experience. We biked and hiked through the mountains, passing through villages that exhibited a very different lifestyle, some so remote that the residents walked four hours to buy and sell their farm output, and where every family had a large herd of goats. Even with electricity, a recent addition, it was primitive living but everyone seemed happy and self-sufficient. Makes you think. Then we went to the ocean where we saw goats in trees and played golf at a new, very upscale development around a beautiful course. Everything was à la carte including the tees and range balls, very different from a U.S. experience. In Marrakesh we communed with snake charmers in a square that was the site of a bombing only a few weeks later. We walked the souks, the little shops that were organized in a confusing labyrinth. That kind of experience makes you realize that all cultures are not like Nebraska.

Our extended DeJonghe/Aaker family each year had a skiing vacation at Bear Valley near our Murphys homes in the winter and a summer vacation that varied from year to year. Some were in Hawaii or Tahoe but the best for me were the two summers we spent on a lake north of Toronto. We got the whole extended family, including the DeJonghes, in a lake outside Toronto for a week of water sports, golf, eating, relaxing, and watching the kids enjoy the camp activities. In one class they fished off the dock and each caught at least three fish—that is the way to learn fishing. I went swimming each morning, once with my watch—my watch, thanks to Andy, now says "Don't get me wet" when I turn it on.

The nearby golf course was called the Rock—some holes had a rock that was one hundred by fifty yards. Cut into a forest, it was dramatic and challenging. The nice thing about golf is that it gets you out into great settings.

Boating was a big part of the scene and it brought back my boating from Minnesota days. I was driving the boat and feeling really good until I hit a submerged rock that we later learned had an obscure buoy guarding it. My reputation took a hit that it would ill afford.

It is special to get together with this group of some twenty-one people with roots that go back years.

I grew up with fifteen cousins, as described in chapter two, but really reconnected some forty-five or so years later. The main vehicle would be a trip to Minneapolis for business or to see a Cal football game. One of my cousins, Linda or Karen, would organize a "reunion" dinner that included some bike and golf outings where we'd really spend quality time together. I got to know my cousins all over again. We reminisced about our incredible parents and grandparents and our summer vacations, and were joined by my favorite people, Mabel (my aunt) and Bjarnie (my uncle--laughing and enthusiastic as always). On one trip I made sure that my kids got to spend quality time with them. This stimulated my organizing a Black Hills cousins bike adventure. It went better than I could have hoped thanks to the Dakota Black Hills biking firm. Three cousins made it—Bud, Doug, and Bob Nielsen—and we almost had three more. Joined by Kay, brother Paul, Doug's wife, and local biking buddies Bob Blaine and John Sears and wife, we biked past Mount Rushmore, just hung out, and got way too close to a herd of buffalo.

Another reconnect was my fifty-year Fargo reunion. Most definitely looked older—can't understand why I don't age like the others. The only classmate still working besides me was John Altenburg, an ophthalmologist from Florida, who was still operating on eyes. I told him that he needed to keep it up because I did not want to be the lone ranger. It was fun seeing some friends I had not seen for fifty years, and it is so pleasant to be around Minnesota lakes. I have golfed regularly with Tom and Sharon Wright, Dick and Janice Johnson, and Karen Cornell Bopp and her husband in a Palm Springs weekend outing, and irregularly with Larry Swenson, but the others I don't see. Most are retired and living a satisfying life, but one that would be too sedentary and not stimulating enough for me. One told me that a normal day is a walk around a lake and crafts. Didn't sound fun.

A fun trip for Kay and me was to go to Dubai. The excuse was a World Economic Forum meeting of their some seventy councils—I was on the brand and marketing council. Like many WEF initiatives we were charged to save the world. After a slow start our council may end up doing some good. The best part, however, was a chance to interact with some very interesting people from very different backgrounds tackling different problems. One council addressed the migration that will be caused by the droughts from global warming. Several others were focusing on the financial meltdown that had just occurred and how to prevent it from reoccurring. The prognosis was not encouraging.

We got to experience Dubai, which was a mindblower—absurdly opulent hotels, manmade islands, indoor skiing (even when the summer temperature is 125 degrees), great golf courses, water taxis, and beaches that would make Hawaii jealous. We made a lunch reservation at the top of the signature sail hotel, the Burj Al Arab, where we could view the new construction that was coming to an abrupt halt. Some former Prophet clients who had worked for a major real estate developer told about how they would sell office space for $20 million to Russians, who would come with cash in suitcases to pay. And how developers would sell out buildings before they were built and use the money to start more. All that stopped abruptly when the bubble burst. Dubai became so destitute that it had to be bailed out by Abu Dhabi.

We took a side trip to Qatar where Tom Aaker (cousin Bud's boy) is a high powered Charter Standard banker and extreme athlete. Among other things Tom has run a marathon around the North Pole (the only event he would not want to repeat), has done the Paris-Brest-Paris ninety-hour 1200 km bike ride (where you have to do three rides during the past year, one of which is 600 km, just to qualify), and just got back from running five consecutive marathons on soft sand on temperatures over 110 degrees carrying his bedding. He was fresh as a daisy.

It was fascinating to see the lifestyle in Qatar and the way women interact and dress. We played golf at night under the lights, a first. The women on the course wore Western clothes but not on the streets. We saw some covered women leaving to go to London; they changed clothes immediately upon entering the plane and became very Western. Most decisions in Qatar are made by two extended families while meeting late at night in social/business settings. People adapt.

I am not much of a hiker—hiking seems like work while biking is fun—but we did a heli-hiking trip in a gorgeous part of the Canadian Rockies (where a disturbing amount of time was spent talking about grizzlies, the sightings, and incidents). We also have hiked in the foothills around our place in the gold town Murphys sometimes at the Big Trees park, where 1,000-year-old trees hold forth, and in Downieville, where the DeJohnge's Shangri-La is located.

Reflecting

Professionally, the past seven years have been wonderful. I really enjoy what I do. There is nothing better than hanging out and talking brand and business strategy with really bright, involved people or in writing books, articles, or blogs about new ideas, frameworks, or perspectives that hit me as interesting. It is just fun. And being around young, interesting, likeable people and watching up close an organization grow and achieve is a real treat. Getting to go to interesting and sometimes exotic locales and be treated occasionally like a celebrity is not bad either. There is also a reward in suspecting (or hoping) that my ideas are making a difference—that they help in a small way to counter the relentless and self-defeating short-termism that pervades business. I do all the biking, golfing, skiing, and reading that I want. So why change a good thing? There is no thought of retiring.

And it is all about family. We are so blessed to have been lucky with our Dejaaker extended family and three girls who are so talented professionally, such wonderful wives and mothers, and such giving and fun people. And Kay gets much of the credit. In addition to being a treasured wife and friend, I see so much of Kay in the kids. One father's day Jan and Joyln took me mountain biking and rode at my pace as well, and Jennifer took me for a hike without her phone. Special. The grandkids are a total joy at least 95 percent of the time. Life is good.

Looking forward to the next seven years. Stay tuned.

Index of Names

A

Aaker, Al, 47, 50, 51, 99
Aaker, Alice, 48
Aaker, Arleen, 49, 103
Aaker, Bill, 47, 48, 50
Aaker, Blanche, 46, 51, 56, 64
Aaker, Bud, 46, 47, 130, 132, 422, 423
Aaker, Dick, 47, 48
Aaker, Doug, 47, 49, 50, 274, 422
Aaker, Ed, 47, 48
Aaker, Ellen, 51
Aaker, Embrikk, 57, 58
Aaker, Ester, 61
Aaker, George, 47, 56, 60, 61, 63, 113
Aaker, Guri, 57, 58
Aaker, Helena, 50, 99, 102
Aaker, Ida, 4-10, 37, 38, 42, 44, 59, 62, 63, 64, 65, 66, 70, 71, 73-77, 80, 107, 133, 134, 207, 208, 256-261, 332
Aaker, Janet, 47, 49
Aaker, Jennifer, ix, 72, 76, 81, 84, 101, 132, 143-146, 153, 167, 172, 203-208, 213, 224, 226, 247-255, 262, 263, 267, 275, 278, 291, 310, 313, 328, 330,
331-336, 364, 367, 368, 375, 377, 378, 383, 384, 386, 388, 403, 404, 414, 415, 416, 419, 424, 435
Aaker, John, 46, 47, 132, 274
Aaker, Jolyn, 65, 105, 125, 204-209, 212, 247-253, 256, 259, 263-267, 269, 274, 312, 314, 316, 320, 322, 326, 330, 331, 332, 334, 361, 367, 375, 376, 377-380, 384, 385, 404, 410, 424, 435
Aaker, Kay, ix, 4, 35, 65, 66, 75, 120, 127-146, 188, 192-199, 200, 203, 204, 207, 208, 209, 211, 213, 214, 217, 240, 242, 245, 246, 249, 250, 251, 252, 255, 256, 259, 260, 262, 267, 269, 270, 271, 303, 313, 323, 326, 329, 331-336, 361, 367, 369, 375-379, 384, 387, 388, 400, 401, 419, 420, 422-424, 435
Aaker, Marie Jeglum, 37, 52-56
Aaker, Mikkel, 56, 57
Aaker, Ole Younger, 56, 57, 58
Aaker, Ole, 37, 42, 53-58, 61, 71
Aaker, Oscar, 5, 6, 9, 18, 37, 47, 48, 49, 50, 59, 67-73, 75, 77,

About the Author

David Aaker is the vice-chairman of Prophet, professor emeritus of Marketing Strategy at the Haas School of Business, UC Berkeley, and advisor to Dentsu Inc. The winner of career awards for contributions to the science of marketing (the Paul D. Converse award), marketing strategy (the Vijay Mahajan Award), and the theory and practice of marketing (the Buck Weaver Award), he has published over one hundred articles and fifteen books, including *Strategic Market Management, Managing Brand Equity, Building Strong Brands, Brand Leadership* (coauthored with Erich Joachimsthaler), *Brand Portfolio Strategy, Spanning Silos*, and *Brand Relevance: Making Competitors Irrelevant* (named by S&B as one of the top three marketing books of 2011) and blogs on marketing issues at davidaaker.com and HBR.org. His books have sold over a million copies and have been translated into eighteen languages. Cited as one of the most influential authors in marketing, Professor Aaker has won awards for the best article in the *California Management Review* and (twice) in the *Journal of Marketing*. An authority on brand equity and brand strategy, he has been an active consultant and speaker throughout the world and is on the Board of Directors of the Food Bank of Contra Costa and Solano. He lives with his wife, Kay, in Orinda, California, close to the families of his three daughters, Jennifer, Jan, and Jolyn.

CPSIA information can be obtained at www.ICGtesting.com
Printed in the USA
LVOW121118020112

261888LV00001B/6/P